Religion in China Today

Religion in China Today

Policy and Practice

Donald E. MacInnis

ORBIS BOOKS

Maryknoll, New York 10545

The Catholic Foreign Mission Society of America (Maryknoll) recruits and trains people for overseas missionary service. Through Orbis Books, Maryknoll aims to foster the international dialogue that is essential to mission. The books published, however, reflect the opinions of their authors and are not meant to represent the official position of the society.

Copyright © 1989 by Donald E. MacInnis
Published by Orbis Books, Maryknoll, NY 10545
Manufactured in the United States of America

Library of Congress Cataloging-in-Publication Data

MacInnis, Donald E.
    Religion in China today : policy and practice / Donald E.
MacInnis.
        p.   cm.
    ISBN 0-88344-594-8. — ISBN 0-88344-645-6 (pbk).
    1. China — Religion — 20th century.   I. Title.
BL1802.M29   1989
291'.0951'09048 — dc20   89-38900
                                                                           CIP

Contents

Foreword

One of the great surprises of China after Mao has been the efflorescence of religious belief and practice. It is a surprise not only for many Chinese Communists, whose scientific materialist ideology teaches them that religion is destined to wither away with the advance of history, but also for many Western observers of China. Heirs to the same rationalist, Enlightenment tradition that Karl Marx drew upon, Western social scientists have tended to underestimate the role of religion in the modern world. Modernity dissolves religion, they have been wont to say. In the modern world *homo religiosus* yields to *homo economicus* and *homo politicus*. According to this way of thinking, the Chinese people would have been too busy dealing with their many political and economic problems over the past decades to worry much about religion. They would not have found it worth their while to hold on to religion in the face of vigorous government efforts to discourage and to suppress it. Even if a pre-revolutionary generation of religious practitioners secretly held on to their customs, a new generation grown up in a thoroughly secular society would have no interest in religion.

But the recent history of China has confounded such expectations. Ever since the establishment of the People's Republic, religion in all its forms has been systematically discouraged, and during the Cultural Revolution it was intensely persecuted. Yet with the death of Mao and the end of the Cultural Revolution era, all kinds of religious practices are springing back to life. Throughout the countryside, peasants are reviving the old marriage and funeral rituals, celebrating traditional festivals, sometimes calling on the services of sorcerers and shamans, and even in some places rebuilding local shrines and temples. On a more formally organized level, Buddhist temples and Islamic mosques are being refurbished and a surprising number of young people are entering training to become monks, nuns and imams. Despite enormous obstacles, the Catholic and Protestant churches have survived and are growing. Enough Communist Party and Youth League members are forsaking atheism for religious belief that the Party has had to issue anxious directives about how to stem this tide.

Even as it perhaps gives inspiration to people of faith around the world, the revival of religion in China thus challenges well-established social theories. This informative new book by Donald MacInnis will give scholars much food for thought. Dr. MacInnis has been studying about China for more than four decades. Nearly two decades ago, when the study of religion was only peripheral to the interests of Western scholars of contemporary China, he compiled and published an important set of primary source documents on religious policy and practice from the early years of the Communist era through the Cultural Revolution. In this new book, he draws on all his accumulated knowledge and experience to document the multifarious forms of religious life emerging in the contemporary PRC.

His earlier book described religion on the defensive, beleaguered by a powerful government determined to systematically control it and, sometimes, fanatically to eradicate it. In an ironic reversal, this new book describes a government on the defensive, puzzled by the blossoming of so many new flowers of religious thought, worried about the consequences of this flowering for its political control, at a loss to explain or reliably to constrain such an outgrowth of popular religious vitality. On the other hand, most of the religious people whom Dr. MacInnis has interviewed for this book seem cautiously hopeful about the future of their practices.

This book allows us no easy explanations for the survival and revival of religion in China. As Donald MacInnis surveys the wide range of religious practice and belief in the People's Republic, it becomes clear that the meanings and motivations associated with rural folk religion are far different from, say, those associated with urban Protestantism. Each religious tradition has to be understood in its own terms, as a particular response to the general failure of the bureaucratic party-state to provide any satisfying experience of moral community or any plausible sense of transcendent meaning.

Allowing no easy explanations, this fascinating collection of data pushes us toward hard, but potentially very fruitful intellectual work. In recent years, there has developed in the West a widespread "post-modernist" dissatisfaction with positivistic social theories that assume an unbridgeable gap between religious belief and scientific reason and between religious practice and the instrumental behavior that supposedly forms the foundation of the modern world. Sharing this dissatisfaction, many historians, anthropologists, and other scholarly specialists on China have begun to take greater interest in the religious dimensions of pre-modern and early modern China. Out of this new research are coming a host of new insights into the complexities of Chinese cultural traditions and social organization throughout history—and a host of stimulating scholarly controversies as well. It portends an intellectual revolution of sorts in Sinology, with all the confusion and uncertainties, as well as the opportunities for progress that revolutions promise. Due to lack of information, scholars have not generally extended such revolutionary intellectual developments to analysis of the religious dimensions of contemporary China. Donald MacInnis's book will do much to remedy the lack of information. China studies—and the academic study of religion in general—will become more exciting because of it.

RICHARD MADSEN
University of California, San Diego

Preface

While this book follows an earlier work on the same subject written in 1970-71 (*Religious Policy and Practice in Communist China*; New York: Macmillan, 1972), because of the great changes that have taken place in both religious policy and practice in China since 1979 and the access to information now available, it is much more than an update of that book. Whereas in 1971 the turmoil of the "cultural revolution" had not yet abated, and its leaders, bent on eliminating religion once and for all, had totally suppressed all public religious activities and banned all published writing about religion, in recent years, under the restored policy of freedom of religious belief, revival is evident among all five officially recognized religions, as well as among folk religions and superstitions, and a flood of articles and books on religion has appeared in the Chinese press. Moreover, the country has opened its doors to visitors, including social-science researchers, so that one can now travel freely throughout China visiting temples, monasteries, churches, and mosques, and interview religious persons without hindrance.

Because information on current religious practice was not available in 1970-71, my earlier book was a documentary history, a selection of source materials available in print, most of them translated from the Chinese press, which documented religious policy and practice from the earliest Communist experience in the 1920s through the 1950s and early 1960s. The purpose of the present work, in contrast, is to provide, in Part I, key documents, articles, and press reports describing the present official policy on religion, and, in Part II, to describe the actual religious situation in China since 1979 using firsthand interviews, scholarly studies, speeches and reports by religious leaders, and translations of Chinese press reports and journal articles.

In conducting research for this book I interviewed persons in ten provinces and two autonomous municipalities (Beijing and Shanghai). Religious adherents, both clergy and laypersons, were quite willing to talk, as were scholars engaged in research on religion. Only once was I turned down for an interview, and that was with an official of a provincial Religious Affairs Bureau.

Even so, it was difficult, as is explained in the introduction to Part II, to obtain reliable religious statistics, because, in most cases, not even local clergy know them, and published figures can vary widely, as can be seen in the section on Tibet. Statistics on religion will be available, I was told, when a nationwide survey, part of a priority emphasis on research on religion called for in the current Five-Year Plan for Economic and Social Development, is completed in three to five years.

An outside researcher can learn a great deal from interviews, particularly from friends and others who trust him, but there are limitations as well. First, government officials, if they consent to an interview, tend to talk in generalities. Even religious adherents, clergy and laity, know little more than what is happening in their own immediate religious community. The larger picture, including such phenomena as the so-called Catholic underground church, the widespread Protestant house meetings, sectarian tendencies in any of the religions, and isolated examples of illegal or highhanded treatment of believers by local officials would be known, if at all, by hearsay only. For some of them, lingering fears from suffering and repression endured during the "cultural revolution" are inhibiting, I was told; they can't be sure it won't happen again.

As for the written word, the magnitude of published materials on religion since 1979 is seen in a bibliography of 374 articles on religion from Chinese journals and newspapers since 1952, published in *Zongjiaoxue Yanjiu* (Studies & Research on Religion), volume 2, 1986, by the Center for Research on Religion at the University of Sichuan. Dramatically reflecting the changing political climate of those years, 35 of these articles were published in the fourteen-year period, 1952-1966, not one was published between 1966 and 1977, and the remaining 339 appeared between 1978 and 1984.

In addition to the national journals of each religion—*Fa Yin* (Buddhist), *Zhongguo Yisilanjiao* (Islamic), *Tian Feng* (Protestant Christian), and *Zhongguo Tianzhujiao* (Catholic)—the Catholics and Protestants publish research journals, *Tianzhujiao yanjiu ziliao huibian* (Collected Catholic Research Materials) and *Jinling shenxuezhi* (Nanjing Theological Review).

Ten centers or institutes for research on religion which publish books and periodicals have been set up, each with a special focus: Urumchi, Islam; Shenyang, Russian Orthodox Church; Xi'an, Daoism; Kunming, minorities' religions; Shanghai, Christianity; Nanjing, Christianity; Chengdu, Daoism; Lhasa, Tibetan Buddhism; and Beijing, world religions.

Thanks are due to my employers, the Maryknoll Fathers and Brothers, for granting a one-year working sabbatical based in Hongkong to complete the necessary research, including forays into China, for writing this book. I'm grateful to numerous friends in China, old and new, who helped arrange interviews and locate published materials; to the staffs of the Universities Service Centre and the Holy Spirit Study Centre in Hongkong; to the Chinese friends who worked with me on translations, Tam Waiyi, Zheng Xi'an, and Yu Linkai; to John Tong and my Maryknoll colleagues in China research in Hongkong, Elmer Wurth, Peter Barry, and John Cioppa; to Janice Wickeri, who provided a translation of "Document 19," and to Melvyn Goldstein, Cynthia Beall, Helen F. Siu, and Stevan Harrell, who shared their recent field research with me; to my colleagues at Maryknoll, New York, Jean-Paul Wiest, Cathy McDonald, and Susan Perry; and to Richard Madsen who read the completed manuscript, offered incisive suggestions, and wrote the foreword. Finally, my thanks to Helen MacInnis for entering bibliographical information on 784 documents into this project's dBase III+ database, an invaluable aid in the final task of organizing and writing.

HEILONGJIANG

● Harbin

● Changchun
JILIN

Shenyang ●
LIAONING

(INNER MONGOLIA)

NEI MONGGOL

BEIJING
Beijing

Hohhot ●

Lüda
(Dalian)

HEBEI
Shijiazhuang ●

TIANJIN
Tianjin

● Yinchuan

Huang He

SHANDONG
Jinan ●

Taiyuan ●

SHANXI

zhou

JIANGSU

Xi'an ●
SHAANXI

Zhengzhou ●

HENAN

ANHUI

Nanjing

Shanghai ●
SHANGHAI

HUBEI

Hefei ●

Chang Jiang (Yangtze River)

Chengdu

Wuhan ●

Hangzhou ●

ZHEJIANG

Changsha ●

Nanchang ●

JIANGXI

GUIZHOU

HUNAN

Fuzhou ●

FUJIAN

Tai-pei ●

● Guiyang

Xiamen ●

TAIWAN

GUANGXI

GUANGDONG
Guangzhou

● Nanning

Hong Kong (U.K.)

Macao
(Port.)

HAINAN DAO

PART I

Religious Policy since the Cultural Revolution

Introduction

Unlike countries that have neither a state religion nor a bureaucracy for government supervision of religion, China does have a religious policy and a hierarchy of State and Party organs for implementing that policy. The purpose of the Religious Affairs Bureau, set up in 1954 under the State Council with branches at provincial and local levels, is to serve as the government's agent in dealing with religious groups to carry out religious policy. The RAB, through its Party committee, including the director, is also accountable to the Party's United Front Work Department. In a Socialist state like China, the RAB is an essential intermediary between the religious groups and various government agencies, providing assistance in such tasks as evicting illegal occupants of churches, mosques and temples. It is said that the RAB also interferes in the internal affairs, even the finances, of local religious groups, although this may be slackening as the religious bodies strengthen their own administrative systems. Some RAB cadres are said to have an anti-religion bias, viewing all religious believers with suspicion and obstructing, rather than implementing, the policy of freedom of religious belief. Judging by numerous articles in the press since 1979, some of them included in this volume, government and Party officials are trying to educate these recalcitrant cadres.

While the religious rights of every citizen have been written into every PRC constitution since 1954, both the wording and implementation of those rights have varied through the years. From the early 1950s religious bodies and believers suffered increasing restrictions on their freedom to carry on religious activities, until all religions were summarily closed down at the onset of the "cultural revolution" in 1966. Many clergy and lay members were harassed, imprisoned or sent to labor camps, and public religious services were not resumed until 1979, following the Third Plenum of the

1

Eleventh Party Congress. The new constitution, adopted in 1982, included Article 36 on religious freedom, and "Document 19" [Document 1 in this volume] was circulated by the Party center that same year, inaugurating a new period of religious tolerance that continues to the present. Documents included in Part I indicate that Party and government policymakers recognize the self-defeating nature of attempts to suppress religion.

Part I of this book contains the basic policy documents, statements by State and Party policymakers and religious leaders, excerpts from a textbook designed to explain the official view of religion to young people, and definitions of religion published recently in Chinese encyclopedias, dictionaries, and books on religion. From these we get a clear picture of the official view of religion and religious policy, which is grounded in classical Marxist language and exegesis.

Ideally, a study of religion and religious policy since the "cultural revolution" should be organized under the journalist's "five W's": Who makes and implements policy? Where and when is it made, revised, or rewritten? What, exactly, is it, and how is it actually carried out? Why is it felt necessary to have such a policy, with its concomitant bureaucracy and restrictions on the full freedom to practice and propagate one's own religion in any way one pleases? Regrettably, while information available now provides partial answers to these questions, we can't know the whole story, and must content ourselves with the ample, if incomplete, fund of information in State documents and other Chinese publications, augmented by firsthand observation and interviews.

"Document 19," the most definitive statement on religion and religious policy ever issued by the Chinese Communist Party or government, was circulated internally through Party channels throughout China in 1982 by the Central Committee of the CCP. The entire text, translated from *Selected Documents of the Third Plenum of the Eleventh Central Committee of the CCP*, is reprinted here as Document 1. The theoretical framework of the many speeches and essays on religious policy published in the Chinese press since 1982 is based primarily on its positions.

"Document 19" is directed to Party and State cadres at every level to stimulate reflection on past experience, good and bad, and to provide policy guidelines for study so cadres will adopt "correct and effective methods" for carrying out the policy on religion.

Section 1 is a summary of the standard Marxist analysis of the reasons for the emergence, growth, and demise of religion.

The second section describes the five religions of China, noting ways in which the "five characteristics" of religion apply to each of them. Religion is (1) complex, (2) mass-based, (3) long-lasting, and has implications for relations with both (4) ethnic nationalities and (5) the nations of the world. The "five characteristics," which were first suggested in the 1950s by the late premier Zhou Enlai and a well-known religious theoretician,

Li Weihan, appear over and over in theoretical essays on religion and religious policy.

The third section sums up the successes and failures of the Party's work with regard to religious questions. It particularly condemns "leftist errors" (beginning in 1957), especially during the "cultural revolution," when the leftists "totally repudiated the Party's correct religious policy." The basic task now is to properly carry out the religious policy and to bring all religious believers together for the "common goal of building a modernized, powerful Socialist state."

Section 4 sets forth the Party's understanding of what the policy of freedom of religious belief does and does not mean.

The next section presents the problem of "winning over, uniting, and educating [politically] the religious professionals" and of redressing injustices perpetrated against them.

The sixth section calls on Party cadres and others to help all religions recover their places of worship and restore them to normal use, while setting the limitations for religious activities and differentiating between the "administrative control" of the Religious Affairs Bureau and the strictly religious functions of each religious organization.

Section 7 explains the organization, role, and purpose of the patriotic religious organizations, such as the Chinese Buddhist Association.

In the eighth section, the Party and State promise to help in setting up seminaries for the training of young clergy "who fervently love their homeland, support the Party's leadership and the Socialist system, and possess sufficient religious knowledge."

The following section spells out why Party members cannot be religious believers, with special attention to the problems of cadres working among ethnic nationalities belonging to one religion or another.

Section 10 explains the importance of the three world religions, Buddhism, Islam, and Christianity, represented in the country, for China's international relations, with a warning to watch out for "hostile religious forces" from abroad infiltrating into China. "The present task is that of developing friendly relationships with foreign religious groups while maintaining our policy of independence."

Finally, "Document 19" closes with a political homily, warning its readers that the "successful handling of the religious question" depends on strengthening the Party's leadership, the work of government organs responsible for religious affairs, and the use of the Marxist viewpoint to carry out scientific research on religious questions.

We have, then, some answers to the "five W's". Who determines religious policy? At the top, the Central Committee of the Party. Who implements the policy? Party and State cadres at various levels, and the Religious Affairs Bureau, with national, provincial, and local offices. Who actually does the theoretical analysis and writes the policy? Theoreticians who "carry out scientific research on religious questions." According to some sources, the most important of these is the Institute for Study of World Religions in the National Academy of Social Sciences in Beijing.

What is the policy? "Document 19" spells that out in detail. Why is it necessary to clarify and correctly implement this policy? Because the support of all religious citizens is important for the building of a united, strong, and modernized Socialist nation; the "five characteristics" of religion, moreover, demonstrate that the religious question cannot be lightly brushed aside or forcefully suppressed. How will the policy be successfully carried out? Only with the full and informed support of Party and State cadres at every level.

Implementing the Policy on Religion

We are quite clear on what the correct, official policy on religion is. We also know that it is the expressed intention of State and Party authorities to carry out that policy. Overall, great progress has been made in recovering, repairing, and reopening churches, temples, mosques, and monasteries; in restoring normal religious activities; in opening seminaries and training schools for new clergy; in publishing religious scriptures and periodicals; and in other related activities. However, many vandalized religious buildings have not been restored, and squatters still occupy others; religious activities are confined to houses of worship; limits are placed on the number of novice monks and clergy; and religious publications are few when compared to earlier times.

The government has provided large sums of money for the repair of houses of worship and other religious buildings, the replacement of cemeteries destroyed in the 1950s, the repayment of back salaries to wronged clergy, and other assistance in restoring the normal functions of religion, although, as noted above, the implementing of these policies is uneven, depending on local officials.

However, only five religions are singled out for protection under the constitutional guarantee of freedom of religious belief: Buddhism, Daoism, Islam, and Protestant and Catholic Christianity. Other religious sects, including at least two brought into China by outsiders in recent years, have been suppressed and their outside sponsors expelled. Religious sects have been at the center of political uprisings in the past, and this government wants religious activities confined to places of worship, with no direct ties to foreign religious agencies. Moreover, traditional popular religious cults, at one time pervasive throughout the countryside, are not included among the protected religions; but, as is pointed out in Part II, they are once again flourishing in the towns and villages, ignored by local officials.

As has been the case since the early 1950s, there are no foreign missionaries, and no schools, hospitals, or other institutions under religious management, nor are there organizations or activities (such as sabbath schools and youth groups) for young people under eighteen. Religious activities are restricted to the formal places of worship, and radio broadcasting and other forms of public evangelism are forbidden. While meetings of small groups for religious worship in homes are usually permitted, and, particularly in the case of Protestant churches, volunteer lay leaders provide important assistance for the clergy, there have been situations in which house meetings or similar activities have been forcefully stopped by local officials.

"Call for a New Look at an Outdated Religious Policy" [Document 16], a speech by Zhao Puchu, President of the Chinese Buddhist Association, to the Chinese People's Political Consultative Conference in March 1988 speaks directly to such problems. Describing the government's system of management and administration of religious work as "old and outdated" and the laws governing religion as incomplete, he calls for the drafting of a new law on religion. As of this date, that legislation has not been written, although, according to Mr. Zhao, several religious leaders are preparing a draft proposal to present to the lawmakers. "We must . . . turn all religious bodies into true people's organizations," he said, "which are under the leadership of the Party and government, but can independently carry out their work according to their own characteristics . . . . The key point is to protect the proper rights of religious believers and religious bodies, and their temples and churches."

Section I

Official Party and State Documents

Introduction

After thirteen years of total suppression, the policy of freedom of religious belief was restored by action of the Third Plenum of the Eleventh Party Congress in December 1978. Churches, mosques and temples began to reopen the next fall, a trend that gained momentum in 1980 and subsequent years. In 1982 a Party directive on religious policy known as "Document 19" was circulated widely through Party channels. While the actual document never appeared in a public journal, an edited version was published in the official Party journal, *Red Flag*, on 16 June 1982.

In that same year a revision of the national constitution, which included an article defining the policy on religion, was adopted [Document 4]. The publication of the statement by Peng Zhen, vice-chairman of the National Constitution Revision Committee (at the Standing Committee of the National People's Congress on April 22, 1982, commenting on Article 36), underscores the importance placed on publicizing its contents at that time:

Citizens enjoy freedom of religious belief. The revised draft restores the relevant stipulations set out in the 1954 constitution, but more clearly and concretely. In our country, citizens may believe in religion or disbelieve, but politically they have one thing in common, that is, they are all patriotic and support Socialism. ... The State protects legitimate religious activities, but no one may use religion to carry out counterrevolutionary activities or activities that disrupt public order, harm the health of citizens, or obstruct the educational system of the State ... [and] no religious affairs may be controlled by any foreign power [NCNA in English, April 18, 1982].

The main difference between the article on religion in the current constitution and the 1979 version is the elimination of the phrase "freedom not to believe in religion and to propagate atheism," a significant liberalization that was brought about by pressure from a group of national religious leaders.

Another action, which for the first time put teeth into the guarantee of freedom of religious belief, was the inclusion of Section 147 in the new

7

Penal Code, which stipulates a sentence of up to two years in prison for State officials who are convicted of illegally depriving citizens of their right to freedom of religious belief [Document 5]. Article 165 of the same Penal Code provides that persons who "use superstition to spread false rumors and swindle people" must be strictly dealt with and punished as the law provides.

Numerous articles on religion and religious policy appeared in the Chinese press in the early 1980s, stressing both the rights and limitations on freedom of religious practice. One distinction, difficult to clarify, was the difference between religious and superstitious activities: one is protected and the other is not [Document 3]. That problem still perplexes Party and State cadres at local levels, as will be seen in the section on Superstition and Religion: Theoretical Analysis in Part II.

One indication of the importance placed on the new religious policy has been the appearance of hundreds of articles on the topic in the Chinese press after a hiatus of many years. Another has been the assistance given by the government in the recovery, repair, and restoration of churches, mosques, temples, monasteries, and clergy training schools, also widely reported in the press. The celebration of such religious festivals as Christmas, Corban, and the birthday of Buddha or Guanyin are regularly noted in the official press. "Document 19" and two other lengthy articles on religion were included in Selected Documents of the Third Plenum of the Eleventh Central Committee, published in 1979 [Documents 1, 2, and 3]. Finally, we learn from the introductory chapter of a 1987 book reporting the results of numerous field studies on the religious situation in various localities in China that research on religion has been given top priority in the Sixth Five-Year Plan for Economic and Social Development: " 'That research on large theoretical and practical questions regarding the establishment of Socialist modernization in China should be particularly strengthened,' and research on religion was placed first in a list of twelve key topics" [Document 23].

Document 1

"Document 19" was first published in Selected Documents of the Third Plenum of the Eleventh Party Congress, 1982.
Translated by Janice Wickeri.

To: all provincial and municipal Party committees; all Party committees of autonomous regions, greater military regions, provincial military regions, field armies, ministries, and commissions within State organs and the general headquarters of the Military Commission of the Central Committee;

all Party committees within the armed forces and within all people's organizations:

The Secretariat of the Central Committee has recently studied the religious question and has drawn up a document entitled The Basic Viewpoint and Policy on the Religious Question during Our Country's Socialist Period. This document sums up in a more systematic way the historical experience of our Party, positive and negative, with regard to the religious question since the founding of the People's Republic, and clarifies the basic viewpoint and policy the Party has taken. Upon receipt of this document, Party committees of all provinces, municipalities, and autonomous regions, as well as those of the ministries and commissions of the Central Committee and State organs concerned, should undertake conscientious investigation and discussion of the religious question, and should increase supervision and prompt inspection of the implementation of each item related to this policy.

It is the belief of the Central Committee that following from this summation of the religious question, our Party needs to make further progress in summarizing its experience in all other aspects of its work, as well as of its work in each region and department. It should be affirmed that since the smashing of the "gang of four," and especially since the Third Plenary Session of the Eleventh Central Committee, our Party has achieved significant results from the summing up of its own historical experience. The "Resolution on Certain Questions in the History of Our Party Since the Founding of the People's Republic" passed by the Sixth Session of the Eleventh Central Committee is a distillation of this kind of result, marking the completion, in terms of ideological leadership, of the Party's task of restoring order. Viewed from another aspect, however, that is, taking our Party's work on all fronts, all regions and departments, the work of summing up our historical experiences is quite insufficient.

It is the hope of the Central Committee, therefore, that Party committees at all levels, most importantly at the provincial, municipal, and autonomous region levels, will, together with the first-level Party committees and organizations of the Central Committee and ministries and commissions of State organs, concentrate their main efforts within the coming two to three years on doing well the task at hand. They should undertake conscientious investigation of the work in those regions and departments for which they are responsible, systematically summing up their historical experience, positive and negative, shaping this into a set of viewpoints and methods in which theory and practice are intimately combined and which are suitable to conditions in their regions and departments.

It is the belief of the Central Committee that we need only earnestly grasp this key link and expand painstaking efforts in order to achieve new results and effectively raise the ideological and theoretical level of all Party members, who will then adopt correct and effective methods of work and open up a brand-new era as our country goes about the great task of building Socialism in the remaining twenty years of this century.

Central Committee of the Communist Party of China
31 March, 1982

Document 19: The Basic Viewpoint and Policy on the Religious Question during Our Country's Socialist Period

March 1982

I. Religion as a Historical Phenomenon

Religion is a historical phenomenon pertaining to a definite period in the development of human society. It has its own cycle of emergence, development, and demise. Religious faith and religious sentiment, along with religious ceremonies and organizations consonant with this faith and sentiment, are all products of the history of society. The earliest emergence of the religious mentality reflected the low level of production and the sense of awe toward natural phenomena of primitive peoples. With the evolution of class society, the most profound social roots of the existence and development of religion lay in the following factors: the helplessness of the people in the face of the blind forces alienating and controlling them in this kind of society; the fear and despair of the workers in the face of the enormous misery generated by the oppressive social system; and in the need of the oppressor classes to use religion as an opiate and as an important and vital means in its control of the masses. In Socialist society, the class root of the existence of religion was virtually lost following the elimination of the oppressive system and its oppressor class. However, because the people's consciousness lags behind social realities, old thinking and habits cannot be thoroughly wiped out in a short period. A long process of struggle is required to achieve great increases in production strength, great abundance in material wealth, and a high level of Socialist democracy, along with high levels of development in education, culture, science, and technology. Since we cannot free ourselves from various hardships brought on by serious natural and man-made disasters within a short period of time; since class struggle continues to exist within certain limits; and given the complex international environment, the long-term influence of religion among a part of the people in a Socialist society cannot be avoided. Religion will eventually disappear from human history. But it will disappear naturally only through the long-term development of Socialism and Communism, when all objective requirements are met. All Party members must have a sober-minded recognition of the protracted nature of the religious question under Socialist conditions. Those who think that with the establishment of the Socialist system and with a certain degree of economic and cultural progress, religion will die out within a short period, are not being realistic. Those who expect to rely on administrative decrees or other coercive measures to wipe out religious thinking and practices with one blow are even further from the basic viewpoint Marxism takes toward the religious question. They are entirely wrong and will do no small harm.

II. The Religions of China

There are many religions in China. Buddhism has a history of nearly 2,000 years in China, Daoism one of over 1,700 years, and Islam over 1,300 years, while Roman Catholicism and Protestantism achieved most of their development following the Opium Wars. As for the numbers of religious adherents, at Liberation there were about 8,000,000 Muslims, while today there are about 10,000,000 (the chief reason for this is growth in population among the ten Islamic minorities). At Liberation there were 2,700,000 Catholics; today there are over 3,000,000. Protestants numbered 700,000 in 1949 and are now at 3,000,000. Buddhism (including Lamaism) numbers almost the entire populations of the ethnic minorities of Tibet, Mongolia, and Liao Ning among its adherents. Among the Han race, Buddhism and Daoism still exercise considerable influence at present. Naturally, out of the total population of our country, and especially among the Han race, which accounts for the largest number of people, there are a considerable number who believe in spirits, but the number of those who actually adhere to a religion is not great. If we compare the number of religious believers at the time of Liberation with the present number overall, we will see that overall there has been somewhat of an increase in absolute numbers, but when compared with the growth of the population there has been a decline.

But in our appraisal of the religious question, we must reckon fully with its definite complex nature. To sum up, we may say that in old China, during the long feudal period and the more than one hundred years of semicolonial, semifeudal society, all religions were manipulated and controlled by the ruling classes, with extremely negative results. Within China, the Buddhist, Daoist, and Islamic leaderships were mainly controlled by the feudal landowners, feudal lords, and reactionary warlords, as well as the bureaucratic capitalistic class. The later foreign colonialist and imperialist forces mainly controlled the Roman Catholic and Protestant churches.

After Liberation there was a thorough transformation of the socioeconomic system and a major reform of the religious system, and so the status of religion in China has already undergone a fundamental change. The contradictions of the religious question now belong primarily to the category of contradictions among the people. The religious question, however, will continue to exist over a long period within certain limits, will continue to have a definite mass nature, to be entangled in many areas with the ethnic question, and to be affected by some class-struggle and complex international factors. This question, therefore, continues to be one of great significance which we cannot ignore. The question is this: can we handle this religious question properly as we work toward national stability and ethnic unity, as we develop our international relations while resisting the infiltration of hostile forces from abroad, and as we go on constructing a Socialist civilization with both material and spiritual values? This, then, demands that the Party committees on each level must adopt toward the religious question an attitude in accord with what Lenin said, "Be especially alert," "Be very strict," "Think things through thoroughly." To overestimate the seriousness or complexity of the question and so panic, or to ignore the existence and complexity of the actual question and so let matters drift, would be equally wrong.

III. The Party's Handling of the Religious Question since Liberation

Since the founding of the People's Republic of China, there have been many twists and turns in the Party's work with regard to the religious question. In general, although there were some major errors, after the founding of New China, and for the seventeen years up to the "cultural revolution," the Party's religious work achieved great results under the direction of the correct guiding principles and policies of the Party Central Committee. We did away with imperialist forces within the churches and promoted the correct policy of independent, self-governed, and autonomous churches, as well as the "Three-Self Movement" (self-propagation, self-administration, and self-support). The Catholic and Protestant churches ceased to be tools of the imperialist aggressors and became independent and autonomous religious enterprises of Chinese believers. We abolished the special privileges and oppressive exploitative system of feudal religion, attacked and exposed those reactionaries and bad elements who hid behind the cloak of religion, and made Buddhists, Daoists, and Muslims break away from the control and manipulation of the reactionary classes. We proclaimed and carried out a policy of freedom of religious belief, enabling the broad masses of religious believers not only to achieve a complete political and economic emancipation alongside each ethnic minority but also enabling them to begin to enjoy the right of freedom of religious belief. We carried out a policy of winning over, uniting with, and educating religious personages, and thus united the broad masses of the patriotic religious personages. We also assisted and supported religious people to seek international friendship and this has had good, positive effects.

Since 1957, however, leftist errors gradually grew up in our religious work and progressed even further in the mid-sixties. During the "cultural revolution" especially, the antirevolutionary Lin Biao-Jiang Qing clique had ulterior motives in making use of these leftist errors, and wantonly trampled upon the scientific theory of Marxism-Leninism and Mao Zedong Thought concerning the religious question. They totally repudiated the Party's correct policy toward religion, in effect since the founding of the People's

Republic. They basically did away with the work the Party had done on the religious question. They forcibly forbade normal religious activities by the mass of religious believers. They treated patriotic religious personages, as well as the mass of ordinary religious believers, as "targets for dictatorship," and fabricated a host of wrongs and injustices which they pinned upon these religious personages. They even misinterpreted some customs and practices of the ethnic minorities as religious superstition, which they then forcibly prohibited. In some places, they even repressed the mass of religious believers, and destroyed ethnic unity. They used violent measures against religion which forced religious movements underground, with the result that they made some headway because of the disorganized state of affairs. A minority of antirevolutionaries and bad elements made use of this situation and, under cover of religious activities, boldly carried out illegal criminal activities, as well as destructive antirevolutionary movements.

After the smashing of Jiang Qing's antirevolutionary clique, and especially since the Third Plenary Session of the 11th Party Central Committee, the correct guiding principle and policy toward the religious question of our Party was restored step by step. In implementing and carrying out our religious policy, we have opened both Buddhist and Daoist temples, as well as churches and religious sites. We have restored the activities of the patriotic religious associations. We have won over, unified, and educated religious personages. We have strengthened the unity between believers and nonbelievers in each ethnic group. We have righted wrongs and have launched a movement for friendly relations internationally among religious believers as well as resisting infiltration and like doings from hostile religious forces from abroad. In all this, we have undertaken a large number of tasks and have obtained remarkable results.

In this new historical period, the Party's and government's basic task in its religious work will be to firmly implement and carry out its policy of freedom of religious belief; to consolidate and expand the patriotic political alliance in each ethnic religious group; to strengthen education in patriotism and Socialism among them, and to bring into play positive elements among them in order to build a modern and powerful Socialist state and complete the great task of unifying the country; and to oppose the hegemonism and strive together to protect and preserve world peace.

In order to implement and carry out the Party's religious policy correctly and comprehensively, the main task now at hand is to oppose "leftist" erroneous tendencies. At the same time, we must be on our guard to forestall and overcome the erroneous tendency to just let things slide along. All Party members, Party committees on all levels, especially those responsible for religious work, must conscientiously sum up and assimilate the historical experience, positive and negative, of the Party in religious work since the founding of the People's Republic. They must make further progress in their understanding and mastery of the objective law governing the emergence, development, and demise of religion. They should overcome every obstacle and difficulty and resolutely keep the religious policy of the Party on the scientific course laid out for it by Marxism-Leninism and Mao Zedong Thought.

IV. The Party's Present Policy toward Religion

The basic policy the Party has adopted toward the religious question is that of respect for and protection of the freedom of religious belief. This is a long-term policy, one which must be continually carried out until that future time when religion will itself disappear. What do we mean by freedom of religious belief? We mean that every citizen has the freedom to believe in religion and also the freedom not to believe in religion. S/he has also the freedom to believe in this religion or that religion. Within a particular religion, s/he has the freedom to believe in this sect or that sect. A person who was previously a nonbeliever has the freedom to become a religious believer, and one who has been a religious believer has the freedom to become a nonbeliever. We Communists are atheists and must unremittingly propagate atheism. Yet at the same time we must understand that it will be fruitless and extremely harmful to use simple coercion in dealing with the people's ideological and spiritual questions — and this includes religious questions. We must further understand that at the present historical stage the difference that exists between the mass of believers and nonbelievers in matters of ideology and belief is relatively secondary. If we then one-sidedly emphasize this difference, even to the point of giving it primary importance — for example, by discriminating against and attacking the mass of religious believers, while neglecting and denying that the basic political and economic welfare of the mass of both religious believers and nonbelievers is the same — then we forget that the Party's basic task is to unite all the people (and this includes the broad mass of believers and nonbelievers alike) in order that all may strive to construct a modern, powerful Socialist state. To behave otherwise would only exacerbate the estrangement between the mass of believers and nonbelievers as well as incite and aggravate religious fanaticism, resulting in serious consequences for our Socialist enterprise. Our Party, therefore, bases its policy of freedom of religious belief on the theory formulated by Marxism-Leninism, and it is the only correct policy genuinely consonant with the people's welfare.

Naturally, in the process of implementing and carrying out this policy which emphasizes and guarantees the people's freedom to believe in religion, we must, at the same time, emphasize and guarantee the people's freedom not to believe in religion. These are two indispensable aspects of the same question. Any action which forces a nonbeliever to believe in religion is an infringement of freedom of religious belief, just as is any action which forces a believer not to believe. Both are grave errors and not to be tolerated. The guarantee of freedom of religious belief, far from being a hindrance, is a means of strengthening the Party's efforts to disseminate scientific education as well as to strengthen its propaganda against superstition. Furthermore, it should be emphasized that the crux of the policy of freedom of religious belief is to make the question of religious belief a private matter, one of individual free choice for citizens.

The political power in a Socialist state can in no way be used to promote any one religion, nor can it be used to forbid any one religion, as long as it is only a question of normal religious beliefs and practices. At the same time, religion will not be permitted to meddle in the administrative or juridical affairs of state, nor to intervene in the schools or public education. It will be absolutely forbidden to force anyone, particularly people under eighteen years of age, to become a member of a church, to become a Buddhist monk or nun, or to go to temples or monasteries to study Buddhist scripture. Religion will not be permitted to recover in any way those special feudal privileges which have been abolished or to return to an exploitative and oppressive religious system. Nor will religion be permitted to make use in any way of religious pretexts to oppose the Party's leadership or the Socialist system, or to destroy national or ethnic unity.

To sum up, the basic starting point and firm foundation for our handling of the religious question and for the implementation of our policy and freedom of religious belief lies in our desire to unite the mass of believers and nonbelievers and enable them to center all their will and strength on the common goal of building a modernized, powerful Socialist state. Any action or speech that deviates in the least from this basic line is completely erroneous, and must be firmly resisted and opposed by both Party and people.

V. The Party's Work with Religious Professionals

To win over, unite and educate persons in religious circles is primarily the task of religious professionals. It is also the essence of the Party's religious work and most important condition and prerequisite for the implementation of the Party's religious policy. Throughout the country at present, there are about 59,000 professional religious, with affiliation as follows:

Buddhist monks and nuns, including lamas about 27,000
Daoist priests and nuns over 2,600
Muslims about 20,000
Catholics about 3,400
Protestants about 5,900

Due to many years of natural attrition, the present number of professional religious has greatly decreased when compared to the number at Liberation. Their class origin, experience, beliefs, and political ideology are quite diverse, but, in brief, we can say that by far the great majority of them are patriotic, law-abiding, and support the Socialist system. Only a very small minority oppose the constitution and Socialism to the extent of colluding with foreign antirevolutionaries and other bad elements. Many of these professional religious not only maintain intimate spiritual ties with the mass of religious believers, but have an important influence over the spiritual life of the masses which should not be ignored. Moreover, as they carry out their more formal religious duties, they also perform work which serves the people in many ways and which benefits society. For example, they safeguard Buddhist and Daoist temples and churches and protect historical religious relics, engage in agriculture and afforestation, and carry on the academic study of religion, and so on. Therefore, we must definitely give sufficient attention to all persons in religious circles, but primarily professional religious, uniting them, caring for them, and helping them to make progress. We must unrelentingly yet patiently forward their education in patriotism, upholding the law, supporting Socialism, and upholding national and ethnic unity. In the case of Catholics and Protestants, we must strengthen their education in independence and self-government of their churches.

We must make appropriate arrangements for the livelihood of these professional religious and conscientiously carry out the pertinent policies. This is especially true regarding the well-known public figures and intellectuals among them, for whom we should speedily implement our policy to supply them with appropriate remuneration. We must pay very close attention to and reexamine those injustices perpetrated against persons in religious circles and among the mass of religious believers which have not yet been redressed. These must be redressed in accordance with the facts, especially those more serious ones which may have grave consequences. These must be firmly grasped and speedily resolved.

We must foster a large number of fervent patriots in every religion who accept the leadership of the Party and government, firmly support the Socialist path, and safeguard national and ethnic unity. They should be learned in religious matters and capable of keeping close links with the representatives of the religious masses. Furthermore, we must organize religious persons according to their differing situations and capabilities, respectively, to take part in productive labor, serving society, and in the scholarly study of religion. They should also take part in patriotic political movements and friendly international exchanges. All this is done in order to mobilize the positive elements among religious circles to serve the Socialist modernization enterprise.

With regard to those older religious professionals whose term of imprisonment has been completed or whose term at labor reform has ended, as well as those who have not yet been approved to engage in professional religious activities by the religious organizations, each case must be dealt with on its own merits, according to the principle of differentiation. Those who prove to be politically reliable, patriotic, and law-abiding, and who are well-versed in religious matters, can, upon examination and approval by the patriotic religious organizations, be allowed to perform religious duties. As for the rest, they should be provided with alternative means to earn a living.

Marxism is incompatible with any theistic worldview. But in terms of political action, Marxists and patriotic believers can, indeed must, form a united front in the common effort for Socialist modernization. This united front should become an important constitutive element of the broad patriotic front led by the Party during the Socialist period.

VI. Restoration and Administration of Churches, Temples and Other Religious Buildings

To make equitable arrangements for places of worship is a means of implementing the Party's religious policy, and is also an important material condition for the normalization of religious activity. At the time of Liberation, there were about 100,000 places of worship, while at the present time there are about 30,000. This figure includes Buddhist and Daoist temples, churches, and meeting places of simple construction as well as places of worship built by religious believers themselves. The present problem is that we must adopt effective measures, based on each situation, to make equitable arrangements for places of worship. We must systematically and methodically restore a number of temples and churches in large and midsize cities, at famous historical sites, and in areas in which there is a concentration of religious believers, especially ethnic minority areas. Famous temples and churches of cultural and historical value which enjoy national and international prestige must be progressively restored as far as is possible, according to conditions in each place. But in those places where believers are few and have little influence or where churches and temples have already been demolished, we must work out measures which suit the conditions and do things simply and thriftily according to the principle of what will benefit production and the people's livelihood. After consultation with the mass of religious believers and important persons in religious circles, and with the voluntary support of the believers, we should set aside rather simply constructed places of worship. In the process of restoring places of worship, we must not use the financial resources of either country or collective, outside of government appropriations. And we must particularly guard against the indiscriminate building and repairing of temples in rural villages.

We should also direct the voluntary contributions of the mass of religious believers for construction work, so as to build as little as possible. Much less should we go in for large-scale construction lest we consume large sums of money, materials, and manpower and thus obstruct the building up of material and spiritual Socialist civilization. Of course we should not demolish existing structures, but fully consult with believers and important persons in religious circles concerning them in order to reach a satisfactory solution based on the actual situation.

All normal religious activities held in places so designated, as well as those which, according to religious custom, take place in believers' homes — Buddha worship, scripture chanting, incense burning, prayer, Bible study, preaching, Mass, baptism, initiation as a monk or nun, fasting, celebration of religious festivals, extreme unction, funerals, etc. — are all to be conducted by religious organizations and religious believers themselves, under protection of law and without interference from any quarter. With approval of the responsible government department, temples and churches can sell a limited quantity of religious reading matter, religious articles, and works of religious art. As for Protestants gathering in homes for worship services, in principle this should not be allowed, yet this prohibition should not be too rigidly enforced. Rather, persons in the patriotic religious organizations should make special efforts to persuade the mass of religious believers to make more appropriate arrangements.

All places of worship are under the administrative control of the Bureau of Religious Affairs, but the religious organizations and professional religious themselves are responsible for their management. Religious organizations should arrange the scope, frequency, and time of religious services, avoiding interference with the social order and the times set aside for production and labor. No one should go to places of worship to carry on atheist propaganda, nor to incite arguments among the believing masses over the existence of God. In like manner, no religious organization or believer should propagate or preach religion outside places designated for religious services, nor propagate theism, nor hand out religious tracts or other religious reading matter which has not been approved for publication by the responsible government department. In order to ensure further normalization of religious activities, the government should hereafter, in accordance with due process of law, consult fully with representatives from religious circles in order to draw up feasible religious legislation that can be carried out in practice.

Major temples and churches famous for their scenic beauty are not only places of worship, but are also cultural facilities of important historical value. Responsible religious organizations and professional religious should be charged with making painstaking efforts to safeguard them by seeing that these monuments receive good care, that the buildings are kept in good repair, and the environment fully protected so that the surroundings are clean, peaceful, and quiet, suitable for tourism. Under the direction of the responsible government department and religious organizations, the income derived from alms and donations received by these temples and churches can be used mainly for maintenance. A part of this income can even be used as an incentive and reward for professional religious in charge of such places who have been outstanding in this regard.

VII. *The Patriotic Religious Organizations*

To give full play to the function of the patriotic religious organizations is to implement the Party's religious policy and is an important organizational guarantee for the normalization of religious activities. There are a total of eight national patriotic religious organizations, namely: the Chinese Buddhist Association, the Chinese Daoist Association, the Chinese Islamic Association, the Chinese Catholic Patriotic Association, the Chinese Catholic Religious Affairs Committee, the Chinese Catholic Bishops' Conference, the Chinese Protestant "Three-Self" Patriotic Movement, and the China Christian Council. Besides these, there are a number of social groups and local organizations having a religious character. The basic task of these patriotic religious organizations is to assist the Party and the government to implement the policy of freedom of religious belief, to help the broad mass of religious believers and persons in religious circles to continually raise their patriotic and socialist consciousness, to represent the lawful rights and interests of religious circles, to organize normal religious activities, and to manage religious affairs well. All patriotic religious organizations should follow the Party's and government's leadership. Party and government cadres in turn should become adept in supporting and helping religious organizations to solve their own problems. They should not monopolize or do things these organizations should do themselves. Only in this way can we fully develop the positive characteristics of these organizations and allow them to play their proper role and enable them, within constitutional and lawful limits, to voluntarily perform useful work. Thus they can truly become religious groups with a positive influence, and can act as bridges for the Party's and government's work of winning over, uniting with, and educating persons in religious circles.

Furthermore, in order to enable each religion to meet expenses under a program of self-support and self-management, we must conscientiously carry out the policy stipulations governing income from house and property rentals. As for the contributions and donations made by believers, there will be no need to interfere as long as they are freely offered and small in quantity. But professional religious should be convinced that private possession of religious income from temples and churches is not allowed and that any action that forces contributions to be made is forbidden.

VIII. *Educating a New Generation of Clergy*

The training and education of the younger generation of patriotic religious personnel in a planned way will have decisive significance for the future image of our country's religious organizations. We should not only continue to win over, unite with, and educate the present generation of persons in religious circles, but we should also help each religious organization set up seminaries to train well new religious personnel. The task of these seminaries is to create a contingent of young religious personnel who, in terms of politics, fervently love their homeland and support the Party's leadership and the Socialist system and who possess sufficient religious knowledge. These seminaries should hold entrance examinations and admit upright, patriotic young people who wish to devote themselves seriously to this religious profession and who have reached a certain level of cultural development. They should not forcibly enroll persons unwilling to undertake this profession or lacking in the necessary cultural educational foundation. Those young professional religious personnel who prove unfitted for this profession should be transferred elsewhere.

All these young professional religious should continually heighten their patriotic and Socialist consciousness and make efforts to improve their cultural level and their religious knowledge. They should loyally implement the Party's religious policy. They should show respect to all those upright, patriotic professional religious of the older generation, and conscientiously study and imitate their good qualities. These older and upright patriotic religious professionals should, in turn, cherish these younger patriotic professional religious. In this way the younger ones will become integrated into the patriotic progressive elements of the religious world, and, under the leadership of the Party, will become the mainstay ensuring that religious organizations follow the correct direction in their activities.

IX. Communist Party Members and Religion; Relations with Religious Ethnic Minorities

The fact that our Party proclaims and implements a policy of freedom of religious belief does not, of course, mean that Communist Party members can freely believe in religion. The policy of freedom of religious belief is directed toward the citizens of our country; it is not applicable to Party members. Unlike the average citizen, the Party member belongs to a Marxist political party, and there can be no doubt at all that s/he must be an atheist and not a theist. Our Party has clearly stated on many previous occasions: A Communist Party member cannot be a religious believer; s/he cannot take part in religious activities. Any member who persists in going against this proscription should be told to leave the Party. This proscription is altogether correct, and, as far as the Party as a whole is concerned, its implementation should be insisted on in the future. The present question concerns the implementation of this proscription among those ethnic minorities whose people are basically all religious believers. Here, implementation must follow the actual circumstances, and so make use of proper measures, not oversimplifying matters.

We must realize that although a considerable number of Communist Party members among these ethnic minorities loyally implement the Party line, do positive work for the Party, and obey its discipline, they cannot completely shake off all religious influence. Party organizations should in no way simply cast these Party members aside, but should patiently and meticulously carry out ideological work while taking measures to develop more fully their positive political activism, helping them gradually to acquire a dialectical and historical materialist worldview and to gradually shake off the fetters of a religious ideology. Obviously, as we go about expanding our membership, we must take great care not to be rushed into recruiting devout religious believers or those with strong religious sentiments. As for that very small number of Party members who have shown extreme perversity by not only believing in religion but also joining with those who fan religious fanaticism, even to the point of using this fanaticism to oppose the four basic principles, attack the Party line and its aim and policy, and destroy national integrity and ethnic unity, persons such as these have already completely departed from the standpoint fundamental to Party members. If, after having undergone education and criticism, they continue to persist in their erroneous position or feign compliance, then we must resolutely remove them from the Party. If they have committed any criminal acts, then these must be investigated to fix responsibility before the law.

Even though those Party members who live at the grass-roots level among those ethnic minorities where the majority believe in religion have already freed themselves from religious belief, yet if they were to refuse to take part in any of those traditional marriage or funeral ceremonies or mass festivals which have some religious significance, then they would find themselves cut off and isolated from the masses. Therefore, in applying those precepts which forbid Party members who live among these ethnic minorities from joining in religious activities, we must act according to concrete circumstances, according to the principle of differentiation in order to allow Party members to continue to maintain close links with the masses. Although many of the traditional marriage and funeral ceremonies and mass festivals among these ethnic minorities have a religious tradition and significance, they have already essentially become merely a part of ethnic custom and tradition. So long as our comrades, especially those living at the grass-roots level, mark clearly the line between ideology and religious belief, then they can show appropriate respect to and compliance with these ethnic customs and traditions in their daily lives. Of course, this does not mean that those customs and traditions which prove harmful to production or to the physical and mental health of the masses should not be appropriately reformed in accordance with the desire of the majority of the people. But to lump these ethnic customs and traditions together with religious activities is not right and will be harmful to ethnic unity and to the correct handling of the religious question.

All Party members must come to the profound realization that our country is a Socialist state made up of many ethnic minorities. Each minority and each religion is differently situated with regard to this question of the relationship between religion and the ethnic minorities. There are some ethnic minorities in which nearly all the people believe in one particular religion, Islam or Lamaism, for example. Among these peoples, the question of religion and ethnicity is frequently intertwined. But within the Han race, there is basically no relationship between ethnic background and Buddhism, Daoism, Catholicism, or Protestantism. Therefore, we must become adept in distinguishing very concretely the particular situation of each ethnic group and of each religion, and in sizing up the differences and relationships between ethnicity and religion, that we may proceed correctly in our handling of them. We must certainly be vigilant and oppose any use of religious fanaticism to divide our people and any words or actions which damage the unity among our ethnic groups. If our Party cannot with clear mind and firm step master this particular question in the present great struggle as we strive to lead such a great nation of so many ethnic groups as ours forward to become a modern Socialist state, then we shall not be able with any success to unite our peoples to advance together toward this goal.

X. *Criminal and Counter-Revolutionary Activities under the Cover of Religion*

The resolute protection of all normal religious activities suggests, at the same time, a determined crackdown on all criminal and antirevolutionary activities which hide behind the facade of religion, which includes all superstitious practices which fall outside the scope of religion and are injurious to the national welfare as well as to the life and property of the people. All antirevolutionary or other criminal elements who hide behind the facade of religion will be severely punished according to the law. Former professional religious, released upon completion of their term of imprisonment, who return to criminal activities will be punished again in accordance with the law. All banned reactionary secret societies, sorcerers, and witches, without exception, are forbidden to resume their activities. All those who spread fallacies to deceive and who cheat people of their money will, without exception, be severely punished according to the law. Party cadres who profit by these illegal activities will be dealt with all the more severely. Finally, all who make their living by phrenology, fortune telling, and geomancy should be educated, admonished, and helped to earn their living through their own labor and not to engage again in these superstitious practices which only deceive people. Should they not obey, then they should be dealt with according to the law.

In dealing according to the law with all antirevolutionary and other criminal elements who lurk within religious ranks, Party committees on each level and pertinent government departments must pay very close attention to cultivating public opinion. They should make use of irrefutable facts to fully expose the way in which these bad elements use religion to further their destructive activities. Furthermore, they should take care to clearly delineate the line dividing normal religious activities from criminal ones, pointing out that cracking down on criminal activities is in no way to attack, but is rather to protect, normal religious activities. Only then can we successfully win over, unite with, and educate the broad mass of religious believers and bring about the normalization of religious activities.

XI. The International Relations of China's Religions

Buddhism, Islam, Catholicism, and Protestantism, which occupy a very important place among our national religions, are at the same time ranked among the major world religions, and all exercise extensive influence in their societies. Catholicism and Protestantism are widespread in Europe, North America, and Latin America, and other places. Buddhism is strong in Japan and Southeast Asia, while Islam holds sway in several dozen countries in Asia and Africa. Some of these religions are esteemed as state religions in a number of countries. At the present time, contacts with international religious groups are increasing, along with the expansion of our country's other international contacts, a situation which has important significance for extending our country's political influence. But at the same time there are reactionary religious groups abroad, especially the imperialistic ones such as the Vatican and Protestant foreign-mission societies, who strive to use all possible occasions to carry on their efforts at infiltration "to return to the China mainland." Our policy is to actively develop friendly international religious contacts, but also to firmly resist infiltration by hostile foreign religious forces.

According to this policy of the Party, religious persons within our country can, and even should, engage in mutual visits and friendly contacts with religious persons abroad as well as develop academic and cultural exchanges in the religious field. But in all these various contacts, they must firmly adhere to the principle of an independent, self-governing church, and resolutely resist the designs of all reactionary religious forces from abroad who desire to once again gain control over religion in our country. They must determinedly refuse any meddling or interfering in Chinese religious affairs by foreign churches or religious personages, nor must they permit any foreign religious organization (and this includes all groups and their attendant organizations) to use any means to enter our country for missionary work or to secretly introduce and distribute religious literature on a large scale.

All religious organizations and individuals must be educated not to make use of any means whatsoever to solicit funds from foreign church organizations, and religious persons and groups in our country as well as other groups and individuals must refuse any subsidy or funds offered by foreign church organizations for religious purposes. As for donations or offerings given in accordance with religious custom by foreign believers, overseas Chinese, or compatriots from Hongkong and Macao to temples and churches within our territory, these may be accepted. But if it is a question of large contributions or offerings, permission must be sought from the provincial, urban, or autonomous-area governments or from the central government department responsible for these matters before any religious body can accept them on its own, even though it can be established that the donor acts purely out of religious fervor with no strings attached.

We must be vigilant and pay close attention to hostile religious forces from abroad who set up underground churches and other illegal organizations. We must act resolutely to attack those organizations that carry out destructive espionage under the guise of religion. Of course, in doing so, we must not act rashly, but rather investigate thoroughly, have irrefutable evidence at hand, choose the right moment, and execute the case in accordance with lawful procedures.

The new task we now face is that of developing friendly relationships with foreign religious groups while maintaining our policy of independence. The correct guiding principles and policies of the central government and the Party provide the essential basis for doing this type of work well. We should handle the domestic religious question realistically and effectively, strengthen our study of the history of world religion and its present situation, and make efforts to train talented people able to engage in international religious activities. Facts have proven over and over again that if we handle the domestic situation well, then all hostile religious forces from abroad will have little or no opportunity to exploit the situation to their own advantage. Then the international contacts undertaken by religious groups will make smoother and sounder progress and the positive function they should have will be given full play.

XII. The Role of the Party and State Organs in Handling the Religious Question

The basic guarantee for the successful handling of the religious question is the strengthening of the Party's leadership. The Party's religious work is an important constituent of the Party's united front and of its work among the masses since it touches upon various aspects of social life. This demands that Party committees on each level must vigorously direct and organize all relevant departments, which include the United Front Department, the Bureau of Religious Affairs, the Bureau of National Minorities, the Department for Politics and Law, the Departments of Propaganda, Culture, Education, Science and Technology, and Health, as well as the Labor Unions, the Youth League, the Women's Federation, and all other mass organizations, in order to unify ideology, knowledge, and policy. The Departments must each take responsibility for their own work, but act in close coordination and take a realistic grasp of this important task in order to conscientiously and unremittingly carry it through to a successful conclusion.

We must strengthen the government organs responsible for religious affairs, to enable all cadres who give themselves to this particular work to study the Marxist theory of religion in a systematic way, to thoroughly understand the Party's fundamental viewpoint and policy on the religious question, to maintain close relationships with the mass of religious believers, and to consult on equal terms with persons in religious circles in order to cooperate and work together.

An important constituent of the Party's theoretical work on religion is the use of the Marxist viewpoint and method to carry out scientific research on the religious question. An important task for the Party on the propaganda front is the use of Marxist philosophy to criticize idealism (which includes theism), and to educate the masses, especially the broad mass of young people, in a dialectical and historical materialist and scientific worldview. To do this, we must strengthen our propaganda in scientific and cultural knowledge as these relate to an understanding of natural phenomena, the evolution of society, and of human life, with its old age, sickness, death, and ill and good fortune. An indispensable aspect of the Party's theoretical foundation is the establishment of theoretical research teams armed with Marxist ideology for the study of religious theory which would strive to set up organizations for religious research and make use of related university disciplines. Of course, when we publish articles in newspapers and magazines on the religious question, we should adopt a prudent attitude so as not to violate the present policy nor to offend the religious sensibilities of the mass of believers. Those in academic circles should respect the religious mentality of those in religious circles, whereas those in religious circles should also respect the research and propaganda activities carried on by academia in its Marxist interpretation of religion.

The central authorities of Party and State emphasize once again that all Party members must clearly understand that the Party's religious policy is not just a temporary expedient, but a decisive strategy based on the scientific theoretical foundation of Marxism-Leninism and Mao Zedong Thought, which takes as its goal the national unification of the people for the common task of building a powerful, modernized Socialist state. Under Socialism, the only correct fundamental way to solve the religious question lies precisely in safeguarding the freedom of religious belief. Only after the gradual development of the Socialist, economic, cultural, scientific, and technological enterprise and of a Socialist civilization with its own material and spiritual values, will the type of society and level of awareness that gave rise to the existence of religion gradually disappear. Such a great enterprise naturally cannot be accomplished within a short period of time, nor even within one, two, or three generations. Only after a long period of history, after many generations have passed, and after the combined struggle of the broad masses of both believers and nonbelievers will this come about. At that time, the Chinese people, on Chinese soil, will have thoroughly rid themselves of all impoverishment, ignorance, and spiritual emptiness, and will have become a highly developed civilization of material and spiritual values, able to takes its place in the front ranks of mankind in the glorious world. At that time, the vast majority of our citizens will be able to deal with the world and our fellowmen from a conscious scientific viewpoint, and no longer have any need for recourse to an illusory world of gods to seek spiritual solace. This is precisely what Marx and Engels have predicted — that there will be an age when people will have freed themselves from all alienating forces controlling the world and will have come to the stage when they will consciously plan and control the whole of social life. This is also what Comrade Mao Zedong meant when he said that the people, relying on themselves alone, will create a new age both for themselves and for the world. Only when we enter this new age will all that shows a religious face in the present world finally disappear. Therefore, each of us Party members, from generation to generation, must put forth all our best efforts in the struggle to bring about this brilliant future.

Document 2

Fully Implement the Policy of Religious Freedom

From Selected Documents of the Third Plenary Session of the Eleventh Party Congress, 1979. *First published in* Renmin Ribao (*People's Daily*), 17 October 1979. *Translated by Zheng Xi'an and Donald MacInnis.*

The policy of religious freedom is the basic and long-standing policy of our nation and Party for dealing with religious questions. The constitutions adopted by each of the National People's Congresses since the founding of the People's Republic of China have stipulated that citizens should enjoy freedom of religious belief. That provision legally guarantees freedom of religious belief for each citizen, and at the same time sets forth the law by which we deal with religious questions. In the days when Lin Biao and the "Gang of Four" ran rampant, this policy of the Party was seriously violated and the rights of citizens regarding freedom of religious belief were rudely trampled. Today, a situation of stability and unity has emerged all over China. People of all [ethnic] nationalities are engaged in the new Long March toward the four modernizations, and to correctly understand and carry out our Party's policy for religious freedom in an all-around way is of vital importance for the task of uniting the broad masses of believers and patriots in religious circles, and for mobilizing the masses to make full contribution to the four modernizations.

I

The main religions of the world, Buddhism, Christianity and Islam, have long histories in China. A considerable number of people are religious believers, particularly among the peoples of the minority nationalities. Religion still exercises a rather strong influence upon these people, and the influence of religion is quite widespread in the world as well.

Our Party has always paid great attention to the issue of religion. In the period of new democratic revolution Comrade Mao Zedong time and again expounded on Marxist-Leninist religious theories, and our Party set up a correct line and a series of concrete policies to handle religious questions.

After the Liberation of our entire country, the Party's policy on freedom of religious belief was written into the program of the CPPCC and the constitution of the People's Republic of China, and religious belief has been respected by the state and protected by law. The people's governments at every level have done a great deal of work, earnestly carrying out the policy of freedom of religious belief. The broad masses of religious believers, together with all the people of China, have made contributions on various fronts to the Socialist cause, securing political liberation for themselves and becoming their own masters in economic affairs. Chairman Mao, Premier Zhou Enlai, Committee Chairman Zhu and other State leaders have granted many interviews to people from religious circles, giving them important instructions, encouraging them to oppose imperialism and love their country, and to make their contributions to the Socialist motherland. According to the wishes of the broad masses of religious believers, each of the [major] religions in our country, with the help of the government, has established its own religious or patriotic organizations, has launched powerful patriotic anti-imperialism movements, has changed the situation of Chinese churches formerly under the control of exploiting classes at home and abroad, has abolished the system of feudal privileges and exploitation in religious circles, and has achieved independent and democratic management of their religious affairs.

Religious leaders have not only done a great deal of work in helping the government implement the policy of freedom of religious belief, but have also made great progress in their own political thinking. Finally, the revolutionary line of the Central Committee of the Chinese Communist Party has played a dominant role in the achievements accomplished in religious work.

Nevertheless, Lin Biao and the "gang of four" have, in recent years, seriously violated the policy of freedom of religious belief. They recklessly trampled on the religious theories of Marxism-Leninism and Mao Zedong Thought, have violated the religious policy, stopped religious activities, and even claimed that "religion no longer exists," and that "religion has disappeared into the museum of history." They rudely interfered with people's religious beliefs, closed and tore down churches and temples, forcefully prohibited the normal activities of religious believers, and tried to wipe out religion by administrative decree. They took enemies for friends and friends for enemies; they confused the two contradictions [antagonistic and non-antagonistic] which are, in fact, of different natures; they called patriots among the religious leaders and believers "monsters and demons" and "objects of dictatorship" and denounced them with cruel accusations. Categorizing them as counterrevolutionaries, they dealt them merciless blows, setting up a great many unjust, fake, and erroneous cases based on fabricated charges.

They broke up the unity of the minority nationalities by forcefully prohibiting the practice of some of their customs, calling them superstitions. They committed outrages of many kinds against religions, violating the Socialist legal system, wrecking the Party's reputation for being practical and realistic, damaging relations between the Party and the broad masses, breaking up the [professional] religious workers, creating disorder among class groupings, dampening the Socialist enthusiasm of numerous religious believers, and seriously affecting production.

Meanwhile, one group of people, taking advantage of the chaos wrought by Lin Biao and the "gang of four," made money for themselves by exploiting the people through illegal superstitious activities playing on the religious sentiments and inflicting personal losses on the masses. These are the people who provided the social foundation for the activities of Lin Biao and the "gang of four," and some of them also were part of the "fight, smash, and rob" gangs.

Since the smashing of the "gang of four," the policy of freedom of religious belief has been restored. This is welcomed by the broad masses of the people. However, up to this very day, the extreme Leftist line of Lin Biao and the "gang of four" still has strong influence over some government cadres in some places. It will be a longtime task to wipe out these widespread pernicious effects.

II

Lin Biao and the "gang of four" violated the religious policy, putting forth the extreme leftist slogan "Wipe out religion," which had disastrous political effects and is anti-Marxist in theory.

Marxists do not believe in religion. They hold that religion is idealism, diametrically opposed to materialism and science. But, on the other hand, Marxism has always held that religion is the product of history, with its own objective laws of birth, growth, and disappearance. Only when the cognitive and social sources which bring about the birth and growth of religion diminish will religion finally wither away. Meanwhile, it should be understood that religious belief is an ideological matter, and that the great majority of religious believers are laboring people. Their different beliefs do not interfere with their economic contributions or hinder their political unity.

As Lenin pointed out in *Socialism and Religion*, "Unity in this revolutionary struggle of the oppressed class for the creation of a paradise on earth is more important to us than united views among the proletariat about paradise in heaven." The basic way to solve the problem of religion can only be to unite with the broad masses of the people, including the religious believers, to completely wipe out exploitation, to develop a high level of science and technology, to significantly raise the level of the people's material and cultural life and ideological consciousness, and thus to gradually eliminate the sources by which religion comes into being and grows. Historical experience has proved that this is the only correct way to deal with the religious question and to unite with the broad masses of people so that they may take part in Socialist revolution and social construction.

With regard to Article 36 of the national constitution, some people speak only about the freedom not to believe in religion but do not speak about, or dare to speak about, the freedom of religious belief. They obviously hold a partial view. Some comrades are afraid of being labeled "Right deviationists" or "capitulationists" if they advocate freedom of religious belief. This shows that the widespread pernicious influence of Lin Biao and the "gang of four" has not been completely wiped out. The correct explanation of Article 36 of the constitution should be: To believe or not believe in religion is a personal affair of each individual; each citizen has freedom to believe in religion as well as freedom not to believe in religion; religious believers will not be discriminated against. All religions are politically equal; there is no dominant religion, and none is allowed.

Other people think that freedom of religious belief means freedom to believe in the mind and heart, but that there is neither need nor permission for outward expression of that belief. This is also wrong. Since religious belief is legally permitted, then certain religious activities (such as reading of scriptures, public worship, observing religious festivals, etc.) and religious organizations and systems should be allowed. As long as these activities do not interfere with production and social order they should be permitted. They should also be allowed, in accordance with practical situations, to have places in which to carry on their religious activities, for that is their legal right.

Article 36 of our constitution also stipulates the "freedom to propagate atheism." This does not mean that the propagation of theism is prohibited. Comrade Mao Zedong said, "We allow various opinions among the people; that is, there is freedom to criticize, to express different views, and to advocate theism or atheism (i.e., materialism)." Therefore, religious professionals should be permitted to preach religious doctrines in places for religious activities such as churches and temples. Atheistic propaganda should not be carried on in churches, temples, and places for religious services; it is even more improper to force others to accept atheism by harsh and simplistic methods. In this way we can avoid the useless disputes between believers and nonbelievers which affect unity.

While citizens enjoy religious freedom, they must, at the same time, conscientiously support the united leadership of the people's government, the independence and unity of their motherland, and the policies that reflect the will of the people which safeguard the normal order in their work, production, and life. Any act that uses religious superstitition to upset stability, unity, and the four modernizations is wrong and cannot be permitted. Article 147 in our newly published criminal law stipulates that "state functionaries who illegally deprive citizens of their religious freedom and drastically encroach on the customs of the minority nationalities will be sentenced to imprisonment or held in custody for up to two years." Article 165 stipulates that "Sorcerers, witches, and those who spread rumors or swindle people of their money or property are to be imprisoned, held in custody, or kept under surveillance for up to two years; for serious cases, the sentence will be imprisonment for two to seven years."

This makes it clear that we must correctly and comprehensively understand and exercise the democratic rights of freedom of religious belief, and must educate those who distort the religious policy, using superstitious practices in violation of the law, jeopardizing social order or production. We must check their activities and, for serious cases, punish them in accordance with the law.

III

To carry out the Party's policy of freedom of religious belief and to properly deal with this question, we should, at the present time, understand the following points:

1. We must be fully aware of the characteristics of religion, that is: its long-standing nature, its mass nature, its nationalities [ethnic] nature, and its international and complex natures (for short, its five characteristics). The religious question can never be solved by means of a few political movements or administrative decrees. We can rely only on persuasion and education to deal with ideological issues, not mandatory decrees, only the democratic method, not force or dictatorship. To do otherwise will not only fail to solve such questions, but can be very harmful.

2. We must strictly distinguish between the two kinds of contradictions [antagonistic and nonantagonistic]. Generally speaking, the religious question is a problem among the people, an ideological problem. There are few counterrevolutionaries now using the guise of religion. We must draw a clear line of distinction between political problems and those of religious belief, as well as the line between general political problems and problems between the enemy and ourselves. We must not politically discriminate against religious believers. Nonbelievers and believers are politically equal. Lenin pointed out long ago that "there should be no differentiation of rights

among the citizens, and any reference to a citizen's religious belief should be completely expunged from formal [state] documents."

To use religion to carry out sabotage is not a question of religion, but a question of violating the law. We must keep sober-minded on this question. The few evildoers and counter-revolutionaries who use religion always fear the unity of the masses of the people and the implementation of religious policy. In their anti-Socialist aims, they provoke religious hostility. We must not relax our vigilance. As long as we implement the policy of freedom of religious belief, respect the proper religious activities of the believers, and strengthen the administration of religious activities, we can make it very difficult for counterrevolutionaries and evildoers to hide themselves among the masses of people, creating disturbances and sabotage. We can unite with the people to strike blows at the enemy and consolidate the proletarian dictatorship in our country.

3. Religions in our country, particularly Islam and Lamaism, have considerable influence among the minority nationalities. Nationality and religion are of two different categories, but they overlap. We must pay sufficient attention to these two points. It is absolutely forbidden to uphold feudal privileges in order to solve nationalities problems; nor should we regard nationalities problems as religious problems and handle them in the same way.

4. Patriots among religious circles are a component of the united revolutionary front of our country. It was totally correct for our Party to adopt the policy of unity, education, and reform toward religious persons, for it has been a success. Along with the progress of the Socialist revolution and social construction in our country, most patriotic religious persons, educated through revolutionary practice and political studies, have made great progress in supporting the leadership of the Party and taking the Socialist road. Since the smashing of the "gang of four" they have endorsed the Central Committee of the Party, they support the general tasks of the new period, adhere to an anti-imperialist and patriotic stand, love their motherland, abide by the law, and enthusiastically support the goal of modernization for our country. Therefore we must pay close attention to carrying out the religious policy for these people, taking further steps to unite with them in the march toward the goal of four modernizations, fully mobilizing their enthusiasm and creating the proper conditions for them to contribute their efforts. Of course, in the new Long March, religious personages have to continue to study and remold their thinking in order to continue making progress.

5. We must continue to strengthen the ideological and political work among the broad masses of believers and patriots in religious circles. We must give them Socialist education, teach them to love their motherland and abide by law, promote science and culture among them, teach them to love the Party and to love Socialism, and to take active roles in the cause of Socialist revolution and Socialist construction. At the same time we must

raise their ideological consciousness through participation in practical struggles. However, while carrying out this propaganda and education, we must resolutely avoid hurting the religious feelings of the believers, and, even more, avoid forcing people to give up their religious belief.

The question of how to deal with the masses of religious believers is not one of finding a method of work or thinking, but a question of mass viewpoint. All of us should give our attention to this work. We must earnestly carry out the Party's policy [among religious believers], help them to solve practical difficulties, and guide them to participate in Socialist construction.

The fate of our country and our people will be decided by whether or not we can accomplish the four modernizations in this century. People all over China are, at present, making great efforts. We believe that as long as we can strengthen the Party's leadership and do our work well, the broad masses of believers and patriots in religious circles will surely keep to the Socialist road, support the Party's leadership and the dictatorship of the proletariat, conscientiously abide by the laws and regulations of the government, support the present situation of stability and unity, and, led by the Central Committee of the Party, contribute to the realization of the four modernizations.

Document 3

Religion and Feudal Superstition

From Selected Documents of the Third Plenary Session of the Eleventh Party Congress, 1979. *First published in* Renmin Ribao *(People's Daily), 15 March 1979. Translated by Zheng Xi'an and Donald MacInnis.*

Recently our newspaper office has received some letters from readers asking, "What is religion and what is superstition?" "What is 'freedom of religious belief' as pledged to citizens by the Constitution, and what is this 'feudal superstition' that we should oppose, or even prohibit?" After visiting comrades in charge of leading offices in religious affairs and religious research, we have prepared this response for our readers, based on their opinions.

The Editors, *Renmin Ribao*

All worship directed to mysterious supernatural powers may be called superstition. Religion is superstition, but not all superstitions are religion. For instance, various feudal superstitions are not religion.

All religions are illusory, erroneous reflections created by humans who experience fear and helplessness when faced by the forces of nature and society. The negative functions of religion become all the more salient as human beings enter a class society, with its exploiting classes and religious professionals. It makes the broad masses of laboring people resign themselves to mistreatment and oppression, submitting to the will of Heaven in the class struggle and their struggle with nature. Therefore Marxism holds that religion is the opium that drugs the people's spirit, which is used as a tool by the exploiting classes in their domination of the people. Marxists have consistently opposed religion in any form.

But, for the broad masses of people, religion is a matter of world outlook closely connected with idealism. The solution of this problem is linked to a long-term process which includes the withering away of social classes and the dissemination and progress of science and culture. Before religious believers completely change their idealistic beliefs, we must acknowledge, allow, and respect their beliefs in order to help lead them, through Party and government propaganda, education, and social practice [actual experience] of belief vs. nonbelief, superstition vs. science, idealism vs. materialism, to draw correct conclusions and rid themselves of these spiritual shackles. The actual practice of the past twenty-nine years since Liberation has fully proved the correctness and effectiveness of the Party's policy. This is also the starting point of Article 36 in the new Constitution which says, "Citizens enjoy the freedom to believe in religion, and also the freedom not to believe and to propagate atheism." Hereafter we should firmly carry out this policy.

In doing that, we must distinguish religion from feudal superstition. By religion, we chiefly mean worldwide religions, such as Christianity, Islam, Buddhism, and the like. They have scriptures, creeds, religious ceremonies, organizations, and so on. These religions have histories of thousands of years. They have extensive influence among the masses of the people, particularly among people of minority nationalities. Religious freedom, first of all, refers to these religions.

Our nation's religious policy guarantees freedom to take part in normal religious activities for all religious professionals and believers, but they have to abide by government policy and laws. They are not allowed to interfere with the freedom of other people (including the freedom not to believe in religion), to interfere in politics and public education, or to bring back the system of feudal exploitation and oppression which has been abolished since Liberation. Even more, we must not permit class enemies to use religion to carry out counterrevolutionary activities and other unlawful practices. Therefore the government must strengthen supervision over religious organizations.

By superstition we generally mean activities conducted by shamans, and sorcerers, such as magic medicine, magic water, divination, fortune telling, avoiding disasters, praying for rain, praying for pregnancy, exorcising demons, telling fortunes by physiognomy, locating house or tomb sites by geomancy, and so forth. These are all absurd and ridiculous. Anyone possessing rudimentary knowledge will not believe in them. Since Liberation, these activities have been losing ground among the people, but some years ago, due to the interference of Lin Biao and the "gang of four," these things have been increasing again in villages where the "disaster" ["cultural revolution"] was serious. In one or two places the daily life and economic output of the people have been affected and their mental and physical health have suffered. We must not neglect these activities. They must be suppressed. We must criticize and educate the shamans and sorcerers, dealing sternly and striking resolutely in such cases. They are absolutely forbidden to carry out superstitious activities on the pretext of religious freedom. Education is the main way to help working people who are cheated by these superstitious activities.

It is true, real life is much more complex than simple concepts and definitions. There still are, among the people, certain long-standing activities such as ancestor worship and belief in ghosts and deities. Although they are a kind of superstition, we generally do not prohibit them by administrative decree as long as they do not affect collective political and economic activities; rather, we solve the problems by patient persuasion and lasting education in science, culture, and atheism.

In dealing with the problem of religion and feudal superstition, we must make a strict distinction between contradictions among the people [nonantagonistic] and those between the enemy and ourselves [antagonistic].

At the same time, by carrying out the policy of freedom of religious belief, we must unite with the masses of believers in a better way in the common struggle toward the goal of the four modernizations.

Document 4

Article 36, Religious Policy

From Draft of Revised Constitution of the People's Republic of China. *NCNA in Chinese, 27 April 1982. In FE 7014, 29 April 1982, and reprinted in China Study Project* Documentation, *No. 8, May 1982, p. 3.*

The draft of the revised Constitution of the PRC was announced by NCNA on 27 April. Article 36, on religious belief, runs as follows:

Article 36: Citizens of the PRC enjoy freedom of religious belief.

No organ of state, mass organization, or person is allowed to force any citizen to believe or not to believe in religion. It is impermissible to discriminate against any citizen who believes or does not believe in religion.

The state protects legitimate religious activities. No person is permitted to use religion to conduct counterrevolutionary activities or activities which disrupt social order, harm people's health, or obstruct the educational system of the country.

Religion is not subject to the control of foreign countries.

Document 5

Penal Code, Section 147: On the Crime of Illegally Depriving People of the Freedom of Religious Belief

Reprinted from the Supreme People's Procuratorate, Department No. 2, Guangming Ribao Publishing House, Beijing, 1986, pp. 339-42, in Zhongguo Tianzhujiao *(The Catholic Church in China), December 1987. Translated in China Study Project Journal, Vol. 3:1, April 1988, pp. 49-51.*

China is a united country consisting of many nationalities, and each nationality has its own customs and practices. It is a country of many people covering a wide area, with many religious sects and differences of religious belief. For this reason, guaranteeing a citizen's freedom of religious belief and having respect for the customs and practices of minority peoples is a major question which has relevance to the implementation of equality between nationalities and to the bringing together of all nationalities and religious sects in the struggle to achieve the four modernizations. China's constitution clearly states that citizens of the Chinese People's Republic have the freedom of religious belief, and that no government organization or social body, or any individual, may force a citizen to believe in religion or not to believe in religion, nor may they discriminate between citizens who are religious believers and citizens who are not (Chinese Constitution, Article 36, Paragraphs 1 and 2). The constitution also states that each nationality has the freedom to retain or to change its own customs and habits (Constitution, Article 4, Paragraph 4). In order to ensure that citizens will enjoy the above-mentioned rights, China's penal code specially provides that State officials who deprive people of their religious freedom or interfere with the customs and practices of minority nationalities in serious circumstances will be punished.

The crime of illegally depriving people of the freedom of religious belief means serious acts undertaken by State officials to deprive other people of their freedom of religious belief illegally.

The crime of interfering with the customs and practices of minority nationalities means serious acts undertaken by State officials to destroy the customs and habits of minority nationalities by forceful means. . . .

2. Correctly recognizing and dealing with the customs and practices of minority nationalities.

Section 147 of the penal code states that State officials who illegally deprive people of the freedom of religious belief or who encroach upon the customs and practices of minority nationalities shall, if the offenses are of a serious nature, be liable to imprisonment or labor reform for a period not exceeding two years.

Document 6

New Regulations Governing Offenses against Public Order

Xinhua, 5 September 1986. In FE 8363, 13 September 1986, and reprinted in China Study Project Journal, Vol. 1:3, November 1986, p. 28.

The regulations were adopted by the Seventeenth Session of the Standing Committee of the Sixth NPC on 5 September 1986. The only clause directly relating to the religious situation is contained in Article 24, and reads:

People who commit one of the following public offenses will be detained for not more than 15 days, fined not more than 200 *yuan* or given a warning:

1. People who knowingly buy stolen goods.

2. People who resell train, bus or steamer tickets.

3. People who contravene the government's prohibition by smoking opium or giving or taking injections of morphine or other narcotic drugs.

4. People who use feudalistic or superstititous means to disturb public order or gain property by cheating, but whose offense does not deserve criminal punishment.

5. People who drive other people's motor vehicles without permission.

Section II

Statements by Religious Policymakers

Introduction

Translations of four articles on religious policy by authorities at national and provincial levels typify a host of similar articles published in recent years.

Document 7 is a radio report of a speech by a provincial party leader, Liu Zhengwei, who justifies the religious policy on practical grounds: it is necessary to unify all the people for building a "powerful, modern socialist country."

Document 8 was written by a research scholar, a staff member of the Institute for Study of World Religions of the National Academy of Social Sciences, and published in the Party monthly, *Red Flag*. After noting several reasons for the new policy on religion, he, too, cites pragmatic reasons for the policy. Believers and nonbelievers alike have common economic interests, and allowing freedom of belief will "arouse all the more the enthusiasm of the masses of believers . . . [for] working concertedly to implement the four modernizations."

Finally, we have an excerpt from an important speech given in 1983 by the late Director of the Religious Affairs Bureau, Qiao Liansheng, to the delegates attending the national Catholic Representatives Meeting in Beijing. Section 5 of his speech has been selected for translation because it articulates the official position regarding alleged control by foreign missionaries of the churches in China before 1949, singling out the Vatican as the worst example of foreign religious forces "serving the ends of imperialism and colonialism."

Document 7

Liu Zhengwei Speaks at Religious Work Conference

Hunan Provincial Radio, 27 March 1986, in JPRS-CPS-86-033, 25 April 1986, p.64.

Yesterday morning [26 March 1986], at the closing ceremony of the provincial conference on religious work, Liu Zhengwei, deputy secretary of the

Hunan Provincial CPC Committee, emphatically pointed out: CPC committees and government organizations at all levels must further strengthen leadership over religious work, continuously and firmly grasp the implementation of the Party's policies toward religion, and make still greater contributions toward the four modernizations and the great cause of the unification of our motherland.

Liu Zhengwei said: Over the past few years, our province has seriously implemented the Party's official policies toward religions; enhanced understanding of the importance of religious work; reversed verdicts on grievances, trumped-up cases, and miscarriages of justice affecting people in religious circles; and solved the problems left over from history. In the aspect of implementing the policies toward religions, it has made arrangements for sites for religious activities, solved the problems of the self-support of some religious organizations, and, at the same time, trained a number of young patriotic religious workers. Religious organizations and some temples, mosques and churches have provided services for production, done social and public welfare work, and made certain contributions toward our province's four modernizations.

As for the problems existing in our province's religious work, Liu Zhengwei said: Regarding religious problems, some comrades are still affected by Leftist ideological influence and take a laissez-faire attitude. They set the implementation of the Party's policies toward religion against the building of the two Socialist civilizations. Thus, this has directly affected the correct and all-round implementation of the Party's policies toward religion. We must seriously study the spirit of the relevant documents of the central authorities and unceasingly heighten understanding of the importance of religious work.

He said: The fundamental starting point and underlying objective in our implementation of the Party's policy on freedom of religious belief and in our dealing with all religious problems are to unite all people who profess religion and those who do not, and to concentrate their will and energy for the target of building a powerful, modern Socialist country.

Document 8

Why Must China Practice Freedom of Religious Belief?

By Lei Zhenchang, Red Flag, *No. 5, 1 March 1981. Translated in* China Study Project *Bulletin, No. 16, July 1981, pp. 17-20.*
Lei Zhengchang is a staff member of the Institute for World Religions, Beijing.

Some people point out: China is a Socialist country with Marxism-Leninism-Mao Zedong Thought as its guide. Communists are atheists. Why has China adopted the policy of allowing freedom of religious belief?

It is true that Marxism-Leninism-Mao Zedong Thought is the thinking guiding our Party and our country. Marxism is thoroughgoing materialism. Not only is it in disagreement with the religious idealist world outlook, but also it attempts gradually to emancipate those who believe in religion from the fetters of religion. Opposing theism is the elementary principle for all materialists and Marxists. However, the existence of religion is caused by ideological understanding, in addition to economic factors. The viewpoint which holds that religion will disappear by itself very quickly with the development of economic construction, science, and technology is unrealistic. For this reason, it is necessary to lay down correct principles and policies on religion. Freedom of religious belief is one of these principles and policies.

As stipulated in the constitution, freedom to believe in religion is the basic policy by which our Party and our country handles religious problems. As set forth in this policy, every Chinese citizen enjoys freedom to believe in the religion of his choosing; he enjoys freedom to believe in one sect or another of the same religion; he enjoys freedom to believe in religion today and not to believe in it tomorrow, and also freedom not to believe in religion today but to believe in it tomorrow; a clergyman enjoys freedom to preach theism in a house of worship, and an atheist enjoys freedom to propagate atheism. Whether he is a believer or not and whether he believes in one religion or another, a citizen of the PRC, according to the constitution, has the duty to love his motherland and support Socialism and the leadership of the Communist Party. Today, we are required to work with one heart and one mind and unite to implement the four modernizations under the leadership of the CCP and to build our country into a modern Socialist power with highly developed democracy and civilization. For this reason, religious activity should be clearly defined. That is, religion should neither intervene in politics, education, and marriage nor resort to exploitation and oppression. Religious organizations are not allowed to receive subsidies or gifts from foreign religious bodies. That is to say, religious organizations should be patriotic and free, and should only deal with questions of religious belief.

This policy of allowing freedom to believe in religion is a correct policy formulated on the basis of the fundamental Marxist principles, after making a scientific analysis of religions and in the light of the actual conditions in our country.

First, Marxists have carried out a profound scientific investigation of religion by treating it as a social phenomenon and analyzing the social and ideological causes of the birth and development of religion. They hold that religion is an outcome of oppression by nature and society and a backward world outlook caused by man's failure to understand the objective laws of nature, society, and mankind in given historical conditions. Religion will not disappear before man can effectively resist and conquer oppression by the forces of nature and society, and as long as this oppression, a root cause of the birth and development of religion exists. Of course, religion will not exist forever. Religious influence weakens and eventually disappears with the development of production, the flourishing of science and technology, the improvement of people's material and cultural lives after the overthrow of the exploiting system, and the heightening of the people's ideological consciousness and cognitive power. However, this will take a very long time. As long as religion exists, there will be people who want to believe in it. This is an objective fact. At present, quite a large number of people in China believe in religion. We must respect this objective fact and proceed from the actual situation to consider and draw up a relevant policy.

Second, religious belief is chiefly a question of ideological understanding. An ideological problem can be solved only by means of persuasion and of increasing ideological consciousness. It is a waste of effort to forbid religious belief or "exterminate" religion by administrative order. For different reasons, many people in China and abroad formerly tried to suppress religion by rigid tactics, which might succeed in putting down religious activity for a short while, but, on the contrary, this aroused religious fanaticism and promoted religion. Engels severely condemned the attempt to "exterminate religion," calling it a stupid way to "serve God." For this reason, as long as there are people who believe in religion, the State should respect their religious belief and allow them freedom to believe in religion.

Apart from this, the overwhelming majority of believers are working people. They differ from Marxists in world outlook, and from nonbelievers in understanding. However, this does not prevent people from having a common economic interest and having the same political orientation. To Marxists, the common economic interest and same political orientation mean much more than difference in religious belief. In fact, generally speaking, the contradiction between believers and nonbelievers and between theists and atheists among the Chinese people is not acute and has never developed into nationwide religious conflict. This has been so during the period of the new democratic revolution and during the Socialist period. Almost all believers in our country favor Socialism, and support the leadership of the Communist Party. Particularly at present, implementing the four modernizations and building our country into a prosperous Socialist power are not only the eager hope of nonbelievers, but also the sincere wish of believers. Practicing the policy of allowing freedom to believe in religion will arouse all the more enthusiasm of the broad masses of believers and lead them to join the other people of the country in working concertedly to implement the four modernizations.

We should also see that China is a multinational country, where different religions are practiced. In our country, religion is often linked with the historical development and customs and habits of some minority nationalities. For example, ten nationalities, including the Hui, Uyghur, and Kazakh, are Islamic; people of the Tibetan, Mongol, Dai and Uyghur nationalities generally believe in Buddhism (including Lamaism); and the Christian religion has extensive influence among the Miao, Yu, and Yi nationalities.

Therefore, we should not confuse nationality with religion, but we should realize that nationality issues are closely related with religious issues. Carrying out the policy of allowing freedom to believe in religion is of vital significance in solving correctly nationality issues, strengthening unity among nationalities, and consolidating and developing the Chinese nation as one big family.

Lastly, religion is not only a kind of ideology. It also generates a formidable social force in the international political field. About 61 percent of the world's population are believers. Religion holds a decisive position in social matters in those countries which have designated state religions. Practicing the policy of allowing freedom to believe in religion in our country will promote friendly communications and cultural exchanges between the Chinese people and the people of other countries, strengthen unity and cooperation between China and the Third World countries, and greatly benefit the cause of opposing hegemonism and protecting world peace.

These are reasons why our Party and country practice the policy of allowing freedom to believe in religion. Thus, this policy is not an expedient but a fundamental step to handle religious issues. It is not a short-term but a long-term policy. It is not spurious but real. Of course, religious activity and feudal superstitious activity should be distinguished from one another and dealt with differently. Religion is a kind of superstition, but feudal superstitious activity is not religious activity. Formerly, the reactionary superstitious sects and all witchcraft and sorcery were banned and forbidden to resume activity. Those who spread fallacies to deceive people or make use of feudal superstitious activity to swindle money out of people or harm people will be dealt with or punished by law according to the seriousness of their offenses.

Document 9

Concerning Questions about Control of Religious Organizations and Affairs by Outside Forces

Speech by Qiao Liansheng, Director of the Religious Affairs Bureau, to assembled delegates, National Catholic Representatives Meeting, Beijing, April 1983. This is Section 5 of the speech, translated from Zhongguo Tianzhujiao *(The Catholic Church in China), No. 7, 1983. Translation by Donald MacInnis.*

Two themes dominate Qiao Liansheng's speech: preventing the restoration of foreign influence and power in the Chinese Catholic Church; and maintaining the independence, self-direction, and self-governance of the Chinese church and reinforcing the patriotic service of all Catholics in support of Socialist nation building.

To maintain our nation's strength and power, and to undergird the independence and selfhood of all religious organizations in our nation, the restoration of foreign religious influence and power must be prevented. It is essential that we utilize the joint forces of all churches to assure that "no religious organizations or religious affairs shall be controlled by foreign forces."[1]

There are historical reasons for bringing this up, as well as current reasons. It is based on our country's policy of absolute independence and selfhood toward the outside, and our nation's history of over 100 years of oppression by foreign imperialism. Even in recent years hostile outside forces have directed a series of destructive (sabotage) actions against us, [forcing us] to defend the independence, peace, and rights of our nation. Therefore this regulation must be obeyed and implemented by all religious organizations, with no exception for the Catholic Church.

Reflecting on the history of our nation since 1840, it is difficult for one to forget over 100 years of Catholic and Protestant propagation in China, coinciding with the aggressive incursions and oppression of imperialism against China, no different from a nation under semicolonialism and semifeudalism.

The Catholic and Protestant churches of that period served as the vanguard and tool of imperialist aggression. No one can deny these historical facts. For the past 100 and more years there have been, in the circles of the Chinese Catholic Church, persons with patriotism and national self-respect who consistently and diligently sought for political means to escape from the road of control and domination by all foreign church powers, advocating a self-supporting, self-governing church. But, because of the semicolonial status of all China at that time, this advocacy had absolutely no chance of success. In 1949, all the peoples of China, under the leadership of Mao Zedong, chairman of the Chinese Communist Party, after a protracted and bitter struggle, finally overthrew the rule of imperialism, feudalism, and bureaucratic capitalism (three great mountains), with the great victory of the new democratic revolution and the founding of the People's Republic of China. Since then, the people have seized national authority, becoming the rulers of the nation; national independence made it possible to free the Chinese Catholic Church from foreign church powers, and especially to cast off the control of the Vatican. Progressive, patriotic members of the Catholic clergy and laity joined the people of our nation to protect its independence and integrity, resolutely taking the road of an independent, self-guided, and self-governing church. The Vatican's long-standing control used the Chinese Catholic Church to serve the ends of imperialism and colonialism, ruthlessly repressing the inexorably emerging achievements of the Chinese people. The result was wave after wave of determined people sacrificing lives and blood, a great treasure. Can it be that we still hope to replay this history? Do we wish to fall again into such bitter times? Certainly not! No one in our entire nation would reply otherwise.

We oppose the domination of Chinese churches by any foreign power, including the Vatican. The Vatican is a nation with particular, monarchical, authoritarian political characteristics, called by the name "Vatican State." It is historically the seat of the pope, the symbol of the power of the pope. The reality of the so-called pope is the monarchical power of this [sovereign] state. This state mixes politics with all religious matters, masquerading under a religious guise. All religious manifestations of the Vatican, all instructions and so on have a political color; all are in political service to its colonialism. Against this, the Catholics of our nation and other citizens must be sufficiently alert and informed to make accurate analyses so as never to allow a monarchical political party with the status of a nation to become the partner of faith, because of one's allegiance to Catholicism, or to blindly follow and serve, and thus be hoodwinked by politics, even to betray our nation.

The Vatican is an enemy of the Chinese people, which came only to serve the expansion of colonialism in the twentieth century, supporting Germany, Italy, Japan, France, and Spain. When Japanese militarism invaded China, dividing our nation's soil by force of arms, when the puppet government of Manchukuo was established in our northeastern provinces, the Vatican was the first to give diplomatic recognition. After the founding of the People's Republic of China, the Vatican maintained a hostile attitude to new China, and from the beginning carried on a series of wrecking [sabotage] activities toward our nation; friends of Catholicism seated here know that very clearly. In recent years, they [Vatican] have used all possible opportunities, on the one hand to put forth a posture of reconciliation with

China, on the other hand to increasingly engage in undercutting the people's democratic powers in our nation and to engage in activities designed to wreck [sabotage] and alter the Socialist system of our nation. Not long ago just such a gang of counterrevolutionaries wearing the outer garments of the Catholic Church was uncovered. There is much factual evidence that the Vatican has never given up its plotting to control the Chinese Catholic Church, even to "changing the structure of Chinese Socialism," and restoring the colonial system in our nation, to serve the ends of modern-day imperialism. Therefore, in the struggle of Chinese Catholicism against the imposition of foreign domination, it is clearly a political question, a question of loving or not loving our country.

For more than thirty years the cause of independence, self-guidance, and self-government of our country's Catholicism, and the undertaking to change the long-standing colonialist nature of the Chinese Catholic Church, have been very successful. Today's Chinese Catholic Church is already completely in the hands of Chinese clergy and laity, a church governed entirely by Chinese themselves, with great influence and voice, able to bring together and educate the broad membership of Catholics for participation in the building of Socialism in our nation. They have equal status with Catholic churches in other countries. The clergy, religious, and members of the Chinese Catholic Church today will never again become "citizens" of a foreign country, never again be "living on the China mainland," so-called subjects of a foreign church, but will have powerful, patriotic self-respect and self-image, and fervently love our Socialist nation, and offer all of their strength to build Socialism in our nation, to the great glory of the people of the People's Republic of China. During the ten years of chaos ["cultural revolution"], many Catholic friends suffered grievous harm, but surely the great majority of friends [here] firmly believe in the Party's and government's policy of freedom of religious belief, and firmly believe in the correctness of the position of self-guidance and self-government in the church. In this profoundly important aspect you have received the respect of the people. In following the course of independence, self-guidance, and self-government, the Party and government's policy of freedom of religious belief is making steady progress, and Catholics who formerly were skeptical of an independent, self-guiding, self-governing church or even were opposed to it are also going on the same road now with the majority of Catholics. To agree with the Chinese Catholic Church's road of independence, self-guidance, and self-government, and to expand the patriotism of church members, is a fine thing. At the same time we offer welcome and support.

Note

1. From Article 36 of the new constitution, adopted by the National People's Congress, December 1982. Article 36 sets forth the official policy on religion.

Section III

Provincial Regulations for the Supervision of Religious Activities

Document 10

Regulations for the Administrative Supervision of Places of Religious Activity in Guangdong Province

While there is not, as yet, national legislation that defines the rights, responsibilities, and limits for religious activities, some local regulations, not now available in Chinese publications, have circulated outside China. The most detailed of these was published in Zhong Lian (China Catholic Communication, Singapore), No. 16, December 1988, and is reprinted here. Since Bishop K. H. Ting refers to these regulations in an interview (Document 98), we assume that this document is authentic.

Chapter I: General Principles

Article 1: These regulations have been enacted in order to protect normal religious activities according to the constitution of the People's Republic of China and relevant national laws and statutes, in keeping with the actual situation in our province.

Article 2: Citizens have freedom of religious belief. No one is allowed to force others to believe or not to believe in religion. There should not be any discrimination against either citizens who believe or citizens who do not believe in religion.

Article 3: The religious affairs departments of the governments at every level exercise administrative leadership over places of religious activity.

Chapter II: Places of Religious Activity

Article 4: The term "Place of Religious Activity" refers to Buddhist monasteries and temples, Daoist monasteries and temples, Islamic mosques, Catholic and Protestant churches and meeting grounds (hereafter abbreviated to temples and churches), religious schools, and simple religious activity points where the believing masses meet together.

Article 5: Both reopened temples and churches and newly established simple religious activity points must apply for registration to the department in charge of religious affairs of the people's government at county level or above.

To run religious training classes, application for registration must be made to the department in charge of religious affairs of the people's government at city level or above. The opening of a religious school must be reported to the Religious Affairs Department of the Provincial People's government. When the above-mentioned applications have been approved and registered, their legal rights and privileges come under the protection of the law; those which have yet to be approved must not conduct religious activities.

Article 6: Places of religious activity which have been permitted to open by the people's government before the promulgation of these regulations, if they have not yet gone through a registration procedure, must undergo registration procedures with the department of the people's government in charge of religious affairs.

Article 7: Places of religious activity and religious training classes which want to alter the approved registered content of a course of study, must inform the department in charge of religious affairs of the people's government at the county level or above for ratification.

Article 8: Construction of new temples or churches must be approved by the Religious Affairs Department of the Provincial People's Government.

Chapter III: Supervision of Religious Venues

Article 9: Places of religious activity which have been approved and opened should form, under the guidance of the patriotic religious organizations, a supervisory body consisting of both religious professionals and religious believers to implement democratic supervision.

Article 10: Places of religious activity must respect the national constitution, laws, and policies; safeguard national sovereignty and unity; safeguard ethnic cooperation; and uphold the principles of independent self-government and self-management (of religion). They are not to engage in activities which oppose the Socialist system, disrupt social stability, or cause damage to the physical or mental health of citizens.

Article 11: Places of religious activity should accept the direction of the departments of cultural relics, urban planning, public security, and parks and gardens in protecting the cultural relics, buildings, facilities, grounds, and so on of that place. They should also do the work of security and fire prevention.

Article 12: Any renovation, reconstruction, or extension of churches and temples must be approved by the department in charge of religious affairs of the people's government at the county level or above.

Requisitions of any temple or church, or its monuments, pagodas, tombs, walls, gardens, or compounds, should be fully negotiated with the religious body in possession of the ownership or usage rights, and reported to the Religious Affairs Department of the Provincial People's government for approval. Maintenance of temples and churches should be reported to the government department in charge of religious affairs for the record.

Any actions under the above provision which involve the departments of cultural relics, urban planning, and parks and gardens should at the same time be reported as provided by the regulations to the relevant responsible departments for approval.

Article 13: No unit or individual is allowed to occupy or destroy a place of religious activity. Without the permission of the supervisory body of the temple or church and the department of the people's government in charge of religious affairs, no unit or individual is allowed to set up a place of business or of a service trade or to conduct exhibitions or display wares and so on.

Article 14: The shooting of films or videos within the property of a temple or church must have the consent of the department in charge of religious affairs of the people's government at the city level or higher. If they are units classified as protected cultural relics, the filming should also be reported to the cultural department for approval.

Article 15: The finances of churches and temples should be managed by democratic supervision, and a comprehensive budgetary system should be established and perfected. No person is allowed to appropriate for themselves the income of a temple or church.

Article 16: Approved and opened temples and churches may operate services such as guest houses, snack bars, and kiosks, and may manage sideline agriculture, forestry, and husbandry industries. However, they must be run according to the relevant policies and regulations of the government.

Chapter IV: Religious Professionals

Article 17: "Religious professionals" refers to Catholic bishops, priests, and nuns, Protestant pastors and evangelists, Buddhist monks and nuns, Daoist monks and nuns, Islamic imams, and other people of religious occupation who have the permission of the patriotic religious organization at county level or above and who have reported for the record to the department of the people's government in charge of religion.

Article 18: Daoist and Buddhist temples should set a personnel quota in line with their concrete needs. The personnel quota for those classified as prominent national temples must be reported to the Provincial People's Government for approval. Personnel quotas for other temples will be approved by the people's government at the county level or above. Additions to personnel within the quota limits must be agreed to by the government department in charge of religious affairs.

Article 19: Religious professionals and graduates of religious schools may, after receiving the consent of the department in charge of religious affairs of the people's government at the city level or above, be allocated by the patriotic religious organization of the province or city, according to the need, to work in a relevant place of religious activity.

Article 20: Religious professionals who go out of the province to conduct religious activities must gain the consent of the Religious Affairs Department of the Provincial People's Government. Those who go beyond their own city or county must have the consent of the department in charge of religious affairs of their city or county people's government. Religious professionals who take up temporary residence in a church or temple must declare their temporary address to the public security organ of the place, according to the relevant regulations.

Chapter V: Religious Activities

Article 21: The normal religious activities of approved and opened places of religious activity are under the protection of the law. No unit or individual is allowed to spread atheistic or antireligious propaganda within places of religious activity.

Article 22: No one is allowed to conduct feudal superstitious activities falling outside the definition of religion, such as divination, sorcery, fortune telling, or interpreting omens, within a place of religious activity.

Article 23: With consent of the department in charge of religious affairs of the people's government, religious professionals may, according to the custom of the religion, conduct the necessary religious rites for believers in cemeteries, funeral parlors, hospitals, or believers' homes.

Article 24: No person is permitted to engage in propagating religion or in religious activities, or to distribute religious propaganda, in any public place other than opened places of religious activity and the places mentioned in Article 23. It is not permitted to make use of religion to conduct activities which hinder the state education system or the educational order in schools.

Article 25: Religious activities in places of religious activity should be presided over, and religious duties performed, by religious professionals checked and ratified at the time of their application for registration. Whoever receives religious professionals coming from other places to lead any religious activities or to preach or to expound scripture must first apply to the department in charge of religious affairs of the people's government at the county level or above. People who are not religious professionals are not allowed to perform religious duties.

Article 26: The patriotic religious organizations at every level can send out personnel to conduct religious activities in places of religious activity under their jurisdiction.

Article 27: Any printing or publishing of religious literature, audio, or pictorial materials must have the consent of the department in charge of religious affairs or the people's government at city level or above, and be handled in accordance with the relevant regulations of the publications department.

Article 28: Religious organizations may sell or distribute approved religious literature, audio, or pictorial materials, religious utensils, and religious art in their own temples and churches.

Article 29: Compatriots from Hongkong and Macau, Taiwan compatriots, overseas Chinese, Chinese with foreign nationality, and foreigners who are religious believers, may practice their religious life-style in opened temples and churches in our province, but they must abide by our national constitution, laws, and the relevant regulations of the particular place of activity. They are not to propagate religion or distribute religious propaganda materials without authorization.

Article 30: Voluntary offerings and donations made within the country to places of religious activity according to religious custom by compatriots from Hongkong and Macau, Taiwan compatriots, overseas Chinese, Chinese of foreign nationality, and foreigners who are religious believers can be accepted. Religious organizations and places of religious activity which receive contributions from religious bodies or individuals in Hongkong, Macau, Taiwan, or foreign countries must, after gaining the consent of the department in charge of religious affairs of the people's government at the county level or above, report them for approval to the relevant provincial departments according to the regulations.

Chapter VI: Supplementary Articles

Article 31: Concerning violations of these regulations: light offenders will undergo criticism and education by the department in charge of religious affairs of the people's government; violations of the Penal Ordinance for the Control of Public Order of the People's Republic of China will be dealt with by the public security organs: violations which constitute a crime will be investigated for criminal responsibility by the judicial organs.

Article 32: Those who on their own initiative and without permission construct temples or churches or organize religious activities will be ordered to cease by the department of the people's government in charge of religious affairs. Those who do not comply with this order will be dealt with by force by the public security organs according to the seriousness of the case.

Article 33: The above rules will be effective from 1 May 1988.

Section IV

Religious Policy and Ethnic Minorities

Introduction

While only 6 percent of the Chinese people belong to minority nationalities, a total of sixty million people are scattered among fifty-four ethnic minority groups, many of them living in remote but strategic areas along the four-thousand mile border with the Soviet Union. Moreover, since ten of the fifty-four minority groups are Muslims, an estimated twenty million people, it is important that visitors from Muslim countries be assured that fellow Muslims in China are free to follow traditional religious practices. Their sense of well-being is important as well for domestic unity and harmony: in past years there have been Muslim uprisings in China.

The first of the three articles selected for this section, written for the *Journal of Central Nationalities College* in Beijing, calls on its readers to correctly understand and implement the religious policy among minority nationalities, using the "five natures" of religion as a typology. The religious situation among the nationalities is complex; it is long-term in nature, mass-based, and has significant international implications. In dealing with these people, it is important to correctly differentiate between the religious issue and the nationalities issue, and between religion and such customs as birth, marriage, and funeral rites, dietary patterns, and festivals.

The writers make the further point that the "reform of the social economic system and the reform of the feudal exploitative system in religion" has brought such changes that the "religious contradiction" is no longer an antagonistic contradiction, that is, a contradiction between the people and the enemy. "Now, the contradiction on the religious issue has become primarily a contradiction among the people," one that can be resolved without using force or violence.

The next article was also written for a scholarly journal, *Social Sciences in Yunnan*, published by the Minorities Institute in Kunming. Section 6, excerpted here from a long article called "The Nationalities Problem in the Period of Socialism," also referring to the issue of religious contradictions, makes the point that the correct handling of these contradictions is directly related to common economic development and prosperity for all nationalities: "Doing it this way will be beneficial in arousing the enthusiasm of the minority nationality masses and in promoting common development

50

and prosperity for all nationalities ... and in helping the laboring people of all nationalities to be liberated from the shackles of religion." That is, the "religious contradiction" will be resolved peacefully and in its own good time.

Finally, the *China Pictorial* article on the Muslims in Beijing describes the respect now shown for Muslim customs and dietary laws. Muslims are supplied with extra flour, oil, beef, and mutton during their three annual religious festivals, and Muslims are appointed to local leadership posts.

Document 11

Correctly Understand the Religious Issue among the Minority Nationalities and Thoroughly Implement the Party's Policy on Religion

By Liu E, He Ren, and Wang Guodong in Zhongyang Minzu Xueyuan Xuebao (*Journal of Central Nationalities College*), *No. 3, 15 August 1982, pp. 13-18. Translated in FBIS, 28 April 1983, pp. 31-46.*

I. The Situation of Religious Belief among Our Country's Minority Nationalities

Among our country's minority nationalities, many of them have religious beliefs. The major religions that are practiced in the areas inhabited by minority nationalities are Buddhism, Islam, Christianity, Catholicism, Shamanism, the East Pakistan religion, Daoism, and the Orthodox Eastern Church. Among them, Buddhism has enjoyed nearly 2,000 years of history in our country, Daoism has had over 1,700 years of history, and Islam has had over 1,300 years of history, while Catholicism and Christianity have developed more extensively primarily since the Opium War. ... In the old China, speaking overall, in the protracted feudal society and for more than a century of semifeudal and semicolonialist society, many religions in our country had once been controlled and employed by the ruling class and had played an extremely passive role. After Liberation, through the reform of the social-economic system and the reform of the feudal suppressive and exploitative system in religion, the condition of our country's religions has undergone a fundamental change. For instance, the situation in the past of an all-nationality belief in Lamaism or Islam among some nationalities has changed. Now, many people have freed themselves from the shackles of religion and have become materialists and atheists. Or, for instance, in some areas inhabited by nationalities, the system of integration of the church and the State and the feudal system of suppression and exploitation which the religious temples and clergy practiced toward the masses of believers before Liberation have been abolished. Now, the contradiction on the religious issue has become primarily a contradiction among the people. This is a tremendous change. It is wrong to not recognize this change. However, the religious issue will still exist within a definite realm over a long period of time and has a definite mass characteristic to it. In many places, it is still interwoven with the nationalities issue, and is still influenced by the class struggle within a definite realm and by the complex international environment. Thus, whether or not the religious issue is handled appropriately will have an important influence which we cannot overlook on the unity among the nationalities and the stability of the nation, as well as on the building of a Socialist material and spiritual civilization. It is also wrong and very dangerous to not recognize such a situation.

II. Correctly Understand the Objective Laws of the Birth, Development, and Withering Away of Religion

... Our party has precisely proceeded from the [above described] laws of development of religion and taken into consideration the religious beliefs of our country's minority nationalities in adopting the policy of freedom of religious belief.

In our country, the religious issue is an issue that has a nationality character and a mass character to it. Some religions, such as Islam and Lamaism, have many followers, and among some nationalities the people of the entire nationality are believers. The influence of religion has deeply pervaded the various aspects of these nationalities, including the economy, culture, and social life. This influence of religion is oftentimes also interwoven with the nationalities issue. When religious discrimination and religious struggle take place among different nationalities, they very easily bring on conflicts and struggles among the nationalities. That is to say, religious belief is not a small matter of individuals or a small number of people, but is an important matter involving many people and, in particular, involving the majority of workers, peasants, and laboring people.

Among the religions that the various minority nationalities in our country follow, many are international in character. For instance, of the four major religions of the world, Buddhism began in ancient India, Islam began in today's Saudi Arabia, Christianity began in the Roman Empire, and Catholicism was [later] separated from other branches of Christianity. These religions are separately followed by people of many countries and nationalities throughout the world. Among them, some are even regarded as the state religion in some countries. Whether or not we do a good job regarding religion has a significant meaning in expanding our international contacts and our country's political influence.

These characteristics of religion, plus its long-term character, make up its complexity. Historically, some leaders of the oppressed nationalities and oppressed people once made use of the banner of religion to mobilize and organize the oppressed masses of people to wage struggle against the oppressors. In our country, in the last years of the Eastern Han Dynasty, the leaders of the Yellow Turbans Uprising, Zhang Jue and his brother, made use of the Road to Peace; at the close of the Qing Dynasty, Hong Xiuquan, the revolutionary leader of the Kingdom of Heavenly Peace [the Taiping Rebellion], made use of the Church of God; the Yihetuan Movement made use of Daoist incantations; and so on and so forth. These were methods of employing the form of religion to mobilize the masses of peasants to stand up and resist the suppression and rule of the feudal landlord class and imperialism. In order to mobilize the masses on a broader and more effective scale, and in order to increase their own authority and explain the rationality and righteousness of the struggle for resistance, the leaders of the uprisings put a religious cloak over the struggles. In this way, the inevitability of the class struggle was mingled with religion. Nevertheless, such conditions could not explain how religion itself has any positive meaning. Besides, in the European Middle Ages, in many places, philosophy, politics, and the law were lumped together with theology and were made subjects of theology. All these factors constituted the complexity of the religious issue. In modern times, colonialists and imperialists use religion as their tool to carry out aggression against and colonialist rule over the weaker and smaller countries and nationalities. Some churches have become their espionage organs. Some missionaries, priests, and nuns have formed special detachments for carrying out subversive, aggressive, and counterrevolutionary sabotage activities under the guise of religious activities. This is a category of contradiction that is different in nature from the issue of belief of the broad masses of religious believers. However, in real life, these two issues are often mingled together. Such a situation also brought complexity to the religious issue.

These realities of religion and the religious issue exist objectively. In the long historical period in the future, these conditions will continue to exist. Furthermore, because religious belief is an issue of ideological understanding, the contradictions of the religious issue have become primarily contradictions among the people in the new period of Socialism. In solving the issue of ideological understanding among the people, we can only use the democratic method of persuasion and education. The purpose of studying and emphasizing these conditions of the religious issue is to correctly understand and have a good grasp of the trend of development of religion and the religious issue and bring it to people's attention so as to adopt an attitude of discreet, rigorous, and careful consideration toward the issue. Thus, on the one hand, we should not exaggerate the gravity and complexity of the issue and panic, and yet, on the other hand, we must not belittle the existence of practical problems and their complexity, lower our guard, and let the issue go unchecked. . . .

In the course of implementing the policy of freedom of religious belief, we must correctly differentiate between the religious issue and the nationalities issue and handle them accordingly. Some people confuse nationalities with religion, saying "the Hui nationality is Islamic," "Islam means the Hui nationality." This is totally wrong. Religion is an ideology and nationality is a people's community that embraces four characteristics. Religion does not have an absolute link with nationality. A religion can be followed by people of many nationalities. For instance, there are ten nationalities in our country who believe in Islam, but we cannot say that these ten nationalities are therefore one nationality. The people of one nationality also can follow several different religions. Among them, there are also some people who may not believe in any religion. For instance, among the Han nationality, some people believe in Christianity and Catholicism, some people believe in Daoism and Buddhism, and some people are not religious. But we cannot say that they are different nationalities. Furthermore, religious beliefs may change, and change of religious belief does not change the nationality component. For instance, the Uyghur nationality followed Manichaeanism, Ao Jiao, Buddhism, and Nestorianism before it followed Islam. The Mongolian nationality followed Shamanism before it followed Lamaism. If we confuse nationalities with religion, we not only have made a mistake in our understanding, but will make the issue more complex, which will be unfavorable to the Party's religious work and work with nationalities.

We also should not confuse religious belief with customs and habits. The Party and government treat the customs and habits of various nationalities the same way they treat religious belief, with the policy of respect and protection. Our country's citizens have freedom of religious belief. The various nationalities also have the freedom to preserve and reform their customs and habits. In terms of the spirit of the policy, there is no difference in essence between the two. However, we should not regard customs and habits as religious beliefs. Without a doubt, some nationalities have certain customs and habits, such as food abstention, festive activities, and marriage and funeral rites, that are definitely related to religious and feudal superstition. Some are originally religious disciplines. For instance, the nationalities who believe in Islam do not eat pork and the blood of animals, and do not eat animals that die on their own. Some festivals are also religious disciplines. However, as time goes by the original meanings are lost and they become customs and habits of the masses. Under the circumstance we cannot look at them as either an issue of religious belief or feudal superstition. The differentiation of the two will have an important meaning for the Communist Party members and the masses of nonbelievers among these nationalities. It is inappropriate to confuse the customs and habits of a nationality with religious activities without being analytical about them, and is unfavorable to the unity among nationalities and to the correct handling of the religious issue.

Document 12

On the Nature of the Nationalities Problem in the Period of Socialist Construction

By Yang Jingchu in Yunnan Shehui Kexue *(Social Sciences in Yunnan), 4 July 1982. Translated in FBIS, 2 March 1983, p. 117 (excerpt).*

. . . Sixth, nationality contradictions of religious belief seemingly have no connection with nationality development and prosperity. In fact, they are directly related to common development and prosperity for all nationalities. Generally speaking, religious belief in itself is not a question of nationality, because one nationality can simultaneously believe in several different religions, and different nationalities also can simultaneously believe in a certain religion. The reason that religious belief in our country has become a nationality question is because there are some minority nationalities in which most people believe in a certain religion, influencing the production, livelihood, customs and habits, and ideological state of the whole nationality, and religion is often interwoven with nationality questions. Before Liberation many minority nationalities in our country had their own religions, separately believing in Islam, Buddhism, Protestantism, Catholicism, and polytheism and other primitive religions, and some religions to this day still have a rather strong influence among working people of all nationalities.

Document 13

Policy toward Beijing Muslim Settlement

In English in China Pictorial, *Beijing, January 1983, p. 137 (excerpts).*

According to statistics recently published by the Beijing Municipal Statistics Bureau, Beijing has more than 300,000 residents who belong to the country's 54 ethnic groups; the Huis, who number some 180,000, make up the majority. Some Huis live among the Hans and other ethnic people in and outside the city; others live in compact communities near Niujie (Ox) Street and other places.

The Party and government have stood for a policy of ensuring equality and strengthening unity among all nationalities and a policy of freedom of religious belief. Religious activities in China are protected by law. Faithful Muslims are called to prayer five times a day, and on important occasions such as the end of Ramadan, Corban, and Djumah (every Friday) they all come to the mosque for congregational prayers. The mosque's imam is often invited to preside over marriage and funeral services or butchering rites in the people's homes. During their religious festivals, the Muslims are supplied with more flour, vegetable oil, beef, and mutton than rationed.

Thanks to the government's education in its policy toward nationalities among the people, disputes between the Hans and Huis in the area are seldom heard of. They respect each other's customs, oblige each other, and live in harmony.

The Party and government often appoint Hui cadres to leadership posts in their area. Today, most of the leading posts in the Niujie neighborhood office are held by Huis. For the Muslims' convenience, the government has in recent years opened a new department store selling specialties for them, a butcher's shop selling beef and mutton, a restaurant, and some snack bars. The hospital and secondary school for the Muslims have now regained their former names (they were changed during the "cultural revolution") and are growing steadily.

Section V

Statements by Religious Leaders on Religious Policy

Introduction

Three statements by religious leaders, Catholic, Protestant, and Buddhist, have been selected from the many now available in print. Bishop Fu Tieshan, the Catholic bishop of Beijing, has often been interviewed for the Chinese press as a spokesman for the Catholic Church in China. Bishop K. H. Ting, President of the China Christian Council and Chairman of the Chinese [Protestant] Christian Three-Self Movement, has spoken many times in many countries about China's religious policy and its relationship to the growth of the church in China since 1979. Mr. Zhao Puchu, a distinguished poet and calligrapher, is President of the Chinese Buddhist Association. All three are members of the National CPPCC.

These religious leaders all speak of the changes that have taken place for each religion since Liberation, and particularly since the "cultural revolution." Bishops Ting and Fu were writing early in the post-Mao period, 1980 and 1981, respectively, while Mr. Zhao Puchu's address was given at the national assembly of the CPPCC in March 1988. The revival and growth of both Catholic and Protestant Christianity was just beginning when Bishop Ting said, in his paper, that eighty Protestant churches had been repaired and reopened in the entire country; today the figure is at least five thousand, with more opening almost every day. The same kind of restoration and revival has taken place in other religions.

Bishop Fu's address was given at the ecumenical conference "A New Beginning" held in Montreal in 1981. Ten Catholic and Protestant church leaders from China joined 150 other participants from around the world for nearly a week of meetings. Bishop Ting spoke, but his paper, reprinted here, was written a year earlier. The "fourteen points" presented in this paper represent the position of China's Christians today. They are thankful for the improvement of the standard of living for themselves and all Chinese people since Liberation. They regard the policy of religious freedom as reasonable, and are grateful for the Communist Party policy which "emphasizes the common ground while preserving differences." They are proud of their three-self independence, no longer needing or accepting help from foreign mission societies; they are financially self-supporting and there are no missionaries working with the churches in China. They are proud, as well, of the postdenominational unity of the churches. While there is not yet a "United Church of China," neither are there denominations, although denominational loyalties still prevail in the hearts and religious practices of many of the older Protestant Christians. With total Christian membership still only a fraction of 1 percent of the population, they see the enormity of the tasks that lie before them; yet they have made great progress, and, while acknowledging the problems, face the future with hope and faith.

One theme that returns over and over in the speeches, interviews, and writings of China's Catholic and Protestant leaders is their insistence on total separation from dependence on foreign mission societies for financial subsidies or missionary personnel. Bishop Ting writes: "Ours is a very small Church with limited financial resources, but we are able to support ourselves. The strength of our position lies in the fact that we will not do anything beyond our ability and thus be forced to become parasitic."

The other three religions, Buddhism, Daoism, and Islam, were autonomous and self-supporting long before Liberation, so the threat of what is called missionary imperialism poses no problem for them. Instead, Mr. Zhao Puchu, in his address to the national assembly of the CPPCC in 1988, spoke directly and with surprising candor of continuing problems in the carrying out of religious policy, particularly at local levels, where the recovery of religious buildings is stalled by stubborn work units occupying the buildings and dilatory or hostile local officials. He describes in detail a particularly egregious case of high-handed and erroneous mishandling of religious policy by the mayor of Kaifeng, who refused to allow a visiting delegation of Japanese Buddhists to worship in the Xiangguo Temple in Kaifeng, saying that it was only a museum. "The mayor apparently did not care about the international political implications involved, nor about how his decision would affect hard-won Sino-Japanese ties of friendship," said Mr. Zhao. This case raises an important question: Do some government and Party officials want only a museum-type religion to survive in China?

Document 14

There Is New Freedom of Religious Belief in New China

By Bishop Fu Tieshan, in A New Beginning, *Theresa Chu and Christopher Lind, editors, Canada China Programme, Toronto, 1983, pp. 27-28.*

China is a country that has several religions: Catholicism, Protestantism, Buddhism, Daoism, and Islam, all of which are regarded as equal. Believers and nonbelievers work together on a basis of friendship and mutual respect. Although atheists and theists hold different opinions in matters of faith, they share the same basic interests in the political, economic, and cultural realms of life. The great goal of building a strong, prosperous, and modernized native land has created close ties between us Catholics and the Chinese people as a whole. To strive together toward such a common goal is the foundation on which we are united as one people.

New China came into being and continues to grow under the leadership of the Chinese Communist Party. It is common knowledge that Chinese Communists are atheists. However, the people's government respects the democratic rights of the people, including the religious belief of the Christians. Accordingly, it has formulated a long-term, stable policy which is welcomed by Christians as well as people of different ranks in China.

We Catholics, like other religious believers, are citizens of a sovereign nation. We have the power to make decisions in our own households. There are three Catholic bishops who are members of the National Political Consultative Conference, and one of them is a delegate at the National People's Congress. There are quite a few bishops, priests, and laypeople who are delegates at the People's Congress and/or at the Political Consultative Conference on various levels of province, city, and county. The People's Congress is the national assembly of China and its delegates are elected from among the people. Bishop K. H. Ting, here present, is a member of the standing committee of the National People's Congress. Mr. Lu Weidu, a Catholic layman, is a member of the Standing Committee of the Shanghai Municipal People's Congress. The Political Consultative Conference is an advisory organ of our government. It is composed of members representing different political parties, different fields of industry, commerce, literature and arts, education, various religions, minorities, overseas Chinese, and compatriots of Hongkong and Macau. Delegates of the Catholic Church participate in discussions with other delegates representing their respective constituencies. They discuss questions regarding the general policy of the nation, finances, and budgetary statements. They also voice their opinions and requests in religious matters. Their opinions are valued. I myself have frequently participated in the activities of Beijing's Political Consultative Conference along with Protestant ministers, Muslim imams, Buddhist monks, Lamas, and others.

Our freedom of religious belief and normal religious activities are protected by constitutional and penal law. In my case, for example, I was in the minor seminary on the eve of Liberation. In new China, I continued my life in the seminary for six years until I received the grace of ordination. As a priest, I did pastoral work for many years until the end of the seventies when again God gave me a special grace, that of being consecrated a bishop. My personal experiences should be sufficient to prove there is freedom of religious belief in China.

For thirty years, the government has backed the church's principle of self-support. Buildings used by the church are taxfree. But during the ten years of turmoil, the satanic Lin Biao and the "gang of four" disregarded constitutions and penal codes and ruined different policies, including that of the freedom of religious belief. The "gang of four's" irrational actions brought untold damage to our country and people. Now, history has judged them correctly, and once more the policy of freedom of religious belief has been restored.

I understand that since the crushing of the "gang of four," the people's government has taken positive measures to implement the policy of freedom of religious belief. Help has been meted out to different local churches to overcome difficulties so that church buildings can be repaired and sacraments administered to people. At present, over eighty Catholic church buildings have been repaired and are functioning. Once more, people receive the different sacraments. Still more churches are being prepared for reopening. Those clergy and laity who suffered persecution during the "cultural revolution" because of the counterrevolutionary policies of Lin Biao and Jiang Qing are having their cases reopened and reexamined in view of their rehabilitation. Unfortunately, Bishop Zhao Zhensheng of the diocese of Xian Xian, Hebei Province, died during the "cultural revolution." He has been rehabilitated during the earlier part of this year. A memorial meeting was solemnly held in Shijiazhuang and a high mass was solemnly celebrated in Beijing's cathedral for Bishop Zhao, jointly sponsored by the Chinese Catholic Patriotic Association, the Church Affairs Committee, the Bishops' Conference, and the Beijing diocese. St. Peter said: "Live as free men, yet without using your freedom as a pretext for evil; but live as servants of God" (1 Pet. 2:16).

Just as it is in other countries, in new China too it is not allowed to infringe upon the interests of the country and the people in the name of religion. Cases of serious offense may result in imprisonment. All are equal before law. The overwhelming majority of clergy and laity love their country and abide by its laws. They observe the instruction contained in the Scriptures: "Remind them to be submissive to rulers and authorities, to be obedient, to be ready for any honest work" (Titus 3:1).

Catholics in China share all the rights of citizenship, on the one hand, and fulfill their responsibilities, on the other. In the political life of the nation, they are masters. They are not discriminated against because of their religious belief. In matters concerning education, jobs, army service, and other areas, they enjoy the same rights as nonbelievers. They work hard to contribute to nation building both in the spiritual and the material aspects of our civilization. At work they live up to the noble spirit of loving God and neighbor. They witness to the good news of Jesus Christ.

Document 15

Fourteen Points from Christians in the People's Republic of China to Christians Abroad

By Bishop K. H. Ting, in A New Beginning, *Theresa Chu and Christopher Lind, editors, Canada China Programme, Toronto, 1983, pp. 108-16.*
   The "Fourteen Points" were originally presented by Bishop Ting in a conversation with Rev. Andrew Chiu and Rev. Arthur Wu of Hongkong on 12 December 1980.

There has already been a good deal of reporting on the Chinese Christian situation and on our guiding principles, but there is still some confusion among fellow Christians overseas, including those in Hongkong. I would like to present some of our views.

1. New China

We Chinese Christians take a positive attitude toward new China. It is not as it was before Liberation, when we took a negative attitude toward the cause of the Chinese people's liberation as a result of misinformation and misunderstanding. Christians cannot deny that new China has brought many good changes to the Chinese people. For over thirty years the price of our food and other necessities has basically been stable. In the past, there were many Chinese people who did not have enough to eat. Now, although special delicacies may be out of reach, our 900 million people have enough to eat, so that there is no longer the need for people to go scrounging for roots and tree bark. Our approximately 10 percent of the world's arable land feeds almost 25 percent of the world's people. This must certainly be regarded as an amazing accomplishment, even though it is not a miracle. In the past, many people were without adequate clothing. On the streets there were rickshaw pullers, beggars, and other poor people who often went barefoot in the rain and snow. Now there are no more rickshaws or beggars, and everyone has shoes and adequate clothing, even a cotton-padded jacket for the winter. The jacket may be patched, but it is no longer worn by several generations as it was before. People's thinking and mental outlook have also undergone significant changes. Despite the ten-year catastrophe, the level of people's mortality and self-respect is much higher than it was before Liberation.
   For poverty-stricken people deprived of their rights for thousands of

years, to have made mistakes in their first attempt at governing a vast country is only natural. But mistakes cannot stifle the wisdom and character of a people which has stood up. There have been many shortcomings in the thirty-year history of new China, and more than a few mistakes. But summing up both our negative and positive experiences and learning from them, we will once again move forward. Thus, those people overseas who gloat over our misfortunes are really too shortsighted.

For us, patriotism is not just the love of an abstract ancient country with a long history. It is first and foremost a love for new China. Our positive attitude toward new China is genuine and based upon facts. The clamor of certain persons overseas who say that our patriotism is pretentious with the aim that the church may survive is insulting to us. Of course, our patriotism is not without a prophetic and critical character. It does not mean blind praise for everything in our motherland.

2. The Policy of Religious Freedom

We regard the policy of religious freedom in new China to be a reasonable one. Communists do not have a high regard for religion, and we harbor no illusions about the Communist Party on matters of religious faith. But the Communist Party is a good political party which aims at uniting the Chinese people. For the sake of national unity, it maintains a respect for the people's customs and special characteristics, including religious ones. It would benefit neither national unity nor Socialism if this respect were neglected. The Communist Party understands this better than anyone else and, therefore, advocates the policy of "emphasizing the common ground while preserving differences." "Emphasizing the common ground" refers to the common ground of patriotism. "Preserving differences" means a recognition of and respect for the differences among people, and refraining from trying to eliminate them. Just as the differences between the national minorities and the Han Chinese cannot be eliminated, neither can those between believers and nonbelievers. Therefore, the Communist Party maintains a policy of religious freedom. We consider this to be a policy as good for religion as it is good for the country.

I am of course speaking of the Communist Party and not of the "gang of four." The "gang of four" is not the Communist Party and the Communist Party is not the "gang of four." The "gang of four" wished to eradicate religion, but the Communist Party seeks to protect religious belief by adopting the policy of religious freedom. Since the smashing of the "gang of four," we are returning to the Communist Party's original policy of religious freedom. Overseas there is the mistaken idea that the religious policy of the Communist Party itself has changed or loosened up. This confuses the Communist Party with the "gang of four," and is of no help for coming to a correct understanding of new China. Today, the Communist Party is leading the people throughout China in revolution and reconstruction, and the "gang of four" has been put on trial in the people's court. To speak of the two as one and the same really creates a lot of confusion.

3. Organizations in New China

China is a properly constituted country. Each of the organizations listed below has its own proper function and sphere of authority, and these should not be confused.

1. The National People's Congress (NPC) is our supreme national legislative body. Only the NPC is empowered to approve and revise the constitution, the marriage laws, the penal code, the civil code, and other laws. Appointments of important officials, such as the premier, vice-premiers, and department heads, must also be approved by the NPC. Deputies to the NPC, which may be both Party and non-Party members, are elected by each province. There are deputies who are religious believers.

2. The Chinese People's Political Consultative Conference (CPPCC) is our political consultative body. While NPC deputies are elected by each province, members of the CPPCC come from every corner of Chinese society. Membership is drawn from the youth, women, workers, peasants, and soldiers; from the Communist Party and democratic parties; from cultural, athletic, scientific, and religious circles; and from the national minorities, overseas Chinese, and people from all walks of life. The CPPCC is an important institution for the promotion of Socialist democracy and an important organ of the United Front. There is within the CPPCC a religious group, comprised of Buddhist, Islamic, Daoist, Catholic, and Protestant representatives. The 46th article of the present national constitution stipulates, "Citizens enjoy the freedom to believe in religion and the freedom not to believe in religion and to propagate atheism." Members of the CPPCC religious group are dissatisfied with this article, which preserves a lingering influence of the "gang of four" period, and have made a proposal that it be changed. If this proposal for modifying the wording of Article 46 of the constitution is passed by the next session of the NPC, then we will be happy. If not, we will continue in our efforts.

3. The State council is the administrative, or executive, organ set up under the NPC. It is the central government of our country.

4. The Religious Affairs Bureau (RAB) of the State Council is set up expressly for the handling of the religious affairs of the State Council. It does not deal with the faith, life, and work of Buddhism, Catholicism, Protestantism, and all other religions. There are some people overseas who, consciously or not, have created confusion by saying that the RAB of the State Council supervises us and that Chinese Christian churches and organizations are parts of the RAB. This would be totally at odds with our social and political system. The bulk of the work of the RAB is to represent the state and the government in implementing the policy of religious freedom. For example, when we want to open a church, the RAB assists us by

negotiating with all parties concerned. Or, when we need special paper for the printing of Bibles, the RAB helps us arrange for its purchase. In 1980, we bought 82 tons of paper for the printing of 135,000 Bibles. As we will be printing more Bibles in 1981, the RAB will continue to help us with the purchase of paper and arrangements for meeting our printing needs. The RAB of the State Council only handles the religious affairs of the State. As to the development of the Chinese Christian Three-Self Patriotic Movement and the administration of the Chinese church, these are our own concerns.

5. One important organization in the life of our country is the Chinese Communist Party. It is the leading force behind the Chinese revolution and national reconstruction. This leadership is not forced upon the people. After much investigation and study, the Party puts its proposals regarding principles and policies before the NPC, the CPPCC, and the people for their study, revision, approval, or adoption. Party members through their exemplary role mobilize the people for the implementation of the adopted policies.

6. The National Committee of the Chinese Christian Three-Self Patriotic Movement (hereafter the Three-Self Movement) is the patriotic association of Chinese Christians ourselves, not a governmental organ. That there are friends overseas who think of the Three-Self Movement as a department of the RAB is the result of the distortion made by certain individuals. The Three-Self Movement was founded by Chinese Christians ourselves. Although there were some missionaries and Chinese church leaders who advocated Three-Self before Liberation, the Three-Self principle of the Chinese Church could not be implemented full-scale under the historical conditions which prevailed at that time. When Y. T. Wu and others launched the Three-Self Movement after Liberation, they did receive appreciation and encouragement from Premier Zhou Enlai. But this certainly does not mean that the Communist Party told the Chinese church to launch such a movement.

7. We have also set up the China Christian Council for the pastoral needs of the Chinese churches. This is the church affairs organization of Chinese Christians.

In sum, organizations in China are properly constituted and the differences and relationships among them should be clearly noted. Our Chinese churches are independent not only of foreign churches but also of the NPC, the CPPCC, the government, and the Party. It is wrong for people outside China to say that the Three-Self Movement is an "official church." China has no "official church." The Chinese church is run by Chinese Christians ourselves. It is understandable that those who adopt a hostile political attitude toward new China would call the Chinese Church, which generally supports new China, an "official church." We regard the term "official church" to be a political expression with which to attack new China. Among the many churches of the world, ours is not one which can be labeled an "official church."

4. Religion and Imperialism

Religion has been exploited by colonialists and imperialists in their aggression against China. We have not denied the scientific character of this assertion. Many of our policy decisions today are related to this fact. This is no longer a question which requires much explanation inside China. Even overseas, more people are today recognizing this fact.

5. Our Three-Self Principle

We are resolved to uphold the reasonableness and justice of Three-Self for the Chinese church. On the basis of past history it is necessary for the Chinese church to follow the Three-Self road. Today, for the Chinese church to bear witness to the gospel among the Chinese people, self-government, self-support, and self-propagation are also necessary. We cannot return to the old situation representing a "foreign religion." Following the ten-year catastrophe, we are returning to our guiding principle of the fifties, not that of the forties. It is wrong for those people outside China who long for a return to the past to think that we are returning to the forties. A return to the forties would mean discarding Three-Self, again making Christianity a "foreign religion." In returning to the guiding principle of the fifties, we wish to continue to uphold self-government, self-support, and self-propagation, and to make the Church one which is well-governed, well-supported, and well-propagating, too.

6. The Unity of the Chinese Church

The present unity of the Chinese Christians is unprecedented. When I first came to Nanjing in the early fifties, there were still many denominations, separated by deep divisions. The members of one denomination in particular would not even pray with the rest of us. Now, the brothers and sisters of this group are not only willing to pray with us, but even to share the sacraments together. The unity which has emerged in the Chinese church is closer than ever before. We are no longer separated by denominational walls. We do experience "how good and beautiful it is for brothers and sisters to dwell in harmony."

The number of churches which have been reopened is still quite small, perhaps not more than eighty at present in the entire country. But Christians have not stopped gathering together, as many meet in their homes. It is a tradition in the Chinese church for Christians to gather in homes to pray and read the Bible. Even in the past when there were many churches, people still liked to worship in their homes in addition to going to church.

When I was little, my mother used to ask friends, relatives, and neighbors over to our home once a week for a worship service. There was an increase in such gatherings in homes during the "cultural revolution" period. We found there were twenty-five home-worship gatherings in Nanjing alone. Although many Christians now go to the churches which have recently been reopened, there are in Nanjing, for instance, still five such home-worship gatherings. Some older people find that it is inconvenient to go to services in churches because of the distance they would have to travel. Others prefer the intimacy of the home-worship gatherings, while still others attend both types of worship. Frequently, people record a church service to take back to listen to in their home-worship gathering.

There are people outside China who are not thankful to God that the Chinese church is more united now than ever before, but instead try to split the Chinese church by dividing it into a "Three-Self Church" and a "House Church." Why should the simple question of where one worships be turned into a contradiction between the home and Three-Self? Does the fact that first-century Christians all worshipped in their homes mean that they would oppose the Three-Self principle and rely on support from foreign quarters? Today in China, no matter where Christians gather for worship, the vast majority are patriotic and seek to defend and implement self-government, self-support, and self-propagation. When there were twenty-five home worship gatherings in Nanjing and the local committee of the Three-Self Movement called a meeting, those who attended the home-worship gatherings all came.

We are pleased to tell you that now, after these ten catastrophic years of the "cultural revolution," the Chinese church is even more united. Christians saw with their own eyes that many leaders of the Three-Self Movement were harassed by the "gang of four" because of the church, and yet they did not complain or advertise it. It was also these leaders who did what they could to preserve Bibles. Such actions could not but inspire people and deepen our unity in Christ. China being a big country with many Christians, it will always be possible to find a few people who disapprove of or oppose Three-Self. But today, the center of opposition to Three-Self is not within China, but overseas.

We Chinese Christians have chosen the road of postdenominational unity, not because we are better than anyone else, but because we live in our particular historical situation. In retrospect, we can only say that this has been a result of the leading of the Holy Spirit, who has allowed us to bathe in the ocean of God's grace.

7. The Work We Have before Us

The Chinese church does not only want to be self-governing, self-supporting, and self-propagating, but well-governed, well-supported, and well-propagating. We must make up for lost time and do our pastoral work well.

Each day we receive many letters asking us to send pastoral workers, and requesting Bibles, hymnals, devotional materials, and theological literature. These are the calls of Macedonia which we must give heed to. Chinese church workers have a great deal of work ahead. Our churches must have good services of worship; there must be better spiritual nurture for laypeople; we must witness faithfully to the people around us; and we must be deeply concerned for the welfare of the Chinese people. To do all this we have set up the China Christian Council. It is not a church, but an ecclesial organization for the service of Christians. We cannot proceed at a faster pace than one permitted by the present capacity of the Chinese church. There are some questions, the sacraments and orders for example, over which we are unable to arrive at a unanimity of opinion all at once. But there are many other matters which do await our common initiative.

We have begun to print Bibles and have republished the *Tian Feng* periodical. The seminary has published teaching materials for nationwide theological education by extension, and it is also in the process of recruiting students. A newly edited hymnal has also come out for temporary use. Books for the training of laypeople are now being edited. So the China Christian Council and the Three-Self Movement both have a great deal that they would like to do.

8. Evangelistic Work in China Is the Responsibility of the Chinese Church

We do not approve of those people overseas who try to mold public opinion into thinking that they should send missionaries back to China. No matter how large the population of China is and how small our church is, the responsibility for spreading the gospel and building up the church in China is the mission of Chinese Christians. We will not invite missionaries to China from overseas. We wish to declare that no group or individual overseas should engage in evangelistic activity in China without the expressed consent of Chinese church authorities, who retain responsibility and jurisdiction in this area.

There was recently the case of an American passing out religious tracts on the streets of Guangzhou who drew the attention and intervention of the police. Then he got angry and said that China had no religious freedom nor freedom for missionary work, and he threatened to telegraph president-elect Reagan requesting that America cut off its "financial aid" to China. We believe this person was in the wrong. If a large number of foreigners all acted in a similar fashion, then what would become of the image of Christianity in China? Would it not once again be regarded as a "foreign religion"? Would that not wipe away Chinese Christians' thirty-year efforts in promoting Three-Self? Therefore, we feel sensitive over the question of missionary work in China.

All missionary and church activities, including radio broadcasts beamed at China, which are carried on willfully and unmindful of Chinese church authorities, are expressions of disrespect and unfriendliness. It is not we who are closing the door of the gospel in China. We are but learning the lessons of history. We uphold self-government, self-support, and self-propagation as the road of an independent and self-administered church in order to guarantee that the door of the gospel may be open and remain open in China. It would simply be self-destructive for the Chinese church to return to a colonial status, and that in the long run is to shut the door of the gospel. And for this American to speak of mutually beneficial trade as "financial aid" is just arrogance and lack of education.

9. Overseas Church Groups' Activities with Non-Christian Chinese Enterprises

Some church-related groups overseas are now in the process of negotiating with Chinese schools, hospitals, factories, communes, and other enterprises for cooperative investment and exchange programs. We would not have any opinion if these groups were not church-affiliated, providing that they were not injurious to our national sovereignty. But we are concerned when church-related groups are so involved. For example, can those church groups which are engaged in activity of a technical nature in China honestly say that they have no goal of bearing witness or doing mission work? Insofar as it is in the nature of a church to be involved in things, how can their people deny having that goal, even if it is not explicitly stated in the contract? This has serious implications for a whole series of questions. One is a question of Christian ethics on the relationship between means and ends. Another is the harm which could be done to the Three-Self principle of the Chinese church if our jurisdiction is violated. There are priests, ministers, and nuns who came to China to teach English who have said that English teaching is their method and means but that their real purpose is evangelism. Is it honest for them to conceal their identity? Is it right that they should not consult the Chinese church and, in some cases, should even have attacked us?

We cannot rely on foreigners for the preaching of the gospel and the building up of the church among the 900 million Chinese people. Let the church take root today in Chinese soil, so that tomorrow it may blossom and bear fruit. Foreign churches, by doing missionary work in China in unauthorized ways, will be going against the direction chosen by Chinese Christians thirty years ago and will have a damaging effect on Three-Self. We are deeply concerned and must study the matter more carefully.

10. No Return to Denominationalism

We feel that the Chinese church can only go forward and not backward. The denominational consciousness of Chinese Christians has been quite weak. I myself am an Anglican, and there are many Christians and church workers in China who are also Anglican. But I don't know of any who wants to restore the Anglican church.

There are a small number of people overseas who have worked to restore their particular denominations in China, but they have not found popular support among Chinese Christians. We would like them to stop working to that end.

When former missionaries come to China, it is natural for them to seek out people they have known who belonged to their particular denominations. This is something we can understand. But let them not go so far as to attempt to revive denominational feelings and loyalties, thus inviting misunderstanding and unpleasantness.

11. International Relationships

We are a small church with many responsibilities within China. We think our major efforts must be devoted to our domestic work. We wish to immerse ourselves in our work so as to push this experiment of ours forward. Then, perhaps sometime in the future, we will be able to speak of some contribution to the international Christian community. But for now, our international commitments must be limited, meaning that we must differentiate and be selective.

We want to have contacts and exchange for the purpose of mutual learning with church groups and individuals overseas who have a friendly attitude toward new China and who respect the Three-Self principle of the Chinese Christians. But we will adopt a different attitude to those individuals and groups who are unfriendly toward new China and oppose our Three-Self principle. Today we are making observations which will enable us to accurately differentiate one from the other. We are by no means suggesting that we regard only those who approve of everything that new China does as friendly. What we are looking at is their basic attitude in recent years. People can change, and we will not dwell on the past or settle old scores. We like our friends to grow more and more numerous.

12. Our Participation in International Organizations and Conferences

Here we must differentiate too, and, because of our limited resources, be selective. There are a number of organizations and conferences which have taken a friendly attitude toward us in which we have not been able to participate. We have also not been able to invite many friendly church groups from overseas for visits in China. We ask for our overseas friends' understanding in these matters.

13. Material or Financial Contributions from Abroad

Ours is a very small church, with limited financial resources, but we are able to support ourselves. The strength of our position lies in the fact that we will not do anything beyond our ability and thus be forced to become parasitic. But because our Chinese church is now already self-supporting and independent, there is probably no longer the need to maintain a simple "closed-door policy" on the question of receiving contributions. We are pondering over the wisdom of accepting certain contributions from friendly church groups and persons overseas, with no strings attached and with due respect for the independent stance of our church, simply as an expression of the universality of our Christian fellowship. This may stop the slander of our enemies and dispel the misunderstanding of our friends, too.

Contributions would have to be from groups and individuals which are friendly toward new China and our church, and there could be no strings attached. I think we can open the door a little to allow people to make contributions to our local churches. But larger amounts should generally be handled by the China Christian Council, perhaps for its pastoral-work fund, because we could not allow foreign contributions to create or restore disparities between rich and poor churches. This tentative idea will be discussed by the leaders of the Three-Self Committee and the China Christian Council. If it is put into effect, it would certainly be carried out with extreme care, and we hope our friends overseas will be able to understand.

There are some people overseas who presumptuously speak of financial contributions in the name of saving the Chinese church, playing up their own role by going so far as to solicit contributions for this purpose. We want to declare that we have not and will not entrust anyone overseas to solicit contributions for the Chinese church. We basically believe that our church should be content with what it has, enjoying its poverty and thriftiness. It should live within its means by relying primarily upon contributions from Chinese Christians. We are opposed to making a big thing out of the financial problems of the church, which would obscure its true character and witness.

14. Differentiation among China Programs in Overseas Churches

There are many "China programs" in churches overseas which seem to take quite different attitudes toward China. We are observing and studying these programs so that we may differentiate among them. We are very grateful for the good work which some of them are doing. But there are also others which in name are engaged in research, in the promotion of prayer for China, and in the work of Christian fellowship, but in actuality are collecting intelligence, spreading hate-China propaganda, and seeking to infiltrate China and violate our church's jurisdiction. This tells us that we must not only listen to what they say, but also watch their actions. We must be careful observers and draw the necessary line of demarcation.

We will not disappoint those who are friendly toward us, and we will treat them in a friendly manner. Together with them in true Christian fellowship, we can more deeply enter into Christ's abundance and grace.

Document 16

Call for a New Look at an Outdated Religious Policy

A Speech by Zhao Puchu to the Seventh National Chinese People's Political Consultative Conference in Beijing, 31 March 1988; from Sing Tao Standard, *Hongkong, 4 April 1988. Translated by Donald MacInnis in* Tripod, *No. 46, August 1988, pp. 56-63.*

On 31 March, Mr. Zhao Puchu, President of the Chinese Buddhist Association and vice-chairman of the Chinese Association for Promoting Democracy, addressed the entire assembly of the Chinese People's Political Consultative Conference as official spokesman for nearly sixty delegates representing various religious constituencies. Speaking with great candor, he pointed out serious problems still remaining in the implementing of the policy of freedom of religious belief and called for the drafting of a new law governing religion in China.

Mr. Chairman and Members:

Allow me to speak on behalf of the members [of this body] from religious circles.

We fully agree with Vice-Chairman Qian Xueshen's report on the work of the Standing Committee of the Sixth Chinese People's Political Consultative Conference, and we fully support Acting Premier Li Peng's report on government work given at the First Session of the Seventh CPPCC.

We are highly encouraged by the great achievements in state and foreign affairs of the Standing Committee of the Sixth CPPCC and of the State Council in the past five years, and in the goals for reforms, tasks, and principles set for the next five years. Under the Party's leadership, religious believers among all the national minorities will join together, striving to make further contributions on the basis of past achievements, for the unity of the nation, for the development of the national minorities, and for world peace.

The five major religions in our country have millions of believers among many ethnic groups. The entire population of at least a dozen ethnic minorities living in the border areas are religious believers. There are four world religions in China. Two-thirds of the world's people are religious believers. Religion has made great contributions to our nation's history and culture, leaving a rich and brilliant legacy. Religion is related to the fields of politics, economics, and culture; it is longlasting, and has relationships with the masses as well as international relationships.

Practice has proven that, if we are to maintain and develop political stability in China, there is an enduring need for full implementation of the policy of religious freedom, unifying the great majority of religious believers and inspiring them to love their country and build Socialism. This will have great significance and positive effects in deepening and fostering reforms, opening up foreign relations, ensuring a stable development of the national economy, promoting the unity of the nation, and securing world peace.

For these reasons, and because it accords with the basic spirit of the documents of the Thirteenth Party Congress, we believe that there are three main leadership tasks in religious work which must be carried out.

The First Major Task: Continue To Implement the Policy on Religion

Since the Third Plenary Session of the Eleventh Party Congress the Party and government have taken on a large and difficult task and have achieved great results in carrying out religious policy and making some important policies and regulations. We religious members of the CPPCC, and religious organizations and leaders at all levels, have also done good work in investigating, drafting laws, policy making, and solving actual problems in the course of helping Party and government bodies.

But the work of carrying out religious policy has moved slowly and unevenly; it still faces great obstacles and problems when compared with the implementation of other policies. The task of carrying out the policy on religion is far from completion, with many difficulties and unsolved problems that still must be dealt with.

As we continue to carry out religious policy, the first problem requiring a solution is the need for more places for religious activities. The level must be reached where there are enough such buildings in every place to meet the needs of religious believers, as well as to maintain relationships with foreign religious circles. Places which were closed or were occupied and remodeled for other uses during the "cultural revolution" must be returned. Government leaders should give priority to the needs of religious believers and not to those units which occupy their buildings. There is an urgent need to return and reopen these buildings, and this problem must be solved quickly.

Equally important is the problem of those places which require restoration, clarification of ownership rights, and economic compensation. We must properly and carefully deal with the problem of those places that were originally designed for religious activities, such as Buddhist temples and shrines, but where religious activities no longer take place. This happened in some places before the "cultural revolution," but the current problem is primarily the result of the "cultural revolution." On the one hand, those temples which have reopened with the permission of state and local governments are limited in number and are insufficient to meet the religious needs of Chinese and foreign Buddhist visitors. On the other hand, many temples that were closed or occupied by other units during the "cultural revolution" still have not been returned.

Some highly influential temples which were occupied [by other units] before the "cultural revolution" and should be reopened are still occupied. Some have even been remodeled for other purposes. This situation is not normal and is a problem that must be solved. It is both unrealistic and irresponsible to suggest that only those temples already on the list for reopening are needed, while others need not be reopened or can be destroyed.

Before the "cultural revolution," many famous old temples were designated as ancient cultural relics which should be protected, but this did not change their nature as places for religious activities, nor did it change the rights of Buddhist circles to administer them. Temples were originally built as places for religious activities. Only later were they occupied by other units and listed as protected cultural antiquities. But because they were designated as such, the occupying units assumed the rights of administration and ownership. When asked by Buddhist circles to return the temples for their original functions and restore them to their original state, they refused, saying that the temples had been "turned over for their use" because of their status as protected cultural antiquities, and that anyone seeking to recover them would have to get permission from the occupying units. Is this reasonable? That's too much!

There is one paragraph in Document 101 which talks about the relationship between protected cultural antiquities and places of religious activity. Vice-Chairman Panchen and I think there are many problems with this paragraph, but there are still those who defended this paragraph in the Seventh National People's Congress. So then Panchen and I wrote a letter to Acting Premier Li Peng regarding this problem. The State Council and the Party's Central Secretariat have taken notice of this and are investigating the problem.

There are places of religious activity on famous Buddhist and Daoist mountains like Wutai Shan, Emei Shan, Putuo Shan, and Jiuhua Shan. Although these mountains have beautiful scenery, the main attraction which has made them famous at home and abroad for believers and tourists alike is not their scenery but their religious characteristics, the site of the four bodhisattvas. If their religious features were damaged, the scenery of Jiuhua Mountain could not match that of its neighbors Huang Shan and Putuo Shan, for it's just a small island in an archipelago of islands. There are many mountains larger and more splendid than Wutai and Emei, so plans for developing famous Buddhist and Daoist mountains must preserve and protect their religious features and special characteristics, thus benefiting both religion and tourism. If we turn these mountains into nothing but tourist attractions, the tourist business will suffer as well.

Speaking of places of religious activity, there are very large problems in the religious affairs of Henan Province. Their two most famous temples, Baima Temple in Loyang, which was the first temple built after Buddhism came to China, and Shaoling Temple in Dengfeng, belong to the ancient

Chan [Zen] sect. There are many problems relating to these two temples, especially Shaoling. The present situation is very bad. The first monk to arrive from Taiwan in recent years, having made arrangements to stay in Baima Temple, could not bear the present conditions he found in Henan. No matter whether he himself was partially to blame or not, it does point out that great problems exist there that have to do with the work of the local leaders.

In Kaifeng there are two other famous temples, Xiangguo and Tieta, yet these temples have not yet been made available to Buddhists for religious activities. The Venerable [*Fashi*] Jin Yan of Kaifeng, aged ninety-six, is chairman of the Henan Buddhist Association and an honorary council member of the Chinese Buddhist Association. For years he has gone around to many places asking for the return of at least one of these two temples, but to date the problem remains unsolved. This religious elder, who has a high reputation in Buddhist circles, still lives in a shabby little private house.

There is a Xiangguo sect in Japan which recently sent a group to visit the Xiangguo temple in Kaifeng. The local government asked Master Jin Yan to accompany them as the acting abbot of the Xiangguo temple, but this title was given only on a temporary basis.

This year friends from the Xiangguo temple in Japan also asked to visit the Kaifeng temple. I heard that after receiving their request, the mayor of Kaifeng gave instructions to inform the Japanese Buddhists that the Xiangguo temple is not a place for religious activities, and they would be welcome to come simply as sightseers, but not to worship there. The mayor apparently did not care about the international political implications involved, nor about how his decision would affect hard-won Sino-Japanese ties of friendship, nor did he show awareness of the important contributions toward the normalization of diplomatic relations between the two nations that Buddhist circles in China and Japan have made. This shows his ignorance about religion and his political immaturity.

The second problem requiring a solution is the matter of the buildings, their contents, and the property belonging to Buddhist temples. Temples and attached buildings are defined as "social property." There is no regulation for such ownership in the current national constitution, so it is described as "state property." This regulation has become the excuse for arbitrary occupation of temples and their buildings [by other units]; therefore, this regulation must be corrected. In some of the temples which have been permitted to reopen, the property line is limited to the eavesline of the buildings only; their mountain and forest lands have yet to be returned to them. They need to have new, reasonable boundaries drawn up and title deeds to their land given to them. Some cultural relics and other items taken away during the "cultural revolution" have not yet been returned. All must be returned and compensation paid for any that have been lost.

The third problem has to do with the way intellectuals in religious circles are treated. Each religion has a number of intellectuals who are engaged in research, teaching, and editing. Some are scholars and experts with high academic and cultural credentials, yet the problems with regard to their professional titles, status, and proper treatment have still to be solved. Some religious professionals who work in religious organizations, institutes, and cultural units, and even some leaders of these organizations, receive only a small living allowance, but no salaries. They do the same work as non-religious personnel in those units but they do not receive the same pay. This problem must be solved.

There are great difficulties in carrying out religious policy. The main reason for this is that Leftist influences in the thinking of some people have not yet been completely wiped out. These people do not yet understand that during the primary stage of Socialism the de facto existence of religion and its development is inevitable, and they do not understand the five natures of religion as it exists in China today, that is, its mass, ethnic, international, complex, and long-lasting natures. Nor do they understand that the starting point for religious work is to respect and protect the religious freedom of believers, to unite religious believers with all the Chinese people to build Socialism with Chinese characteristics, and to avoid the use of force aimed at weakening or wiping out religion.

Some new leaders among our comrades know little about religious work, but they do know the Leftist line on religion. Some comrades advocate an open economic policy, but they have fossilized thinking when it comes to religious questions. Moreover, the government's system of management and administration of religious work is old and outdated, and the laws governing religion are incomplete.

The Second Major Task: Carry Out Systematic Reforms

For a long time the administrative and management systems for religious work have suffered from malpractice and overcentralized power. The Party and government have taken over religious work. This situation is not appropriate for the current policy of reform and openness. The core problem of reform, according to the principles and spirit of Party General Secretary Zhao Ziyang's report to the Thirteenth Party Congress, is to separate party from administration, and administration from enterprises; to reform the personnel system of cadres; to clarify the relations between Party, administrative organs, and mass organizations; and to carry out a policy of the "separation of politics and religion." "Separation of politics and religion" means separation of the functions of government administrative departments from religious organizations and temples; it does not mean our nation still has a sociopolitical system in which religion and politics are merged. The key to solving the problem of separating politics and religion lies in clarifying the leadership role of government administrative departments and the role of religious bodies, who should carry out independently religious activities according to their own special characteristics.

The administration of churches and temples should be given over to religious believers themselves. We must systematize this policy. The government religious affairs departments provide leadership on religious questions for all government administrative units to implement the policy of freedom of religious belief, guaranteeing and supervising the implementation of the constitution, laws, regulations, and policies, in order to harmonize relationships of religious with other sectors of society. We must change the administrative and management system and the methods which regard religious bodies as administrative units, and turn all religious bodies into true people's organizations which are under the leadership of the Party and government but can independently carry out their work according to their own characteristics. They should be able to enjoy the right to administer their own personnel, property, and religious affairs according to the constitution, laws, and policies of our government. Only in this way can we strengthen and improve the leadership of government administrative departments and at the same time give full play to the functions and vitality of religious organizations.

The Third Major Task: Strengthen the Law on Religion

The problem of drafting a new law on religion is urgent. Only with such a law can the constitutional right of freedom of religious belief for all citizens, with protection under the law, be guaranteed. Only with such a law can problems between religious believers and non-believers, and between the masses and religious professionals, be solved according to law, for whoever breaks the law will be punished.

The first step in drafting a good law on religion is to further emancipate our thinking by breaking loose from old bonds which were once regarded as untouchable. We must demonstrate the basic need for systematic reform of the work of administering religion, to widen our views and to develop new concepts and move into a new context. The key point is to protect the proper rights of religious believers and religious bodies, their temples and churches. During the process of drafting this law, the lawmakers must consult persons from religious circles and listen to the opinions of religious workers and legal experts. At present the Religious Affairs Bureau under the State Council has already organized a special group to carry out this task, and religious bodies are doing their best to help them. Several religious leaders are preparing a draft proposal of this law for presentation. I believe that a religious law which reflects Chinese characteristics and which can correctly define the relationship between government and religion under Socialist conditions will appear in the near future.

Thank you.

Section VI

Marxism, Religion, and Communist Party Membership

Introduction

Two articles, one from a 1981 Fujian newspaper, the other from a textbook on religion published in 1984, rehearse the ideological, political, and practical reasons why Party and Youth League members cannot be religious believers. The question often arises, and can be found again in the section on Youth and Religion in China Today in Part II of this book.

How does it happen that Party members convert to religion? According to Document 18, the loss of social discipline during the period of "leftist" leadership, the wrecking of the Party's work caused by the "gang of four," and the failure to educate Party members in basic Marxist teachings are at the heart of the problem. How to remedy the situation? Those religious fanatics who refuse to give up their religious convictions should be expelled from the Party. As for the others, they should be led to study Marxist theory and Party teachings with the goal of establishing a "firm Communist worldview." At the same time, the Party should help these members to solve the practical problems of their lives, such as ill health and marriage problems, and "make them really feel the love, concern, and warmth of the Party. . . . We cannot simply abandon this group of comrades, but should bring their political activism into full play, and at the same time . . . help them to acquire a dialectical and historical worldview and gradually throw off the bonds of religious ideology."

Document 17

Party and Communist Youth League Members Should Conscientiously Resist the Influence of Religious Ideas

By Ye Shuangyu in Fujian Daily, *23 October 1981. Translated in* China Study Project *Bulletin, No. 17, December 1981, pp. 27-29.*
The article reiterates the known policy that Party membership is not compatible with religious belief. It is an important statement in that it makes clear the ideological and political criteria on which the policy of freedom of religious belief is based.

The freedom of religion is our Party's consistent policy. While continuing to clear up the Leftist influence, we should correctly implement the Party's policy on religion. However, what merits attention is that in some parts of our province religious activities have gone beyond the bounds permitted by law and some religions have even infiltrated into our Party and CYL [Communist Youth League] organizations and have recruited believers among Party and CYL members. We must pay close attention to this matter. Each and every Party and CYL member must conscientiously resist the influence of religious ideas. . . .

Marxism, the CCP's guiding ideology and theoretical basis, was established and has been developed in the course of criticizing idealism and other decadent ideologies. It is a crystallization of social progress and human civilization. . . . The philosophic basis for Marxism and Communism is dialectical and historical materialism, which is the essence or core of the proletarian world outlook and thoroughly atheistic. It stands diametrically opposed to the idealistic theism consisting of religion and various feudal superstitions. The most fundamental viewpoint of dialectical and historical materialism is that man's social being determines his consciousness and the masses of people are the makers of history and the real masters of the world. Without the scientific truth of Marxism and dialectical and historical materialism there would have been no CCP, not to mention its correct leadership. . . . We are now undertaking the great cause of the four modernizations. Today, we need the guidance of Marxism-Leninism-Mao Zedong Thought as we did while striving for the victory of the new democratic revolution. This is where the vital interests of the entire people lie. Dialectical and historical materialism—the most thoroughgoing atheism—was, is, and will be the only world outlook of us Communists.

We uphold atheism, oppose theism, and do away with superstitions; this is determined by the nature of our Party. Communist Party and CYL members must not believe in religion or join a church, which is the Party's and the CYL's most fundamental requirement for each and every Party and CYL member. When a Communist Party or CYL member believes in religion or joins a church, it essentially means that he has renounced his Marxist world outlook, thus forfeiting his minimum qualifications for Party or CYL membership. Therefore, it is absolutely impermissible for Party and CYL members to believe in religion or join a church. As for a very small number of Party and CYL members who believe in religion and participate in religious activities, we should do painstaking educational work among them and persuade them to give up their religious belief and to quit church activities. Those who refuse to do so should be persuaded to withdraw from the Party or the CYL. We must do this work meticulously, not in an oversimplified way.

Some people say, "The Constitution stipulates that citizens enjoy freedom to believe in religion. Since Party and CYL members are also citizens, they should therefore be allowed to enjoy this freedom." This view not only cannot serve as the basis for allowing Party and CYL members to believe in religion, but exactly shows that those holding such a view lack a basic understanding of the nature, guiding ideology, basic tasks, and components of the Communist Party and the CYL. True, Party and CYL members are citizens. However, there is a big difference between Party and CYL members on the one hand and citizens on the other because the latter cannot be called Party or CYL members. A Communist Party member in particular should not be confused with an ordinary person. Engels said that Communists are called practical atheists. As far as belief is concerned, Communist Party and CYL members not only should not believe in any religion but should regard it as their unshakable duty to publicize atheism.

In view of the long history of religion and its mass and national character and complexity, our Party and government have laid down and upheld the basic policy of freedom of religion and have formulated such regulations as permitting legal religious activities, dealing blows to and banning illegal religious activities, banning religion from interfering in politics and education, forbidding the inculcation of religious ideas into young people's minds, and prohibiting religious activities from disrupting production and public order. This policy and the regulations show that our Party trusts the masses, has respect for history, and proceeds from reality. The policy on religion, like other correct policies, should not go beyond the stage of historical development or fail to take the consciousness of the masses into account. However, it cannot be said on account of this that our Party has changed its understanding of the essence of religion and has given up its ideological struggle against religion. Particularly in our province, which is open to the outside world and in which a special economic policy is being implemented, the religious forces from abroad are stepping up their infiltration into the interior of the province; they are establishing a relationship with people, gathering information, and carrying out illegal activities. We must not lower our guard and give up the struggle against them.

Each of us Communist Party and CYL members must firmly establish the Communist world outlook, cherish great ideals, uphold materialism and atheism, conscientiously resist the influence of religious ideas, unite with patriotic personages in religious circles, and isolate and hit hard at those reactionaries who carry out illegal disruptive activities in the garb of religion, in order to maintain stability and unity and to promote the four modernizations.

Document 18

Communist Party Members Cannot Be Religious Believers

From Zongjiao Mantan *(Brief Talks on Religion), Zhejiang People's Press, third edition, 1984, pp. 124-31. Translated by Donald MacInnis.*

In recent years situations have arisen in a number of places where Communist Party members, even some basic-level cadres, have become religious believers. They read "the Bible," offer prayers, solicit donations, build shrines and temples, and worship Buddha [*qiu shen bai fo*]. Some of them not only take part in religious activities themselves, they also pull other people into their religion, increasing the membership. These actions have a very bad influence on the masses.

We must understand that this is not a normal phenomenon. The appearance of this phenomenon is due to errors of the longstanding "Leftist" leadership, in particular the negative consequences of the wrecking of the Party's constructive work caused by the counterrevolutionary gang of Lin Biao and Jiang Qing; it also is a result of relaxing our work in politics and thought, and neglecting the education of Party members in the basic teachings of Marxism and the Party. This should arouse the full concern of all levels of Party organs and the broad membership of the Party, because it reflects the ideological confusion of certain Party members and some new aspects of religious activities at the present time.

The very nature of the Party determines that Party members must be atheists and cannot be members of a religion.

Everyone knows that the Chinese Communist Party is the vanguard of the Chinese working class; its historical mission is to destroy all systems of exploitation and exploiting classes as well as all unfair and unreasonable social phenomena in our nation, and bring about a Communist social system. The basic principles and nature of our Party determine that members must be atheists and cannot be religious believers. We will discuss the reasons why Communist Party members cannot be religious believers.

First, a religious worldview is directly contrary to the Communist world-view. The Chinese Communist Party takes Marxism, Leninism, and the thought of Mao Zedong as its guide and compass, upholding the scientific worldview of dialectical and historical materialism. Marxism is the only scientific theory for understanding and reforming the world. Only Marxism can scientifically reveal the laws of historical development of human society, show clearly the historical position and great mission of the proletariat, and point out the direction and the way to be taken by the proletariat and the working class in the struggle to change the old world and build a new one. Our Party is the party of the progressive working class; not only is it a party founded on the working class but it is also a party that uses the weapons of Marxist theory. A Communist Party member must guide his own life and work by firm belief in, and by adopting the standpoint, view-point, and methods of Marxism, Leninism, and the thought of Mao Zedong in order to correctly understand society and nature. This is the Party spirit which is required of every Party member.

But religion is a thought system diametrically opposed to science and atheism. In the words of Marx, it is a kind of "topsy-turvy worldview." All religions believe that mankind cannot understand or grasp the real world and its permutations, since everything in human experience, including hu-man life and prosperity, disasters, and death, is considered to be unpre-dictable divine mystery controlled by "God" [shangdi], "true God," [zhen zhu] or Buddha. Humans are powerless in the face of "gods," and can only subordinate themselves to divine manipulation. The [alleged] existence of mystical supernatural forces is an absurd and distorted reflection of the forces of nature and society. In old China religion was the tool by which the dominant classes oppressed and hoodwinked the people, tying them tightly in a spiritual bondage. So a Communist Party member should be an atheist fighter, using dialectical materialism to expose the illusions of theism, and leading the people to gradually dispel the fog and bondage of religion. To give up this fighting task and believe in religion is to abandon the Party's scientific worldview and to lose the advanced nature of a Party member.

Next, it is contrary to the highest ideals of Marxism and our present struggle for a Party member to believe in religion. The ultimate goal of our Party is to bring about a Communist social system. The goal of our Party during the present period of struggle is to build a modernized, high-level, civilized, democratic, and socialist nation. This is an important stage of Communist development and is the universal wish of the whole Party and all the people after years of struggle. Party members should be the vanguard of the working class, with a Communist consciousness firmly based in the long-range ideals of Communism and of total struggle. Under the leader-ship of the Party's correct way, direction, and policy, they should give themselves completely, with whole heart and spirit, to spreading the spirit of serving the people, uniting with the masses, immersing self in hard work, plunging wholeheartedly into the great struggle to build a modernized nation, and in every way giving full play to the role of being a model and vanguard, to research new conditions, to resolve new questions, and to use their own wisdom and two hands to clear away the obstacles to building a modernized nation on the road ahead.

But religion is vigorously preaching that the real world is illusory, insignificant, and that human life is "like the life of a mayfly," brief and ephemeral, without meaning. Religion induces people to give up interest in the present life and to cease all efforts to find happiness and prosperity in this world. If a Party member believes this kind of propaganda, how can he give himself to the untiring struggle of the Party in the cause of modernizing China? How can he be a vanguard of the working class worthy of the name? . . .

In summary, if a Party member believes in religion he is going in the opposite direction from the Party and is not worthy to bear the name of Party member. A Party member should arm himself with a scientific worldview, and become a materialistic, atheistic, heroic fighter who never stops in the struggle to bring about the highest ideals of Socialism and Communism.

The fact that the Party carries out the policy of freedom of religious belief does not mean that Party members are free to believe in religion.

"Doesn't our national constitution guarantee freedom of religious belief?" Some Party members use this as the reason to justify their own religious belief. Or, when the Party organs get them together to teach them to give up religious belief and withdraw from religious organizations, some people still believe that this "violates the stipulations of the constitution."

This, in fact, is a confused understanding without foundation. Lenin said: "Religion is not a private matter when it relates to the party of the Socialist proletariat. Our Party is the liberating alliance of vanguard fighters with the working class. This alliance cannot, indeed must not, fail to be aware of the ignorance, nonsense, and lack of consciousness of religious believers. We insist on total separation of church and state, using pure ideological weapons, indeed using nothing but ideological weapons, our words and publications, to engage in the struggle with the miasma of religion. Like the Russian Social Democratic Party, we have established our organizations precisely so as to fight against anything that religion does to hoodwink the workers. We say that ideological struggle is not a private matter, but is a concern of the entire Party and the entire proletariat" [*Selected Works of Lenin*, vol. 10, p.64]. This is a basic attitude of the working-class party and its members for dealing with religion.

It is true that we should resolutely carry out the policy of religious belief set forth in the constitution. Communist Party members should be models in obeying the constitution. But there are national laws for the nation, and Party rules for the Party. Besides obeying the national constitution, a working-class-party member must faithfully carry out the duties of a Party member, unconditionally obeying the Party program, Party constitution, and other rules of the Party, or he cannot be a Communist Party member.

It should be pointed out that the stipulation in our national constitution on freedom of religious belief refers to citizens of China. Party members are not ordinary citizens, nor are they ordinary workers among the masses; they are the vanguard of the working class with Communist consciousness, who maintain an important criterion of the Communist vanguard, namely, loyalty to and faith in Marxist scientific truth and in no way believe in religious theology. If one believes that religion is a private matter as it relates to the Marxist Party, and that freedom of religious belief is all right for Party members, then one is downgrading the Party to the level of any ordinary mass organization and downgrading Party members to the status of any ordinary citizen; how can one then speak of the vanguard nature of the Party and the leadership example to be set by Party members? If one says that some Party members insist on believing in religious theology because they enjoy the freedom of religious belief of ordinary citizens, then he is arranging his own funeral as a Party member. Since he cannot enjoy his "freedom" and at the same time remain in the Party, he must resign from the Party. So we must make it very clear that a Party member cannot retain religious belief; he cannot believe in religion, or attend any religious activity or any religious organization. This upholds the principle of the vanguard nature of the Party and the Communist purity of the Party's troops.

Some comrades ask, "Can members of the Communist Youth League believe in religion?" The answer also is negative. We know that the CYL is a mass organization of vanguard youth which assists the Party under the leadership of Marxism, Leninism, and Mao Zedong Thought. CYL members should assiduously study and acquire knowledge of culture, theory, science, and technology, and establish a historical and dialectical materialist worldview, faith in science, love of truth, and a wholehearted ideological commitment to serve the people; they should strive to be shock workers in building a Socialist material and spiritual civilization, rather than religious believers who reject the world. By its very nature the CYL determines that its members cannot at the same time be religious believers.

Party organs should educate Party members who are led astray into religion to give up their religious belief.

Since Party members cannot believe in religion, then how should Party organs correctly deal with Party members who have already joined a religion?

It must be said that there are some Party members who believe in religion who are truly odious. Not only do they believe in religion, they instigate religious fanaticism, even to the point of using religion to stir up opposition to the four basic principles, the Party's way, its direction, and its policies. These people, whose standpoint as a Party member has already perished, should be expelled from the Party if they don't change, or if they continue to say both "yes and no" [feign compliance] after going through criticism and education.

Aside from these few we should look at some other Party members who are religious believers, especially those whose political consciousness and ideological thinking are questionable, because they have not sufficiently studied the theories of Marxism and basic knowledge of the Party, have not established a firm Communist worldview or outlook on life, and cannot find a clear way out or a rational explanation of the difficulties they meet in daily life. Engels said, "There are bound to be people of every class who search for spiritual liberation and consolation as a substitute for material liberation in which they have lost hope"(Selected Works of Marx and Engels, vol. 19, p. 334). We must first give these comrades adequate education in the Party's way, direction, and policies, in a Marxist and atheist worldview, and in basic knowledge of the Party, so that they can know clearly what direction to go, see the road ahead, and strengthen their faith. We need to help them to draw a clear line between atheism and theism, to know the essence of religion and its illusory and deceptive nature, and raise their political and ideological consciousness.

At the same time we should thoroughly and meticulously analyze and understand the reasons why these comrades believe in religion in order to strengthen the ideological work directed against religion. The Party organs should help to solve problems encountered by Party members in their work, daily lives, marriage, health, and so on, and make them really feel the love, concern, and warmth of the Party. The Party should help them to give up religion and resign from religious organizations of their own free will. If these comrades obey the admonitions of the Party and give up their religious belief and in fact do engage in earnest study and concrete work, then they should not be looked down upon. But if they still hold on to their religious belief after undergoing a period of study, they should be expelled from the Party according to the basic principles of the Party organization. This is absolutely necessary in order to preserve the purity and the vanguard nature of the Party organization and its membership.

As for those national minorities where the entire population are religious believers, enforcement of this policy of course must be carried out according to actual conditions, adopting appropriate measures. There is no simple way to deal with this. One must look at the fact that there are still a significant number of Party members among the national minorities who, although they follow the Party's road, and actively carry out the Party's work and follow the Party's regulations, are still unable to completely free themselves from religious influences. We cannot simply abandon this group of comrades, but should bring into full play their political activism, and at the same time conduct patient and painstaking ideological work, helping them to acquire a dialectical and historical worldview, and gradually throw off the bonds of religious ideology. As Party membership grows in number, it is of course necessary to take very seriously the fact that excessive pressure should not be used to bring religious believers who have pronounced religious feelings into the Party.

These principles are equally appropriate in dealing with members of the Communist Youth League. The CYL organization should thoroughly study the reasons why some members believe in religion and should give them earnest help to give up their religious belief by patient and convincing teaching. If, after receiving education over a period of time, they are still unwilling to give up their religious belief, they can be expelled from the League. The League should be careful the way they handle the expulsion so as not to hurt their feelings.

Section VII

Policy on Avoiding Waste and Extravagance in Religious Practices

Introduction

One of the arguments used by Chinese Marxists, who find no utilitarian value in religion, is that it wastes time and money that could be better spent contributing to the nation's gross national product. Since the constitution guarantees freedom of religious belief, it also, by implication, guarantees the right to have and build places of worship. However, permission to refurbish and reopen churches long used for other purposes and to use scarce land and building materials to erect new churches, temples, and mosques must be granted by the government. The Religious Affairs Bureau, at local or provincial levels, is the mediating agency between the religious group and relevant government offices. It is not clear who sets the quota on how many such buildings can be built, or what the deciding factors are, but we know that there is a shortage and that many religious districts and dioceses are waiting for permission to repair and reopen decrepit churches and temples or build new ones. Even so, new churches, temples, and shrines are springing up in many places, causing concern in government circles. Moreover, excessive spending on weddings, funerals, and religious festivals is seen as unnecessary extravagance, which indeed it often is, leading to long-term indebtedness for an entire family.

Again, it is hard to draw the line between legitimate religious activities and illegal superstitious practices. Document 20 warns against wizards and witches who infiltrate some localities "in the name of the gods," intimidating people into giving them money, spreading fallacies, and upsetting social order.

Finally, we have an argument that materialists would find hard to refute: that rural areas with a shortage of schoolrooms would do better to build schools than spend money on new shrines, temples, and family tombs.

Document 19

Shanxi Party Committee Issues Circular on Extravagance and Waste around Religious Festivals

Shanxi Provincial Radio, 29 December 1985. Translated in JPRS-CPS-86-014, 28 January 1986, pp. 83-84.

The general offices of the Shanxi Provincial CPC Committee and Shanxi Provincial People's Government have jointly issued an urgent circular on the strict prohibition of extravagance and waste and of giving banquets and gifts around New Year's Day and Spring Festival.

The circular says: It will soon be New Year's Day 1986 and the Spring Festival. The number of commemorative meetings, receptions, and tea parties in all places will obviously increase. The problems of giving banquets and gifts and of extravagant eating and drinking in some places and units have frequently arisen. This runs counter to the spirit of the circular of the general offices of the CPC Central Committee and State Council. A high degree of attention by CPC committees and governments at all levels must be drawn to this.

With a view to resolutely curbing the unhealthy trends of extravagance and waste and of giving banquets and gifts, after studies by the provincial CPC Committee and provincial People's Government, they issued a circular saying the following:

1. Around New Year's Day and the Spring Festival, the provincial CPC Committee and provincial People's Government must not hold receptions and group meetings for the purpose of mutual congratulations around these holidays. Except for the necessary army-people get-togethers and receptions for foreign guests and overseas Chinese, and [words indistinct], departments concerned at the provincial level and prefectures and cities must not hold tea parties and receptions. When these are necessary, they must hold them in a thrifty way and provide only tea.

2. Leading cadres at all levels must not extort anything from the lower levels or purchase Spring Festival goods at low prices. The lower levels are not allowed to give banquets and gifts to the higher levels under any pretexts. It is essential to advocate holding weddings in a thrifty way and to oppose holding weddings extravagantly, and to oppose all extravagance and waste. It is imperative to strictly deal with the serious cases in which leading cadres who give extravagant banquets and extort engagement gifts under the pretext of weddings, which produces very bad efforts.

3. Party and government organs and leading cadres at all levels must act as models in implementing the instructions of the central authorities, State

Council, provincial cpc Committee, and Provincial People's Government on improving work style, take the lead in establishing good work style, and promote a basic improvement of Party style and the general mood of society.

The circular demands that all places and departments seriously inspect all activities arranged around New Year's Day and the Spring Festival and correct as soon as possible anything which does not conform to the above spirit.

Document 20

Indiscriminate Building of Temples in Rural Areas Should Be Curbed

By Wu Ming in Nanfang Ribao, *5 June 1983. Translated in FE 7049, 11 June 1982 and reprinted in China Study Project* Documentation, *October 1982, pp. 46-47.*

Several days ago, I was on a business trip to other places and discovered smoke curling up from some newly built temples in rural communes and production brigades where men and women, young and old, come to worship. An old comrade who traveled with me observed that this practice was far more common than in the 1950s. As far as I know, the indiscriminate building of temples has increased the economic load of the masses and encouraged feudal superstitious activities in the rural areas. Many commune members strongly object to this. However, some cadres in these localities are indifferent to this phenomenon and say, "The State has built large temples, and so the peasants have built small ones. Why should we bother about this?" It seems quite necessary to discuss the question of whether or not we should interfere in the indiscriminate building of temples in the rural areas.

What does "the State building large temples" actually mean? It seems that in the past few years, some famous temples which exert a great influence and are valuable cultural relics have been repaired in some localities. These famous temples are not only places of religious activities, but have always been places of historic interest and scenic beauty which the masses like to visit very much. They are being repaired in implementation of the Party's religious policy by providing necessary places for normal religious activities and to preserve historical relics so that there may be more beautiful places to visit. However, we should make it clear that when the State approves the repair of some famous temples, it does not mean that the State encourages the building of temples, and much less does it mean that the resources and funds of the State or collectives can be used to build temples.

Respecting and protecting the freedom of religious belief is the Party's basic policy on religion. However, we oppose the indiscriminate building of temples. At present, many localities have engaged in large-scale construction of temples, wasting a lot of manpower, materials, and funds. This is very harmful. A commune in Haifeng county, for example, has recently built over fifty new temples. Some villages have built temples for the Earth God, temples for Erlang, temples for the God of the Southern Heaven, temples for Guangong, temples for the Holy Mother, and so on. The building of a new temple costs 2,000 to 3,000 *yuan*.

After a temple is built, the so-called celebration activities of giving theatrical performances again need thousands of *yuan*. The money is subscribed from the villagers. The commune members have to bear expenses for building the temple and for giving the performances. Besides, they also have to provide food and lodgings for their relatives who come to see the performances. Consequently, some commune members have to sell rice and even borrow money for such purposes and they pour out endless grievances. How can we not interfere in these activities?

What is noteworthy is that after the temples are indiscriminately built in some localities, some wizards and witches begin to make trouble. In the name of the gods, they blackmail those who do not subscribe money by putting up notices stating that "such and such persons will have no son." So the masses dare not disobey them. Under the pretext of restoring temples, some wizards, witches and lawless elements wantonly occupy schools, medical centers, and headquarters of production brigades and production teams and put up notices everywhere, spreading fallacies to deceive people. This has seriously impaired normal social order and production. What they are doing has greatly exceeded the range of religious activities. Their activities should be resolutely banned and offenders who have seriously violated the criminal law should be punished according to the law.

Implementing the religious policy and protecting the freedom of religious belief should never be interpreted as slackening the propaganda of atheism. We are duty bound to educate the peasants with Marxism and to strengthen the building of a spiritual civilization in the rural areas so that the peasants may shake off ignorance and superstition. We should properly work to curb the indiscriminate building of temples in the rural areas. It is wrong to remain indifferent and not to interfere.

Document 21

Building Temples or Schoolhouses?

China Daily, *1 June 1987, p.4.*

In recent years, there has been a craze for building temples in the countryside, while the improvement of poor-quality schoolhouses has been ignored. There is a striking contrast in some villages — the temple is the best building, while the school is the worst. An article by Jia Dechang in *Economic Daily* commented on the phenomenon. Excerpts follow:

Some poverty-stricken areas pinned their hopes of becoming rich on spiritual blessings, instead of relying on their own efforts.

A pavilion for the "god of heaven" was built in a village when there was a drought. The villagers wanted to petition the god for rain, but while doing so they missed the right season for planting.

The craze has also found its way to some comparatively rich areas such as Wenzhou in Zhejiang Province, which is famous for its highly developed township-run economy. Apart from building temples, some people there even use cement to build tombs for themselves. A few young people have gone so far as to build high-quality tombs for themselves although they are only in their twenties.

This is a waste of labor and money. There are still many who are struggling just to feed themselves, although the living standard of most farmers has improved. It is of no help to the collective or the individual to throw money into building useless temples.

In the May 4th Movement of 1919, the pioneers of democratic revolution devoted themselves to the struggle against feudalism and superstition. Just after the founding of new China, the farmers rose to pull down temples and destroy idols in the agrarian reform. Later on, ideological education was given to farmers to counter superstition.

Why should feudal superstitions revive today?

The opinion that this is the outcome of the development of market-oriented economy and the open policy is groundless.

This is not a new problem, but an old one left in history.

Administrative measures are not enough to combat superstition. The scientific and cultural level of the nation must be raised.

Education is the most important means of improving the cultural level.

Education is undeveloped in the countryside, and the average schoolhouse area for primary- and middle-school pupils is far from the standard set by the State.

The State pays 100 million *yuan* every year for the building of school-houses for primary and middle schools in remote and poor areas. This aid began in 1983.

However, schoolhouses in most primary and middle schools in the countryside are in poor condition, and this affects the development of education.

Education in the countryside would take on a new look if the craze for building temples could be turned into one for building schoolhouses.

Section VIII

Religion and Religious Policy Explained in a Textbook for Young People

Introduction

Zongjiao Gujintan (Religion Yesterday and Today) is a 235-page book, written in short chapters and easy style, published in the Friends of Youth Series by the Shanghai People's Publishing Co. in 1985. Its purpose is to provide basic information about the origins of religion, the development of the great world religions, the religions of China, and answers to basic questions about the religious policies of China under Socialism. This last section is translated here.

The author makes it clear in the introduction to the book that he writes from a Marxist viewpoint: "The theories of Marxism about religion gave clear direction for my research. ... If we use the methods and viewpoints of historical and material determinism to analyze concretely the facts of ancient and contemporary religions of China within definite historical periods, then we can cut through all kinds of fog and obfuscation to see that sources for the birth and evolution of religion are not found in heaven but are here among humankind."

After a concise historical overview of religion among the Han Chinese, the author addresses a series of questions about religion and religious policy since Liberation. Why does the constitution guarantee freedom of religious belief? It is "to ensure that questions of religious belief are personal matters for all citizens," for the basic task is "to strengthen the unity of the entire nation, both believers and non-believers, to carry out the modernization and unification of our country for the sake of China."

Which religious activities are considered normal, and why should temples, monasteries, and churches be repaired and reopened? The answers to these and similar questions are utilitarian, pragmatic, with never a reference to the spiritual needs or spiritual contributions of religious believers, although the list of normal activities includes worship, prayers, and preaching. If the religious policy is to be carried out, places of worship will be needed. But (and much more space is given to this line of reasoning), many of these churches, temples, and monasteries are famous "both inside and outside China for their historical and cultural value" and should be preserved. And many of them are, in fact, tourist meccas with thousands of

92

visitors each year, including many from abroad. Religion is a cultural artifact that earns both foreign exchange and international goodwill.

Illegal superstitious activities are defined, differentiating such "superstitious customs" of the rural people, as worshiping ancestors from the illegal activities of shamans and sorcerers. Patient education and "vigorous building of a Socialist spiritual civilization" will eventually take care of this heritage of old habits and customs.

Finally, the young readers of this book are given reasons why members of the Party and Communist Youth League cannot be religious believers. "The basic task of the CYL is to educate young people in the spirit of Marxism. When an advanced young person joins the CYL he has already made the free choice not to believe in religion. He has already consciously become an atheist, not a theist."

Document 22

Excerpts from *Religion Yesterday and Today (Zongjiao Gujintan)*

By Zhang Sui; a volume in the Friends of Youth Series, Shanghai People's Publishing Co., 1985, pages i-iii, and 219-35. Translated by Tam Waiyi and Donald MacInnis.

Preface

Religion is both a historical phenomenon and an ideology which has had a heavy influence on the development of human history down to the present time, when many people still believe in various religions. What then, after all, is this false, illusory, and upside-down reflection of objective existence? What influence has religion had on the course of human history in different historical periods? Why is it that religion still has a protracted existence in society under Socialism? These questions have aroused my deep interest in religious research.

In my daily life and work I come into contact with many young friends who are eager to learn, including university students, young workers, teachers, cadres, journalists, editors, and librarians. They express their deep desire to know the basic principles, viewpoints, and facts about religion, having encountered many religious questions and religious phenomena in their daily lives, such as: visiting famous mountains and temples, where they saw impressive, gilded statues of Buddha; or hearing the sounds of pipe organ music while passing by a church; or viewing religious works of art by great masters displayed at art exhibitions; or seeing religious themes portrayed in movies, television, and novels; or in meeting devoted religious believers among their circle of young acquaintances. I have been inspired by contacts with these young friends to write this book.

Because there are many religions with long histories, and many volumes of sacred scriptures, both in China and elsewhere in the world, it is impossible to carry out a thorough and systematic exposition of religion in this small book. Rather, we will take a few cases to represent the whole, dividing the book into three sections: exploration, information, and policy, explaining and discussing those questions in which young people have interest and need for understanding. We wish to provide the reader with a general understanding of religious questions and religious policy, and basic information about the birth and the spread into China of the three great world religions—Buddhism, Christianity, and Islam. We will also speak of the emergence and development of indigenous Daoism in China, and of questions related to the religious policies of China under Socialism.

It is said that religion is a very complex historical phenomenon. If we just go around in circles focusing on the grotesque and bizarre religions, we will certainly feel befuddled. But if we use the methods and viewpoints of historical and material determinism to analyze concretely the facts of ancient and contemporary religions of China within definite historical periods, then we can cut through all kinds of fog and obfuscation to see that sources for the birth and evolution of religion are not found in heaven but are here among humankind. In this way all kinds of strange religious phenomena can be clearly explained.

With regard to religious questions, it is the basic policy of the Party and the State to respect and protect freedom of religious belief. This is clearly stipulated in our national constitution. The essence of the policy of freedom of religious belief is that each citizen has freedom of choice; it is a personal matter for each citizen. We must carry out this policy of dealing with religious questions, and base it on a firm footing so that all religious believers and nonbelievers alike will enthusiastically love Socialist China and join together in the common struggle towards the goal of building a strong, Socialist nation.

It has been a learning exercise for me to write this book. The theories of Marxism about religion gave clear direction for my research. The result of the research work of scholars of religion, history, and archeology have enriched my knowledge, clearing the paths of my thinking and informing me greatly.

Since my [scholarly] level is limited, I'm afraid it is impossible to avoid errors and shortcomings in this work. I sincerely ask that all readers, specialists, and senior scholars will freely offer suggestions. . . .

What Is the General Situation of Religion in China?

Many religions have entered and spread throughout China. Buddhism has a history of about two thousand years in China, Daoism over seventeen hundred, and Islam over thirteen hundred years. Christianity came to China as early as the Tang dynasty, but it did not really spread throughout the nation until after the Opium Wars. In the course of their dissemination in China, these organized [systematic] religions evolved in different degrees, reflecting special aspects of Chinese culture. But whether historically or in the present time, the number of believers belonging to these organized religions has amounted to only a small proportion of our total population. Statistically, there are about ten million Muslims, over three million Catholics, and three million Protestant Christians [in China today]. It is difficult to compile accurate statistics on Buddhists, while Daoists in China are very few, and not very influential. Some of the national minorities are believers in primitive religions.

Looking at religions geographically, they occupy about two-thirds of the area of our country. Catholic and Protestant Christians are found mainly in central, south, north, southwest, and east China, and in Beijing, Tianjin, and other districts. Tibetan Buddhism is found mainly in the Tibetan Autonomous Region and the areas of Qinghai and Gansu provinces, the Inner Mongolian Autonomous Region, the western part of Sichuan province, the northwest part of Yunnan province, and other districts inhabited by Tibetans.

Theravada Buddhism is found mainly in southern Yunnan and neighboring regions. Buddhism among the Han Chinese is found in all parts of China, but the number of real believers among them is very small. Muslims inhabit broad areas of China, mainly the Xinjiang Uyghur Autonomous Region, the Ningxia Hui Autonomous Region, Qinghai, Shaanxi, Yunnan, and other provinces where the Hui minorities live. There are ten national minorities in China in which almost the entire population are Muslims: Hui, Uyghur, Kazakh, Dongxiang, Sala, Kirgiz, Uzbek, Pao'an, Tartar, and Turkic.

Believers in primitive religions are still found among over thirty national minorities in China, mainly in the Tibetan Autonomous Region; Yunnan, Sichuan, Guizhou, and Hunan Provinces; the Guangxi Zhuang Autonomous Region; Guangdong, Taiwan, and Heilongjiang provinces; the Inner Mongolian Autonomous Region; and other provinces and districts. The reasons for the historical and geographical spread of the religions in China and the situation of primitive religious belief among the national minorities before Liberation, as well as that of other religions, are all intimately related.

There are "five characteristics" of religion in the period of Socialism in China. These were proposed by Comrade Li Weihan after completing his analysis of the religious situation in China. These are: its mass nature, its democratic nature, its international nature, its protracted nature, and its complex nature. In order to know how to deal with religious questions under Socialism it is very important to understand these "five characteristics.". . .

What Are the Special Features of Religion among the Han Chinese?

Since most Chinese are ethnic Hans it is very important to analyze the situation of religion among them. We will give a general picture of that situation in this chapter.

THE FIRST CHARACTERISTIC

The main impression we get from the legacy of ancient deifications inherited from the time of the Xia people, the ancestors of the Hans, is that such legendary figures as Pan Gu, Nu Huo, and Fu Xi Si, were human and not divine [people and not gods]. Although there are some divine elements in this tradition, they are mainly used to describe the contributions and achievements of these traditional personages in technology, craftsmanship, military prowess, and so on. In fact they represent the "humanization" of the level of productivity of certain historical periods, as they had developed. Among the deities of the ancient Chinese people, there were numerous legends about the Yellow Emperor, the Yen Emperor, and such other legendary figures such Sui Rensi, Yu Changsi, Shen Lingsi, but many national groups in China regard them simply as great people, and consider themselves to be their descendants. This is different from the tradition of the ancient Hebrews [Israelites], who regarded themselves as descendants of "God" [Jehovah]. For example the "History of Wei," one of twenty-four volumes of the "Ancient History of China," which records the origins of the Xianbei nationality who once lived in north China, says that these people were descended from one of the twenty-five sons of the Huang Emperor, Changyi, who was ruler of the north. There was a Xianbei Mountain, hence their name. Obviously there is nothing about divinity in this legend.

THE SECOND CHARACTERISTIC

The proportion of Han religious believers among China's total population has been quite small for over two thousand years up to the time just prior to Liberation. Although the worship of Buddha and other deities among the Chinese people has been quite widespread, they have never limited themselves to a single religion or sect; rather, they have worshiped Buddhism's "Amitofu" and "Guanyin," Daoism's god of wealth, the "stove god," and the "three gods" of prosperity, longevity, and good fortune, [fu, shou, lu]. The "nonexclusivity" of religious belief among the Han Chinese is one of the few characteristics of their religious beliefs.

THE THIRD CHARACTERISTIC

Although there are not many followers of systematic religion among the Hans, concepts of "gods and ghosts" and "soul and spirit" were rather widespread before Liberation, when the people stood in awe of many gods and ghosts, and gave heavy religious content to their funeral ceremonies. These ideas about "gods and ghosts" and "soul and spirit" are still influential today.

THE FOURTH CHARACTERISTIC

The ruling class throughout China's history has never legally forced one religion, a so-called state religion, on all the people. This is true for each of the many emperors from Qin and Han down to the Qing. Although there were many believers in various deities and practitioners of Daoism's "eternal life," the ruling thought system of the emperors, beginning with Han Wu, was Confucianism. Many emperors used religion to reinforce their rule, hoping to gain the protection of the gods by worshiping them. But whenever the forces of organized religion threatened the control of the ruling class, they either put strict limitations on it or stamped it out. Four times in the history of the Han Chinese there were incidents of "exterminating Buddhism" [mie fo]. Strong and prosperous dynasties were tolerant of organized religion and followed policies of "treating everyone alike" and "accepting things of diverse nature." The Tang Emperor Tai Zong, the Yuan Emperor Shi-zu, and the Qing Emperor Kang Xi all followed such policies.

Although there are many historical records showing how the ruling class repressed the religions of the people, most of them were not for religious reasons but because of other things that happened which had a direct connection with the people's religion.

THE FIFTH CHARACTERISTIC

In the Han society it was the ruling thought system, Confucianism, which imposed restraints on the development of organized religion. The principle concept of Confucianism, the concept of "the will of heaven" and the general principles of feudalism, were in conflict with the teachings of Buddhism and the other great religions. The Confucian concept of "the will of heaven" was spread among the people by the feudal literati. These included such ideas as "Fate determines life and death, heaven [tian] determines prosperity and wealth" and "People can try, but success depends on heaven"; such ideas controlled the actions of the people. This "heaven-determined fate" way of thinking led many of the people away from reliance on religion to reliance on themselves to "change" their own destiny. This is one of the reasons why there weren't many followers of organized religion among the Han Chinese. . . .

Why Have There Been Fundamental Changes in the Religious Situation in China?

During the long period of feudal society in China, and the semifeudal, semicolonial society of the years 1840-1949, the use of the major religions as a prop was an important factor in maintaining the system of exploitation by the ruling class. The landlords, slave owners, counterrevolutionary war-lords, and bureaucratic capitalists principally used and controlled Buddh-ism, Daoism, and Islam. Later, the forces of foreign colonialism and imperialism principally used and controlled the Roman Catholic and Prot-estant churches. . . . .

After the establishment of the People's Republic of China, the Party and State adopted a policy of freedom of religious belief, which is the basic policy for dealing with religious questions. After a series of major social changes, and reforms in the religious system, the religions of China have been profoundly transformed.

First, following the destruction of the exploiting classes and the exploit-ing system under Socialism in China, the class sources of religion have been eliminated. Generally speaking, religious questions have now become in-ternal questions of thinking and belief.

Second, China has become a strong, great, and independent Socialist nation. The foreign Protestant and Catholic imperialist forces have been cleared away. The many patriotic members of these churches have mounted anti-imperialism campaigns, and now follow the road of independence, autonomy, and self-propagation. There are now eight national religious organizations: the Chinese Buddhist Association, the Chinese Daoist As-sociation, the Chinese Islamic Association, the Chinese Catholic Patriotic Association, the Chinese Catholic Church Affairs Commission, the Chinese Catholic Bishops' Conference, the Chinese Protestant "Three-Self" Pa-triotic Movement, and the Protestant China Christian Council.

Third, since there is economic benefit for all, religious believers and nonbelievers work hard together with the Party and the State for the four modernizations. A great change that has taken place in Socialist society is the respect given to religion and the guarantee of social status for religious believers. This is reflected in the religious thought of each religion, and is principally shown in the joining of love of country with love of religion. The fact that all religious workers participate in the great cause of Socialist nation building is seen in such slogans as "Love your nation, love religion; glorify God and benefit all the people" (Protestant circles) and "We share with others the joy and benefit of this our holy land" (Buddhist circles). Such slogans have received enthusiastic support and response from great numbers of religious believers.

In summary, this section explains how the religious situation in China has been fundamentally transformed. . . .

How Can We Correctly Understand the Policy of Freedom of Religious Belief?

On 4 December 1982, the Fifth Session of the Fifth Plenary of the National People's Congress approved Section 2, Article 36 of the revised national constitution, under the heading "The basic rights and obligations of citizens." Article 36 reads:

All citizens of the People's Republic of China enjoy freedom
of religious belief.

No organ of state, mass organization or person is allowed to force any citizen to believe or not to believe in religion. It is not permitted to discriminate against any citizen who believes or does not believe in religion.

The State protects legitimate religious activities. No person is permitted to use religion to conduct counter-revolutionary activities or activities disruptive to social order, harming people's health, or obstructing the educational system of the country.

Religion May Not Be Subject to the Control of Foreign Countries.

This article of the national constitution sets forth the basic policy for dealing with religious questions in China during the Socialist period. We must fully and correctly understand this policy. What is freedom of religious belief? Citizens of the People's Republic of China have freedom to believe in religion and freedom not to believe in religion; they can believe in this religion or in that religion; they have the right to believe in one or another of the various sects within a religion; those who are unbelievers have the right to believe in religion and those who are believers have the right to give up their religious belief. The long-term policy of the Party and State is to respect and protect freedom of religious belief.

We should clearly understand that the essence of this policy of freedom of religious belief is to ensure that questions of religious belief are personal matters for all citizens. By making freedom of religion a basic right of citizens, the constitution is making it very clear that this is a matter of personal choice for each citizen. All normal religious activities and religious beliefs are protected by the constitution. No one can force citizens to believe or not to believe in religion; there can be no bias against citizens who believe or against citizens who do not believe in religion.

Religious believers and nonbelievers alike share equally in the political and economic benefits of the great household of our Socialist nation. We all join efforts under the leadership of the Chinese Communist Party and the people's government in the struggle to build a strong, modernized Socialist nation. We should not neglect nor deny the basic political and economic benefits for either religious believers or nonbelievers, for if we do we forget that our basic task is to strengthen the unity of the entire population (including both religious believers and nonbelievers), and to carry out the modernization and unification of our country for the sake of China! No one is permitted to use force in dealing with questions of religious belief; to do so will not only fail to solve questions relating to belief, thinking, and the spiritual world, but it will increase misunderstanding among religious believers and nonbelievers, will harm the unity of all ethnic groups, and damage the cause of Socialist modernization.

The national constitution also clearly stipulates that religion cannot be used to carry on activities destructive of the social order, or injurious to the health of our body of citizenry, or obstructive to our nation's educational system. Religious organizations and activities cannot be controlled by forces outside China. This also is an important part of our religious policy. Only in this way can religious activities move in the right direction.

In summary, only this policy of freedom of religious belief based on the theories and principles laid down by Marxism, Leninism, and the actual conditions in China is the correct religious policy for benefiting the people. We should earnestly study, thoroughly comprehend, and conscientiously carry out this policy.

Which Religious Activities Are Considered Normal?

The national constitution stipulates that the State will protect normal religious activities. So what are normal religious activities? Religious functions carried on by religious believers in religious places such as temples, monasteries, churches, and mosques which are considered normal include: reading scriptures, worshiping Buddha, burning incense, other forms of worship, prayers, preaching, expounding scripture, celebrating Mass, baptisms, observing religious commandments, practicing vegetarianism, seeking grace [cui en], and carrying on religious customs in the homes of religious believers such as meditation, prayers, reading scriptures, fasting, and theological study. All these are considered normal religious activities. These functions of patriotic and self-supporting religious organizations are protected by law, and no one can interfere with them. All religious places (such as temples, monasteries, churches, etc.) are administered [guan li] by religious organizations and religious clergy under the administrative leadership of the Religious Affairs Bureau of the people's government. No one can carry on atheistic propaganda in these temples, monasteries, and churches, or initiate debate about atheism and theism among religious believers. On the other hand no religious organization or person can preach, evangelize, or propagate theism or distribute religious tracts or any other religious publications not approved by government authorities outside those places of worship. . . .

Why Should Temples, Monasteries, and Churches Be Repaired, Restored, and Reopened?

In recent years our country has planned and carried out repairs, restoration, and reopening of a number of temples, monasteries, and churches in various parts of China. This is to completely carry out the policy of freedom of religious belief of the Party and State by providing the necessary material conditions for conducting normal religious activities. It is easy to see that it will be difficult to implement a policy of freedom of religious belief if there are no appropriate places in which to carry on normal religious activities.

Among the temples, monasteries, and churches already reopened, there are many that are not only places of religious activities but are also famous both inside and outside China for their historical and cultural value: for example, Daming Temple in Yangzhou, the Guoqing Temple on Tiantai Mountain in Zhejiang, the Huajue Temple in Xi'an, the Putuo Mountain temples in Zhejiang, the Shaoling Temple on Song Mountain, the temples on Omei and Qingcheng mountains in Sichuan, the Catholic Xujiahui Cathedral in Shanghai, and other famous mountains and ancient cultural sites. These temples, monasteries, and churches are managed by religious organizations and religious clergy under the leadership of the Religious Affairs Bureau of the government.

Many temples, monasteries, churches, and holy places on famous mountains have been fully restored through the careful, meticulous repair work, preservation, and management of specialists. The rare antiquities, precious scriptures, and Buddha figures bright and gleaming with new gilding have been carefully preserved. Not only do religious believers go there to worship Buddha, burn incense, and offer prayers, but even more nonbelievers from among the masses go to these scenic places and visit these sacred sites to enjoy their quiet environment and to study and learn about the ancient and precious cultural and artistic heritage of China.

On visiting the temples, monasteries, and churches in these famous places we should be conscious and respectful of the policy of freedom of religious belief set forth in our constitution and not interfere in the normal religious activities of religious believers and clergy in these places, nor should atheistic propaganda be carried on there. Also, the buildings and cultural artifacts (such as engraved stone steles, sculptures, and paintings) should be protected from damage such as random graffiti or carving. These buildings and artifacts are a precious historical heritage of our nation, the fruits of the labor and wisdom of our ancestors. When young friends visit these places, they should consciously study them from the angles of sociology, culture, fine arts, and so on, in order to enrich their knowledge for their lasting benefit. . . .

How Can We Rigorously Differentiate Normal Religious Activities from Those That Are Superstitious and Illegal?

We have already discussed normal religious activities in previous chapters. No one can meddle with normal religious activities which are protected by law. So what are feudal superstitious practices?

So-called illegal superstitions are feudalistic superstitious practices which hoodwink the masses, spreading fallacies, deceiving the people, cheating and swindling, harming people's lives, corroding people's thinking, corrupting social norms, and undermining the building of a spiritual and material Socialist civilization. Such illegal practices should be abolished according to the law. Nor does the law allow counterrevolutionary practices which have already been abolished to be revived. All destructive, counter-revolutionary activities and illegal, criminal practices which operate under the cover of religion should be resolutely attacked according to the law. Anyone who breaks the laws of the nation, no matter what religious form their actions take, must be punished according to the law. Only in this way can normal religious activities be reliably protected.

As for those persons who depend on illegal superstitious practices for their livelihood, they must be helped and educated so they will give up their evil practices and take part in productive labor, becoming self-supporting workers. Those persons who "use superstition to spread false rumors and swindle people" must be dealt with severely and punished as the law provides, according to Article 165 of the criminal code. We must never "mistakenly take the eyeballs of a fish to be pearls," that is, allow those persons who, pretending to carry on normal religious activities, in fact swindle people and bring harm to the four modernizations with their illegal activities while going scot-free.

Superstitious thinking is still widespread among the masses, and particularly in those districts which are rather backward, where some of the people still carry on superstitious practices such as worshiping their ancestors on New Year's day and other festivals, offering prayers to the gods of heaven, earth, wealth, and the likes. These are questions of ordinary thought and understanding, habits and customs, and should be differentiated from the illegal activities of shamans and sorcerers. Only when these old customs and habits and backward ways of thinking are dealt with by patient and persuasive education, vigorously building a Socialist spiritual civilization by spreading scientific knowledge and promoting the "five sayings and four beauties" campaign, will we begin to solve this problem. . . .

Why Can't Members of the Chinese Communist Party and the Communist Youth League Be Religious Believers?

Since the national constitution stipulates the right to freely believe in religion for all citizens, then why can't Chinese Communist Party and Communist Youth League [CYL] members also be religious believers, because they too are citizens?

We have already noted above that this provision of the constitution has two meanings: citizens have freedom of religious belief and freedom not to believe in religion. When a person becomes a Party member he has already made the free choice not to believe in religion. A Party member is not the same as an ordinary citizen; he is a member of the Marxist political party. Since the Party takes dialectical and historical materialism as its theoretical base, there is no question but that Party members must be atheists, not theists. Therefore Party members must not believe in religion or take part in religious activities.

Those grass-roots Party members who live among national minorities where nearly everyone is a religious believer must draw a clear line of distinction with regard to religion, while respecting and abiding by the customs and habits of the local people in their daily lives. Because weddings, funerals, and holy-day observances of the people all are colored by religious traditions and are an essential part of the people's habits and customs, it is useful for Party members to join with the people in these activities, thereby strengthening unity with the nationalities. This is quite different from actually taking part in religious activities and should be clearly differentiated.

The same reasoning applies to CYL members. The constitution of the CYL stipulates that its members are the helpers and reserve troops for the CCP, who firmly support the principles of the CCP, Marxism, Leninism, and the thought of Mao Zedong as their guide and compass. The basic task of the CYL is to educate young people in the spirit of Marxism. When an advanced young person joins the CYL he has already made the free choice not to believe in religion. He has already consciously become an atheist and not a theist. There is no question about it, CYL members cannot be religious believers nor can they take part in religious activities.

It goes without saying that Marxism is diametrically opposed to any form of theism. We should make unremitting efforts to bring about a scientific worldview and point of view, and a positive, general, scientific, and cultural knowledge among the masses, and especially among the young people, using persuasive propaganda and education.

But in political activities, Marxists and religious believers can and must join together in a united front for the common struggle for Socialist modernization. The facts show that this kind of unification work has been an important part of the Party's broad-scale, patriotic, united-front leadership since the founding of our nation.

Therefore, Party members and CYL members must understand that religion still has its long-term [protracted] nature, even in the period of Socialism, and that they must be models in the way they publicize and carry out the policy of freedom of religious belief set forth by the constitution. It would be even better if they would rally the national minorities with different religious beliefs to join in the common struggle toward the goal of building a strong, modern Socialist country and the great cause of national unity.

Section IX

Definitions of Religion Published in Contemporary China

Introduction

Standard Marxist definitions of religion and explanations for the emergence, growth, and demise of religion are found in every substantial article on religion published in China, usually with liberal quotations from Marx, Lenin, and Engels. Four sources are used in this section, two dictionaries, an encyclopedia, and a book on religion in the Socialist period.

Extensive excerpts from the *Encyclopedia of Religion*, published in 1988, and the introductory chapter of *Religious Questions Under Socialism in China*, published in 1987, particularly the latter, reflect a more scholarly and less doctrinaire approach when compared to the two earlier dictionary definitions from 1979 and 1981.

In his introductory chapter to the Shanghai book, Luo Zhufeng sets the guidelines for this important work, the first volume on religion since Liberation which includes phenomenological studies of religion. The opening sentence, "Religion is both an ideology and a complex social phenomenon," immediately moves this work beyond the dogmatic, clichéd approach found in similar works. While Marxist theory still sets the theoretical framework, the nine field studies (some of them included in Part II of this book) are valuable reports, remarkably free of Marxist dogma and rhetoric, of firsthand investigations by social scientists.

Luo Zhufeng moves beyond economic and social determinism as an explanation of religion and shows his impatience with a strictly theoretical approach to religious research: "Therefore it is not enough to rely on philosophical debate and logical inference for research on religion. Philosophers should come down from their lofty, abstract stratosphere and get close to their research subjects in order to understand the thoughts and feelings of religious believers and the position and function of religion in society."

He develops this entire introductory chapter around the "five natures" of religion. "The special features of religion in new China are summed up in the 'five natures.' ... We must increase and deepen our understanding of these 'five natures' if we are to give clear and practical guidance to this work during the new period of Socialist construction."

Definitions and explanations of the nature and function of religion are more conventionally Marxist in the *Encyclopedia of Religion*. Sections on "The point of view of historical materialism," "The social historical function of religion," and "Religion and science and culture" summarize the Marxist theory of religion, using examples from the history of religions. The remaining sections begin with the "five natures" of religion, used to describe religion in Socialist China and the conditions for religion in a Socialist society, concluding with an elucidation of the policy of freedom of religious belief. "No Socialist government supports a specific religion. At the same time, religions are forbidden to interfere in civil government, judicial procedures, or public schools. In short, this policy aims to unite all persons, both religious believers and others, for the common goal of building a powerful, modern Socialist nation. This is both the beginning and the end of the government's policy on dealing with religious issues."

Document 23

Chapter 1 of *Religious Questions under Socialism in China*

Shanghai Academy of Social Sciences, 1987, pp. 1-9. Translated by Zheng Xi'an and Donald MacInnis.

I

Religion is both an ideology and a complex social phenomenon. The field of religious research is vast. In China, religious studies is a subject just beginning to open up, while the question of religion under Socialism is a completely new topic for study.

People are faced with many questions in actual life. In China, now that the bases for social classes are virtually destroyed, why does religion continue to exist? Why have the number of religious believers increased in some districts in recent years? What influence does religion have on social life and the building of the four modernizations? How can religion be in harmony with Socialist society, and what are the effects to be expected? How should the Party, government, and the rest of society properly deal with religious questions? These are all questions of general concern for specialists in research on religious theory, as well as for government and Party cadres, for members of religious circles, and for the broad masses of the people.

The Sixth Five-Year Plan for Economic and Social Development of the People's Republic of China included in the section on philosophy and social sciences the recommendation "that research on large theoretical and practical questions regarding the establishment of Socialist modernization in China should be particularly strengthened." Research on religion was placed first in a list of twelve key topics.

This book is a response to that call, an initial exploration of this current and significant subject—the question of religion in China during the Socialist period. . . .

The substance of actual religion is complex. It is usually said that all religions have a concrete, synthesized system, at least a few organized elements, and ideological factors such as a religious philosophy or doctrine, religious rules and morality, and both clergy (religious professionals) and the masses of religious believers. The important factors which constitute religious life are the interacting elements of psychological and religious feelings, rites, organizations, structures, and so forth. These elements are certainly interrelated. It can be seen that religion is not only an ideology, but it is also a complex social phenomenon, one kind of social reality, and an organized part of social life which cannot be ignored.

As a social ideology, religion is not linked, in its origins, only to economic bases; to be restricted by economic bases in fact generates a counter effect, as there are parallel links with other ideologies, political viewpoints, laws, philosophies, ethics, arts, and the like, in society. In differing degrees all these affect the genesis of religion, while the influences that religion has in each of these fields, especially in areas where all of the people are religious believers, or where religion is quite widespread, cannot be underestimated.

In addition to the effects of religious ideology on society, there is an intimate relationship between the existence, growth, and change of religious institutions, religious believers, and religious activities and the growth and change of politics and economics, for example, in a society. Religion is certainly not fixed and unchanging; on the contrary it is constantly undergoing growth and change. Therefore it is not enough to rely on philosophical debate and logical inference for research on religion. Philosophers should come down from their lofty abstract stratosphere and get close to their research subjects in order to understand the thoughts and feelings of religious believers and the position and function of religion in society. Marx investigated nineteenth-century German religion; Engels investigated early Protestant Christian movements and the era of religious revolution under the capitalist class; Lenin investigated religion in Russia. All paid close attention to the unity of religion and society, and theorized about the existence of religion and its social effects from the angle of society itself. They did not look at religions in different times and different societies as if they were all the same, nor did they draw inferences from generalizations.

II

To conduct research on questions about religion in the Socialist period in China, the topic must be placed in a specific and coherent frame of reference. Enormous changes have occurred in human history and in society under Socialism, changes which are bound to affect religion which is carried over from the old society; these, in turn, bring about various changes in religion and related factors, with the result that society is further affected by religion.

Of course all factors bringing change to religion are interrelated, but they are not of equal relevance. To research the conditions, trends, and laws of change which affect religion, one must approach it from every side, and only after grasping the overall reality of religion, the complex relationship of religion and society, can we thoroughly understand the special characteristics of religion under Socialism.

In the early years of national construction, Zhou Enlai, Li Weihan, and others suggested the "five natures" of religion; its mass nature, long-lasting nature, international nature, complex nature, and [minority] nationalities nature. These are of first importance for guiding people to understand and to deal with religious questions. It seems that religion in any social system has these five natures. In fact these five natures have been, from the Marxist point of view, a part of the reality of China since Liberation. When summed up scientifically, these religious characteristics have special implications.

China is a nation with many religions. The three great world religions, our own Daoism, and the various religions of the national minorities all have their believers, a total of over one hundred million. This many religious believers among the masses unquestionably poses a mass question. There are middle-aged and elderly people, workers, peasants, and intellectuals among them. Some of the people who could not stand the suffering caused by the oppression of the exploiting classes in the old society sought comfort in religion, showing little interest in social revolution.

Under Socialism, however, religious believers among the masses actively take part in Socialist construction, helping both politically and economically. But they still hold their religious beliefs, take part in religious activities, and have special needs for places of worship, religious scriptures, publications, and so on. In order for these one hundred million religious believers to take part in the great enterprise of the four modernizations, we must not fail to understand their religious feelings or to show concern for their special needs.

There are fifty-five national minorities in China, six percent of our population. They live in the border regions, about 60 percent of the land area of China. A significant number of them live in the regions of the high plateaus, the border plains, and the mountains. The proportion of religious believers among the national minorities ranges from fairly high to very high, while in some groups virtually every person is a religious believer—clearly a situation with a specific "mass nature."

Religious beliefs and minority-group feelings and customs are integrated into an organic whole among these national minorities. Religion sets the norms for their core culture and morality. In the old society, while religion was used by the dominant class to maintain control, it also functioned as a means of resisting oppression from outside. Today, while the situation of all religious believers has certainly changed, the fact is that religion and the national minorities are still intimately related. We must respect and take seriously their religious beliefs, or else it will affect the unity [with the nation] of the national minorities.

Religion is a product of human society. There is scarcely a nation on earth without at least one national minority which has its own religion. According to statistics in the 1980 edition of the *Encyclopedia Britannica* ("A Summary of Religion in the Nations of the World"), there are 2,578,049,960 members in the world's religions, which is 60 percent of the world's population. Many nations once had a state religion, so that even today religion and politics are closely related.

Now that China has initiated an "open policy" toward the outside, religious questions are often involved in matters concerning our international relations, making it imperative that we understand how to deal correctly with such questions. Before Liberation, some of the religions in China were controlled by foreign mission organizations and were used by the imperialists as tools for their penetration of China.

Today this situation is basically changed, and religious enterprises are entirely administered by Chinese religionists. The opening up of international exchanges among religious circles on a basis of equality, friendship, independence, and self-governance has helped to advance understanding and friendship between the people of China and the people of other nations and will help the movement for world peace. But in the course of opening up international exchanges, we must, at the same time, be on guard and resist any actions by hostile foreign forces to use religion against China.

Religion is a long-standing historical and social phenomenon. Why do we speak today of religion's "long-lasting nature?" We do so because even after the overthrow of the exploiting system which had lasted several thousand years, and after establishing a Socialist society, there are still some people who believe that religion has lost the objective social conditions for its existence. They say that we cannot count the days until it disappears altogether, and would adopt simplistic methods of force and coercion to try to wipe out religion. . . .

In the early years after the founding of our country, the complex nature of religion was seen in the relationships between religious and political belief. The key task was how to discern the contradictions between these two disparate natures, and, under the protection of [the constitutional guarantee of] freedom of religious belief, to educate and unite the religious believers and eliminate the political influence of the imperialists and counterrevolutionary elements in our country who were using religion to maintain their control. Religion is still influenced today by the complex international environment and the class struggle which prevails in certain regions. But the main question is how to properly deal with religion, unite the large numbers of religious believers, and vigorously promote the development of China.

The special features of religion in new China are summed up in the "five natures" mentioned earlier. Over thirty years of actual experience have proven over and over that the main reason for the success or failure of our religious work has been how well we understand the "five natures" of religion. We must increase and deepen our understanding of these "five natures" if we are to give clear and practical guidance to this work during the new period of Socialist construction.

Document 24

Chapter 1, "Introduction" of the Religion Volume in the *Chinese Encyclopedia*

Zongjiao *volume in* Zhongguodabaike Quanshu, *Chinese Encyclopedia Publishing Company, Beijing and Shanghai, February 1988, pp. 1-13 (excerpts). Translated by Yu Linkai and Donald MacInnis.*

Introduction

Religion is a social and historical phenomenon, a form of human social ideology. Religion emerged in human self-conscious. When people felt powerless in the face of the forces of nature, society and life, they sought help from supernatural powers in determining their fate and spiritual destiny.

Most religious people are moved by a sense of awe and worship, believing that supernatural forces (such as gods, angels, spirits, or ghosts) exist, and that these supernatural forces influence people's fate. Religions are defined by commonly held beliefs, codes of ethical behavior, rituals, and religious organizations and sects. The emergence and development of religious ideas and practices are determined by certain social and historical conditions. At the same time, religion influences the social life, political structure, cultural habits, and social morality of the nation at any given time. Religion exists in every nation in the world today, a universal social and historical phenomenon.

Estimates place the number of religious believers in the world today at two and one-half billion, three-fifths of the total population. In some nations the majority of the people are religious believers. Religions vary from country to country. There are universal world religions, such as Buddhism, Christianity (including Protestant, Catholic, and Eastern Orthodox branches), and Islam; regional and national religions, such as Judaism, Shintoism, Hinduism, Sikhism, Jainism, Zoroastrianism and so on. There also are many primitive religions such as Shamanism, and the Bon and Dongba sects, etc. Buddhism is spread throughout northeast, southeast and south Asia, accounting for 6.2 percent of all religious believers in the world. Islam, with 17 percent of the world's religious believers, is found mainly in Asia and Africa, especially in western Asia, northern Africa, the south Asian subcontinent and southeast Asian countries. Of the world's religious believers, 34.4 percent are Christians, two-thirds of them in Europe and the Americas. . . .

The Nature and Function of Religion

DIFFERENT POINTS OF VIEW

Many efforts have been made to explore the nature and function of religion. For example, Herbert Spencer called religion a faith with the power to transcend human knowledge. Bradley [Francis Herbert] stressed the function of religion as man's search for benevolence (goodness). Frazier [James G.] said that religion is primarily the use of rituals and prayers to influence the power that controls nature and human life. *Maike Tagete*[translit.] claimed that religion is human sentiment seeking harmony between humanity and the universe. These are some of the ideas about religion which use different approaches; but since they do not examine religion as a social phenomenon, they fail to demonstrate the real nature and cause of religion.

THE POINT OF VIEW OF HISTORICAL MATERIALISM

Historical materialism provides many scientific explanations for the nature, function, and rules affecting changes in religion. Marx and Engels applied the viewpoint of dialectical materialism to the study of social history, and made a great contribution to religious studies. Engels said, "Any religion is the projection of human imagination about the external forces which dominate human life. In this projection, earthly power takes the form of transcendental power." Any organized religion is a social substance. It is part of the superstructure produced and developed on a specific economic foundation. Although religion is "high above or farther away from the material economic base," it is still the distorted projection of the economic base. The origin of religion at each stage of its development can only be found in the material world; that is, the content and function of religion can only be explained by its social relationships, which are formed in economic production relationships.

In a class society, the formation of religious concepts is influenced by the forces of nature and controlled and restricted by the blind and alien forces of the class society. It also comes from the fear, desperation, and misery of the workers brought on by the system of exploitation and from the need of the exploiting class to use it as a spiritual means to benumb and manipulate the masses. Therefore, the main reason for the existence and growth of religion in a class society is class oppression and exploitation.

Apart from the social sources of religion, there are conceptual sources. The spiritual substances worshiped in religion are the abstraction and idolizing of objective matter in human perception, infinitely expanded and then presented after deification, isolating them from nature and objective reality so that they become something absolute, the ultimate cause of the universe — that is, God.

THE SOCIAL-HISTORICAL FUNCTION OF RELIGION

In a class society, the social historical function of religion is very complex; it must be analyzed in a concrete and matter-of-fact way, examining the effect of each religious event on the historical process. Historically, the reactionary exploiting class used religion as a spiritual cornerstone for its domination; however, some revolutionaries also used the banner of religion in their struggles, therefore religion helped, to a certain degree, in advancing historical progress. . . .

RELIGION AND SCIENCE AND CULTURE

Religion has made an important contribution to the advancement of mankind's knowledge and culture. It is closely related to science and social ideologies such as philosophy, literature, art, ethics, etc. Human perceptions of nature and society in earliest times were represented by witchcraft, mythology or religious concepts. In literature this took the forms of poetry, music, dancing for the gods, painting and sculpture. In ancient Greece and Rome, the outstanding architecture was found mainly in sacred temples, tombs and memorial halls. In such cultures, the religious and secular spirit were merged. . . .

Throughout history, religion has influenced each race in spirituality, culture, science, ethics, morals, and customs. In seeking "natural law" and a means for immortality, Daoists objectively contributed to the development of medicine, chemistry, and astronomy. *Chantongqi* is a widely recognized early work. The "Sketch of Zhenyuan Miaodao" recorded the earliest gunpowder experiments in human history. It is widely acknowledged that Daoist theory contributed to Chinese medical theory, and the laboratory skills of the Daoists contributed to the maintenance of health and the curing of diseases. In the ethnic minorities regions of northwest and southwest China, religion has been central in their history, culture, ethics, morals and customs. There are ten ethnic minorities in China's northwest where virtually all the people are Muslims. Although Islam is a foreign religion, it adapted to Chinese traditional culture while keeping its unique characteristics. It has become an indispensable part of our national culture, contributing a great deal to the history, culture, medicine, astronomy, mathematics, and calendar science of China.

Buddhist culture in Tibet is a fundamental part of Tibetan culture, where it has made great contributions in medicine, calendar science, literature, handcrafts, art, painting, sculpture, and the like. The Potala Palace and the Jokhang Temple are masterpieces of architecture. Tibetans adopted the calendar of the Buddhist Mizong sect, combining it with the duodecimal cycle system of the Hans. It accurately records the agricultural seasons.

While Christianity had the reputation of being the tool of the imperialists after coming into China, it did make real contributions to the spread of Western science and culture, for example, establishing hospitals, schools, publications, libraries, and the concept of equality between men and women.

The Characteristics of Religion in China

China is a nation composed of numerous ethnic nationalities and religions, including both primitive shamanistic religions and world religions. The world religions, Buddhism, Islam, and Christianity, all came from outside China. Once established in China, they interacted with Chinese traditional culture and with each other, forming religions with national characteristics. Daoism, a native Chinese religion, spread beyond China to adjoining regions. There has never been a single dominant national religion in China as in some Western nations. China's rulers throughout history followed a policy of tolerance, supporting and protecting religion.

Religious believers today form only a small proportion of China's population. In the northwest and southwest provinces, where national minorities predominate, religion and government administration overlapped over long periods of our history. Religion is closely related to the culture of the national minorities, where believers form the majority of the population.

Among the Han population, which forms the majority of China's people, the main religious tradition is belief in predestination, or fate, and the worship of ancestors. This is the reason why Buddhism and Daoism have never become dominant religions in China. During the Xia, Shang, and Zhou dynasties, great political and economic changes took place. During the earliest agricultural period in China, the people combined their own hard labor with prayers to heaven for favorable weather. In *Shangshu Hong-fan*, it is written, "Their concern is lords, people, and clergy." The will of God and the will of man were placed side by side. After the Zhou dynasty, the Confucianists advocated "governing by virtue, and respect for heaven but not blind belief in heaven." The predominant orthodox ideology throughout Chinese history has been to "respect the gods and immortals, but keep one's distance from them," from the *Analects* of Confucius. Each emperor called himself the Son of Heaven, with all imperial authority granted as a divine right and the imperial power transcending even divine power. The imperial policy toward religion had two purposes, both to use religion and to keep it at a distance at the same time.

Relationships based on blood ties became important after irrigated agriculture was introduced. A patriarchal social system based on kinship and an ethical system based on "fidelity" developed in the Zhou dynasty. Ancestor worship, representing the patriarchal social system, became an integral part of Chinese culture, a custom practiced by every family among the Han people. Some people are religious believers, some are not. People take part in religious practices on occasion, while ignoring religion the rest of the time. They believe in anything from Confucianism to Daoism, from the traditional immortals to various gods, from Buddha to Mary, anything is all right if they think their prayers will be answered. Because of the contradiction between the patriarchal social system and the Confucian emphasis on ethics and moral principles and the religious idea of worshiping supernatural powers, the orthodox Confucian had to suppress the social functions of religion. These characteristics of religious belief which developed throughout China's history still influence the practice of religion among the Han people.

Religion in Socialist China

In the period since the founding of the People's Republic of China in 1949, the exploiting class and the system of exploitation have been wiped out and the Socialist system has been established. The historic changes brought about with the Socialist economic system naturally are reflected in the area of religion. After the forces of imperialism in the church were expelled, the Catholic church became independent and self-governing, and the Protestant church practices the "three-self" principles—self-government, self-support, and self-propagation. After the social-democratic reform, Buddhism, Islam, and Daoism also eliminated feudal privileges and the system of oppression and exploitation. Religion has become a private affair, a personal matter of religious belief. Everyone respects the beliefs of others out of a sense of unity and patriotism, whether religious believers or not, or believers in one religion or another; this is something seldom found in the history of religions, either in China or elsewhere. The subjective world of religious believers has been changed by the new social reality and social practice. At the same time, the patriotic religious believers of all ethnic nationalities have made great progress toward joining in the patriotic united front. Great changes have taken place in the area of religion in China.

CHARACTERISTICS

In a Socialist society religion still has five basic characteristics: its long-term nature, its complex nature, its widespread mass influence, its base among ethnic nationalities, and its international ramifications. Although the class basis for the existence of religion has basically disappeared, the social, psychological and perceptual bases among the people still continue. Since the improvement of the people's material life and the development of science and culture will not take place overnight, the ideology and customs inherited from the old society will not disappear in the immediate future. Moreover, natural disasters and mistakes in the practice of Socialism which frustrate the Socialist movement and cause suffering for the people cannot be avoided. There will be, as well, foreign religious influences, because our Socialist society is involved in complex international relationships. Meanwhile, the people's growing demand for higher levels of material life and culture cannot be immediately met, so some seek for psychological gratification in religion, offering prayers to supernatural powers. The elimination of these nonmaterialist concepts is dependent on the steady growth of economic productivity of the whole society and on the achievement of much higher levels of culture and enriched spiritual life. This means that the conditions for religion still exist and will continue for a rather long time under Socialism.

The Conditions for Religion in a Socialist Society

The people of all ethnic nationalities in China, as well as all religious believers, want to build a prosperous, democratic, and civilized Socialist country. Freedom of religious belief is guaranteed by the national constitution. This is the basic condition for religious harmony in our Socialist society. Some of the moral principles of religion and its ideology are in accord with the requirements of Socialism. Religious ethical norms which accord with traditional ethics and culture should be respected, protected, and promoted. International contacts between China's religions and those outside China improve understanding and friendship between the Chinese people and those in other parts of the world, thus playing a role in safeguarding world peace. Therefore, under specific historical conditions, religion can cooperate with a Socialist society. The great majority [masses] of religious believers love both their religion and their country, obey the laws and regulations of the nation, and support the Socialist system. At the same time, the government enforces the proper implementation of the religious policy, which is essential for mutual cooperation between religion and Socialist society.

The Policy of Freedom of Religious Belief

The citizens of the People's Republic of China enjoy the right to freedom of religious belief. The government follows the policy of respecting and protecting freedom of religious belief. Every citizen has freedom to believe or not believe in religion, freedom of belief in one religion or another, freedom to change one's belief from atheism to religion, and freedom to give up one's religious belief as well. The policy of religious belief as adopted by the Chinese Communist Party is based on the theories of Marxism and Leninism. This policy also accords with the interests of the people, for it stipulates that religious belief is each citizen's private matter, and guarantees their right to freely choose a religious belief.

No Socialist government supports a specific religion. At the same time, religions are forbidden to interfere in civil government, judicial procedures, or public schools. In short, this policy aims to unite all persons, both religious believers and others, for the common goal of building a powerful, modern Socialist nation. This is both the beginning and the end of the government's policy on dealing with religious issues. The People's Republic of China has experienced setbacks in past years. Not until the Third Plenary Session of the Eleventh Party Congress of the Chinese Communist Party was the proper policy on religion put into effect. Since then the theory, policy, and practice of religious affairs have returned to normal.

Document 25

Definition from the *Dictionary of Religion (Zongjiao Cidian)*

Shanghai Dictionary Press, 1981, pp. 712-13. Translated by Zheng Xi'an and Donald MacInnis.

Religion is a social ideology which belongs to the superstructure. Religionists believe in a mysterious supernatural realm and worship superhuman powers which they believe dominate nature and society apart from the real society. Religion emerges when primitive society has developed to a certain stage. At the very beginning it appears as the spontaneous belief of primitive peoples. The very low productive power of primitive society rendered men helpless before natural forces, and the intellect of primitive people was so undeveloped that they could not distinguish the forces of nature from those of mankind, so they personalized the forces of nature that dominated human life, treating them as supernatural deities.

With the evolution of society and history, religion continued to evolve from the earliest nature worship to spirit worship, totem worship, ancestor worship, and the worship of gods; from polytheism to monotheism, the worship of one god who governs all other gods; from tribal religion (such as the shamanism of the Hezhe, Ewenke, and Elenqun ethnic groups, the Ben worship of the Tibetans, the religion of the bushmen of Africa, etc.), to national religions (such as Judaism, Shintoism, Hinduism, etc.), and even world religions (such as Buddhism, Islam, and Christianity). The influence of Chinese Daoism has also spread to other countries.

As religion evolved, religious organizations, religious professionals and clerical hierarchies appeared. Each religion shaped its own creeds, theologies, taboos and commandments, while religious rituals became increasingly complex and diversified.

Historical materialists hold that religion is man-made, an illusory reflection in the minds of believers of an outside power that dominates human life. In class societies, social distress caused by class oppression and the system of exploitation is the chief reason for the emergence and growth of religion. Religion expresses the sighs of the oppressed in response to real sufferings, functioning as an anesthetic which drugs the human spirit. Religious believers hold that their religious faith is everlasting, a divine revelation transmitted to human nature.

Throughout history, the ruling class generally used religion as an instrument to neutralize the people's will to resist. In ancient and medieval times, many nations with slave and feudal systems maintained official state religions. In modern times state religions still exist in many countries. Meanwhile, the oppressed peoples, shackled by traditional beliefs and historical conditions, often seek spiritual comfort in the illusory world of religion, sometimes even using religion as an instrument for revolt.

Religion as a historical social phenomenon follows its own course of emergence, growth, and withering away. Due to the persistence of social and cognitive sources of religion, the illusory religious reflection of the real world will disappear only when Communism is fully realized, when relations in daily life are seen as plain and rational relations between persons and between man and nature, and when the forces of nature and society are no longer alien to humankind.

Document 26

Definition of Religion in *Ci Hai*

Translated by Zheng Xi'an and Donald MacInnis.

Religion is a social ideology. Religionists believe in and worship supernatural deities. It is a distorted and illusory reflection of the forces of nature and society in the human sphere of consciousness. . . . Religion is a historical phenomenon and follows its own course of birth, development, and withering away. When humankind enters the period of Communism, with the total elimination of the exploiting classes and their influence, the sources of religion will disappear, and, with highly advanced material production, culture, and science, religion will naturally wither away.

PART II

Religious Practice since the Cultural Revolution

Introduction

In the summer of 1974 I returned to China for the first time in twenty-five years. The physical, social, and cultural changes were overwhelming. New roads, railroads, factories, suburbs, apartment buildings, bicycles, trucks, buses, irrigation projects, tractors, and rural power lines were visible everywhere. Myriad family farms had been collectivized, and teams of workers tilled the neat, green fields and paddies. We saw no ragged beggars, homeless families, unwashed street urchins, landless peasants pulling rickshaws, or underfed hawkers selling tiny hoards of oddments and sundries. Children attending school were at an all-time high, and, for the first time in modern history, we were told, everyone in China had enough to eat and some kind of medical services.

This was the most secular society we had ever seen. All churches, temples, and shrines were closed, some in shambles, others boarded up or converted to other uses. The Catholic cathedral in Guangzhou was a collection point for garbage, while the Shanghai cathedral served as a storehouse for grain. The "Anti-Lin Biao, Anti-Confucius" campaign was in full swing, and two young women dockworkers in Shanghai, when questioned, enumerated the reasons why Confucius and his teachings were unacceptable in Socialist China.

I asked a young woman, our student guide at a university, if young people still believed in the old religions. She replied, "There is no need to. Since the new society is based on scientific materialism, the old superstitions were proved to be false." Asked whether young people might not be curious, and seek out the old religious believers to "learn from the past" (a slogan current at the time), she replied, "Why would anyone want to discuss the old religions? What do they have to do with our new society? It simply would not interest young people. It's irrelevant."

117

Research Methodology

I returned to China several times in subsequent years, each time astonished by the changes taking place before my eyes. For religious believers, 1979 marked the turning point from total suppression of public worship to a new policy of freedom of religious belief. Churches, temples, and mosques began to reopen that year, and by 1988, my most recent visit, one could find revitalized places of worship everywhere. Young people joined their elders, flocking to the churches and temples. Part II of this book describes the actual religious situation in China today, based on firsthand interviews, scholarly studies, speeches and reports by religious leaders, and translations of press reports and journal articles.

Although the materials published in this volume are selected from a much wider collection, they still can serve as little more than broad glimpses, a sampling of the whole picture. In China today one is quite free to visit religious places and talk with religious people without hindrance; no one monitored my interviews with priests, monks, abbots, bishops, and *ahongs*, or censored my tapes and notebooks. Still, particularly with published materials, one is bound by the limitations of the press in China today. Only one general periodical is published by each of the five recognized religions, although specialized journals, such as the *Nanjing Theological Journal*, are beginning to appear. There are no other religious publications except those published by state-sponsored research centers, and there is nothing comparable to the Gallup Poll or other religious surveys.

A full picture of any one of the religions would include extensive surveys of the clergy and laity to determine who they are, what their faith means to them, how they practice their faith, and what age, class, and other social categories they represent. Chinese social scientists have begun these kinds of field studies, and some of their work is found in this book. In a few more years, we are promised, there will be much more information of this kind available.

Religious Statistics

Statistics for each of the religions can be found in some of their annual reports, in published interviews, and in other sources. Even so, when local leaders are asked, their usual answer is a shrug: they know how many clergy, seminarians, and novices there are, but can never give a precise answer on member statistics. This is even more true for the Buddhists and Daoists than the Christians, for they have no membership ceremonies, like baptism and confirmation, while the Muslims seem to include all members of all Muslim families, whether active in the local mosque or not, so that national estimates range from ten to twenty million or more. In the case of Chinese Catholics, many will not attend mass in the so-called official churches for a variety of reasons, while the proliferation of Protestant house meetings in the countryside, with thousands not listed on the rolls of the churches in some provinces, confounds the statisticians.

What is a Buddhist, a Christian, a Muslim, and how many are there? Each faith has its own answer. A document prepared by the provincial Religious Affairs Bureau, dated April 1988, gives the following membership statistics for Fujian Province:

Total Religious Believers in Fujian Province	635,000
Buddhists	70,000
Protestant Christians	
Baptized	201,000
Preparatory members	168,600
Catholic Christians	188,706
Muslims	1,350
Daoists [no information]	—

The document gives no explanation of its sources or interpretation of this information. For example, since Fujian is said to have the most lively Buddhist revival in China, there must be many more Buddhists than seventy thousand; therefore, one must conclude that this refers only to *jushi*, lay devotees, who live at home, for monks and nuns are listed separately in this table of statistics. As for Daoists, can it be that there are no Daoists in the entire province, or is the definition of Daoist so vague and their organization so amorphous that no one can identify them?

Sects and Heresies

It is difficult to report objectively on sectarian, dissident, or heretical groups within a given religion, because information is not easily available to an outsider. We know, for example, that there are several Buddhist and Muslim sects in China, that the Protestant denominational heritage is still alive in people's hearts, that the Catholic church has its own internal divisions, and that each of these religions has to deal in its own way with heretical tendencies. We also know that secret societies, the source of anti-government uprisings in the past, are forbidden, and that this ruling has been used, in some places, against the assembling of small religious groups in homes or elsewhere outside the regular places of worship. These topics are beyond the scope of this book.

The Topics

What is included, then, and what is left out? A glance at the Table of Contents shows sections on the five officially recognized religions, Judaism, popular religion, Confucian studies, religious surrogates (a category which includes superstition, atheism, socialist spiritual civilization and Marxism as a faith), and finally, youth and religion.

Other categories, which were dropped for lack of space, were rites and customs, including weddings, funerals, burials, etc.; religion in literature and the arts; religious model citizens and "five good" families; the spiritual-pollution campaign; religion-sponsored social-service projects; and what has been called the crisis of faith since the "cultural revolution," although this is dealt with tangentially in the section on Youth and Religion.

Within each major topic, "Buddhism in China Today," for example, documents and interview transcripts were selected with the aim of presenting a representative picture of the religious life of each faith, based on reports by responsible church and state leaders at national and provincial levels, the published results of scholarly investigations, and firsthand reports on the local religious situation provided in interviews with monks, nuns, abbots, imams, priests, pastors, seminarians and lay believers, including young people.

Because the most critical problem facing each of China's religious communities is the shortage of clergy due to the laicizing of many monks, nuns, and other religious personnel in the 1950s and 1960s, the closing of all seminaries and training institutes for many years, and the age and health problems of many surviving clergy, a section is included under each religion which reports on the recruitment and training of new clergy and the role of lay volunteers.

Religious Surrogates

Since even in the most secular of societies, everyone, even anarchists, believes in something, and people continue to search for a transcendent dimension, four categories of nonreligious beliefs are included under the heading, "Religious Surrogates in China Today."

The revival of superstitious practices, judging by the number of articles in the Chinese press, is a widespread phenomenon which both worries and puzzles the authorities. How could this happen, after years of education in Marxism, atheism, and scientific and historical materialism? Thirteen documents translated from the Chinese press describe what is happening, explain why it is happening, distinguish religion from superstition, and suggest ways of dealing with the revival of superstition.

The sections on atheism, Socialist spiritual civilization and Marxism as a faith present six articles from the Chinese press describing how to promote atheism among the masses as well as Party members, the reasons why Party members cannot be religious believers, and the campaign called "Building a socialist spiritual civilization" which engulfed the country a few years ago. Finally, an interview on a bus in Yunnan Province reveals the views of one young working woman on Marxism and religion.

Qigong, traditional Chinese slow-motion exercises used for physical fitness and for healing, cannot be classified as either a religion or superstition, but because of its current popularity and its religious origins, it is mentioned here as a religious surrogate.

Youth and Religion

Again with a look to the future of religion in China, there are seven documents translated from the Chinese press in a separate section on "Youth and Religion in China Today" in which the writers, using the tools of dialectical and historical materialism, search for answers to the question of why do young people still believe in religion, even to the point of wanting to become monks, nuns, priests, and pastors?

Buddhism in China Today

Section I

Buddhism at Local and Provincial Levels

Introduction

The section on Buddhism at Local and Provincial Levels consists of excerpts from interviews with two Buddhist abbots and two responsible officials of provincial Buddhist Associations from three provinces, Fujian, Yunnan, and Sichuan. In each case the interviews were unmonitored, conducted in the seclusion of a guest room in the interior of the temple.

We covered a range of subjects, all related to the present state of Buddhism in China and its prospects for the future. As with other religions in China today, the two most urgent priorities are the need to recover, repair, and reopen places of worship and to train and ordain new personnel to replace laicized, deceased, and aging clergy.

Every religious person in China, whether clergy or layperson, can tell personal horror stories of the "cultural revolution." Clearly, it was the intention of the organizers of the campaign against religion to wipe it out completely. Public worship services were suppressed for thirteen years, 1966-79. Members of the clergy were, in nearly every case, forced to leave their temples, churches, and monasteries; some were imprisoned, others were placed in labor camps, and all were forced to find secular jobs in order to survive.

Aftermath of the "Cultural Revolution"

Temples, churches, and monasteries were closed and converted to other uses. Some suffered savage attacks and depredations, and, in many cases total destruction. The devastation wreaked by marauding Red Guards on the buildings and religious artifacts of the ancient and famous Guanghua Temple in Putian, Fujian, which I visited, was almost total. Their entire library of ancient Buddhist scriptures, together with the hand-carved wood

123

blocks used for printing, was destroyed. In Chengdu, I was told, only two key temples were protected by the national government; many others were destroyed or converted to other uses. The great Zhaojue Temple complex became a zoo and public park. Now, with financial aid from the government, it is being partially restored, although the city zoo still occupies much of the property.

Other famous temples, such as the Yuntong Temple in Kunming where I interviewed the general secretary of the provincial Buddhist association, were protected by order of Premier Zhou Enlai himself and suffered little damage. Even so, many of the Yuntong Temple buildings had been taken over for other uses, and repairs and restoration were still in process here as elsewhere.

According to published reports and eyewitness accounts, the temples, shrines and monasteries of Tibetan Buddhism suffered the most damage and destruction of all religions in China. Edward Gargan, for example, writing in the *New York Times* [14 June 1987], said that all but a handful of the 6,254 monasteries and temples in Tibet in 1957 had been demolished.

The problem of clergy shortage is as critical as the shortage of places of worship. The most vibrantly active Buddhist temple I visited, the Nanputuo Temple in Xiamen, has two Buddhist academies, one to train monks, the other, nuns. According to the abbot, there are seventy men and sixty women novices enrolled in courses ranging from two to four years, depending on how much previous schooling they have had. Some will go on for further study after graduation, perhaps to the national Buddhist Institute in Beijing. What will happen to the others? "Some will remain to serve this temple, some will stay on to teach a new class of novices, and the rest will go their own way."

In response to a question about motivation of the young novices, the abbot gave several reasons. Most of them, he said, come from families with a strong Buddhist heritage. Others are searching for solutions to personal problems, such as ill health, disappointments in life, or family discord. Some, he candidly admitted, are hoping to find a way to go abroad, and, indeed, some of them do find jobs in Buddhist temples in Southeast Asian countries.

Monks, Nuns, and Lay Buddhists

As noted in the Introduction to Part II, there are statistics for monks and nuns, but not Buddhist laity. According to the abbot of Nanputuo Temple, about 1,000 young Buddhists nationwide are enrolled in regular schools, studying to become monks and nuns. There are two other Buddhist academies in Fujian, one in Putian with 60 men, and one in Fuzhou with 100 women. Otherwise, except for Buddhist academies in certain large cities, novices in Fujian as elsewhere are either taught one-on-one by a local monk or in small, short-term training classes (peixunban) organized in temples or monasteries.

Nanputuo Temple typifies the problem of clergy shortage. Out of a total of 140 resident monks and nuns, only 10 had taken their vows before the "cultural revolution"; the others are still in training, called "small monks" and "small nuns." The temple complex is staffed by an additional 70 hired day workers.

The general secretary of the Buddhist Association in Sichuan had no provincewide statistics, but told of a plan to publish results of a nationwide survey of religion in three to five years. In Sichuan Province, he said, there are between 1,000 and 2,000 monks, including novices, far from enough to serve the 110 temples and monasteries now open and serving the Han Chinese. The Tibetan Buddhists in the province are better off, he said, with over 600 temples, large and small, open and staffed.

In Fujian there are 10,000 monks, including novices, in the temples and monasteries (chujia), and about 60-70,000 Buddhist jushi (lay devotees), according to Abbot Puyu of Drum Mountain. Forty years ago there were not that many. More people come to the temples now to "burn incense" than forty years ago, he said.

How many come for worship at the temples? The only statistics are the number of gate tickets sold, about 10,000 on the first and fifteenth days of each lunar month at the Wenshuyuan Temple in Chengdu, and 30,000 in a two-day period celebrating the birthday of Guanyin at the Nanputuo Temple in Xiamen, which I witnessed, in part (see introduction to Document 29). But no one can say how many are Buddhist worshipers, how many are simply repeating inherited customs and how many are merely curious visitors.

Finances

In Sichuan, the general secretary said, the government gave generously for repairs and rebuilding of damaged temples and monasteries: 15 million yuan for the two Tibetan autonomous regions where the destruction was most severe, and 6 million yuan for the rest of the province. Additional subsidy was provided for building a road and repairing temples on the sacred Mount Omei, but that was primarily to facilitate tourism. Otherwise, all temples and monasteries are self-supporting: "Each temple supports itself [yi miao yang miao]." Income from donations, temple and monastery enterprises, and other sources was 900,000 yuan in 1987.

The Future

When asked about the future of Buddhism in China, the abbot of Nanputuo Temple expressed optimism, basing his answer partly on the survival of Confucian and other traditional values and partly on the fact that "people will always need religion, even under Socialism. This is quite evident now in the people's reaction to the 'cultural revolution.' "

Abbot Puyu, in the Yongquan Temple, Drum Mountain, Fujian, said: "Religion will not disappear. If it does, it will only be temporary, the result of forceful repression by rulers trying to gain control. . . . Religion will not disappear."

Document 27

Interview with the General Secretary of the Buddhist Association of Yunnan Province

In May 1988, I interviewed the general secretary of the Buddhist Association of Yunnan Province at his office in the Yuntong Temple, Kunming. We spoke in Chinese. He was a young man, unmarried, a recent university graduate.

Q. How did you get this job?
A. I was appointed by the government after graduating from the university. My major subject was Chinese literature. I am not a Buddhist and my home is not in this province.

Q. What are the functions of the provincial Buddhist Association [CBA]?
A. The CBA is the highest Buddhist body. If any temple or monastery has a problem they come to the CBA and we help them by going to the authorities. Our job is under the United Front. It is also our duty to receive visitors from abroad.

Q. Is the CBA responsible to the Religious Affairs Bureau under the State Council?
A. Yes, at the provincial level; it also is under the provincial United Front Department.

Q. What are your duties?
A. I'm the general secretary.

Q. Who is in charge of the provincial CBA?
A. Master Dao Shulong, age fifty, is the head of the CBA here. He is in Beijing now, attending a meeting of the national CBA.

Q. Who pays your salary?

A. The provincial United Front Department. I only receive 60 *yuan* a month, but I'm not married. I'm still single.

Q. Is there still an age limit for marriage?
A. Yes, twenty-two for women and twenty-five for men. But it varies from place to place.

Q. Are there any marriage restrictions for Buddhists?
A. Yes, for monks and nuns; it depends on whether they leave home [*chu jia*] or stay at home [*zai jia*]. If they leave home and enter the temple and take vows, they can't marry. Many young people can't take that hard life, and after some years they walk out. Others are *jushi* [lay devotees]. They are still "at home." They may wear monk's robes and look like monks, but they do not shave their heads or take vows. They study Buddhism on their own, can marry, and usually have other jobs. Of course when monks or nuns want to marry they give up their vocation [*huan shu*] and return to secular life.

Q. Are you from a Buddhist family?
A. No.

Q. Then you do not believe in Buddhism?
A. No. But in old China people really didn't know what their religion was. They just prayed to the gods, any gods, and burned incense because it was their tradition. They didn't know what they believed, Buddhism or Daoism or what.

As for me, I work in a religious job, and I can make a clear distinction, what religion is and what it is not.

Buddhists in Yunnan

Q. Are Buddhists mainly from the city or countryside?
A. Both, but mainly from the countryside.

Q. What is the age range?
A. Mostly older people.

Q. In which parts of China today is Buddhism most active?
A. In Fujian Province, especially in Fuding district. The economy is better in the coastal provinces; they have more money. In Yunnan there are many Buddhists, but our economic development lags behind Fujian and Guangdong. It is harder to find support for temples and monasteries here.

In Xishuangbanna, near the Burma border, it is the Dai tradition for each family to send one boy to a temple for a period of service. They must go, for a few days, or weeks or months, and some for their whole life. The community supports them, so there is no problem of finding financial support. Monks in the temples receive special treatment. Families take turns providing food for them, so they have no financial problems. This system is called *tuobo* [alms support].

Q. What about the Tibetan Buddhists?
A. Their life is much harder than in other provinces, so the life of the monks there is harder.

Q. Are there any Daoists in Yunnan Province?
A. Only a few, in the Baoshan district.

Youth, Religion, and Morality

Q. I find that some Chinese young people are interested in religion. Do you see any benefit in religion?
A. In my personal opinion, there is no benefit; it's just a spiritual crutch [*jingshen jituo*]. But there is some value in believing in Buddhism in order to study Buddhist traditions, because Buddhism had a big influence on Chinese culture. But if it is just burning incense and kowtowing, that is meaningless.

The purpose of our seminars and training classes is to lead them to study Buddhism in the right way, not just going through meaningless motions like burning incense. There is a Buddhist saying, *"Suiyuan so bie, suiyuan so sheng,"* which means, "Our present life and the way we die are determined by our previous life, by chance, really." But I don't believe this. Our life is given to us by our parents, not by the gods, and we can determine the kind of life we live by ourselves. We don't have to believe in fate.

My birth, my coming into this life, was not my decision, but my parents'. *"Sui yuan"* means that birth and death are decided by chance. Our birth is, indeed, by chance; there is no prior life, no reincarnation, so it is useless to pray for a better next life. Since our life is given by our parents only, there is no question of a soul or fate [*linghun, mingyun*].

If one has intelligence, knowledge, and good morals, one can have a good life. I think that life, based on one's own merits, will become better and better under natural [not metaphysical] conditions [*ziran tiaojian*]. So there is no such thing as fate. We have to work hard. Buddhist teaching says that one must believe in Buddhism in order to be a good person. But you don't have to be a Buddhist to be good. Our country has asked us to learn to be good persons by emulating Lei Feng [a young soldier, renowned for his selflessness, who gave his life on behalf of his comrades]. The results are the same. People shouldn't believe in superstitious things.

Buddhist Study Class for Youth

Q. Do you have a Buddhist Academy [*foxueyuan*] in this province?
A. No, we only have a training class [*peixunban*].

Q. How many students are there? How long do they study?

A. It depends on the budget. We have about twenty students in this class. If we have more money we can go for one or two years. When young people want some training in Buddhism we can open a short-term course for them for a few weeks. A Buddhist academy usually has a three- or four-year course. A training class is different; it usually goes for half a year to a year, but seldom two years.

Students in a training class are usually junior-high-school graduates. We divide them into classes according to their level of schooling.

Q. Are there any women students?

A. Yes. In Dehong [a Yunnan locality] there are many women believers. The people in Dehong are members of an ethnic minority group. We will open a training class for them soon.

In Kunming the training-class students are all men. There are about twenty in the present class, all from Kunming and two nearby cities. We don't recruit from other places because we have a problem, not enough teachers or money. This is because the school and temple were closed for such a long time. We don't have housing for teachers or students. Our dormitory space is insufficient, because the whole temple complex was turned into a public park during the "cultural revolution," and given back to us only four years ago. When we got it back, we had no classrooms or dormitories. We are still building and repairing. The training class began last year.

Q. Do monks do the teaching?

A. Yes. There are three *fashi* [masters] here. They are the teachers.

Q. Were there any training classes before last year?

A. Yes, before the "cultural revolution". We had a Buddhist academy [*foxueyuan*] before 1949.

Q. How many monks are there in this temple?

A. There are twenty, young and old, but only three are qualified to teach.

Q. Are there any nuns?

A. Yes, but very few. In Tongchang, Baoshan district, there are more nuns. Baoshan is near Burma.

Q. Are the students in your training class all Han Chinese?

A. Yes, all are Han. In Yunnan, the people living in the interior of the province are Han. The minority people live in the border regions. In some border areas the people can't speak the national dialect, so if we accept them here as students, they have a language problem, they can't understand the teachers.

Buddhist Temples and Monks in Yunnan Today

Q. How many Buddhist temples in Yunnan are open now?

A. I don't have an exact number. Each district has at least one or two temples open for the public. Every small town or village has its own small temple or shrine where the people can pray (*bai-bai*) and burn incense. These are with government permission.

Q. Are there open temples and monasteries in every part of Yunnan Province?

A. Yes, there are about a hundred open temples now.

Q. How many monks are there in Yunnan now?

A. We have no accurate statistics, because they move around, they come and go. There are about five hundred Han Chinese monks, young and old, and more than four thousand among the minority groups in the border areas. But the figure is imprecise because some monks go into a temple one day and leave the next. Of course many of the "small monks" among the ethnic minority groups are only temporary, and return home when their volunteer training period is over.

Q. Among the five hundred, how many are old and how many are novices or new monks?

A. They are mostly young people. About a third are older.

Red Guard Depredations during the "Cultural Revolution"

Q. Did the Red Guards cause any damage to temple buildings in Kunming?

A. Very little. The cultural relics in the temple buildings were not seriously damaged. The Red Guards broke the stone lions in the Qiongzhu Temple [outside the city], that's all. These temples were under protection, designated as "First-Class Historical Cultural Relics," so we were better off than other places. Premier Zhou Enlai gave personal orders not to destroy cultural relics in Yunnan, so they were better protected.

The Red Guards burned the name labels of the five hundred *lohans* [immortals] in the Qiongzhu Temple. Now no one can remember the names. The old scholars are dead, and even the researchers can come up with only a few names.

Q. Was there damage to this temple complex?

A. No, not much. The local government turned this into a public park, which changed its function. It no longer looked like a temple. Now we are restoring it to its original state.

Q. What about the Guanyin Temple in Dali, which we visited?

A. Yes, the *pusas* [statues] were badly damaged. They have been replaced with new ones, and some are not yet finished.

Temple Finances

Q. Who paid for repairs to the temples?

A. The government paid part of the expenses. But the construction techniques for temples are different and more costly than for other buildings. The government based their estimates on the cost of ordinary buildings, so we didn't have enough money to repair and replace the carvings, the gold leaf, and other special features. The rest of the money comes from personal contributions.

Q. Do overseas Chinese help?

A. Yes, but not as many as in the coastal provinces. The Nanputuo Temple in Xiamen (Amoy) has been given many cars and minibuses by overseas Chinese. But Yunnan is too remote, not many of them come this far.

Motivation for "Small Monks" (Novices)

Q. We met four "small monks" in Dali. What is their motivation? Are they, perhaps, just looking for a job? Or do they really want to become monks for religious reasons?

A. Young people make this decision mainly for religious reasons, not just to find a livelihood. Young people today have jobs, especially now, after the open-door policy; they can easily find a job, either in the government or private sector.

But while some may go there for religious reasons, others may not like the struggles of life in the world and want to escape from reality. These people won't stay long in the temple or monastery, because they can't take the hard life there. They don't really have a religious faith. Only those with real religious faith can endure the temple life.

Q. It seems that monks from remote places can wander around the country freely, like Tian Ran, the monk in Dali whose original home was in Manchuria. They really have a very free life, don't you think?

A. Yes, some young people who want to become monks think they would like that life-style. Today there may be twenty monks in our temple, tomorrow some may be gone. They will go on to another temple, and if they like it, they can ask to stay there.

Zhao Puchu [president of the Chinese Buddhist Association] made a proposal in a recent meeting about "Regulations for Monks": any monk who goes to another province should first have official permission in writing from the provincial CBA. Otherwise monks will flock to the good temples, and the less desirable ones will remain empty.

Q. Is it true, as the abbot in a Fujian temple told me, that some young monks enter the monastery because they want to go abroad, to countries of Southeast Asia?

A. Yes, that's true for young monks in the coastal provinces, Fujian, Zhejiang, Jiangsu. Their teacher-masters [*shifu*] often have gone to Singapore, Hongkong, the Philippines. They want to follow them. They are waiting for a chance to go abroad. When I was studying in Fujian I knew about this situation. Last year several of those monks from the Xiamen temple went abroad. I knew them when I was a university student there. A monk-teacher from the Xiamen Buddhist Academy went to the U.S. last year. I knew him; he was the dean.

Q. I talked with some "small monks" in Dali. They seemed to have a good spirit. How many will persist and become monks?

A. Since you are a specialist, I can give you a frank answer. It's hard to say, people's minds are always changing. I can't really answer this question. It depends. Can he get used to the hard monastic life? Personal relationships are important. If he tires of the temple life, he will quit.

It also depends on the stage of economic development of the region. The coastal areas are better off than we are here in the interior. People don't have extra money here to contribute, and few overseas visitors come here. Without such donations, the life of the monks will be harder. If life gets harder, some will quit.

This is true not only for Buddhism; other religions have the same problem. Last year I visited a Christian theological seminary, a Buddhist institute, and a Muslim training college, all in Sichuan Province. All these young students have open minds. The old teachings and traditions are not suitable today, they think. So there is a clash between them and the older conservatives. If life in the temple is good, they'll stay, if not, they'll leave. I think that religious motivation among those students is not that strong.

It's the same among students in other places. For example, only a minority of the first forty graduates of the Beijing Buddhist Institute have become monks. That's the highest graduate-level Buddhist institution in China. Some of them have taken other jobs, and some just went home.

Document 28

Interview with the General Secretary of the Buddhist Association of Sichuan Province

By Donald MacInnis in Chengdu, 9 July 1988.

I interviewed the general secretary of the provincial Buddhist Association and a religious historian at the CBA office in the Wenshuyuan Temple in Chengdu on 9 July 1988. We spoke in Chinese.

They are working on a history of Buddhism in China, and discussed various theories regarding dates and origins of earliest Buddhism in the province, using two lines of evidence: one, folk history and written records, the other, grave excavations.

During the "cultural revolution" the monks and nuns, barred from religious activities, were forced to find secular jobs, usually doing manual labor. All religions were affected, although the Lamaist temples and monasteries in the two Tibetan autonomous regions of Sichuan suffered the worst depredations at the hands of roving Red Guard bands attacking the "four olds" (old habits, ideas, culture, and customs).

In Chengdu two key temples were saved, but many others were destroyed or converted to other uses. The great Zhaojue Temple, was converted into a zoo and park. Now, with generous financial aid from the government, it is being restored in part, although the city zoo still occupies much of the property. A few monks had stayed and worked in the zoo, continuing their religious life. Now the temple has about eighty monks, young and old.

Statistics

I asked about numbers, restored temples, active monks and nuns, novices, and finances. They do not have accurate figures, they said; the government will publish the results of a national survey of religion in three to five years.

There is insufficient clergy, between one and two thousand monks and nuns, young and old, including novices, to serve the 110 open temples and monasteries of the Han Chinese in the non-Tibetan regions of Sichuan. The two Tibetan autonomous regions of the province are better off, with over 600 temples now reopened and staffed. The rate of restoration and reopening of temples in Sichuan is "comparatively good," they said.

They have no statistics on the number of faithful Buddhists, although ten thousand come to this temple on the first and fifteenth days of each lunar month, and "several thousand" each day. No one can say how many are Buddhist worshipers and how many are simply curious visitors. However, each of the two days I visited there, hundreds of elderly men and women were seated on benches in the shaded courtyard adjoining the kitchen, chatting, sipping tea, and eating simple bowls of vegetarian food. Perhaps it was merely a comfortable place for senior citizens to gather and socialize, but for some of them, who fingered prayer beads as they sat there, it was clearly more than that.

Clergy Training

There are three levels of training: the tutorial system [peiyang], with a novice studying under a master in a local temple; short-term training classes [peixunban] in temples; and Buddhist academies or institutes [foxueyuan].

Sichuan Province has no Buddhist academy, but two schools for monks and nuns have been opened in recent years. One, for training nuns, has 40 students in a three-year course. The other, for Lamaist monks, has 150 students in a three-year course. While there are plans to open a Buddhist academy in Sichuan with a three-year course for Han Chinese, there now is only a two-year training class (peixunban), with 40 students here at the Wenshuyuan Temple.

There is a shortage in both numbers and quality. "We need to raise the quality level of our monks. Young monks in their twenties with inadequate training now become the heads of temples and monasteries. The head monk of this temple is only in his twenties."

Lamaist Buddhism in Sichuan

The statistics given for Buddhism in Sichuan before 1949 do not include the two Tibetan autonomous regions. There are "several tens of thousand" lamas in those two regions, as many as several hundred in a single monastery, and several dozen each in smaller ones, he said.

The Buddhist Association: Finances and Administration

All temples and monasteries are now administered by monks, and all are now self-supporting. The guideline is, "Each temple supports itself" [yi miao yang miao]. If money is needed, they ask the Religious Affairs Bureau. "We have no money. The CBA belongs to the Buddhists; it is our organization, not the government's. If a temple or monastery needs help, we request it for them." Local income from donations and other sources last year was 900,000 yuan.

The government, he said, gave generously for repairs and rebuilding of damaged temples and monasteries: 15 million yuan for the two Tibetan autonomous regions and about 6 million yuan for the rest of the province. In addition, the government gave ten million yuan for repairs to the twenty-five temples on Omei, the sacred mountain, and another 7 million *yuan* for building a vehicle road to the top, since the former long, steep climb was too much for the elderly and handicapped. Mount Omei, of course, is a major tourist attraction which generates considerable income.

Nearly half of the hundred counties in Sichuan now have Buddhist Associations. Some counties have no temples or monasteries, hence no Association. Sichuan has over thirty delegates assigned to the national representatives meeting of the CBA. Only the Tibetan Buddhists have more. This was a matter of pride for the general secretary, who said that his province had a better showing than Fujian, which is renowned for the vitality of Buddhism.

Document 29

Interview with the Abbot, Nanputuo Temple, Xiamen (Amoy)

By Donald MacInnis, January 1988.

Using Chinese, I interviewed the abbot of the Nanputuo Temple in Xiamen in January 1988, during the two-day celebration of the birthday of Guanyin, which takes place three times a year on the nineteenth day of the second, sixth, and ninth months of the lunar calendar. Thousands of people were working their way through the temple complex day and night, whole families, old people, young people, an almost equal number of men and women. Most of them were offering incense before the various sacred images and burning spirit money in the big bronze kettles; others were simply curious visitors. It was an astonishing sight, as if thirty-nine years of Socialism and Marxist propaganda against religion had never happened. I stood transfixed for nearly an hour, watching faces, intent, focused on the tasks of lighting incense and moving from image to image, bowing with lighted bundles of incense, placing a few sticks in the crowded pot, then moving on to the next shrine, climbing from level to level. It was an orderly crowd, pressing shoulder to shoulder in astonishing numbers, a constant flow, moving on and up in a slow, purposeful circumnavigation of the temple complex. Novice monks and nuns, clothed in gray ankle-length gowns, stood by in each court and alcove offering assistance and selling incense and paper spirit money.

When I interviewed the abbot on the second day, he told me that attendance was down slightly this year, because they had raised the price of an entrance ticket from five to thirty *fen* [cents]. Even so, they estimated that thirty thousand would attend the festival.

As I waited in the antechamber for the abbot to appear, I talked with

the elderly monk who kept me company. It was his duty, he said, to enter-
tain guests. He told me that about thirty monks had remained at the temple
during the "cultural revolution." They survived on food raised on the property—rice, sweet potatoes, and vegetables. Since this famous temple had
been designated for protection from the marauding Red Guards, there was
very little damage, and no sacred books were lost. One large image of the
Maitreya Buddha facing the front entrance required regilding, but the government, he said, procured the gold leaf for them.

The number of resident clergy had risen to about 140, he said, including
70 male and 60 female novices enrolled in the two novitiates. Only about
10 elderly monks remained from earlier times; the others are dead, he said.
The temple is staffed by an additional 70 hired day workers.

He is illiterate, he said. Most of his generation had no education. There
was a movement begun by the Abbot Taixu about sixty years earlier when
they began to educate monks, but many older monks opposed it, saying
that meditation [zuo chan] was sufficient.

"All your novices seem very devout," I said. "Not all of them," he replied. "The young women are more devout, but not all the men. The young
generation is not as devout as the older one."

I asked about their novice-formation program in his Buddhist academy.
There are nineteen teachers, thirteen of them monks and the others laypersons. The novices study for two years. Some will go on for further studies, perhaps to the Buddhist Institute in Beijing, some will remain to serve
this temple, and some will stay on to teach other novices. The rest will go
their own way. "They are free to go to any temple or monastery in China."

A novice monk told me their daily schedule. They rise at 4:00, eat breakfast at 6:00, and retire at 9:30 in the evening. They spend two hours reading
scriptures [nian jing]. I asked about meditation. He said that, as students,
they have no time for that, but of course the monks meditate. "Meditation
is good for the body and the mind," he said. "It calms you down and reduces
anxiety. Abstinence from meat is also good for you."

Besides serving as abbot of one of China's largest temples, the abbot of
the Nanputuo Temple is president of the Fujian Buddhist Academy, president of the South Fujian (Minnan) Buddhist Academy, president of the
Xiamen Buddhist Association, a member of the standing committee of the
national Chinese Buddhist Association, and abbot of the Yong Quan Temple on Drum Mountain, near Fuzhou, replacing Abbot Puyu, who recently
retired.

The Abbot's Life History

Q. Please tell me about your life history.

A. I am seventy-eight years old. My home was Liaoning, in the northeast
[Manchuria]. Why did I become a monk? In 1939, at age thirty, I made my
decision, provoked by the Japanese attack on China. As a school principal

in Antung, I lived under the Japanese in what they called "Manchukuo" and refused to join their puppet "Save China Association." I went to a monastery in Liaoning and offered myself as a novice monk. Later I went to monasteries in Beijing and Qingdao, where I studied in a Buddhist academy. I already had a degree from a normal college. After three years' study, I graduated and moved to the Gaoming Temple in Yangzhou. After three years I came to the Nanputuo Temple.

Nanputuo, A "Key" Temple in China

Q. Why was Nanputuo Temple spared from Red Guard attacks during the "cultural revolution"?

A. Nanputuo is a "key temple," one of 14 key temples in Fujian. There are 142 key temples nationwide, both Buddhist and Daoist, counting those in Han areas only, but not those in Tibet and Inner Mongolia. In fact, only 2 other temples in Fujian were granted protected status during the "cultural revolution," one in Quanzhou and one in Fuzhou.

Temple Finances

Q. What are the sources of funding for operating the Nanputuo Temple and the academy for training novice monks and nuns?

A. We have sufficient income to meet all our needs from entrance tickets, contributions from the faithful, and profits from services, such as the vegetarian restaurant, hostel, shops, and bookstore. We can ask for up to 40,000 *yuan* per year from the government for building repairs if we need it.

We once had many acres of rice and vegetable fields, but these have been taken over by the government for other purposes. In fact, on the city plan our land is now within the perimeter of the adjoining Xiamen University.

Motivations of Young Novice Monks and Nuns

I asked him what were the reasons motivating young people to enter the novitiate. He gave several reasons:

Most of them choose the vocation because of strong Buddhist family influence, he said. Others want to follow a religious life because of traumatic personal experiences suffered during the "cultural revolution." Others enter the novitiate because of ill health, having tried both Chinese and Western medicine without success. Some say they see the need for monks and nuns to serve as successors for the older generation.

There are other motives too, he said. Some hope to go abroad this way, and in fact many have done so, going to Hongkong, Macau, Singapore, Indonesia, Malaysia, and other places where there is a need for Buddhist monks. The government allows them to go if they have a valid invitation to serve a temple or monastery.

Some want to study Buddhism because life is cruel. Buddhism has a long and rich history, and they want to learn truth from Buddhism.

Q. How do you select your students?
A. We interview each student. They must have a sincere faith.

Q. What is the length of training?
A. We are in the process of extending the period of study to six years. At present, those with primary-school education must study six years, those with junior-middle-school, four years, and senior-middle-school, two years. We also have a three-year graduate-study program. After finishing here, they can take the examination for study at the Beijing Buddhist Institute. We now have seven students there. We have sent at least one student to Beijing from every class since the "cultural revolution."

Women Novices

Q. How many women are studying to become nuns?
A. We have sixty-five young women enrolled in two classes. This year our first class will graduate. Unfortunately we have no room for further students, although we have many more applicants.

Q. What will they do after graduation?
A. Some will remain here to teach. Some will teach elsewhere, while others will go to serve other monasteries [*miao*] or set up their own. There is a shortage of nuns and they are much needed. Sometimes they are pulled out before graduating here to help in a monastery. There are many more women volunteers than men. Almost all come from the rural areas; in fact, we have none from Xiamen City.

Buddhist Students Nationwide

Q. How many students are there nationwide?
A. There are about a thousand Buddhist novices, men and women, studying in regular classes today. We have ninety men and sixty women here. Putian has sixty men, Fuzhou has one hundred women in three classes, but no men. Seventy men are enrolled in the top-level Beijing Buddhist Institute. Shanghai has fifty men and thirty women; Suzhou has sixty men; Nanjing has sixty or seventy men, and there are fifty women studying in Sichuan. A formation program for thirty men and seventy women opened two days ago at Chaozhou in Guangdong.

Q. What about pre-novitiate training classes [*peixunban*] for women?

A. Yes, there are two kinds of such classes. One is called "culture class" [*wenhuaban*], for primary-school graduates, and the other is a higher level class. Quanzhou and Sianyu [two nearby cities] have over seventy young women each in such classes.

The Future of Buddhism in China

Q. What is your view of the future of Buddhism in China?

A. I am optimistic, for these reasons: First, the Confucian tradition, culture, and values system prepares our people for Buddhism. Next, Chinese people have a profound respect for their ancestors, and this also is conducive to Buddhism. Finally, people will always need religion, even under Socialism. This is quite evident now in the people's reaction to the "cultural revolution."

Q. Will there be sufficient young volunteers to replace your generation of monks and nuns?

A. Yes, we have many, especially in Fujian Province. But we still don't have enough. With limited personnel and resources, we have far more applicants than we can train, especially women.

Document 30

Interview with Abbot Puyu, Yongquan Temple, Gushan, Fujian

Donald MacInnis interviewed the recently retired Abbot Puyu (Universal Rain) twice in early 1988 at the Yongquan Temple on Drum Mountain (Gushan) near Fuzhou.

Q. What is the difference between Han Buddhism and Tibetan Buddhism?

A. There is a difference, because their language, lifestyle, and culture are different. The basic content of Buddhism is the same among all the ethnic groups, only their cultures and lifestyles are different.

Q. You say the content is the same; then Buddhism in Tibet and Fujian Buddhism are the same?

A. Yes, the same, because there is only one Buddhism. Buddhism is the same religion everywhere in the world. It's not like Christianity and other religions which have many sects and branches. After all, every religion has only one purpose. Christianity has only one purpose, too, even though it has many branches. Although some groups broke away from the Roman

Catholic church (one is called "new" and the other "old") they have the same purpose, everyone calls them Christianity. Their teachings are the same. Buddhism has many branches too, but their teachings are the same. Just as every nation has many rivers, but they all flow into the sea, so all branches of Buddhism rise from one source and flow in one direction. But each people has its own ways of religious practice. These various ways differ from one nation to another, but the basic doctrines are the same.

Q. I was told that in Xishuangbanna young children, ten or twelve years old, leave home to become monks for a few months.

A. Yes, it's true. Later they can return home, marry, and take an ordinary job. Then they will live a different life-style. It's the same in Thailand and Burma.

Q. Are they called monks?

A. Yes, but monk [*heshan*] is only a Han transliteration from ancient Indian language. No matter what nationality, the meaning is the same, only the pronunciation is different. *Heshan* in Han Chinese means one who teaches doctrine to others. Lama is the Tibetan and Mongolian name for *heshan*. We usually call people who "leave home" [*chujia*] *heshan* or *lama*.

Q. If a young boy, ten or twelve, "leaves home" for three or six months to live in the temple, then returns home and marries, can he be called "monk"?

A. No, he is called a *fojiaotu*, a lay Buddhist. *Heshan* means one who really leaves home, abandons family life, and lives in the temple or monastery.

Q. I have another question. What do believers in any religion really believe? What is the substance of religious faith? Can you answer for Chinese Buddhists?

A. It's mainly the same among all religions, with small differences. . . . Chairman Mao Zedong once said, "Everywhere in China there are people who go to the temple only to *shan nan xin mi* [come to the temple with good intentions but are not necessarily believers] and burn incense. They don't know the basic doctrines of Buddhism. They live the same kind of daily life as anyone else. But there also are some devout Buddhists who live at home, not in the temple, called *jushi* [lay devotees]. Lay Buddhists can't be called "monks." Monks perform the functions of running the temples and monasteries.

Q. I was told that there are about one hundred monks here. Is that right?

A. We have no fixed number, they come and go.

Q. So they are free to come today and leave tomorrow?
A. Yes.

Q. Do they have a *hukou* [residence certificate]?
A. Yes, they can transfer their *hukou* from one temple to another.

Q. Do they need authorization from the abbot *[fangzhang]*?
A. Yes, not the *fangzhang*, but the monk in charge of the temple, the *miaozhang*. Each temple has its own regulations.

Q. It seems that monks have more freedom than ordinary people.
A. Yes, that's true. There are rules and regulations, though.

Q. What do you mean?
A. Christianity has the Ten Commandments. Buddhism also has Ten Rules, but they are not the same. They are the basic rules of Buddhism. Besides these Ten Rules, we have the Five Ordinary Rules. With all these rules, monks are not free to do anything they wish. They must obey the laws of our nation as well. Otherwise they would be too free. "Free" doesn't mean *suibian* [do as you wish]. Without rules and regulations there is no point in having an abbot. And there are many other smaller rules for monks and nuns in China besides the basic rules and regulations.

Q. What branch of Buddhism is practiced here?
A. The Caodong Sect of Chan Buddhism. But the temple master [*zuchi*] and other jobs are the same in every temple, differing somewhat between large and small temples.

Q. Do you have study classes for novice monks here?
A. Yes. After the Third Plenary Session of the Eleventh Party Congress, the policy on religion was once again put into effect. Since then we have had three training classes (*peixunban*) to study the Buddhist disciplines [*jielu*].

Q. What is the difference between a training class and a Buddhist academy [*foxueyuan*]?
A. One is short-term, the other long-term.

Q. What is the term for your training class here?
A. One year. The Buddhist academies have two systems. One is a preparatory course, the other is the standard course. There is also a postgraduate course in Beijing. Every big temple has training classes, and there are several Buddhist academies in China.

Q. What is the purpose of a training class?

A. There are two purposes: to learn the methods and meaning of religious exercises; and to learn about the administration of a temple. Also, to learn about patriotism and obedience to the laws of the nation. We also train some students to go on for study at the Buddhist academies.

Q. What are the educational levels of your novice monks?
A. They come to us from both junior and senior middle school.

Q. Do any novice monks come here from college?
A. Very few.

Q. After completing a training class, do they go on to a Buddhist academy?
A. Those who pass the entrance examinations can do so.

Q. How many are there in a training class?
A. About twenty, sometimes as many as forty.

Q. All male?
A. Both male and female. The women prepare for the nunnery [*nigu miao*]. Some temples only have nuns.

Q. You have already had three training classes? What percentage go on for further study?
A. They go in two directions. Some return to their home temple to work there. Some continue their studies in the Beijing Buddhist Institute, or go to a Buddhist academy in their province, after passing the entrance exam.

Q. When I visited a temple in Dali and talked with the monk in charge of a small class of novices, I was surprised at the paucity of study materials, only two books. This didn't seem to be a regular training class [*peixunban*]. Is that true? Are there exceptions?
A. Besides recruiting students for the training classes in the big temples, every temple may have its own training class, because of travel difficulties. There can be a small class like that one.

Q. What is the future of the five major religions in China?
A. Religion is the belief of the people, and they are free to believe. This can't be stopped by force. The country also belongs to the people. No matter what party rules the nation, if you go against the will of the people, you'll have problems. Since people have the right to freely believe, how can they be stopped? So, in light of the current reality in China, we have a constitution which guarantees freedom of religious belief. No matter who is in charge of the government, they can't interfere with the people's religious belief.

Q. What you have said is the government side. What do you think about the people — their future regarding religious belief? Modernization has negative influences on religious belief in Europe, Taiwan, and other countries where Christian numbers have declined.

A. In each nation there are those who believe, and others who don't. Nonbelievers do not feel the need of religion, while believers do feel the need. When Sakyamuni was on earth, there was a need for religion. How does religious belief arise? From the negative side of life. When life goes well we don't feel the need. But happiness and misfortune, good and evil, are not absolute opposites; they are not seen in the same way by different persons. Rich people won't believe in religion, that's true. But there are different kinds of rich people.

Religion will not disappear. If it does, it will only be temporary, the result of forceful repression by the ruler trying to gain control. But later, when he wants the hearts of the people, the ruler needs to allow freedom of religious belief. The Earth is only a tiny speck in the universe. Scientists acknowledge that there are many stars and planets that men have never visited. Religion will not disappear.

Q. I agree, everyone needs religious faith. But most of the youth in China and many in my country don't see any relevance in religion for them. They are busy with their own affairs.

A. Never mind. That's only a temporary situation. People's lives will change. When they meet difficulties they have to believe in something, then they will turn to religion. In this way they will find a spiritual anchor. Religious belief will generate religious power to meet the needs of people's lives.

Q. You are now over seventy-five. What about the problem of successors? Will your generation of clergy and believers be followed by another?

A. According to Sakyamuni, this is decided by heaven. By "heaven" we mean "nature," which means we, ourselves, have to raise up our successors — a double meaning. Talking about successors is not as simple as just recruiting disciples [*tu di*]. You have to select the right persons. By that I mean to see if they have the potential. They are not sent by God, nor is it arranged by God, but by us humans. Still, we cannot say that God has nothing to do with it.

Q. In Christianity we say that clergy receive "God's call" to the ministry.

A. It's the way you strengthen your belief. You put everything on God, waiting for him to arrange it.

Q. No, it's not that simple. God gave us brains and hands.

A. What you Christians call God, we call Sakyamuni; it's only a difference in name. Americans have their heaven. Chinese have their heaven, which is really only the earth. But our heaven and earth are only tiny specks in the universe. We don't know where heaven really is.

Q. What about your successors?

A. Don't worry about it. It's only a temporary matter. Take myself, Puyu. If I retire, from a political point of view we call it retirement; but in the temple, I'm a retired old monk, still living here in the temple. Never mind what my title or responsibility is, I still live here. I'm still the monk Puyu. I don't have any duties, but I still enjoy the same treatment; people still come to see me. It's not really retirement, like government and factory workers who retire and live at home. This is my home.

Q. What do you mean by speaking of religious revival from the political angle?

A. It means the implementation of the religion policy and the political status of religion. Before Liberation, monks did not participate in political affairs, such as the National People's Congress or the CPPCC, nor did they join any other activities in society. After Liberation this changed.

Q. Is this good?

A. Yes, of course it is good. Not every monk in the temples is superstitious. The constitution stipulates that monks are citizens like everyone else. So their political treatment is better now. This is very different from before the "cultural revolution." Before I retired, I was a member of the CPPCC beginning in the 1950's, and of the NPC at both the provincial and municipal levels in Fujian and Fuzhou. I was not the only religious person, there was another one, two of us. After the "cultural revolution," with its negative influences, I was the only religious delegate; I was even a member of the national CPPCC.

Though I am now retired, and not in charge of the temple, I am still a member of the Fujian CPPCC, as is the new abbot. The political status of Buddhists is much better and completely different from before Liberation.

Q. Compare Buddhism now with before Liberation.

A. From what point of view? From the political and social angle, the status of Buddhism has improved. Only a few people still think that Buddhism is a feudal superstition. The government does not view Buddhism as superstitious. They respect religion. Only a few cadres have a contrary view of religion.

During different dynasties many rulers tried to cut down the number of temples. There are several examples in history [he gives examples from the Tang, Song, and Qing dynasties]. Chairman Mao led the revolution, but he didn't order the temples to be abolished. It was the "gang of four" which damaged many temples, and not only temples, but the whole national economy. After the "cultural revolution" some temples are still in ruins, especially in the mountain areas. But the government also gives money to repair temples. This seems to be a contradiction, to destroy them then rebuild them.

The main decisions are made by the temples and monks themselves. If the monks have a low level of education and administrative skills, there will be problems in managing the temple, and its development will be affected. These are not political influences, but internal personnel problems.

The Panchen Lama once said that in some places there are still people with leftist ideas. They are disobeying the law; they are responsible for tearing down temples.

Q. Are there any newly built temples?

A. Yes, the Guanghua Temple in Putian; they rebuilt some badly damaged buildings there.

Q. My meaning is, entirely newly built?

A. No, the present level of the economy, and government policy, do not allow construction of new temples.

Q. Not allowed?

A. That's correct, not allowed. In the rural areas land is needed for farming; there is no room for building new temples. Food production is more important. In former times we didn't have so many people, and we had more open land. Some people even turned their homes into temples, but the situation is completely different today. Nowadays the number of monks and nuns is decreasing, and some temples have no one in charge. We don't have enough personnel to staff new temples.

Because of the "gang of four," the number of monks decreased. Since the Third Plenary of the Eleventh Party Congress the number of monks and nuns is on the increase, but they all go to larger temples, and many smaller temples are empty. So we can't build new temples, because we have no one to staff them.

Q. I've been told that in Tibet there are many new temples.

A. The situation is different there. There is plenty of land, and politics and religion overlap in Tibet. In the Han areas, politics and religion are kept separate.

Q. Can you compare the number of monks and nuns now with the numbers before Liberation?

A. We don't have precise statistics. In Fujian there are about 60-70,000 Buddhist *jushi* [devotees] "at home" and about 10,000 monks and nuns are in temples and monasteries [*chujia*]. Forty years ago there were not that many. More people now come to the temples to burn incense than forty years ago. At that time the temples did not sell incense. Now some temples even make incense for sale.

Q. On a normal day, how many people come here to burn incense?
A. I don't know. Because this is an open temple, people have to buy tickets. Not all visitors burn incense; but certainly more than before.

Q. Are monks allowed to make visits in the homes of Buddhists?
A. Yes.

Q. But in the case of death—for death rites?
A. No [*buxing*]. Yes, our government has a policy of freedom of religious belief. But no one is allowed to influence others. If you have a death in your family, if you invite a monk to "read scriptures," your neighbor, who does not believe in religion, may overhear it and be influenced. This could create conflicts. So we never go out of the temple to "read scriptures." That's the regulation. But some monks do visit Buddhist homes, because that is the custom. Before Liberation it was very common to have Buddhist rites in the homes; no one interfered. Other people enjoyed these spectacles.

Q. Such as public funeral processions through the streets?
A. Yes. Formerly, Christian preachers could preach in people's homes, but not now, for the same reason. This is to protect religious freedom.

Q. Can you compare the number of open temples now with the number before Liberation?
A. Now there are regulations for temples; before Liberation there were no regulations.

Q. Who sets the limit on how many temples will be open?
A. The Chinese Buddhist Association. Why were no temples designated "open" before Liberation? Because then there were no regulations about tourism and temples. Now the government, to protect the temples from damage by nonbelievers, designates certain temples as "open." The government does not interfere in the management of temples.

There are two meanings for "open": one refers to temples and monasteries open for tourists; the other refers to those approved for teaching Buddhism.

Q. I met a monk who said he opened a new temple in Nanping.
A. That is not a new temple, it's an old one. He is just reopening it. It's like a temple in Fuzhou which was torn down to build a highway; now it is rebuilt elsewhere as a new temple.

Q. So the CBA determines the number of open temples?

A. Yes. Take Fujian for example; there are fourteen big temples, all open, and many more small temples. In Fujian many farmers and fishermen are religious believers. So in the rural areas there are more and more temples reopening.

Section II

Reports by the National Buddhist Association

Introduction

Two reports from the national Chinese Buddhist Association, one given in 1982 and one in 1987, have been selected for reprinting here. There is no indication how delegates are chosen, but this is called a "national representatives meeting," with delegates from each province. The 1982 report lists five major tasks of the national CBA: to help the government to implement the policy of freedom of religious belief; to train Buddhist monks (nuns not mentioned); to produce and circulate Buddhist scriptures and other publications; to foster Buddhist research; and to promote friendly exchanges with Buddhists from various countries.

There is no evidence here that the national CBA exercises direct control over the functioning of temples and monasteries, or even over provincial and local clergy-training schools. Like local Protestant churches, Catholic dioceses, and Muslim mosques, each seems to operate in semiautonomous fashion within its own national community. However, according to Abbot Puyu (Document 30), the CBA does have the authority to determine how many temples will be reopened. "Now there are regulations for temples and monasteries," he said. "Before Liberation there were none." Nor is it allowed, he said to build new temples at this time. There are regulations, as well, prohibiting religious services in homes, once a normal function of Buddhist monks.

In 1982, a fund for propagating Buddhism was approved for the purpose of financing the training of Buddhist monks, the expansion of theological research, the publication of Buddhist books and periodicals, and the renovation of major Buddhist monasteries and temples. As with the Chinese Muslim community, donations would be solicited from Chinese benefactors in Hongkong and overseas, as well as inside China—a radical difference from the Chinese Christian churches, which do not accept financial support from agencies abroad.

Document 31

The Work of the Chinese Buddhist Association, 1982

By Zhao Puchu, President, in Fa Yin *No. 4, July 1982. Translated in China Study Project Documentation No. 10, March 1983, pp. 33-35.*

Buddhist Association Meeting, May, 1982

A) THE WORK OF THE CHINESE BUDDHIST ASSOCIATION DONE IN THE PAST YEAR AND MORE

1. It has been the primary task of the Association to help the government in implementing the policy of freedom of religious belief in the past year and more.

2. It has been an important and urgent task of the Association to nurture Buddhist priests so as to meet the needs of Buddhist work in China and abroad.

3. Publications and circulations of Buddhist scriptures, books, and images:

Since the Jinling Buddhist Xylograph and Printing House reopened last year it has printed and circulated 10,789 Buddhist scriptures and books. In the meantime, under the direction of Panchen, Vice-chairman of the Standing Committee of the NPC and Honorary President of the China Buddhist Association, sixteen kinds of Tibetan scriptures and five kinds of Tibetan Buddhist images are to be printed. In addition, a circulating office was set up in the Fayuan Monastery in Beijing to sell Buddhist scriptures, books and images. Moreover, for the purpose of improving and developing publications and circulations of Buddhist scriptures, books, and images, a discussion meeting was held a few days ago before the second session of the Association.

4. New developments in Buddhist academic research:

i) The periodical *Fa Yin* produced four issues last year with a circulation of 8,000 copies each issue. There were 6,000 subscribers from provinces, cities, and autonomous regions throughout China; and overseas subscribers came from ten countries and districts. It received more than 400 articles, nearly 10,000 letters, and donations of 13,000 *yuan*. Since this year it has become a bimonthly publication. The circulation has expanded to 12,000 copies each issue.

ii) The completion of the catalog of "Fanshan Buddhistic Stone Scriptures," a scripture based on the Tripitaka of Liao dynasty. In the course of related work, the only existing copy of another scripture which has long been considered lost was discovered.

iii) The participation in the work of the Buddhist section of the religions volume of *Chinese Encyclopedia*; the publication of *Buddhism in China*, Vol. 2, and other Buddhist scriptures and relevant books.

iv) The Chinese Buddhist Books and Relics Library has a collection of 120,000 volumes of books, including various Tibetan scriptures and some rare scriptures of the Tang, Song, Yuan, Ming, and Qing dynasties. The library also provided some local monasteries and temples with Buddhist images and articles, urgently needed for their renovation.

5. Friendly exchanges with Buddhists from various countries have been developed; the contacts with Chinese in Hongkong, Macau, and overseas Chinese have been strengthened.

Starting from last year, the Association has received 1,758 foreign guests, Chinese in Hongkong and Macau, and overseas Chinese of 190 delegations from nineteen countries and districts; and dealt with 481 international telegrams.

B)ARRANGEMENTS FOR WORK TO BE CARRIED OUT WITHIN THIS YEAR

1. To concentrate on carrying out the relevant documents transmitted from the State Council so as to continue to help the government fulfil the policy of freedom of religious belief; to help the Bureau of Religious Affairs under the State Council in drawing up a list of major monasteries and temples to be reopened in China (including minority nationalities' regions); to understand and to reflect situations of the implementation of policies on the field of Buddhism in minority nationalities' regions, and to raise suggestions on resolving the existing problems, especially in the area of Tibet.

2. To call on Buddhists conscientiously to study Premier Zhao Ziyang's report on "the present economic situation and policies on economic construction for the future," to raise self-awareness in taking an active part in the construction of Socialist modernization, in which stress is placed on economic construction.

3. To call for efforts to nurture Buddhist personnel, to complete the preparatory work for the training courses for monks in Nanjing this year. (Each course will accept about 200 students and last for about nine months.)

4. To do a good job of circulating Buddhist scriptures and images.

5. To upgrade the quality of the periodical *Fa Yin*; to complete the work related to *Chinese Encyclopedia* and other publications; to prepare to set up the Institute of Chinese Buddhist Literature, History, and Philosophy; to establish a committee of the Fojiao-honghua (Dissemination of Buddhism) Fund to procure money so as to solve the financial difficulties faced by the work of Buddhist academic research, monks' training, publication, and so on.

6. To continue exchanges with Buddhists from other countries.

7. To do a good job of receiving the Tripitaka-Receiving Delegation from the Baolian monastery in Hongkong, and organize a scripture-bearing group to Hongkong.

DECISIONS ADOPTED BY THE STANDING COMMITTEE ON 21 MAY 1982

1. Unanimously and firmly to support the "Draft of the Revised Constitution of the PRC"; especially satisfied with Article 36 of the constitution which has restored the 1954 constitution article.

2. To express satisfaction over the profound work of the Association in the past year and arrangements for work before the end of this year; unanimously to pass the President of the Association Zhao Puchu's report.

3. The China Buddhist Association should make further revision and arrangement for proposing a list of major monasteries and temples to be reopened as places for religious activities in the Han areas, Tibet, and Mongolia.

4. To express great concern for the training of Buddhist priests. Apart from running well the Chinese Buddhist Theological Institute and giving help with the running of its affiliated school in Suzhou (Jiangsu province), the China Buddhist Association should try to complete the preparatory work for training course for monks in Nanjing within this year; and to help and support major monasteries and temples based on their foundations in various areas, including in the districts of Mongolia and Tibet, in playing positive roles in founding Buddhist theological institutes and training courses on their own initiative.

5. To express satisfaction with the discussion meeting on the work of publishing and circulating Buddhist scriptures and books.

6. To agree with tentative measures for Raising Dissemination of Buddhist Funds, and in principle to agree with a name list of the committee of the fund, which were submitted to the Second Session of the Association by the China Buddhist Association.

7. To accept with unanimous approval the proposal of Li Rongxi, Member of the Standing Committee and Associate Secretary-General of the China Buddhist Association, as Vice-president of the Association; Zhou Shaoliang, Committee Member of the China Buddhist Association and director of the Chinese Buddhist Books and Relics Library, as Standing Committee Member of the Association; and Master Jinghui, Editor of the periodical *Fa Yin*, for Committee Member of the Association.

8. To authorize the China Buddhist Association to conscientiously study, determine, and deal with the proposals and suggestions presented by Standing Committee Members and Committee Members of the Association at the Second Session of the Association after the meeting.

The meeting calls on Buddhists of various nationalities in China to propagate the fine traditions of Buddhism, to make more contributions to the fields of theological study, production, loving the country and observing the law, serving the society, promoting human welfare, protecting world peace, practicing the Buddha's teachings, and so on.

TENTATIVE MEASURES FOR RAISING DISSEMINATION OF BUDDHISM FUNDS (PASSED AT THE SECOND SESSION OF THE FOURTH STANDING COMMITTEE OF THE CHINESE BUDDHIST ASSOCIATION)

1. In light of the spirit of Articles 2 and 15 of the constitution of the China Buddhist Association, the Association decides to set up the Fojiao-honghua Fund and draws up tentative measures.

2. The fund is aimed at financing the nurture of Buddhist priests, the expansion of Buddhist theological research and publication of Buddhist books and periodicals, the development of Buddhist cultural enterprises so as to serve the construction of Socialist modernization.

3. Sources of the fund:

To receive donations from local monasteries, temples, Buddhist organizations, the broad mass of Buddhist believers, and persons who are concerned for the Buddhist cultural enterprise in China;

To receive donations from Chinese Buddhists in Hongkong and Macau, overseas Chinese Buddhists, and Buddhists with Chinese origin;

To receive donations from foreign persons of goodwill who are enthusiastic over the enterprise of Buddhist culture.

Other income.

4. Uses of the fund:

To finance the founding of Buddhist educational organizations for monks and nuns (including Buddhist theological institutes, training courses, and other similar types of educational organizations);

To finance the printing of Buddhist images and the publication of Buddhist scriptures, books, and periodicals;

To finance the renovation of major Buddhist monasteries and temples;

To finance other Buddhist enterprises. . . .

Document 32

Fifth National Conference of the Chinese Buddhist Association, 1987

Excerpted from Fa Yin *No. 3, 1987. Translated in* China Study Project Journal *2:3, December 1987, p. 83.*

The Fifth National Conference of the Chinese Buddhist Association was convened from 23 February to 1 March 1987 in Beijing, after the last conference of the Association in 1980. The conference was attended by 300 delegates of various nationalities from all Buddhist sects in China. The conference adopted resolutions for President of the China Buddhist Association Zhao Puchu's report on "Be United, Carry Forward the Fine Traditions of Buddhism and Make Contributions toward the Cause of Building Our Homeland and Benefiting Our People"; and the Vice-President of the Association Zheng Guo's written work report on the fourth Committee of the Association, and the revised Constitution of the China Buddhist Association.

"Buddhists have found a way to integrate Buddhism and Socialism with Chinese characteristics since the Fourth National Conference of the China Buddhist Association. There are two fundamental conditions needed to integrate Buddhism and Socialism: one is that the Party and the State respect and protect Buddhists' right of freedom of religious belief in light of policies and the law; the other is that Buddhists love the country and observe the law, support the leadership of the Party and the State, and positively make contributions to the construction of Socialist material and spiritual civilizations," President of the China Buddhist Association Zhao Puchu said in his report at the conference.

The conference called on all Buddhists of various nationalities in China to conscientiously study and implement the spirit of Zhao Puchu's report; to raise the awareness of patriotism, Socialism and the concept of law; to hold fast to the requirement of the four basic principles to religious believers; to safeguard the stability and unity of the country; to be united in, and carry forward, the fine traditions of Buddhism; to make new contributions to the building of our homeland and benefiting our people; to unite under the four modernizations; and to work toward world peace under the leadership of the Party and the State.

Leaders of the Party and the State Qiao Shi, Chen Pixian, and Apei Awangjinmei met the delegates to the Fifth Conference on 28 February, 1987 at the Great Hall of the People in Beijing.

Panchen Lama was again invited to be Honorary President of the Association; Zhao Puchu was reelected as the President of the Association at the closing session of the Conference. The Conference also elected 16 vice-presidents, namely, Pabala Gelielangjie, Jiamuyang Luosangjiumei Tudanquejinima, Xiarongduobu, Zheng Guo, Ming Zhen, Gongming Jiangbaqurimu, Li Rongxi, Gong Tanglun, Sejiekansu Lunzhutaokai, Jia Ya, Wu Lan, Yuan Zhuo, Long Lian, Dao Shuren, Zhou Shaoliang, and Duojizha Jiangbailuosang; and a new 267-member Committee. The Committee then held its first meeting and elected 71 standing-committee members, with Zhou Shaoliang elected as Secretary General, and Vice Secretary Generals Dao Shuren and You Xiang, It also invited eleven honorary committee members.

Section III

Training New Monks and Nuns

Introduction

Five documents have been selected for this section, three from the Chinese press, one from a Hongkong newspaper, and an essay from a volume published in Shanghai in 1987 based on field studies by social scientists, that examine the reasons why some young people become Buddhists.

We have no overall figures for new Buddhist clergy, men or women, but judging by sample figures provided in interviews enlisting recruits is not a problem. A Catholic bishop in Fujian told me that 8-900 Buddhist monks and nuns had taken vows in Fujian since 1980.

Why are there young Buddhist converts in Socialist China? The Shanghai investigators enumerate several reasons, some of them already mentioned in Section I. The first is the influence of Buddhist families: more than half of the students in one Buddhist academy gave this as their first reason for entering the novitiate. Others are searching for release from despair and world-weariness caused by personal problems in their love lives or by disappointment in jobs or in pursuit of higher education. Some, in fact, enter the Buddhist academies as a substitute for university studies, having failed the entrance examinations.

Others have been influenced by Buddhist novels, painting, music, architecture, philosophy, and martial arts, and enter Buddhist schools to pursue their interest in Buddhist culture.

A number want to be monks or nuns for psychological reasons, searching for a quiet and peaceful life away from the noise and pressures of the cities or the turmoil and tensions of an overcrowded household. (A young monk at the Nanhua Temple in Putian, Fujian, told me that his main reasons for entering the monastic life were to escape from family discord and to secure his livelihood.)

Another reason is the desire to escape the boredom of rural life. Monks are free to travel from temple to temple throughout China, where they are always welcome and receive room and board in exchange for duties performed as transient members of the temple staff. Moreover, some lucky ones can find jobs in temples and monasteries abroad.

Finally, the Shanghai researchers note that an occasional criminal seeks to hide under the robes of a monk, while others, victims of belief in fatalism and superstition, find "absurd and preposterous" reasons to join the novitiate. Some believe they will be reincarnations of long-dead monks and nuns, or wish to join because they "saw a vision."

How should these young people be helped? Basing their responses on materialist assumptions and ignoring any valid spiritual or metaphysical reasons for religious faith, the commentators in the Chinese press offer suggestions on how to help these "misguided" young people return to normal life. Those who seek to flee the world because of setbacks in their personal lives need to find activities that fit their special needs, "activities that will raise their level of culture and ideology and enrich their spiritual life." Those who are influenced by superstitious ideas "know very little about Buddhism," and need basic education in "scientific and cultural knowledge . . . to understand dialectical materialism and to build a correct outlook on life." As for those with a sincere Buddhist faith and commitment, they will become the core group of young Buddhists, and the important question is "how to help them to build a firm, patriotic ideology . . . so as to contribute to the four modernizations."

The remaining documents in this section are stories from the Chinese press reporting on two seminaries for training nuns, the training program as short-term monks for Dai boys in the tribal regions bordering Burma, and a Hongkong newspaper report on the fifteen-day ordination ceremony of 800 monks and nuns at the Nanhua Temple in Guangdong Province in June 1988. Finally, the Buddhist Institute in Sichuan is the first school of higher learning for nuns in China, and 37 were chosen for the first class out of over 1,000 applicants for the four-year course.

Document 33

An Analysis of the Reasons Why Some Young People Become Buddhists

From Religious Questions under Socialism in China, *(Shanghai Academy of Social Sciences, 1987), pp. 200-210. Translated by Zheng Xi'an and Donald MacInnis.*

In recent years, with the implementing of the Party's policy on religion, religious activities in monasteries in various parts of the country have been restored. A number of young people have enthusiastically embraced Buddhism, some even applying to live in monasteries and become monks or nuns.

For example, in Fujian, a province with a long history of Buddhism, the number of monks and nuns exceeded thirty-eight hundred in the year 1982, shortly after the implementation of the policy on religion. Some of them were new converts in the latter years of the "cultural revolution." Besides these, there are many young people now who want to study to become monks or nuns. One Buddhist seminary aroused widespread interest when news of its opening was made public. Many persons wrote letters asking about the nature of the study program and requirements for admission. In a few months over two hundred letters were received applying for admission to study or to become monks or nuns.

Some of the applicants were young women, some even high-school students. In their letters they said that they "admired very much the professional monks and cherished the hope to become devout Buddhists." Others wrote saying that they were "facing the decision on what road to take in life," and, "believing in Buddhism and admiring eminent monks," they were determined to take the examination and strive for the goal of a lifelong religious vocation.

Backgrounds varied among the applicants, from high-school students to unemployed high-school graduates, cadres, and workers, but the vast majority were young villagers. These young people were "born and grew up in the sunshine of the new society." What, then, made them so eager to become Buddhists? Why is Buddhism so fascinating to them that they would want to say goodbye to their dear ones, leave home, and come to live a lonely and boring life?

In our search for answers, some comrades from the Department of Religious Research of the Shanghai Institute of Social Sciences, helped by persons in Buddhist circles and supported by the religious-affairs sections of various regions, have interviewed, since 1982, some young monks and novices, both men and women, in a number of places. We present here a preliminary analysis of their reasons for believing in Buddhism.

The Influence of Buddhist Families

A very important reason that some of these young people came to believe in Buddhism is the influence of family members who are Buddhists. Buddhism has a long history and widespread influence in China. Although our society has experienced world-shaking changes since Liberation, religious thinking as an ideology continues, and will continue for a long time in our society, affecting the minds of some people. The elderly ones, particularly those who came from the old society and had a strong belief in Buddhism, are deep-rooted Buddhists; even disasters such as the ten years of chaos cannot make them give up their belief. The religious faith of these people will always affect those around them, in particular their family members.

A seventeen-year-old young man from Hubei said that he had often listened to his grandfather tell stories. Since the grandfather was a Buddhist, he liked to tell Buddhist stories. As a result, the child wanted to become a monk. As time passed he grew up and his belief in Buddhism deepened, until at last he decided to become a monk and applied to study in a Buddhist seminary.

In another case, a young man from Hunan said, "My parents were faithful Buddhists throughout their lives. Under their influence I made up my mind while still a child to learn about Buddhism and to become a monk. I read the scriptures and prayed to Buddha." It was the influence of his parents' Buddhist ideology which led to his deep-rooted Buddhist faith and his decision to give up his job and enter the Buddhist seminary.

A young junior-high-school graduate in Jiangxi came from a Buddhist family that had practiced vegetarianism since his grandfather's time. His parents had studied Buddhism each morning and evening. His interest in Buddhism grew from his childhood years, when he lay in bed watching his parents at their studies and listened to their chanting. At the age of ten he began to study Buddhist scriptures under the instruction of his parents. His father's religious teacher, a Buddhist monk, often explained Buddhism to him, and eventually he became a young monk.

Other young people were led to a religious vocation by parents or other family members who became monks or nuns. One young man from Ningxia often visited his mother in the monastery after she became a nun in 1961, and his brother who became a monk in 1975. Through their influence he finally made the decision to become a monk himself.

These examples show that one of the most important reasons for young people's religious belief is the influence of older family members. Of over one hundred monks and nuns in a certain Buddhist seminary class, more than half were influenced by Buddhist family members or relatives. In some cases, every member of the family became monks or nuns. In others, several brothers became monks. Some who grew up in temples, nurtured by Buddhism, became monks when adults.

Generally speaking, these young believers are more pious and their religious knowledge is more thorough [than that of their predecessors]. They are the core group of a whole cohort of young believers. The very important question is how to unite with these young people, how to help them to build a firm, patriotic ideology and bring their initiative into full play so as to contribute to the four modernizations.

The Influence of Buddhist Culture and Works of Literature and Art

Religious culture is part of a national culture. Buddhism has a long history in China. Some of our country's best culture is crystallized and preserved in Buddhist culture. The development of Buddhist philosophy has enriched the ideological history of our country, and Buddhist arts, including architecture, painting, music, etc., continue to scintillate today. Buddhist culture is attractive to some young people, arousing their interest in studying Buddhism and eventually leading them to religious belief.

For example, there was a young worker at a certain factory who had won the title of Excellent Youth League Member and Advanced Worker in his factory. Because of his love of literature and the arts he became interested in Buddhist culture. Later he mailed his application to study in a Buddhist seminary. In his letter he said that he wanted to study in a seminary in order to pursue research on the Buddhist dharma; he wished to probe into the essence of Buddhist dharma to learn more of its value in terms of culture and scholarly studies.

Another young man, a farmer, said: "Buddhism, along with ancient medicine, architecture, martial arts, and calligraphy, is part of the brilliant cultural heritage of the motherland. There should be successors [to those who created this heritage]. I am still young, and should learn something [of that heritage]." So he applied for admission to the Buddhist seminary.

Another example is that of a twenty-year-old man from Wuxi who said, "I like reading the ancient literature of our country. I love philosophy, logic, literature, calligraphy, painting, music, martial arts. I know very well that much of the cream of our cultural heritage can be found in Buddhist scriptures. Because we lack trained personnel, this precious cultural heritage is not properly cared for." He would like to study in a Buddhist seminary to acquire relevant knowledge, he said, so that he could pursue a career in this field.

Most young people who think this way have some education and knowledge already and love studying. They hope to absorb the splendid cultural heritage of our nation, and they cherish certain ideals and ambitions. But their basic reason for applying to enter Buddhist seminaries is their hope to further their studies. They are not as pious as those who choose to become monks through family influences, and they lack the ideological preparation for a lifetime vocation as a monk.

Still other young people come in contact with Buddhism and find their interest aroused by reading books, magazines, and works of literature. A seventeen-year-old senior-high-school student said, "Except for reading about monasteries and monks in books and newspapers, and seeing them in films, I have never seen a real monastery or monk. I have learned from my reading that some monks stood up and fought fearlessly and relentlessly against reactionary rulers, some even giving their lives for the motherland and people. The film, *Shaolin Temple* is an example of this."

Another man who is studying Buddhism in a certain temple first came into contact with Buddhism by reading novels. His interest in Buddhism was raised even higher by reading books on predestination, and he finally made up his mind to become a monk. When he was eighteen his parents wanted him to marry, but he was unwilling. He held firmly to his Buddhist beliefs, kept to a vegetarian diet, and finally became a monk.

A monk at a certain monastery in Sichuan loved reading fairy tales when he was a child, stories about fate, predestination, retribution, and reincarnation. Through his reading and the influence of his family he came to the point where he believed that Buddhist teachings give a very thorough and sensible explanation of human life and of the universe itself. As a result he became a Buddhist and entered a monastery.

From these examples we can see that not all young people who wish to study in Buddhist seminaries or preparatory classes, or to enter monasteries, are necessarily religious believers. Quite a few of them are merely curious, and, feeling that there are gaps in their knowledge, are searching for answers. Thus, some people come in touch with religion simply out of their strong desire to learn something. Therefore our comrades who carry on ideological work, particularly among young people, must be concerned when they see young people enter monasteries or come into direct contact with a religion. They should analyze the motives, lead young people to know what religion is, and deal with it in a correct way. Only in this way can they help to implement the Party's religious policy and the cause of Socialism.

There are other matters that deserve our attention, such as the question of how to reinforce research on religion, including the history of religions, ideologies, culture, and the present state of affairs [in religion]. We also need to broaden young people's understanding of religion so that they can deal with religion in a correct way. Religion is a very complex social phenomenon, and for a variety of reasons is shrouded with layers of man-made veils and thus appears quite mysterious. Most of our young people today, including college students, have no idea of what religion is all about.

A certain university has made a survey of some of its students and found that most students do not have the least knowledge about religion, or "know very little" or are "very vague" about it. Young people have a very strong desire to learn, and some young people want to learn about religion. This is only normal. We regret that their desire cannot be met, with the result that they come to know and judge religion by hearsay, or by reading certain literary works. Some of them turn to religious organizations or actually go into the temples and monasteries. Therefore it is proper to make available some knowledge of religion, to introduce some facts about religious history and religious culture to young people. This will help them come to a proper understanding of religion and will also help to implement the party's religious policy.

Another university offered a special study unit on religion in the course on historical materialism. After they had heard the lectures, many students said this special study unit had filled in some blanks in their fund of knowledge. Some of them said that the lectures "made us more fully aware of the beginnings, the nature, the essence, and the normal forms of religion, enabling us to get a clear comprehension of religion so as to correctly understand the Party's policy on religion."

Turning to Buddhism in the Search for Release from Despair and World-Weariness

Socialism has eliminated exploitation and oppression and the social sources for religion. But the many contradictions that remain in actual life often bring problems and disasters to people. One often meets individuals who encounter these problems in the course of their daily lives. Different people approach these contradictions in different ways. Some press onward in the face of difficulties and become stronger. Others, not daring to face real life, lose faith in life or lose courage because of setbacks and turn to religion in the hope of gaining spiritual comfort.

Based on our surveys, the social and personal reasons why young people turn to religion can be summed up as follows:

PROBLEMS OF LOVE AND MARRIAGE

Love and marriage are major events for young people. True love and a happy marriage make life richer and happier, but disappointment in love or an unsuccessful marriage bring endless troubles and pain. How does one deal with the wounds of a broken love affair? A person of strong will can bury such troubles in his heart and transfer his feelings to other spheres. But certain young people take love to be the total content of life. When they suffer disappointments they can find no way out and life becomes meaningless.

For example, a young man in a certain place lost his mother when he was very young. He became acquainted with a fellow student in junior high school. They kept each other company for a long time and were dear to each other, just like sister and brother, and they finally fell in love. Later the girl married someone else and the young man was devastated. After that, he felt that "being young has little meaning for me" and decided to become a monk.

In another instance, a young man in Jiangsu Province about twenty years of age suffered heartbreak because of disappointment in love. He had never thought there would be such sadness and sorrow from a broken love affair, so, lacking the courage to fight against fate, he began to think about becoming a monk. He asserted that he would never fall in love again and would give up the thought of marriage to avoid a repetition of his spiritual trauma. He would become a monk and seek a new life. He did avoid the pain of another disappointment in love, but he did so by choosing to flee from love a second time.

THE PROBLEMS OF GOING ON FOR HIGHER EDUCATION AND OF FINDING A JOB

The hope and ideal of many young people is to go to college. Of course it would be nice to have the chance for further study, to acquire more knowledge, and to make a bigger contribution to one's country and people. But one need not go to college to do that; even if one fails to enroll in college he can make contributions in an ordinary job just the same. However, some young people collapse after one setback, such as failing to pass college entrance examinations, or they find life meaningless simply because they do not like their job.

For example, a certain young high-school graduate failed twice in the college entrance examinations and was waiting at home for employment. He felt depressed and finally turned to religion for help. He said, "The superior Socialist system can never salvage my fate. I will find only disillusionment in this world so I must find my place and live a quiet life."

A young monk now in a certain temple in Sichuan received a similar blow when he failed to pass the college entrance examinations. Although he got a job he thought it was meaningless, saying that young people hope to do something earthshaking. But when they see others entering college and see themselves as inferiors, the only way they can find spiritual surcease is to take the road of Buddhism, and thus he became a monk.

Another young man, originally a student in a big city, settled down for many years in the countryside. Later he was transferred to a mine where the work was hard and conditions poor. When he saw that some of the classmates who went to the countryside with him were sent back to the city, while others entered college, he sighed over the way fate treated different people in different ways. In addition his mother died. Lacking a warm home, feeling miserable, depressed, and disillusioned with the world, he came to a monastery asking to become a monk.

PROBLEMS OF PSYCHOLOGY AND ENVIRONMENT

Life environment can have great influence on the emergence and formation of religious psychology, in particular for some young introverts. When they feel unable to adapt to their environment, they become sick of the world.

A certain young villager came to take his father's place in a job in the city. He was all alone, without family or relatives nearby, and "for the first time he tasted the bitterness of the world and the difficulty of living in society." There are high buildings and broad streets in the city, but for this young man from the countryside, with "not even a small room of his own to live in and no place to walk freely, he suffered as if shut up in a cage." Besides this, the young man "could not bear the sight of people intriguing against each other and selfishly pursuing personal gain. He did not want to live with ordinary people and soil his pristine character." And so he "cut off all worldly goals and decided to devote his life to Buddhism, to burn himself like the incense in the temple."

A young factory worker thought he was "weak," "a sacrifice to political movements," and "the undeserved target of his leaders' anger" as well, so he lost confidence in himself. After several years of reflection he despaired of life in the real world and turned to Buddhism as the only way to "wash away worldly sorrows."

Some people come to believe in religion for purely psychological reasons. Most of them are young women who are generally lonely introverts and prefer to live quietly by themselves.

There was a young woman living in a big city who believed that her own disposition required that she live in a quiet environment conducive to a refined state of mind. This was incompatible with her life in a noisy city. She yearned for a place of retreat and chose Buddhism as her shelter from real life. She said her fondest wish would be to leave her worldly life and convert to Buddhism.

Another woman, who was fond of calligraphy, painting, and music, said, "These would remedy the emptiness in my mind and heart." She felt that everything worldly was disgusting and prosaic. She wanted a quiet and solitary life, and her only hope was to become a nun.

These true stories show that a rich material life is not necessarily equivalent to an abundant spiritual life. While building a Socialist material civilization, we must pay adequate attention to the building of a spiritual civilization which is rich and varied. Those young people who cannot adapt themselves to the world and feel empty-hearted deserve our concern and love; we need to find activities that fit their special needs, raise the level of their culture and ideology, and enrich their spiritual life.

We have listed above the main reasons why some young people become dispirited and world-weary. We need to learn how to cultivate and educate young patriotic believers in religious circles. At present, most patriotic religious believers are aware of the changes from the old society to a new one. They have long received patriotic education and built a strong foundation on patriotism. Whatever the circumstances, they will be firm in their love of the motherland and of their religion.

When we look at the actual situation of young believers, we find that many of them have turned to religion because of setbacks encountered in daily life. Many of them have come to find the world and its ways repugnant and hide themselves from reality. It is a difficult task to give these young people an education which combines "loving the nation" and "loving one's religion." If we can find a good solution to this problem, it will strongly influence how people in religious circles hold to the patriotic road while at the same time loving their religion.

The Influence of Fatalism and Superstition

Fatalism is an idea that has long been current among the Han people. Even women and children know the so-called truisms, "What will be will be, don't try to resist it," and "Life and death are predestined, wealth and poverty depend on the will of heaven." Such sayings still affect the younger generation of new China. Some young people say, "It won't do not to believe it, neither will it do to believe all of it."

There is a family in a certain county of Fujian who believed the fortune-teller when he said they were predestined to become monks. So the husband and wife, together with their child, have abandoned family life for religious vocations in Buddhism.

A twenty-year-old young man also believed that he was destined to become a monk. He sold his properties and became a monk. His wife remarried and a good family was destroyed.

Still other young people believe in Buddhism because of preposterous sayings and fantastic ideas. For example, while recruiting new students, a certain Buddhist seminary found that some of the young applicants claimed that they wanted to become monks and nuns because they were reincarnations of monks and nuns, or they were born of Guanyin [Goddess of Mercy]. Some claimed that they had a "vision" while praying behind closed doors, and came to ask for [divine] "instructions." Some were originally "protecting the incense and the lamps" at a "celestial palace" on a certain mountain, and after being forbidden to do this by the public security officers wanted to go to Emei Mountain to "cultivate their moral character" or to "cultivate themselves according to the teachings."

There were two young men in a certain place in Jiangxi Province studying Buddhism from their "adoptive mother." This "adoptive mother" was very mysterious. It was said that she lived on fruit and water only. She earned money by telling fortunes, physiognamy, and curing illnesses. In fact she was something like a witch.

Another young man said he would find a way to put "God" in people's hearts to enhance the beauty of their hearts. The ideas of these young, earnest Buddhists sharply diverged from traditional Buddhist teachings.

Most of these young people came from culturally backward countryside and mountainous areas. Since their own cultural standards were low, they could easily be influenced by superstitions. Furthermore, they knew very little about Buddhism and did not know the difference between religion and superstition. The facts of these cases should tell us that education for this kind of young person should start from the very beginning: that is, they should be given more scientific and cultural knowledge and helped to do away with superstitions, to understand dialectical materialism, and to build a correct outlook on life.

We should do more to help people distinguish superstition from religion, and to cultivate the ability of young people to tell the difference between normal religious activities and illegal, superstitious religious activities in order to implement the Party's policy on religious freedom. We should ban illegal, superstitious practices that are harmful to people's physical and mental health.

Other Influences

There are still other reasons why some young people come to believe in Buddhism.

For example, some want to enter Buddhist seminaries or training classes because they think it would be nice to be a high-ranking monk who can go abroad. Some want to use religion as a springboard to enable them to move from the countryside to the city and find a position there. Some even publicly acknowledge that they come to study Buddhism for economic reasons.

Some young villagers cannot stand working on the farm at home and yearn for city life. Under the pretext of becoming a monk they want to go to the monastery in a big city in order to enrich their experience. Some Fujian young people have done this. They first became monks in a small temple in their native town or village; next they went to a temple in Fuzhou or to Nanputuoshan Temple in Xiamen; after that they paid visits to other famous temples, monasteries, and mountains. They would stay longer at the good places, while soon leaving the places which they didn't like as well. All this had nothing to do with genuine religious belief; they simply lived on Buddhism.

A very small number of people could not stay on in their home place because they had committed some crime. They hid themselves in the temples in order to get away from legal punishment. These people are very few, yet there have been some.

Young people who believe in Buddhism for these reasons are not genuine religious believers. Although they temporarily stay in temples and monasteries for personal reasons, once they get what they want or find out it is impossible to get it, they vacillate. Of course it is possible that some of them will change and become sincere Buddhists after all.

It can be seen from our analysis that there are many reasons why young people become Buddhists. The depth and breadth of their belief vary according to their experience, life circumstances, and cultural level. In Socialist society religion is a long-lasting social phenomenon. As an ideology it exercises influence not only on those who came over from the old society, but on some of the young people who grew up in the new society as well. These are the ones who will become the core believers of the various religions; therefore their living situation, their ideological changes, the reasons for their belief, and their activities both in society and in their religious groups will be closely connected with the development and changes of religion in the future. To overlook this will be detrimental to our future work.

Document 34

Dai Boys Study in Monasteries

China Daily, *1 June 1988.*

While most Chinese children receive their education in State-run schools, many in southwest Yunnan Province's Xishuangbanna Dai Autonomous Prefecture are sent to practice Buddhism and learn the ancient Dai language in monasteries.

"Only in the monasteries, can our children learn to read the ancient and modern Dai language in addition to studying mathematics, astronomy, calendar-calculation, and medicine on [sic] the Buddhist sutras in the ancient Dai language," said a villager in Menghai County in the prefecture.

The prefecture, which consists of three counties, is home to 200,000 Dai people, most of whom are practicing Buddhists.

They have built 485 monasteries, which accounts for almost one for every village.

"So far there are 5,470 school-age monks in those monasteries," said a prefectural official in charge of education.

In Mengzhe township, Menghai County, for example, school-age monks number 1,054. This means that one out of every four children in the area is learning the ancient Dai language through reading sutras taught by adult monks in the monasteries.

In order to provide the young monks with training in modern science and technology, the prefectural education department has set up special classes in the State-run schools (taught in the Han language) for the school-age monks.

The official said that, "1,545 young monks are currently studying in such classes."

Dulongzhuang, a 28-year-old senior monk in one monastery, said that nine of the 29 monks in his monastery are studying in a Buddhist school.

He added, "The young monks here get up at 7 in the morning and study the Dai language and read the sutras from 8 to 10. Then they go back home to help their families with the farming or do some homework. Those who attend normal classes stay at school during the day and continue with their reading of the sutras into the evening."

But the monk's life is not quite as austere as one might imagine. They may watch TV, go to cinemas, and play sports.

"Although traditional Buddhist taboos prohibited monks from dancing, singing, and playing musical instruments in monasteries, these rules are no longer so strictly observed here," Du said.

When school-age children first practice Buddhism as monks in monasteries, they are called "monks-in-training." They can become true monks only after they are able to recite at least 23 articles from the sutras.

Document 35

Well-Trained Buddhist Nuns

By Ren Ci, in Ming Bao, Hongkong, 6 May 1986. Translated by *Donald MacInnis.*

In the Ten Thousand Rocks Park, covered by the shadows of green trees, a group of two or three nuns in gray Buddhist habits can occasionally be seen strolling around. They are the first generation of fully trained Buddhist nuns ever to study in Amoy.

The South Fujian Buddhist Institute is located where the Venerable Hung Yi taught seventy-four students sixty years ago in the Nanputuo Temple. After five years of hard novice life twenty persons were graduated in 1930. Between 1938 and 1945 a second group of twenty students was enrolled, but most of them were secularized and became teachers, doctors, and workers; some became lay Buddhists [*jushi*]; a few went to Taiwan, where they remain today.

The South China Buddhist Institute and the Wuchang Buddhist Institute were formerly the highest level Buddhist schools in China.

In 1980, at the National Buddhist Representatives Conference, many delegates advocated restoring the South Fujian Buddhist Institute. Zhao Puchu, President of the Chinese Buddhist Association, personally inscribed the dedication board for the school, and the government allocated 500,000 *yuan* for restoration funds. In May last year, the school officially opened and accepted eighty students from all over China, of whom forty were women. This is the first time the South Fujian Buddhist Institute has accepted women students.

The 80 students are divided into two classes, one for men and the other for women. The men's section attends classes in the Nanputuo Temple, while the women study in the Ten Thousand Rocks Temple, quite far from the men's section. After a half year of trial, the number of students has grown to 145; the women students in particular have increased by half to over 60, a truly unprecedented growth.

These sixty women come from every part of China, recommended for study by local Buddhists. The oldest is thirty years old and the youngest is eighteen; all have shaved heads. Since they wear clothing similar to the men students, it is difficult to distinguish women from men, but their conduct is gentle and proper. If they complete six years of study they are then free to find their own work.

If asked why they converted to Buddhism, they all reply, "for salvation from bitterness and hardship" [*jiu ku jiu nan*] and that they are willing to "enter hell." Judging from their own devout manner, it seems that this answer is the truth.

One whose home is in Jilin, in the northeast, a graduate of junior middle school, was introduced to the South Fujian Buddhist Institute by the Buddhist Association of Jiangxi after taking her novice vows in the town of Shicheng. She is determined to study Buddhist law and doctrine until she has mastered it.

Each day these nuns arise at 4:00 A.M. to recite the scriptures and to do their studies, eating breakfast at 6:00 A.M. After eating breakfast, they care for their personal hygiene and then attend two class sessions in Buddhist history and Buddhist scriptures, as well as Chinese language, history, etc., taught by senior scholars and monks from Shanghai, Beijing, and other places. At 4:00 in the afternoon they recite scriptures for an hour and at 5:30 eat supper. Each one is free to choose her evening activities, such as reciting scriptures and studying. After this period of free time, at the sound of the 9:30 bell, each one must spend one hour in silent meditation, with no limitation on meditation time if they wish to extend.

There is no cost to the novice nuns for their food and clothing, for it is provided by the school; in addition each student receives 10 *yuan* a month for personal expenses, which they say is sufficient. Besides the funding provided by the government, a portion of the expenses of the Institute are contributed by the Venerable Hung Quan, the head of the Singapore Buddhist Association.

These novice nuns are not allowed to go outside the school or to walk in the streets alone. On occasion they are permitted to take walks together in the hills, but only in groups of two or more; this probably is to "avoid the unexpected."

The students all wear a round orange badge commemorating the opening of the Buddhist Institute. In the center is a wheel like the wheel of a ship, which symbolizes the endless revolutions of the Buddhist dharma.

Document 36

Buddhist Institute Trains Nuns

By Sha Qing, China Daily, *14 January 1986.*

In the secluded meditation rooms behind the high vermillion walls of Sichuan's Tiexiang Temple, 37 young women aged 20 to 25 commit themselves to the esoteric study of Buddhism.

About seven kilometers from Chengdu City, the Tiexiang temple in 1964 became the Bhiksunis (Nun) Buddhist Institute, the first school of higher education for nuns in China. Venerable Bhiksuni Long Lian, a Buddhist nun, is its head.

Long Lian comes from a rich Sichuan family. In the 1930s she could have gained a rewarding position in the local government; instead she became a nun to escape what she perceived as the corruption in the official-dom.

Long Lian spent decades studying the Tibetan language, English, medicine, poetry and painting. She holds practical views on Buddhism.

"Buddhists should have the opportunity to study their religion," she said. "But there has never before been an institute, although plans for one existed for a long time."

When the institute was set up, it received over one thousand applications for admission from eight provinces. On the principle of putting quality before quantity, only 37 students were accepted, mainly from Zhejiang and Henan.

The applicants first prostrated themselves before Buddhist nuns in their local temples before undergoing the head-shaving ceremony. The most promising were recommended by the local temples to the institute, and the final admissions decided by the institute on the basis of their test scores.

"We accept students no younger than 18 because only at this age are they able to decide their own future," said Long Lian. "Their parents must also give permission."

Like universities, the institute offers four years of academic study. Buddhism, its history, religious cultivation, Chinese and English are part of the course.

Long Lian and a venerable nun from another temple teach Buddhist monastic disciplines. Teachers invited from universities take the other classes. The regimen is not an easy one for the young nuns with only a middle- or high-school education.

The Tiexiang Temple was built in the Ming Dynasty, occupying an area of about seven hectares. The rooms adjoining its east side are used for classes and religious rites. A two-storey building at the back of the temple courtyard is set aside for meditation.

Students usually spend four hours a day in class and the rest of the time is meditation.

Also used for dining, a room for offering sacrifices is next to the class-room.

"There is no ceremony before breakfast," explained Xu Ping, vice-chair-woman of the institute.

But lunch is different. With bowls in hand, students enter the dining room in line. After eating, students must recite scriptures before leaving. All abstain from meat, according to Buddhist discipline.

Each is paid a monthly 20 *yuan* by the Government. Strictly speaking, Buddhists should not take a meal after noon. But the institute thought this might affect the young students' health, so three meals are offered daily.

The meditation rooms double as the students' bedrooms — each shared by four people. Big wooden beds, which students also use for sitting in meditation, have been specially made.

Five hundred disciplines control the students' everyday life. According to rule, their smiles disappear, their eyes are cast downward and they step aside when they encounter a stranger.

Students are allowed to visit town on Sundays but only in pairs. TV is approved for broadening knowledge, but the programmes are "screened" first. Music violates the rule of controlling one's desires, and so is forbidden.

China's many temples need well-educated Buddhist monks and nuns and Buddhism research needs to be improved, said Long Lian. Students from the institute are expected to shoulder that task in the future.

Document 37

800 Monks and Nuns Ordained in Nanhua Temple

By Kathy Chan, Hong Kong Standard, *18 June 1988.*

It was one of the biggest Buddhist ordination ceremonies in post-Mao China. At the end of fifteen days' rites almost 800 men and women were ordained as full monks and nuns in southern China's famed Nanhua Temple some 250 km north of Guangzhou.

But to some of the participants it was something more than mere ritual. For the two officiating senior monks — Abbot Sik Benhuan, eighty-one, and Abbot Jy-din Sakya, seventy-one — it was homecoming to one of the original centers of Chan Buddhism, better known to the world now as Zen. The two abbots had been away for more than forty years.

For American nun Sik Chuanyuan, the former Emma Barrows, fifty-four, it was fulfillment in the final search for the meaning of life.

For Jipu, the forty-three-year-old Shaolin monk, it was fulfillment of another kind — accepting the teachings of Buddha and taking the vows as a prelude to setting up a full-blown Shaolin school of boxing southwest in China.

For many of the others it was the final restoration of Buddhism in its own right after almost forty years of devastation and tight government control.

Or was it?

Day after day the air was thick with incense smoke and the cloying smell of joss. Temple bells rang intermittently. Novices, monks, nuns, and laypersons chanted sutras from dawn to late afternoon.

The uninitiated might find nothing amiss. Especially at the sight of so many young people taking the vows, contrary to reports that only older people are allowed to get so deeply into religion.

But this ought to have been a fifty-three-day ritual. The official explanation for cutting it down to a mere fifteen days is the high cost of feeding so many people — 1,500 *yuan* (HK$3,000) a day.

Traditional Chinese Buddhism requires monks and nuns to have their shaven heads burned by lighted joss-sticks. This is frowned upon by the authorities and has been done away with by the faith. Nevertheless, some of the participants insisted on it and were accordingly scarred.

The fifty-three-day ritual would have allowed the novices to be properly trained in the rites and right behavior. Truncating the whole ceremony had telling effects — many fumbled, forgot table "manners" or fudged their lines. Instead of ten days' training on table etiquette, they had only thirty minutes.

Where there should have been solemnity and dignified chanting, there was now spitting, coughing, neck scratching, shrugging, and yawning all through the rituals.

The cross-shaped complex, on the bank of the Cao Xi and nestling at the foot of a range of hills to the north, is a hygienist's nightmare. Monks, nuns, and laypeople fell ill.

But the faithful preferred not to blame the environment. The sick, they said, were being "punished by the above." A senior monk explained: "Before they are ordained, it is inevitable that some of the novices will disturb the spirits who hang around at such a time to recover debts incurred in previous lives. These debts must be recovered before the novices are fully ordained and come under the protection of the gods."

Whatever the gods and the authorities had in store, most of the novices struggled bravely through their *samanera* and *samaneri* (matriculation rites) in little groups before moving on to the advanced rites of *bhikshu* and *bhikshuni*. Nobody failed.

Then, with the laymen in one big assembly, they chanted and bowed through final *boddhisattva* rituals—the final affirmation of their vows.

It was a colorful affair, without the solemnity which usually accompanies such ceremonies.

Happy Homecoming Tinged with Some Sadness

There couldn't have been a more solicitous monk. Each time Nanhua's abbot, Weiyin, seventy-five, looks ill, Li Zhizhen runs for the doctor. As he did just before the ordination ceremony began.

There also couldn't have been a more repentant man at Nanhua. "I have been a bad monk. Now I want to do something good for the temple and for Abbot Weiyin for the rest of my life," Mr. Li once told the ailing abbot.

But behind his back during the two-week ritual, monks were pointing him out to visitors as "the traitor" and "the government agent."

Although no longer a monk and merely a lay administrator at Nanhua— officially deputy director of the administrative committee—there was no doubt that everyone deferred to him. Right down to one monk getting his permission to take visiting newsmen around the sprawling complex.

As the senior monks tell it, Li, fifty-five, was an orphan of Jiangsu who was cared for by the monks and took to the monastic life at the age of six. At eighteen he found his way to Nanhua, whose fame had spread to all corners of China over the centuries.

"He is a very intelligent man," said one of the senior monks with the barest hint of irony.

"When Mao Zedong ordered the purge of temples in the late 1950s, he and another young monk took the initiative to purge Nanhua.

"Abbot Benhuan was sent to a labor camp. Our present abbot [Weiyin] was tied to a tree and beaten with a big bamboo stick," the monk recalled.

Today, the abbot is a mere walking skeleton, paralyzed on the left side for much of last year.

That campaign against Buddhism led to massive confiscation of temple lands all over the country and the dispatch of thousands of monks and nuns to labor camps. Many were subsequently made to unfrock, and puppet monks were put in charge of temples.

Li, too, was defrocked. Then he was appointed to run the temple, got married, and fathered three children.

Li himself claims a leading role in the "cleanup" of the temple during the "cultural revolution."

"Nanhua escaped being ravaged by the Red Guards. We carried out our own self-criticisms first.

"We wrote big-character posters and put them up on the doors. Then we sealed the temple. The Red Guards came and were satisfied with our self-criticisms. They left us alone."

Li says the whole complex is now under the full control of Abbot Weiyin but sees an important role for himself because "the new people" are not versed in the rituals.

"I learnt from this temple, now I can repay it by teaching others. In this way I can also repent for the wrongs I have done," he said.

But one visiting nun was told by a senior monk that "things are not what they seem to be." The monk added: "Everyone is being closely watched, and not every monk is a real monk."

Before 1949 Nanhua reputedly had three hundred monks and nuns. Its reputation rested on having been home to Huineng, the sixth patriarch of Chan (Zen) Buddhism and the first Chinese monk to attain this rank. All the five previous patriarchs had been Indians.

Huineng preached here for 37 years from 677 AD, just over 170 years after an Indian monk had built the first of nine temples in this complex.

Huineng died here and his embalmed body is still on display in one of the main shrine halls. Huineng had forty-three disciples, who carried Chan to Japan, Thailand, Europe, and North America, where it is now better known as Zen.

Nanhua maintained its tradition as one of the great centers of Buddhist learning until the Communists came to power. But a year before this happened, acting Abbot Jy-din Sakya, then a strapping thirty-one-year-old, was ordered to leave by his master, Xuyun.

Abbot Jy-din came from one of Guangdong's wealthiest families. He was to have joined the newly founded Huangpu Military School, founded by Sun Yat-sen, run by Chiang Kai-shek with Zhou En-lai as its political commissar.

He became a monk instead. With the approach of the Communist armies and his family's prominence, it was thought he would be safer elsewhere.

"Master Xuyun was right. The Communists began to look for me once they came to Guangdong because I had friends among the Kuomintang people," the abbot said.

But he was safely away in Hawaii, his place as head of Nanhua taken over by Abbot Sik Benhuan, who stayed ten years before being sent to a labor camp.

But Abbot Benhuan apparently bears no grudges against the communists. He says: "The period in the labor camp was a consequence of wrongs I did in my previous lives."

Abbot Benhuan spent about eighteen years in labor camps. But he kept the faith. Though forbidden to perform religious duties, he and other monks kept up with their meditations. With a smile, he said: "Who can stop your mind from thinking and working?"

Section IV

Economic Self-Support for Temples and Monasteries

Introduction

Judging by the numerous articles in Chinese newspapers, journals, and books describing the self-support enterprises of Buddhist temples and monasteries, such ventures have been given high priority. Indeed, the concept of "Three-Self" autonomy for all religions is set forth in several documents elsewhere in this work. Unlike the Christian churches, which were dependent for much of their operating expenses on contributions from foreign mission societies, the Buddhist temples and monasteries received very little aid from abroad, and this only in the form of donations by visiting overseas Chinese. That is still an important source of funds, judging by the lists of donors and their generous donations posted in some of the temples visited in 1988; but the approved way is for "each temple to support itself" and "All monks should take part in productive labor," a statement by Zhao Puchu, President of the Chinese Buddhist Association at the thirtieth anniversary celebration of its founding (Document 38).

Why should temples and monasteries be self-supporting, and monks and nuns take part in manual labor? The reasons given are both pragmatic and ideological, although the latter is not stressed now as it was in the 1950s, when all monks and nuns were assigned to manual-labor projects. Certainly, these writers say, they should work like everyone else, but in reality, if they don't organize self-support projects, they won't be able to keep the temples and monasteries open. The extensive farmland once owned by most temples and monasteries which provided their basic food and income has been largely taken over by other units, and the number of able-bodied monks and nuns is greatly reduced. As a result, if they are not famous places visited by many tourists who patronize their shops and make generous donations, they are forced to set up profit-making enterprises.

Many of these are described in the section on self-support projects in Fujian Province. These include handicrafts and manufacturing, like hand-weaving, sewing, bookbinding, boxmaking, ropemaking and a brick and tile works.

A second category is agricultural: growing rice, vegetables, fruit trees, tea plants, medicinal herbs, peanuts, timber, and bamboo.

Another source of income is the sale of incense and paper money burned as prayer offerings, fees for services of crematoriums and cineraria (places for permanent storage of ashes resulting from cremations), and other religious services.

Finally, tourist services are a major source of income for well-known temples and monasteries. In addition to income from gate tickets, many temples and monasteries operate hostels, vegetarian restaurants, soft-drink and ice-cream shops, tea stalls, photo shops, and book and souvenir shops. Those in remote locations which attract few visitors are at a real disadvantage, which can be seen by comparing income figures for 1983.

The Zhiti Temple, with 40 *mu* of cultivated land and 45 monks, had an annual income of 15,000 *yuan*, which allowed 21 *yuan* per month for personal expenses of each monk. The Jinbei Temple, with eight *mu* of land and six monks and nuns, earned 16,000 *yuan*, giving each person 12 *yuan* per month. The Pingxingcan Temple with 29 *mu* of land and 21 monks and nuns (only twelve able to work), earned only 5,811 *yuan*, providing six to ten *yuan* to each worker per month. In contrast, the famous Puquan Temple near Fuzhou, with only eleven *mu* of cultivated land, netted 383,939 *yuan* in 1983, largely from tourist services, giving 30 to 40 *yuan* each month to the monks, while Nanputuo Temple in Xiamen, another famous place, was able to pay 70 *yuan* to each monk, with additional bonuses, and 50 *yuan* a month to novices (seminarians).

An interesting insight into ways in which religion must adapt to its sociopolitical environment is found in a section of Document 39, "Insecticides Conflict with Buddhist Teaching." In a certain county the monks and nuns were unwilling to use insecticides because they believed it would be killing living beings, contravening Buddhist teachings. After studying scientific books and discussing the question among themselves, they agreed that harmful insects are like evil persons and, therefore, could be destroyed. As a result of using insecticides, their harvest exceeded their neighbors'.

What are the benefits of these economic enterprises of the temples and monasteries? The Shanghai researchers conclude that, first, they carry on the fine Buddhist tradition of manual labor. Monks and nuns were long accustomed to tilling fields and doing manual labor, but they got away from that, relying on alms and fees for such religious ceremonies as "making their living from the dead," offering prayers for a tranquil afterlife, and telling fortunes.

Second, clergy participation in such projects sets the proper direction for Buddhism under socialism: "Nonworkers do not eat."

Third, by promoting self-support, the government is relieved of providing subsidies, and heavy demands are not made on the faithful, taking money away from economic investment.

Fourth, the income generated from the projects is used to repair and preserve such cultural antiquities as ancient and famous temples and monasteries.

Finally, some of these projects, such as one that makes a brand-name fruit juice, which is sold widely in the region, contribute to the gross national product and to the four modernizations.

Document 38

All Monks Should Take Part in Productive Labor

*Statement of Zhao Puchu to the Chinese Buddhist Association,
October 1983. Translated in China Study Project* Documentation
No. 13, March 1984, p. 32.

"All able-bodied monks and nuns, in cities or countryside, should participate in productive labor."

Zhao Puchu, President of the Buddhist Association of China, made this statement here this week at a national Buddhist congress in celebration of the thirteenth anniversary of the founding of the Association.

In temples where religious activities had been resumed, he said, monks and nuns should be encouraged to become self-supporting and run temple affairs with offerings at religious services and through productive labor.

The noted scholar said that Chinese Buddhists had the tradition of engaging in agriculture, afforestation, building bridges and roads, and offering services in education, medicine, and social welfare.

"In the early 1950s, many Buddhists and Buddhist organizations won social respect for their achievements in these fields," he said.

"In line with the Buddhist teaching 'repaying the favor of the country and all living beings,' all Buddhists should make greater contributions to temple management, religious activities, training talented Buddhists, publishing Buddhist books and periodicals, doing research in Buddhism and helping China's reunification and international exchanges," he said.

He also called on all local branches of the Association to represent the interests of Buddhists and reflect their opinions and suggestions to the Party and government, as well as educating them to observe the laws and decrees of the country.

Document 39

A Survey of the Productive-Labor Projects of Buddhist Monasteries and Temples in Fujian Province

In Religious Questions under Socialism in China *(Shanghai Academy of Social Sciences), 1987, pp. 188-99. Translated by Zheng Xi'an and Donald MacInnis.*

In April and May of 1984 we conducted field research on Buddhist activities in Fujian province; this essay is a systematic report of those investigations.

Before the "cultural revolution" there was already a tradition in Fujian province of monks and nuns working for income-producing projects belonging to the temples and monasteries. For example, the Buddhist Association of Fuzhou had already developed textile weaving, bamboo crafts, sewing, metalwork, bookbinding, paper-box making, ropemaking, etc.— eight handicraft factories with over five hundred Buddhist workers, including monks and nuns, and men and women believers. Their productivity was excellent.

The temples and monasteries in the suburban districts near the city had organized farming work for the monks and nuns; they raised rice and vegetables, established fruit orchards and tea plantations, and raised medicinal herbs, etc., with the goal of economic self-sufficiency. Other temples and monasteries in the mountain areas also carried on agricultural production with good results.

During the ten years of turmoil all was ruined, the factories were moved away, and agricultural production ceased. After the Third Plenary Session of the Eleventh Central Committeee of the CCP, the current religious policy was gradually put into effect. When the provincial religious-work units and the Buddhist Association restored religious activities, they also set up a variety of productive-labor projects for monks and nuns in monasteries and temples, each one adapted to the particular local situation. This was done in the tradition and spirit of "one day without working means one day without food."

Now, aside from a minority of temples and monasteries that have established rice mills, sewing units, incense factories, etc., and some newly opened handicraft work, the most important projects are in agriculture and services. The temples and monasteries in the mountain districts all have projects for expanding agricultural production, such as rice, peanuts, yellow beans, vegetables, orchards, tea plantations, medicinal herbs, tea-oil plants, timber, and so on.

The temples and monasteries in urban or tourist areas operate various kinds of service projects staffed by monks and nuns, such as hostels, small shops, restaurants, tea stalls, photo shops, etc. Now, with their well-managed productive-labor projects, most of the temples and monasteries in the province are able to "use the monastery to support the monastery." Some raise more food than they need for themselves. Some have surplus income beyond their living costs. Some allocate extra funds from their production projects to repair temple and monastery buildings. Many of the monks and nuns have a new self-image and a new spirit. They are proud that they are "self-supporting workers" and that they make a contribution to the "four modernizations" of our country. The situation and the experiences of the monks and nuns who take part in productive labor in this province are described below.

An Overview of Productive-Labor Projects of Monks and Nuns in Buddhist Temples and Monasteries in Fujian Province

Monks and nuns in temples and monasteries in the mountain districts of Fujian province have the best record in production. These temples and monasteries are located in the mountain districts quite far from the cities, so not many Buddhists go there to worship, and contributions from overseas Buddhists are small. To put it another way, they do not chiefly rely on selling incense and charging fees to support their livelihood; rather, they solve the problem of self-support through productive labor. Most of these temples and monasteries are self-sustaining, not only in food, but also in their other expenses. The living allowance of the monks and nuns is going up, and the agricultural output of some temples and monasteries exceeds that of the average farmer or production brigade of that region.

Some of the tea plantations, forests, and orchards operated by neighboring units, brigades and communes over a period of years were not well managed and were not doing well. When they were given over to the Buddhist monks and nuns to manage, production increased greatly, so people's communes in several other districts contracted their fields and orchards to the temples and monasteries, often with excellent results. Some of these are described below.

THE BUDDHIST ANYANG YUAN [RETIREMENT HOME] OF THE CHONGFU TEMPLE IN FUZHOU CITY

The sixty-five elderly nuns living in this retirement home can be divided into three categories. One group consists of those who are no longer able-bodied but are cared for by the temple. There are forty-five of these. There are ten in the second group, those who work as service personnel, taking care of the general work in the temple and caring for the daily needs of the old people. Ten other persons make up the third group, those who take part in productive labor, operating the crematorium, placing the ashes in repose, and raising rice and vegetables.

Altogether the temple has ten *mu* of land. In 1983 they planted 8.5 *mu* in rice and harvested 13,000 *jin* of rice, averaging 1500 *jin* per *mu*. Two *mu* of vegetables provided all the food they needed. In addition they have three crematoria and one ossarium. Their entire income for 1981 was 24,190 *yuan*: 4,390 from agricultural production, 16,800 from the crematoria and ossarium, and 3,000 from admission fees. They had a surplus after total expenditures of 22,590 *yuan*, which included the living allowances for the elderly nuns, wages for the service personnel, medical expenses, and other costs.

The temple and monastery take full responsibility for the elderly nuns living in the retirement home, including food, lodging (each person has a small room), medical care, and a living allowance beyond their own resources (each person receives eight *yuan* a month from the people's government for the "five guarantees"). [The "five guarantees" pledged by the government for all elderly persons: food, lodging, clothing, medical care, and burial.] The temple itself provides 18 *yuan* for personal allowance, plus 21 *yuan* for food and 5 *yuan* for miscellaneous expenses. The service personnel receive from 35 to 40 *yuan* a month. Those who work in production projects are paid according to their labor, each person averaging over 50 *yuan* a month. This temple has earned a surplus beyond its own needs since 1981.

ZHITI TEMPLE, NINGDE XIAN

This temple, located on a high mountain, now has forty-four monks. Formerly, monks had a hard life there, often resorting to sweet potatoes [rather than rice] for their main food. In recent years they have opened up new farming land and tried various enterprises which have brought big improvements in their livelihood.

They now have forty *mu* of agricultural land on which they raise rice, manage forests, and cultivate tea plantations, herb gardens, and other crops. They have built a power plant to generate electricity for their enterprises and lighting for their personal needs. They harvested over 30,000 *jin* of rice in 1983, including more than 2,000 *jin* given over to the government as their grain quota. Added to that was over 15,000 *yuan* income from tea, medicinal herbs and other products.

In addition to their room and board, each monk received an average of 21 *yuan* per month. Because their production and management was done so well, they received special commendation from the provincial Buddhist Association and other units.

JINBEI TEMPLE, NINGDE XIAN

This temple, with four monks and two nuns, has plans to expand to ten persons. Because they have only a little over 8 *mu* of land they planted

1,200,000 tea plants in 1980 with the goal of self-support. In 1981 their income from the sale of tea was 14,000 *yuan*. Added to this was income from jasmine flowers, vegetables, and over 5,000 *jin* of rice. In 1983 the total income was over 16,000 *yuan*. They are now expanding production by planting two million tea plants, with plans for five million more next year. They also have plans to replant five *mu* of higher altitude tea land in bamboo, jasmine, oil vegetables, and fir trees, aiming for a target income of 10,000 *yuan* per year. Because their production work has been done so well, they have received high praise from local religious work units and the Buddhist Association.

While their work in agriculture has been profitable, they also have a very fine spirit. Refusing to use the money for themselves, the monks and nuns hold to a simple life-style. Aside from their food and clothing, which is provided by the temple, each person receives only twelve *yuan* a month for personal use. They are admired for contributing most of their surplus income for repairing temples and monasteries and preserving famous ancient buildings. Moreover, in addition to earning income from tea production for their own needs, they are contributing to our nation's total output of tea for export, so the local tea administration gave them 3,750 *yuan* for help in expanding their tea production this year. . . .

PINGXINGCAN MONASTERY, FUDING COUNTY

This is a newly built monastery which had been the Pingjiang Buddhist Tea Plantation. They now have sixteen monks and five nuns, most of them elderly. Among them only five are between the ages of eighteen and thirty, with fourteen between fifty and seventy and two over seventy. Only five are fully able-bodied, seven semi-able-bodied, and the rest are unable to do any manual labor. They have 14 *mu* of agricultural land, including 3.3 *mu* planted in paddy rice and fifteen in sweet potatoes. In addition there are tea plantations, forests, and fields planted to yellow beans, turnips, rape, ginseng, tea, vegetables, etc. They now are self-sufficient in grain and vegetables. In 1983 their total income was 5,811 *yuan*, 90.5 percent of that, or 5,511 *yuan*, coming from farm production.

In addition to their food, the monks and nuns receive 72 to 120 *yuan* per year for their labor. Their standard of living is not high, but they have enough for building and repairs, because the monks and nuns insisted that they would not accept their share of the temple's total income for the last three years. This kind of spirit of enduring hardship in order to start new enterprises has been praised by Buddhist circles. . . .

Some monasteries and temples that lack cropland have become tourist areas, and have organized the clergy to provide services for visitors. The Puquan Temple at Gushan, Fuzhou, and Nanputuoshan Temple in Xiamen have been particularly successful in such ventures.

YONGQUAN TEMPLE ON GUSHAN [DRUM MOUNTAIN], FUZHOU

There are about sixty monks at this temple. Since cropland is limited, they cannot expand crop production beyond what is now planted. Land now cultivated includes 3 *mu* of paddy rice, 6 *mu* of vegetables, 8 *mu* of fruit trees, and a few other smaller crops. The priority now is to meet the needs of visitors, with such service enterprises as restaurants, cold drink shops, service shops, etc. Income from these enterprises for 1982 and 1983 was 383,939 *yuan*, sufficient to provide for the basic needs of the temple without outside financial help. Each monk received from 30 to 40 *yuan* a month living expenses.

NANPUTUOSHAN TEMPLE, XIAMEN

There are about fifty clergy at the Nanputuo Temple at present, ten of them veterans (including some with responsibilities in general affairs in the temple enterprises), and thirty-seven novices enrolled in seminary studies. In addition there are over seventy laypersons who come from outside as day workers.

The general-services section is organized into two departments: one includes the larger collective enterprises, the vegetarian restaurant, small bookshop, photography shop, etc. The services section receives income from selling entrance tickets, guest hostel fees, offerings for incense, and contributions. Monks who work in service projects receive an average pay of 50 to 70 *yuan* a month, with additional bonuses and other benefits such as retirement pay. Monthly income from the enterprises averages about 4,000 *yuan* for entrance tickets and over 4,000 *yuan* for incense offerings.

The living expenses for seminarians come from these sources. In addition to receiving their clothing and bedding, seminarians receive a monthly personal allowance of 30 *yuan*, but when contributions from overseas Chinese Buddhists are added, the average rises to about 50 *yuan* a month.

At present, aside from the wages and personal allowances of monks and workers, the main expense is for repairs to the temples and monasteries, and for regilding the Buddhist statues. After these expenses, there is still a surplus, making this one of the wealthier temples in Fujian. . . .

INSECTICIDES CONFLICT WITH BUDDHIST TEACHING

In Ningde County there were some temples and monasteries which raised paddy rice using methods that were better than the neighboring production brigade's, but their harvest was no better, because the monks and nuns were unwilling to use insecticides. They believed they would be killing living beings, and thereby contravening the Buddhist commandments. After the religious affairs cadres of the county had convened a number of meetings, distributed scientific books and materials, started classes in scientific agriculture, and showed films on the use of insecticides and pesticides, they took the monks and nuns to see the good harvests of farmers who used pesticides. After seeing with their own eyes the actual results of using pesticides, they realized this was the way to increase their crop yields. They discussed the question "Is it really taking life to use pesticides against insects? Is it really against the teachings of Buddhism?"

After these discussions, they all agreed that harmful insects are like evil persons, and it is not contrary to Buddhist commandments to destroy them; so they gave up the idea that killing insects is taking life. This year the monks and nuns in Ningde County agreed unanimously to use insecticides and to follow scientific methods of cultivation, with the result that their harvest is larger than that of their neighbors. ...

Benefits Resulting from Economic-Production Projects of Temples and Monasteries

Productive labor by monks and nuns fits in with the demands of the times. It is in the fine tradition of Buddhism, it helps carry out the spirit of "the monastery supports the monastery," it allows monks and nuns to be self-sufficient in food, it helps protect our country's historical sites, and it contributes to the "four modernizations." This is the direction to go and the road to take for Buddhism during the period of Socialism in China.

CARRY ON THE FINE BUDDHIST TRADITIONS

It is traditional in China for monks and nuns to engage in productive labor. Early in the Jin Dynasty monks were engaged in farming. After the Tang Dynasty, the Baizhang Sect of Chan Buddhism established the "Hundred Rules," which made it clear that "one day without work means one day without food." Since then, monks and nuns, following this fine Buddhist tradition, have engaged in productive labor. Because the vast majority of Buddhist monks and nuns throughout history have believed and accepted this, they have happily taken part in productive labor.

The reaction of monks and nuns in Ningde County is an example. They say, formerly we did not do much actual productive labor; instead, we relied on donations from Buddhist laypersons and from fees for Buddhist religious rites, with the result that we were never free from [economic] anxiety, and people looked down on us. Even worse, we were not observing Buddhist tradition, because we had forgotten it. Now, by engaging in productive labor, we have revived this fine Buddhist tradition, changing the opinion of the general public toward us, and achieving what we had really hoped for.

SET THE DIRECTION FOR THE DEVELOPMENT OF BUDDHISM UNDER SOCIALIST CONDITIONS

Despite the Buddhist tradition of monks and nuns taking part in economic production, from the Ming and Qing Dynasties onward, Buddhism went into a decline, and monks and nuns "made their living from the dead," offering prayers for a tranquil afterlife, telling fortunes and gradually separating themselves from productive labor.

Prior to Liberation, most monks and nuns did very little productive labor. After Liberation, during the nationwide land-reform movement, monks and nuns were also allocated cropland. Many of them began to work the land

and became self-supporting workers who raised their own food. From this experience onward, monks and nuns have taken part in economic production, thus setting the direction for the future development of Buddhism, while at the same time responding to the demands of society under Socialism. "Nonworkers do not eat," is a policy of Socialism. Monks and nuns are citizens like everyone else, and therefore must adhere to this policy, which is also in full accord with the Buddhist tradition that "one day without work means one day without food." This, then, should be the direction for the development of Buddhism, for it suits both the demands of our times and the teachings of Buddhism.

EARN ONE'S OWN LIVING, USE THE MONASTERY TO SUPPORT THE MONASTERY, AND LIGHTEN THE BURDEN OF OUR COUNTRY

Another step in carrying out the policy of freedom of religious belief is to open some Buddhist temples and monasteries so that Buddhists can have places to resume their regular religious activities. Units related to this matter have already said that reopened temples and monasteries should be self-supporting. In order to do this right, the monks and nuns should take part in productive labor. In this spirit, Fujian Province has called on all monks and nuns, to the extent of their physical health and strength, to engage in productive labor, with significant results. At present the basic condition for each temple and monastery in the province is "use the monastery to support the monastery."

Ningde County, where most of the monks and nuns are earning more than enough for their own personal needs, is a good example. Not only are the working monks and nuns earning enough for a good living standard for themselves, they are also supporting their elderly colleagues who cannot work, thus relieving society of this burden.

The Chongfu Temple in Fuzhou also has well-managed projects that support forty-five elderly monks and nuns in the retirement home whose final years can now be lived in tranquillity.

PRESERVE HISTORICAL ANTIQUITIES AND CONTRIBUTE TO THE "FOUR MODERNIZATIONS"

Aside from providing for their own livelihood by productive labor, monks and nuns in Fujian province use their surplus income to preserve antiquities by repairing and restoring temples and monasteries, many with long histories. For example, construction began on the Zhiti Temple in Ningde County in the year 862 A.D. near the end of the Tang Dynasty, and was completed more than a thousand years ago in the year 971 A.D. during the Song Dynasty.

Temples and monasteries in Fuqing County, such as the Chaoming Temple and pagoda, are nearly one thousand years old, tracing back to the Southern and Northern Liang Dynasties. These ancient buildings had been in disrepair for many years, and suffered additional damage during the "great proletarian cultural revolution," when most of the Buddhist statues disappeared. If repairs had not been made soon, there was danger that the remaining precious antiquities would disappear forever. But now those temples and monasteries with well-run economic enterprises are taking some of their earnings to repair the buildings and to replace the missing Buddhist statues. This has already brought significant results in the overall preservation of the cultural antiquities of our country.

In addition, temples and monasteries with well-run economic projects contribute to the "four modernizations." Many of them have planted orchards for the production of fruit juice, which adds to our country's exports. The monks of Jinbei Temple have planted many fruit trees in order to increase their production of fruit juice. The grain, fruit juice, and medicinal herbs sold by the monks of Zhiti Temple each year are worth 5-6,000 *yuan*, which is a significant contribution ["adding bricks and tiles"] to the "four modernizations."

Remaining Problems

There are still some problems with regard to the economic-production projects of temples and monasteries in Fujian Province.

1. The expansion of economic productivity of some temples and monasteries is limited by the fact that only a portion of their occupied land has been returned to them, and they do not have sufficient cropland.

2. Some of the new monks and nuns fear hardship and fear manual labor [*pa chiku, pa laodong*]. They would rather roam around than stay in one place and work. Some of them openly say that they are unwilling to work, and prefer to travel and stay at big temples and monasteries.

3. The problem of recruits [new religious personnel] must be solved. Most temples and monasteries do not have enough monks and nuns. In some of them, most of the religious personnel are elderly and unable to work. As a result, the morale of the able-bodied monks and nuns suffers, because they feel that they aren't able by themselves to support their elderly colleagues.

4. How can temples and monasteries that are tourist attractions or are located near big cities, and have utilized the advantages of their location to open up money-earning projects, change the current situation in which they rely on income from selling incense and from contributions by visitors?

Section V

Buddhism in Tibet

Introduction

While it is difficult to separate religion from politics in Tibet, a one-time theocratic state now known as the Tibetan Autonomous Region of China, this section will focus on religion. After the clashes between Tibetans and government forces in Lhasa in March 1988, when 300 monks and nuns were reported arrested, access by foreign visitors was tightened. Unable to make arrangements from Hongkong in August, I flew to Chengdu on a chance, where, after a few days' delay, I was able to book a five-day visit and confined my stay to Lhasa. Aside from personal observations and a conversation with the acting *ahong* at the Muslim mosque (the chief *ahong* was on pilgrimage to Mecca), my main source of information was the head of the Center for Religious Research at the Academy of Social Sciences, Mr. Tseten Lhundop, thirty-eight. By mutual agreement, we limited our discussion to religion.

Published statistics on Buddhism in Tibet today vary so widely that all are suspect. Mr. Tseten Lhundop gave me no precise statistics, saying they are still preparing them, but suggested a figure of as many as 10,000 monks, including novices, in Tibet today. He said that official government figures for 1959 give the following numbers for the three major temples, but that, in fact, they had as many as 10,000 in each at that time: Drepung, 7,700, Sera, 5,500, and Ganden, 3,300.

Edward Gargan, writing for the *New York Times* on 14 June 1987, was told by an old monk that there were more than 3,000 monks at the Ganden Monastery before the 1959 uprising, sometimes as many as 5,000 when the Dalai Lama came. The Ganden complex, with its scores of buildings, was dynamited and completely demolished in the 1960s by the Chinese, writes Gargan. Today, I was told, 300 monks and many volunteers from the laity who give days and weeks at a time are slowly rebuilding this, the holiest place of the Gelukpa sect.

Gargan says there were 6,254 monasteries in Tibet in 1951, and that now all but a handful lie in ruins. Fox Butterfield, writing in the *Times* on 11 October 1987, says there were 3,500 temples and monasteries, and that all but a dozen were destroyed by youthful Red Guards brought in from other provinces of China.

In 1987 testimony during the hearings of the United States Congress on human rights violations in Tibet, William B. Kerr, an American medical doctor who had made an extended visit to Tibet earlier that year, said that "all of the rural monasteries we saw were mere fragments of bombed-out buildings. . . . The total destruction of the vast majority of Tibet's monasteries has led to the irreplaceable loss of the majority of Tibetan religious texts, paintings, religious artifacts, medical texts, history and art work" (unpublished manuscript by Blake Kerr, M.D.).

In "A Look Inside a Xigaze Lamasery," *China Daily*, on 7 August 1985, reported that in Tibet before 1959, "Poor monks numbering more than 111,000 worked hard to maintain buildings and their superiors' comfort, but their efforts contributed nothing to self-sustenance."

In a release in English on 3 January 1986, Xinhua credited the Religious Affairs Bureau as the source for the figure of 1,300 lamaseries which had been opened since 1979. Over 20 million *yuan* had been appropriated by the government for repairing and rebuilding, and "the bulk of China's some 1,000 lamaseries had been desecrated or destroyed in the 'cultural revolution,' " but that "these have been reopened or replaced and 300 new lamaseries have been built."

On 6 August 1985, *China Daily*, citing figures given by the deputy director of the Tibetan Religious Affairs Bureau, reported that 50 monasteries and temples in Tibet, with 3,000 lamas in residence, had been restored and opened, with another 43 under repair. The same article said there were about 2,770 monasteries in Tibet in the 1950s.

Xizang Ribao is quoted in FE 8692 from the Lhasa Tibet Regional Service broadcast of 4 October 1987: "It has been decided to repair and open up a total of 235 temples and monasteries. . . and 178 of them have been repaired and opened. . . . At present there are 14,300 monks living in monasteries in the region."

Stating that there are now 6,600 lamas in Tibet, an article in *Renmin Ribao* dated 12 March 1987 reported that 160 monasteries had been restored and over 500 other religious buildings had been built or rebuilt by the people.

On 17 February 1986, Xinhua described the opening day of the great prayer ceremony, a ten-day celebration that had been suspended for twenty years. "More than 10,000 lamas of various Lamaist sects and hundreds of thousands of followers flocked to Lhasa for the ceremony, which was performed annually until 1966."

At this time, we can only conclude that no one knows how many lamas there are in the Tibetan Autonomous Region, or how many temples and monasteries are back in use. But as any visitor quickly learns, there are many faithful Tibetans on pilgrimage to the main temples.

Revival of Tibetan Buddhism

The article by Goldstein and Beall (Document 41) affirms the revival of religious practice and rebuilding of prayer walls and shrines in the nomadic region of western Tibet. These U.S. anthropologists, who lived for months at a time with the nomads in 1987 and 1988, write: "During the period of our fieldwork in Phala the nomads were free to practice their religion as they saw fit, and religion had again become a part of their lives. . . . Most households have small altars in their tents and prayer flags fly from the tent poles and guylines. . . . Some are also actively supporting the re-emergence of monasticism by donating animals and food to help rebuild small local monasteries, and by hiring monks to conduct prayers."

In "Tibet Enjoys a Religious Revival" (Document 42), Michael Rank writes that officials admit that "the overwhelming majority of Tibetans are practising Buddhists despite thirty years of government propaganda pro-pounding atheism, and that this applies to many Communist Party members as well as ordinary citizens."

One Party member told him, "The Party tells us we should be atheists but I can't help believing in Buddhism. It's part of our tradition and they can't stop me from believing what is in my heart."

When asked, "Who are the religious believers in Tibet?" Mr. Tseten Lhundop replied, "All the people in Tibet are believers, including Tibetan cadres at every level. All believe, except Communist Party members, and even some of them are religious believers. . . . The people are faithful. They come here [to Lhasa on pilgrimage] by the tens of thousands, because we now have both freedom of religion and freedom to travel."

Religious Policy

The dramatic change in religious policy in Tibet was reported by a Hong-kong journalist in October 1983 (Document 43). Tibetan social scientists told him that the fundamental error of the policymakers had been their failure to perceive that Tibetan society was an "integration of politics and religion," which led to further error, linking religion with class oppression. Now, he writes, religious services have been fully resumed, all people can go on pilgrimage to Lhasa, the position of many lamas has been restored, and other restoration activities are under way.

The most recent news on religious policy, which preceded by four months the death of the Panchen Lama in January 1989, was his announcement of the formation of a new national guiding commission for Tibetan Buddhism "to ensure self-governing of the religion and eradication of administrative interference [in] religious activities in Tibet" (Document 44).

New Clergy in Tibet

While figures are not available, visitors are told that many young recruits have entered monasteries as novice monks, and, indeed, they can be seen by visitors in all the open monasteries and temples. When asked why some of them wear the robes of a monk and others do not, a senior monk said that the government had placed limits on the number of monks allowed for each temple. "They get no formal schooling," I was told. "They memorize the scriptures for chanting, and some study English so they can serve as tourist guides. . . . Most temples maintain a tutorial system, the older monks teaching novices. But none have training classes [peixunban]."

A new Buddhist Institute was opened in 1985, with a ten-year course planned, leading to the *geshe* degree. Prior schooling of students ranges from primary through senior middle school.

Document 40

An Interview with the Director of the Religious Studies Center, Academy of Social Sciences, Lhasa

By prior arrangement, Donald MacInnis interviewed the Director of the Religious Studies Center of the Tibetan Academy of Social Sciences, Mr. Tseten Lhundop, thirty-eight, in Lhasa on 13 July 1988. They spoke in Chinese. Tseten had been in his present job five years after completing three years of study in the Beijing Academy of Social Sciences where he studied Marxist theory, history of religion, religious philosophy, Chinese Buddhism, Buddhist logic, Chinese logic, and Sanskrit. They agreed to focus on religious policy and practice, leaving political matters out of their discussion.

After explaining how the government's policy on religion had been implemented since 1979, Tseten responded to MacInnis's questions.

Q. Who are the believers in Tibet?

A. All the people in Tibet are believers, including Tibetan cadres at every level. All believe, except Communist Party members, and even some of them are religious believers. But the level of belief is not the same from one person to another. Some people really don't understand what they believe, and could not explain it.

But the people are faithful. They come here [to Lhasa] in the winter by the tens of thousands, because we now have both freedom of religion and freedom to travel. On the fifteenth day of the fourth month of the lunar calendar several hundred thousand come to Lhasa. Of course, this year [because of the disturbances], we didn't have so many.

Q. Can you tell me about the numbers of monks and novices?

A. We are working on these statistics, but have nothing ready yet for publication. However, there are quite a few, both the young and the elderly, perhaps as many as ten thousand or more. It is difficult for the temples now, because there is a limit on the number of new monks permitted.

Q. Is the limit imposed by the government?

A. Yes, government permission is required. I have heard recently that the government will set a limit on the number of monks allowed for each temple and monastery. Monk-novices must get permission to transfer their residence permit from their home to the temple.

Official government statistics for the year 1959, give these numbers for the three major temples: Drepung, 7,700, Sera, 5,500, and Ganden, 3,300.

In fact, there were really 10,000 in each of these. Many of them left the monastery [were laicized] during the troubles and were married. Many of them still are married, but continue living in the monasteries. However, they can't take part in religious ceremonies, except as ordinary believers. They have secular jobs in the monasteries.

The Tibetans are generous, so monks have no financial problem. Some of them receive as much as several tens of *yuan* a day from the faithful.

During the "cultural revolution" no monks were in the temples; all were out somewhere at labor. Now the temples are slowly reviving.

Q. Will it succeed?

A. One can't be sure [*shuo buding*], because there are not enough properly trained monks. Some young novices live at home and study under a monk in the temple.

Q. Does the government set a minimum age limit of eighteen here, as elsewhere in China, for religious instruction?

A. Not in Tibet. Younger ones can become novice monks.

Clergy Training

Q. Please tell me how new monks are trained.

A. A Buddhist Academy, the first of its kind in Tibet, opened at the Drepung Monastery in 1985, headed by Yuan Zhang, a monk, whose Tibetan name is Bumi Qambalozhub. He is also vice president of the Tibetan branch of the Chinese Buddhist Association. He is a "doctor" of religion, something like a Ph.D. degree [*boshi*], called *geshe*. He earned this degree in 1959, in the traditional debate competition, the same year that the Dalai Lama earned his.

Q. Was there no training school for monks before 1985?

A. No, every temple had classes taught by the monks. Students moved up year by year, from class to class, from temple to temple, some of them for twenty years, following one or the other of the two streams of the Yellow Sect. Classes of students would debate the religious classics, climaxing with the great debate in the three big temples (Jokhang, Ramoche, Drepung) in Lhasa, when several hundred would debate the Five Classics. These debates took place twice in summer and once in winter. Eighteen would be chosen from the final debate competitions for the top honor, the title of *geshe*.

The finalists would be ranked, beginning with first place. There were twenty *geshe* chosen when the Dalai Lama took part. The Bainqen [Panchen] Lama did not earn the title, because he didn't make it to the final competition.

The debates were resumed in 1986, and four *geshe* titles were awarded, out of only twenty or so debaters. This was the first competition since 1959. You can see the shrinkage of monks at this level. Today there are only five or six elderly *geshe* in Tibet out of a total of ten; the others are the new ones. Before Liberation there were eighteen new *geshe* chosen every year.

The new Buddhist Institute that opened in 1985 is administered [*guanli*] by the government. Monks teach religion, but laypersons teach other subjects. It will take at least ten years of study to achieve the rank of *geshe*. The prior schooling of students ranges from primary through senior middle school.

Q. What about the "small monks" [*xiao heshan*]?
A. They get no formal schooling. They memorize the scriptures for chanting, and some study English so they can serve as tourist guides. . . . Monks study the Five Scriptures and religious theory. Nuns memorize the scriptures for the purpose of chanting. Formerly nuns, too, studied religious theory.

Most temples also carry on the tutorial system, the older monks teaching novices. But none have training classes [*peixunban*].

Q. Is Tibetan Buddhism still divided into sects?
A. Yes, there are sects, but most Tibetan Buddhists believe [*xin*] in the Dalai Lama. All homes have his picture, even members of other sects.

In central Tibet most clergy and laity follow the Yellow Sect, while other sects prevail in other places. But Tibetans don't differentiate among the sects; except for members of the Bon sect, they go to any temple or monastery.

Q. Is there any friction among the sects?
A. Yes, if they have some learning, they tend to argue; but this doesn't happen at lower levels.

Q. Please explain how the Dalai and Panchen Lamas differ in role and function.
A. The Dalai Lama is in charge of religious, administrative, and political affairs, while the Panchen Lama only handles religious affairs for the No. 2 Yellow Sect. He is the responsible religious leader in one region only,

with the title of *huo-fo*. He is not a *geshe*. He is married, and is not known for his religious scholarship, as is the Dalai Lama. He is worshiped in his own district and in Qinghai Province.

The Ganden Fawang is the top scholar of the Yellow Sect. He inherits the role of Tsang-gaba, founder of the Yellow Sect. The Ganden Fawang in 1949 was of the 96th generation. He administered the annual Great Prayer Meeting and helped select the Dalai Lama. He had the same rank as Dalai Lama, but only administered religious affairs. He is now dead, and there is no successor because there are no *geshe* from whom to elect a Ganden Fawang. The acting Ganden Fawang is Dr. Bomi, but even he is not qualified to be the Ganden Fawang. Still, he is the highest ranking monk today. The whole system fell apart, especially after 1965.

Temple Destruction

Q. What was the extent of temple destruction during the "cultural revolution"?

A. All temples except Ganden were destroyed or vandalized by Red Guards who came in from China in 1966. Ganden was destroyed by the local people, who looted it, taking anything of value, even the wood timbers, doors, and window frames. Some religious statues were taken to China and sold in Hongkong. Some have been returned from China. [Other sources say that Ganden was demolished by the Chinese, who used explosives to level the entire complex of buildings.]

About half of the temples in Lhasa have been restored, more than ten, the important ones. There were more than twenty before.

Implementation of Religious Policy

Q. Is the policy of freedom of religious belief being implemented now?

A. Yes, it's not bad now, but still not fully carried out. Some local cadres still don't understand the correct policy.

Q. What is the function of the Buddhist Association?

A. It is a mass [people's] organization.

Q. What is the function of the Religious Affairs Bureau?

A. We don't have one in Tibet. Here the Minorities Relations Committee, an administrative office at each level of government, city and district, serves in its stead. They manage [*guanli*] religious affairs, such as government subsidies. The subsidies are generous, but are spread out over many temples and monasteries. However, maintenance of the Potala Palace comes under the Ministry of Culture [*wenhuahui*].

Tibetan Youth and Religion

I asked about youth and religion. He replied that he had fifty classmates in high school. Today, some are interested in religion, and read books, some printed in India, seeking to move beyond the "blind faith," customs and practices of traditional religion. One is a high-level monk in India.

"For educated youth, it's not the same as before, when everyone was a religious believer. Today, young people don't believe very much [*bu tai xin*]; but they do follow the moral teachings, and some read and study about religion, not just repeating inherited forms and practices."

Q. How do you differentiate between superstition and religion?
A. Superstition has bad effects, while religion, with its systematic theory, organization, and beliefs, does not. Buddhism has both blind faith [*mangmu xin*] and intellectual faith [*zhihui xin*].

Q. Is what you call blind faith, superstition?
A. One can't say for certain. Whoever believes in the Three Treasures [*san bao*, that is, *fo, jing, seng*: Buddha, scripture, clergy] is a Buddhist. But it is hard to differentiate. Who are religious believers? At a minimum, they must acknowledge the Three Treasures. They don't have to know the systematic theories and doctrines of Buddhism.

Q. What about offbeat tribal or local religious sects? Are they superstitions or religions?
A. That is hard to say. In any case, we should respect the culture and customs of ethnic minorities.

Document 41

Religion among the Tibetan Nomads

Excerpted from "Nomadic Pastoralism on the Western Tibetan Plateau," by Melvin C. Goldstein and Cynthia M. Beall of the Department of Anthropology, Case Western Reserve University, in Nomadic Peoples *(forthcoming). Reprinted with permission.*

During the commune period (1969-81), there was no attempt to diminish the geographic scope of pastoralism by expropriating nomad pastureland or resettling nomads in agricultural areas. ... However, while full-scale pastoralism continued during the "cultural revolution," expression of the pastoralists' traditional culture was prohibited. The policy known as "de-

stroying the four olds" was energetically implemented with the aim of destroying culture and creating a new atheistic Communist culture. Religious
activities were totally forbidden, religious structures, including monasteries
and prayer walls[1] were destroyed, and the nomads were forced to cut their
braids and even abandon deeply held traditional values, such as the taboo
against women slaughtering animals. This was a terrible period, since food
was inadequate, and their values and norms deliberately turned topsy-turvy.
Chinese policy during this period, therefore, sought to maintain pastoral
production but destroy the social and cultural fabric of the nomads' traditional way of life. . . .

Culture and Religion under the New Policy

The post-1980 Tibet policy of the Chinese government parallels that
implemented throughout other parts of China. It rejects the earlier Maoist
"assimilation" ideology for national minorities, substituting in its place a
policy that accepts the validity of traditional minority culture and religion
within the Communist state. It also eliminates the use of class distinctions
and class struggle. An incident that occurred during our fieldwork in Phala
illustrates the extent to which the latter has been implemented. A former
"poor"-class *upung* nomad who had been an official during the commune
period sold a sheep to a trader before milking it, therein breaking a traditional nomad taboo. Nomads believe that this could affect negatively the
milk production of the entire camp, and another man in the same camp, a
former "class enemy" who had been persecuted throughout the "cultural
revolution" period, became incensed. He started berating the seller and
words soon changed to pushing and fighting. They took the case before the
xiang, the "poor"-class nomad arguing that the "wealthy"-class nomad was
looking down on him because of his class background and was trying to
impose old superstitions on him. The local- and district-level officials were
not impressed with his anachronistic perspective and did not side with him,
but instead fined both men. It is noteworthy that one of those deciding this
case, the senior (elected) *xiang* leader, is a very well-liked former monk of
"wealthy" class background. A great deal has changed in Phala since de-
collectivization.

This is nowhere more evident than with regard to the practice of religion.
During the period of our fieldwork in Phala the nomads were free to practice their religion as they saw fit, and religion had again become an important part of their lives. Each nomad home-base camp has hired villagers to
rebuild its prayer wall or walls, and nomads are again pursuing the cycle
of religious rites that typified the traditional society. Most households have
small altars in their tents and prayer flags fly from their tent poles and
guylines. Nomads make pilgrimages to monasteries and holy sites and travel
to visit lamas without asking anyone's permission. Some are also actively
supporting the reemergence of monasticism by donating animals and food

to help rebuild small local monasteries, and by hiring monks to conduct prayers for them.[2] In Summer, wandering monks and villagers come to the *changtang* to do prayers, carve prayer stones, build walls, and mold clay figurines of debris. Nomad practitioners of traditional Tibetan medicine are also active in the area.

These traditional practices did not reappear all at once or in an orderly fashion. The nomads at first actually feared that the new policy was a devious trick launched to expose pockets of "rightist" thinking, and were reluctant to take the lead and risk being singled out. Change, therefore, occurred only gradually as individual nomads took single actions that in effect tested the general policy. When no protest or punishment came from the district officials above them, the practice in question spread rapidly. The reemergence of nomad "mediums" (individuals whom deities possess and speak through) exemplifies this incremental-change process. This traditional part of the Tibetan Buddhist religious system reappeared in Phala only in the winter of 1987 when an adult nomad in one camp took very ill. Having no medicines, the man was suffering in great pain. Another of the nomads in that camp spontaneously went into a trance and was possessed by a deity who gave a prognosis and explanation of the disease. When no higher level criticism of this event occurred in the ensuing weeks and months, the nomad medium and others made a traditional-style costume worn by mediums, and he is now sought after in cases of serious illness. Ironically, he is one of the few nomads who is very much a supporter of the Communist Party.

Notes

1. These walls are about 10 feet long (or longer) and four feet high, on top of which are piled stones on which prayers have been carved. Nomads do religious prostrations before them as well as circumambulate them to gain merit.
2. There are, however, varying government-set limits on the number of monks that can be recruited in monasteries. This policy is disliked by Tibetans, who see it as a continuing curtailment of their ability to practice their religion as they wish.

Document 42

Tibet Enjoys a Religious Revival

By Michael Rank, Lhasa, in South China Morning Post, *12 August 1983.*

Ask ten-year-old novice lama Awang Quni questions about politics and he will be stumped, but his grasp of Buddhist theology is second to none.

Awang is the youngest of about ten boy novices at Drepung monastery near Lhasa who have been entrusted to lamas for training in accordance with an ancient Tibetan tradition.

Once almost every family sent at least one boy to be a lama, so that about a third of the male population were monks, but the tradition is dying out under the influence of Communism.

Sitting between two elderly lamas in their dark crimson robes, Awang said he knew nothing about the Chinese Communist Party and could not even name the capital of China.

But asked about the Dalai Lama, young Awang showed he had not shirked his theology homework. "He's the reincarnation of Guanyin," he said, referring to the Buddhist goddess of mercy.

Awang also knew the former god-king now lives in India, but admitted he could not identify Mr. Deng Xiaoping, China's present strongman.

Young Awang leads an austere life, studying the scriptures for nine or ten hours a day. He said he had no toys but did sometimes play with other children and also enjoyed painting pictures.

"I plan to study hard and eventually obtain the *geshe* degree," he told reporters who interviewed him in the porch of one of the magnificent halls of the monastery. A Tibetan official explained that the *geshe* degree was roughly equivalent to a Western doctorate.

Awang, who speaks only Tibetan, said he had never been to school and that he was sent to the monastery three years ago by his parents who live in Lhasa.

"My parents want me to be a lama and so do I," said Awang, who is tutored by his uncle, a lama at Drepung for the last forty years.

Awang, a friendly if dishevelled boy wearing shabby Chinese clothes rather than monk's robes, said he did not feel at all afraid as he was besieged with questions by strange-looking foreigners armed with video-cameras and flashguns.

He said his father was a brick-kiln worker and his mother a seamstress and that none of his four brothers were lamas.

All religious activity in fervently Buddhist Tibet was banned during the Maoist "cultural revolution," but monasteries started to accept lamas again three years ago.

Drepung monastery was once the largest monastery in Tibet with ten thousand lamas, but many were expelled after the Chinese takeover in 1951 and yet more were forced out after the 1959 anti-Chinese uprising which caused the Dalai Lama to flee his homeland.

There are now only 233 monks left at Drepung, almost half of them young men who took vows since the end of the ban on organized religion in 1980, when extreme leftist regional leaders were purged and replaced with moderates.

There has been a spectacular religious revival in Tibet in the last three years, and forty-five monasteries with about fourteen hundred lamas are now open.

But this is minimal compared with the twenty-one hundred monasteries before the "cultural revolution," the majority of which were badly damaged or destroyed by Maoist Red guards.

Most of these temples are gone forever, although one of Tibet's most famous monasteries, Ganden near Lhasa, which was razed during the "cultural revolution," is being rebuilt.

A new Buddhist seminary is to open in Lhasa soon to set up training of lamas. About two hundred aspiring lamas and devout laymen recently took an examination to enter the institute.

Officials of the Tibet branch of the Chinese Buddhist Association said only candidates who were devout, reasonably well educated, in good health, and patriotic were eligible to become lamas.

But they said the examination did not include any explicitly political questions.

Officials admit that the overwhelming majority of Tibetans are practicing Buddhists despite thirty years of government propaganda propounding atheism and that this applies to many Communist Party members as well as ordinary citizens.

"The Party tells us that we should be atheists but I can't help believing in Buddhism. It's part of our tradition and they can't stop me from believing in what is in my heart," said one Party member, chatting on the roof of the magnificent Jokhang temple in central Lhasa.

"I am telling you this because I think you should know what things are really like here and not only hear government propaganda."

Perhaps the most dramatic expression of Tibetan religious fervor is to be seen at the main entrance to the Jokhang, where dozens of worshipers prostrate themselves in supplication to the Lord Buddha.

Worshipers include young and old, most of them wearing colorful traditional Tibetan gowns. But they also include a few fashionably dressed youngsters in flared trousers, probably given to them by relatives living in India, home for eighty thousand refugees who fled with the Dalai Lama.

Inside the temple, devotees light yak-butter candles and chant the scriptures. Elaborate statues of Buddhist deities are half-obliterated in the smokey darkness. Many altars are decorated with photographs of the Dalai Lama, now more greatly revered than ever after twenty-four years in exile.

Every monk and lay Buddhist interviewed during a week-long visit to Tibet said he fervently prayed for the god-king's return. Government officials, too, said that a visit from the Dalai Lama could "assist Socialist construction by raising the enthusiasm of the masses."

Document 43

Changes in PRC Policy on Tibet

Hongkong, Wen Wei Po, *8 October 1983. Translated in China Study Project Documentation No. 13, March 1984, pp. 36-37.*

More than thirty years have elapsed since the peaceful liberation of Xizang [Tibet] and twenty-odd years have passed since the suppression of the rebellion and the reform carried out in Xizang, yet the Xizang people sincerely believe in Buddhism and still highly respect the Dalai Lama. This shows that Xizang's religion and nationality problem is rather prominent. Therefore, whether central policies on Xizang can be properly formulated and implemented will only affect the economic cultural development of Xizang, but also influence the will of the people of Xizang and the unification of the motherland.

Concerning this problem, Mao Zedong had an explicit instruction. He said: "In Xizang, before any problems are considered, the matters of both nationality and religion must be taken into full account and all our work must be done steadily with meticulous care." It is a pity that he erroneously launched the "cultural revolution" in his later years, inflicting a tragic catastrophe on the people of Xizang.

During my tour of Xizang, I visited some lamas of the monasteries. I found that the destruction caused by the "cultural revolution" to Xizang can be summed up in the following: 1) Mass religious services were entirely prohibited; 2) The lamas were forced to resume secular life and were sent to labor in the countryside; 3) Large numbers of Buddhist cultural relics, including classical books and banners, gifts and presents sent by the emperors of the Ming and Qing dynasties to Xizang monasteries, were confiscated. The number of classical books damaged and lost was more than the Dalai had taken abroad when he went into exile; and 4) Many monasteries were demolished. The Xizang people were most distressed at the destruction of the Ganden Monastery. The Ganden Monastery, built in the early fifteenth century, is the first monastery of the Yellow Sect. During the "cultural revolution," this huge complex of buildings was turned into ruins after being intentionally demolished. Thousands of lamas of the monastery had to live in exile.

While in Xizang, I visited some Zang nationality social scientists. From their viewpoint, the mistake of the "cultural revolution" was, in general, a fundamental mistake of the guiding ideology. Specifically speaking, there was a lack of scientific analysis of Xizang society, which has an "integration of politics and religion." Consequently, problems of different natures were indiscriminately dealt with, instead of differentiating between them. The close combination of politics and religion has been the tradition of Xizang for several centuries. What is more, one cannot speak of culture without religion in such a society. The mistake of the "cultural revolution" is that stress was laid on linking religion with class oppression, which neglected the fact that religion was the spontaneous belief of thousands upon thousands of people and that the monasteries and temples were also cultural centers in the serf system. As a result, on the premise of "class struggle," the oppressive nature of religion was repudiated, while the normal religious activities of the masses were prohibited.

It is fortunate that the central government and the localities are now trying to make energetic efforts to cure the scars of the "cultural revolution." In light of our own experience, there are the following changes: 1) Religious services of the Xizang people have been fully resumed. The people from all localities can go on pilgrimages to Lhasa. It is said that there are several million pilgrims every year; 2) The positions of many lamas have been restored. Many new lamas are recruited through the Xizang branch of the Chinese Buddhist Association and other temples and monasteries; 3) Many temples and monasteries are being rebuilt, including the above-mentioned Ganden Monastery, which is being gradually renovated; and 4) The protection of Buddhist cultural relics and classical books has been further strengthened. Young, educated Xizang people are also trained to assist the old lamas in sorting out and inheriting the Tibetan classics.

Now, the guiding ideology of the central government has changed remarkably. The key to the problem is whether the policies are properly implemented. Many of the people who were interviewed expressed the view that they agreed with the central government's "Summary of the Forum on Xizang Work." However, concerning religious matters, they suggested that the central government dispatch cadres who are good at carrying out policies, so as to ensure the implementation of policies. After my tour of Xizang, I also had the same feeling.

As mentioned above, many lamas and the Xizang people of the elder generation still cherished the memory of the Fourteenth Dalai. Such a practice not only stems from religious belief, but is also mingled with complicated national feelings. After my tour of Xizang, I could not help thinking about a problem: as the people of Xizang still have profound feelings about the Dalai, the policies of the central government on the Dalai must embody the national feelings of a considerable number of Xizang people who wish for his return. In 1982, on behalf of the central government, Li Weihan (a representative of the central government who participated in the signing of the agreement on the peaceful liberation of Xizang), expressed his views on the Dalai: "We miss the Dalai Lama and our Zang nationality compatriots abroad. They depend on other countries for their living and are separated from their motherland and people. No one with patriotic feelings can bear this situation. We are deeply concerned at their circumstances.

As always, our policy is that all patriots belong to one family, whether they rally to the common cause early or late. The gate of the motherland is wide open to all those who sincerely cherish the motherland." This policy is reasonable and justified and is welcomed by many Tibetan compatriots.

Recently, the Dalai Lama himself has changed his attitude. As well as sending delegations to the motherland, he mentioned twice this year his intention to return to the motherland in 1985. In this respect, we hope that the central government will adopt further measures to strive for the early return of the Dalai to the motherland, so that greater achievements can be attained in the unity of the nation and the unification of the country.

Document 44

Panchen Lama Discloses New Buddhist Commission

Beijing Review *(in English), No. 41, 10 October 1988, pp. 10-12.*

The Panchen Lama disclosed on September 28 that a national guiding commission of Tibetan Buddhism will be set up this year to ensure self-governing of the religion and eradicate administrative interference of the religious activities in Tibet and other Tibetan-inhabited regions, *China Daily* reported.

He also disclosed that he has been keeping contacts through letters and telephone with the Dalai Lama, another spiritual leader of the Tibetans, who has been living in exile in India since 1959 when he fled after an abortive rebellion.

The fifty-year-old Panchen, a living Buddha and also a leading religious figure of Tibetan Buddhism, said that he will be the chief of the guiding commission to be headquartered in Beijing.

The Panchen Lama described the establishment of the commission as one of the "major measures" to stabilize the situation in Tibet and other regions, with Tibetan Buddhism as the main religion.

It will also help develop Buddhism and promote the unity of Han nationality with other national minorities, he said.

Wearing a Tibetan robe and looking very healthy, the Panchen Lama said in his Beijing residence that the Tibetan Buddhism Guiding Commission will mainly be responsible for the religious activities in Tibet and Qinghai, Gansu, Sichuan, and Yunnan provinces.

The traditional interference of religious activities with administrative measures over the years, he said, had not weakened the religious belief of the people. "Instead," he said, "leftism has spurred Tibetan people's feelings toward religion and strengthened their belief. It also did harm to the harmony of nationalities, as religions have close relations with minorities."

To stabilize Tibet, he said, the religious work must be enhanced there. "But it doesn't mean to interfere with administrative measures. We must make the religion self-governing in accordance with the doctrine," he said in fluent Chinese but sometimes through a Tibetan interpreter.

Panchen, also vice-chairman of the NPC Standing Committee, said one of the tasks of the commission is to teach all the monks and nuns to love the country and abide by the laws of the state. "This is the least one expects of a citizen," he said.

"The political attitude of the monks and nuns plays an important role in maintaining stability and unity in Tibet and other regions," he said, recalling that the two riots in Lhasa in September last year and March this year were staged by a handful of monks and nuns under the slogan of Tibet independence.

The Panchen Lama described the general situation of Tibet as "stable and getting better," but stressed that it would be wrong to "sit back and lower our guard" against the separatists, who are few in number but have enough capacity for maneuver, as they have support both at home and abroad.

For the correct and thorough solution of Tibetan problems, he called for real implementation of regional national autonomy, more flexible ethnic, economic, religious, and intellectual policies than the inland provinces, and top priority to the development of agricultural and animal husbandry in the area.

The Panchen Lama said what he advocated about the real autonomy of Tibet "was different in nature" with the so-called independence of Tibet preached by the separatists who attempted to split Tibet from China.

On the five-point statement on human rights in Tibet made by the Dalai Lama and his recent proposal to make Tibet a self-governing democratic entity, with Beijing responsible for foreign affairs and defense, the Panchen Lama said that the heart of these ideas was to split the motherland, using an old Chinese saying to describe these proposals as the same medicine prepared in different ways.

Describing his relations with the Dalai Lama as "good religious friends," the Panchen Lama said that they had been keeping contact in recent years through letters and telephone. When the Dalai Lama was in London in April this year, for instance, he said that they had "frank talks" over the phone.

"I told him that the riots are not advantageous to the interests of the Tibetans and the solution of problems in Tibet. No problem can be solved by means of burning cars or beating people with stones," the Panchen Lama said.

He expressed his hope that the Dalai Lama could use his influence to stop violence and stop such activities as stirring up troubles abroad or planning explosions or assassinations at home.

The Dalai Lama denied his blame over the telephone, saying he opposed any riots and violence but favored peace. As for the plans for violence, the Dalai Lama was quoted as saying, "It was done by some young Tibetans and radical organizations. They in fact do not heed what I say."

When the Dalai Lama asked for leniency to the arrested chief offenders of the riots, the Panchen Lama said most of the people involved in the riots would receive lenient treatment.

He also advised the Dalai Lama to come back to contribute to the development and prosperity of Tibet. "What is the use of making a noise abroad? Persisting in antagonism will do nothing good for Tibet and the whole country, and there is no hope for success," he told the exiled Dalai Lama.

"It is natural that he has accepted some of my suggestions while refusing others," the Panchen Lama said with a smile. "We take different political roads, after all."

He confirms that most of the 300-odd lamas and nuns arrested during and after the Lhasa riots in March this year had been released, leaving only a few still in detention for violating the criminal law.

"We are also considering, within the limits permitted by law, to give lenient treatment to the four involved in killing a policeman during the riot," he said.

Refuting the rumor of new arrests in Lhasa, the Panchen Lama said only a few criminals, such as thieves and robbers, were arrested in recent months.

But he disclosed that some working teams, consisting mainly of Tibetans, were sent to a dozen monasteries in Lhasa which were involved in the March unrest, aimed at consolidating these monasteries and educating most of the monks and nuns.

"While insisting on education of most monks and nuns who had committed light crimes during the riots," he said, "we must not be soft on those instigating the riots."

New measures are being taken in Tibet to thoroughly rehabilitate those who had been labeled unjustly since the 1959 rebellion and particularly during the "cultural revolution" (1966-76), he said.

Document 45

Tibetan College Nurtures Budding Lamas

By Zhu Ling, China Daily, 21 July 1985.

The soft chanting in D-flat of Buddhist sutras instantly grabs the senses of those who venture into a modest compound, nestling at the foot of a barren mountain range on the western outskirts of Lhasa, capital of the Tibetan Autonomous Region.

There is not a soul to be seen in the 190-square-meter courtyard except for a dog tending her litter. Through a nearby window is seated a group of young men, cross-legged and murmuring.

This is the first Buddhism college in the history of Tibet, the center of the Lama sect of Buddhism. The college will be formally inaugurated tomorrow, at a time when there is a shortage of erudite young successors to Lamaism in Tibet, said the college's president, Qiangba Luozhu, sixty-seven. He was recognized as an incarnation of a Living Buddha at the age of eight.

"Now religious freedom has returned to Tibet and our people are freely observing normal religious practices. But most lamas of great learning are in their seventies and few young lamas can understand the Buddhist sutras or do any research on it," he said.

Religious influences can be felt in every vein of Tibetan history and social life, he said. For this reason, bringing up a new generation of lamas to carry on the study of Lamaism and manage the temples and monasteries has become urgent.

The college program is primarily set at ten years, with students devoting 80 percent of their studies to religious philosophy, history, Buddhist sutras, and law and the other 20 percent on the Tibetan language.

After graduation, they will be assigned to religious institutions and lamaseries in Tibet.

In August 1983, 146 students, aged thirteen to twenty-five, were enrolled after exams in the Tibetan language. Another 54 young men will be enrolled next year, said Living Buddha Chemorn Dantsencele, head of the Tibetan Buddhist Association.

He said that the State will cover all expenses. Living expenses alone for each student are estimated at 504 *yuan* a year. The regional government will also contribute funds.

The college so far has six faculty members, four of them senior lamas. Students are enrolled on a voluntary basis with the full agreement of their parents. They must be in good health and prepared to observe religious disciplines — in other words, no drinking, no smoking, and no marriage.

After about six months, the college's president said, several students asked to leave, saying that they had been forced to come by their parents. "We let them go," he said.

In a bedroom to the far right on the second floor, a fifteen-year-old student was reciting a Buddhist sutra with his eyes closed. The twelve-square-meter room had two beds and it was neatly arranged. The boy, Luosang Jingmei, had been a fifth-grade pupil at Lhasa Primary School.

"I want to be a monk with knowledge and my request was okayed by my parents," he said with a shy smile. He is his family's only child, his father a manager at the No. 1 Furniture Plant in Lhasa.

He gets up at 6:30 every morning with the school bell. He recites Buddhist sutras until 8:30, breakfast time.

Nine to 9:30 every morning is housecleaning time. Classes are then held until noon and from 3 to 6:30 in the evening. The students chant in groups or debate in pairs between 8 and 11 three nights a week to deepen their understanding, Luosang said.

Document 46

Youngsters Swell Buddhist Lama Ranks in Tibet

NCNA, in English, 1 March 1985; JPRS-CPS-85-029, 26 March 1985, p. 45.

At the Sera Buddhist monastery, one of the largest in Tibet, 160 young lamas in purplish red *kasayas* sat on the ground in groups of 9 earlier this week talking enthusiastically. In each group, they took turns to ask each other questions. When fellow monks failed to give an answer, the questioner clapped his hands and waved his Buddhist beads above his head in triumph.

These young lamas were having a debate on Buddhist classics, and the main topic was logical reasoning, one of the required courses for students. Debating is considered by the monastery a very important part of the training of young lamas.

Gungjue Dargyai, director of the Democratic Administrative Committee of the Sera Monastery, said there were barely one hundred lamas there a few years ago, and some of them were in their eighties.

In 1983, the monastery began to recruit youngsters willing to devote themselves to Buddhism from peasant, herding, and urban families. This paid off. The 160 new recruits are divided into nine classes and taught by experienced lamas who are well-versed in Buddhist doctrines.

Gungjue Dargyai told Xinhua that all the young lamas were keen students. Apart from participating in religious activities and memorizing the required scriptures in the daytime, they also spent two hours every evening studying on their own.

In the old days, he said, it took a lama twenty or even thirty years to obtain a *geshe*, the highest academic degree of Tibetan Buddhism. But in recent years it was taking only ten years for young lamas to get the degree because they were hard-working and conditions were much better.

Besides taking part in religious duties, the lamas at Sera also raise cattle and grow fruit. Personal income last year came to 1,400 *yuan*, half of which was donated by believers.

Document 47

Most Lamas at Gathering under Thirty

China Daily, *10 March 1987.*

Some 70 percent of the eighteen hundred lamas attending a prayer ceremony here are twenty to thirty years old.

Most of the young lamas have shown a mastery of scriptures and religious rituals in the eleven-day prayer ceremony that started on Sunday.

The first prayer ceremony was initiated in 1409 by Zong Kaba, founder of the Yellow Sect of Lamaism, to revitalize Tibetan Buddhism and promote religious disciplines.

Since 1980 monasteries in Tibet have admitted many young lamas. They had to pass a strict examination on Buddhism before being admitted and receiving further training by veteran lamas.

Some of them have completed in three years the study of scriptures that normally requires five years to complete.

The Tibet Autonomous Region set up a Buddhist college in 1983 to train top clergymen.

The central government has adopted special policies for the Tibet region, where almost all residents believe in Buddhism. It has allocated funds of up to 20 million *yuan* (US $5.4 million) and organized teams to repair more than one hundred monasteries over the past few years.

Daoism in China Today

Introduction

The life and practice of Daoism is the most difficult of all religions in China to describe, because it is the most amorphous. Abbot Puyu (Document 50) says there are very few Daoists in Fujian, and none in Fuzhou. Indeed, the government statistics for all religions in Fujian show no Daoist believers, and, in contrast to Buddhism's 9,650, only 79 priests and nuns. Since the same chart shows only 16 Daoist priests and nuns in 1949, the increase must be due to novices.

Most press reports on Daoism in China today focus on famous mountains, like Huashan (Document 48) and Qingchengshan (Document 55), describing the repair of their temples and the revival of tourism, while the Center for Religious Studies at the University of Sichuan, which specializes in Daoism and publishes a journal, deals only with the theory and history of Daoism.

Even the chairman of the Chinese Daoist Association has difficulty describing the actual practice of Daoism today (Document 49), referring only to young people, particularly young women, who want to be Daoists, and the CDA's plans to organize classes.

Whether from internal decay or devastations brought by events like the "cultural revolution," the erosion of Daoism, described in an interview with a senior Daoist nun in Chengdu in August 1988, is sobering. Of more than one hundred Daoist temples before 1949, only one remains in the city of Chengdu, the Qingyanggong Temple. "The others were destroyed." Only four large temples remain open to the public in the entire province.

When asked about monks and nuns, she said they had more than one thousand in former times (and five hundred at the time of Liberation), but only a few dozen now, most of them young novices who study in the temple under older monks and nuns. The only other clergy-training program, she said, is a one-year course in Beijing, with forty students, all women this year. The previous four classes had all been men.

The vice-chairman of the Shanghai Daoist Association told a reporter (Document 52) that about twenty Daoist temples in China are training priests today. The chairman of the CDA (Document 53) told reporters there were one hundred Daoist monasteries and temples open in China in 1984.

However, as with Daoism in Taiwan and elsewhere, the temples are popular on festival days; 110,000 worshipers (and holiday visitors) jammed the Daoist temple in Guangzhou on Lantern Festival Day in 1985 (Document 57).

Document 48

Ancient Daoism in Modern-Day China

By Julian Baum, Christian Science Monitor, *8 August 1988.*

"People come here from all over the country wanting to be monks," says Cao Xiang Zhen, a Daoist nun and head of the Daoist Association of Huashan.

At least a dozen young men arrived at Huashan last year to work in its temples, says Sister Cao. Huashan is one of Daoism's five sacred mountains, where Daoists have worshiped for two thousand years.

Few of the new arrivals were allowed to stay, however. The natural beauty of the Shaanxi Range and the Daoist life-style, which has been romanticized in Chinese literature since ancient times, attracts more recruits than the association is allowed to accept under government quotas.

Many of the young apprentices are "naughty Daoists," Cao says in a gentle rebuke.

She says that many want to wear the robes and become wandering friars, only to go sightseeing across the country and travel freely from one temple to another as Daoists did for centuries until the Communists came to power in 1949. But this is no longer permitted.

Except for a few Chinese youths, Daoism has lost most of its popular appeal as China's native religion.

A reform-minded Communist Party has tried to strip away mystery and myth from Chinese life, condemning most of the practices of popular Daoism and pushing it into further decline.

As the country tries to "get rich through Socialism," only a handful of youth, often from China's poorest regions, are attracted by an ascetic existence at the fringe of modern life. Few of China's thousands of Daoist temples have survived into the 1980s, and many lack priests.

"Dao is the original force of the universe," says Min Zhiting, deputy secretary-general of the official Chinese Daoist Association in Peking. "We believe in tranquillity, modesty, kindness — that weakness will defeat strength and that softness will win over hardness. . . . "

In its popular forms, Daoism is represented by a pantheon of gods and demons and has absorbed almost every ancient practice known to the Chinese people.

Modern Chinese intellectuals have often been embarrassed by their country's indigenous religion. Liang Qichao, an early twentieth-century reformer, once wrote that Daoism was "a great humiliation," and that its activities "have not benefited the nation at all. ... "

The individualistic life of the Daoists was gradually reined in by the Communists in the 1950s, when monks were forced into collective labor and had to join a state-controlled association.

Since then, the Communist Party has imposed an official version of Daoism which stresses benevolence, patriotism, and public service without the mysticism and superstitious practices.

This "Socialist" Daoism is the creed that is being taught to new recruits, although they also keep in mind the romantic images of Kung Fu heroes who, like oriental Robin Hoods, defeat legions of bandits with their martial-arts skills as immortalized in movies and popular novels.

"The thing I'm most proud of is that whatever we do here as Daoists is for the public and not for the individual," says Lang Chaoshou, a young apprentice on Huashan, echoing the new Daoist ethic.

Mr. Lang is assigned to a temple on Huashan's highest point, the South peak, which rises far above the Shaanxi plain to a height of 7,500 feet.

Like Daoists young and old, Lang says the spectacular mountain scenery has given him a love of nature and reverence for the natural environment, attitudes which are noticeably lacking elsewhere in China.

Document 49

Daoism Is Revived in China

An interview with the chairman of the Chinese Daoist Association; NCNA, in English, 11 July 1983; FE 7386, 15 July 1983; reprinted in China Study Project Documentation *No. 12, October 1983, pp. 40-41.*

A Chinese Daoist leader said today (11 July 1983) that the Chinese ancient religion—Daoism—which is more than seventeen hundred years old, is normalizing its religious activities. Li Yuhang, a sixty-six-year-old senior Daoist from Mao Shan, Jiangsu, is the chairman of the China Daoist Association. He is also a member of the CPPCC and has just returned to his Bai Yun Guan (White Cloud Temple) at Li Bian Men, Beijing, where the association is located, after attending the first session of the Sixth CPPCC. He said that Daoism is one of the five main Chinese religions (namely, Buddhism, Daoism, Islam, Catholicism, and Protestantism) and is an inherent and "locally born and bred" religion in China. . . .

Chairman Li said that his association publishes the *Journal of the Chinese*

Daoist Association, which publicizes Daoist activities and research works. The association also owns a room for research work. He said that Daoism is rich in literature and documents, and the *Collected Daoist Scriptures*, a collection of Daoist classics, has as many as 5,485 volumes which are worthy of research. . . .

Daoism once had its golden age. Its theory and doctrine were highly praised by some supreme rulers in the Han Dynasty, Tang Dynasty, Five Dynasties, Song Dynasty, and Yuan Dynasty. Its fine nihilist thought was favored by the disgraced officials who fell into political disfavor and by recluses. Some rulers who looked for longevity even esteemed the religion, fostered Daoists, and believed in them and alchemists. Therefore, Daoist temples were built all across the land and many Daoist schools of thought strove for popularity.

"Then, the religion declined," Li Yuhang said. "After the founding of new China and after the people's government promulgated and implemented the policy of freedom of religious belief, the China Daoist Association was established in April 1957 for organizing normal religious activities. However, the religion also faced calamities during the "ten chaotic years," and the activities of the association were suspended. At present, normal activities of the association are reviving. The State, though it is in financial straits, has allocated a large amount of funds for the restoration of famous mountains and temples and the protection of Daoist historic sites.

As for the successors [next generation] of the Daoists, he said: "We do not have to worry, as there are many people who want to be Daoists. Basically speaking, there are two main schools of Daoist thought: The Zhenyi (True Unity) sect, which originated from the Wu Dou Mi Dao (five pecks of rice sect) founded by Zhang Daoling in the Eastern Han Dynasty, and the Quanzhen (Complete Purity) sect, which was founded by Wang Zhongyang, a Daoist, and his apprentice, Qiu Chuji in the Jin Dynasty. Priests of the Zhenyi sect are allowed to eat [regular diet] and are not forced to cover their hair and leave home, and are commonly known as the "Daoists of the laity." At present, we have abolished some regulations, taboos, and commandments, while strictly observing the Daoist regulations. Therefore, many young people want to be Daoists, particularly female Daoists. We have organized a special Daoists' class for young males and are planning to organize more special classes for more people. In addition, we plan to organize a female Daoists' class in Wuhan. Thus, they can replace those Daoists who "rise to the Daoist conception of being immortals" (meaning death).

Document 50

Excerpts from an Interview with Abbot Puyu, Yongquan Temple, Fujian

Interviewed by Donald MacInnis; the bulk of the interview appears in Part II, Section I.

Q. What is your impression of Daoism? There doesn't seem any evidence of Daoist religious revival.

A. Daoism is a purely Chinese religion; it didn't come from another nation. Its principles are something like Christianity. They believe people can go to heaven. But the Christian heaven is quite different from the Daoist heaven, as is the Buddhist heaven. Sakyamuni combined the "heavens" of other religions, but the final home for Buddhists is not heaven, but Nirvana.

Chinese Daoists believe they will go up to heaven. Daoism believes "burn yourself and go to heaven." It doesn't mean to burn yourself while alive, or to have your body burnt after death. It means your body is consumed by the fire of your religious zeal and your soul will go to heaven, where you will become an immortal. That is the first principle of Daoism.

Q. What about Daoism today?

A. Daoism was weakened by the development of Buddhism. After Liberation, the number of Daoist believers has decreased. Although they have some new believers, they are not as many as Buddhism. . . .

Document 51

An Interview with a Senior Nun at the Qingyanggong Temple in Chengdu, Sichuan Province

On 15 July 1988 Donald MacInnis interviewed a senior nun at the Qingyanggong Daoist Temple in Chengdu, Sichuan Province. He had witnessed the final public prayer ceremony of that day in the Sanqing Pavilion, performed by eight persons, seven of them nuns, half of them young novices.

The nun said that this is one of seventy-two major Daoist temples built in China throughout history, and that Laozi, the founder of Daoism, personally supervised the building of this temple. Other buildings were added to the temple complex through the years, making it the main Daoist temple in this region. Before the "cultural revolution" there were over one hundred Daoist temples, large and small, in Chengdu, but only this one has been reopened.

Q. How do you maintain the temple?

A. We can't expect the government to provide financial support, so we follow the policy of self-support [*yi miao yang miao*]. We receive generous donations from the people, as much as 10,000 *yuan* or more from a single donor. The temple is not private property; it is neither State-owned nor is it a collective enterprise like a factory. Therefore we have to depend on ourselves to find the resources to administer the temple.

Q. How many temples were there in Chengdu before 1949?

A. We had over one hundred, large and small. Now this is the only one remaining, the biggest one. The others were destroyed.

Q. Are there no temples remaining open elsewhere?

A. Yes, several big temples have been repaired and reopened on Qingcheng Mountain, Guojia Mountain, and Emei Mountain. Together with this one, there are four large temples now open to the public in Sichuan Province.

Q. What about smaller temples?

A. Yes, there are some small temples, but most were destroyed.

Q. How many monks and nuns do you have now?

A. A few dozen, most of them young novices. In former times we had over one thousand; we had five hundred at the time of Liberation.

Q. Are you recruiting and training new monks and nuns?

A. Yes, some monks and nuns serve as tutors for novices. The government asks the elderly monks to train novices. The government also runs a training class for us.

Q. How many years of preparation are necessary to become a nun?

A. Not many. In the past it was quite simple to become a nun. But there are some requirements now. First, a novice must come of her own free will; second, she should have a high-school education. Daoism is not like Buddhism. One can become a Buddhist by simply shaving one's head, but one must have both talent and virtue to become a Daoist monk or nun.

Q. Are there other training programs for nuns and monks?

A. Yes, there is an annual study program in Beijing. There are forty students in this year's class from all parts of the country. We are planning to start a class here too.

Q. There is a Buddhist college in Beijing. Is there also one for Daoists?

A. Buddhism is quite strong in China, so there are many Buddhist institutes. The largest one is in Beijing. There is one near Chengdu as well. But there is no Daoist college.

Q. How many students are there from here in the Daoist class in Beijing?

A. Four women students from our temple and six others from other Sichuan temples are now studying in Beijing. It's unusual that this year's class of forty is all women. Each class in the previous four years was all men, averaging about forty students per class. The men from last year's class have all returned and are assigned to various smaller temples in Sichuan province.

Document 52

Daoists Rebuild the Past

By Lu Ming and Zhang Lei, in China Daily, *9 July 1987.*

He knows they are there, those Daoist hermits dreaming of beauty and feeding on the herbs of life in the deep mountains. In his mind's eye he can picture them in the fragrance of cypress, seeking perfection and immortality, and becoming one with the Dao itself.

But the seventy-one-year-old Daoist priest has more immediate, earthly concerns, and he knows he is not immortal. "I may attain longevity," he said, flashing a smile, "but not immortality."

As Vice-Chairman and Secretary General of the Daoist Association in Shanghai, Chen Liansheng's life has very little to do with *wuwei*, the famous Daoist doctrine of "doing-nothingness" and inactivity.

"Doing-nothingness" is a luxury Chen can't afford, for he has to spend his day compiling Daoist scriptures which have been out of print, attending People's Political Consultative Conference meetings, and conducting services praying for health, good harvests, and peace in the world.

And on top of everything else, he does all he can to train young students recruited from Shanghai's neighboring provinces to learn the tenets of Daoism and become priests at the White Cloud Temple, one of the two temples in Shanghai.

"Now we're caught in a situation when the young crop is still in the blade but the old one is all gone," he said.

About twenty Daoist temples around the country are training young priests these days, Chen said, and each temple usually has fewer than twenty young Daoists.

The only indigenous religion in China, Daoism dates back to the Chinese sage Laozi in the sixth century B.C. It used to have tens of millions of followers in China. It has about thirty million adherents in the world today.

Based on the concept of Dao, the universal force harmonizing nature, this philosophy later evolved into a pantheistic religion of hero worship and mystical rites.

The Daoist church was almost phased out during the "cultural revolution" (1966-76). Chen and eight other priests were kicked out of the White Cloud Temple, but not before they had seen sixteen thousand volumes of Daoist classics, some dating back to the Ming (1366-1644) and Qing (1644-1911) dynasties, seized and turned into pulp at a paper factory.

Of the nine priests banished from the temple, Chen was the only one who lived to return. But he found four of the temple's five halls occupied by a spreading neighborhood.

Chen and the other Daoist priests wasted no time in piecing together the broken sculptures and recovering the scriptures which survived. A collection of thirty-six volumes of Daoist scriptures was reprinted. Daoist music was recorded and put on tape, and young people were brought from Daoist families to study at temples in Beijing, Shanghai, and Wuhan, and in Sichuan Province.

"It was when we came together from all over the country to do a video-tape of Daoist rituals that we realized we had aged terribly," Chen said.

Aging priests

They also found out something else: as the most knowledgeable Daoist priests died, they took with them some of the most valuable parts of this once glorious culture.

According to Chen, most of China's remaining Daoist priests are in their 70s.

The aging of Daoist priests has made it very difficult to find people qualified to teach students, and training is further impeded by the notion that Daoist doctrines must emerge out of a student spontaneously instead of being taught.

Launched in March 1986, the three-year Daoist course at the White Cloud Temple has thirty-one students, with an average age of twenty. The curriculum ranges from Daoist doctrines, rituals, musical instruments, calligraphy, and philosophy to the martial arts and English. After graduation, the students will be practicing Daoism at the two temples in Shanghai.

An ardent and hard-working group, the thirty-one students lead a simple life, getting up at 5:30 A.M. to chant and going to bed at 9:00 P.M. when lights are turned off.

Entertainment consists of one hour's TV news every evening, Chinese chess, table tennis, and every kind of reading that comes to hand, ranging from Daoist classics to martial-art fantasies and Shakespeare.

"The Daoists of the 1980s are different from what they used to be," said Si Xiaojing, a twenty-three-year old student from a traditional Daoist family in Jiangsu Province. "The Daoists of today have talents and intellect."

An avid reader, the young Daoist finds manifestations of the Dao in contemporary Western philosophy, and even quantum mechanics. He is "especially fascinated" by the notion that one is to consume the lowest level of energy so as to preserve natural and human resources—a very Daoist notion.

When not studying, the young Daoists help the older priests take care of the two temples, which are open to Shanghai's more than two thousand Daoist followers.

Document 53

100 Monasteries Reopened

Hong Kong Standard, *12 September 1984.*

China has reopened about one hundred Daoist monasteries and temples, a meeting of the Chinese Daoist Association was told.

Secretary-General Wang Weiye said these included the monasteries of Taiqing in Shenyang, Tianshidong in Sichuan, Yuquanyuan in Shaanxi, and Maoshan in Jiangsu, and the temples of Changchun in Wuchang, Zixiao in Hubei, and Baopu in Hangzhou.

They are served by over three thousand priests and nuns.

Daoism, indigenous to China and over eighteen hundred years old, is the strongest in the rural south.

The Mount Wudang center received seven hundred thousand pilgrims last year.

The association, set up in 1957, implements the government's policy on freedom of religious belief. It has trained sixty priests and published fifteen hundred sets of scriptures and several papers on Daoism.

Local governments have helped restore temples. Beijing's White Cloud Temple has been renovated at a cost of 1 million *yuan* (about US $358,000).

Document 54

Priests Urged To Work in Fields

South China Morning Post, *12 November 1984.*

Daoist priests living in seclusion should work in the fields as well as run their places of worship, China's National Daoist Association said yesterday.

"This is a good way for Daoists to support themselves and contribute to the country's Socialist economic construction," said a resolution adopted at the association's annual meeting.

More than forty Daoists from seventeen provinces and cities attended the week-long session at the White Cloud Temple in Beijing, the New China News Agency said.

Daoism is China's oldest surviving religion, based on the teachings of the sage Laozi in the 6th century B.C.

Along with other faiths, it was suppressed during the Communist Party's 1966-76 "cultural revolution" and the aftermath of that tumultuous decade, reviving only a few years ago.

The government says "a number" of Daoist temples have been restored, but the overall number of temples, priests, and believers is not known.

Document 55

The Current Situation of Daoism in Qingchengshan, Sichuan Province

From Religious Questions under Socialism in China, *pp. 211-13. Translated by Zheng Xi'an and Donald MacInnis.*

Qingchengshan is located fifteen kilometers southwest of Guang County in Sichuan Province. Daoists call it "the Fifth Wonderland," or "the Wonderland of Nine Rooms for Celestials." According to legend, Zhang Lin of the Han Dynasty climbed the mountain, preached there, and erected buildings. This is said to be the way in which Qingchengshan became a Daoist center.

Qingcheng means "green city." The two peaks, Qingcheng and Pengzu, form an axis with two lines of green ridges running southward, embracing what seems like outer city walls from both sides like a chair or dustpan. Outside the walls are crimson cliffs that even strong and vigorous monkeys cannot surmount. Inside the walls there are green trees the year around. The place looks exactly like a city, and so it is called Qingcheng.

Through dynasty after dynasty about seventy temples and monasteries have been built here. Six principal temples still exist: Jiafu Temple, Guchang Temple at the Tianshi Cave, Zushi Hall, Shanqing Temple, Yuanmin Temple, and Yuqing Temple.

During the "ten years of chaos" ("cultural revolution"), the temples and monasteries were closed and the Daoist priests were dismissed and driven out. When the Party's policy on religion was eventually reinstated after the Third Plenary Session of the Eleventh Party Congress, temples and economic-production facilities were gradually returned to the Daoist priests, and religious activities have resumed. Guchang Temple at Tianshi Cave, where the local Daoist Association is located, has been repaired with the help of the government. The mountain path from Qingchengshan to Shangqing Palace has also been repaired and widened. The "Nine Turns," which made access very difficult, are now wide enough for two people to safely climb abreast.

There are about fifty Daoist priests and nuns now at Qingchengshan living in the temples. Ten of them are elderly, while the rest are young men and women. In addition there are about one hundred lay Daoists and workers of different ages helping them maintain the temples.

Not long ago Qingchengshan enrolled a number of young believers who had offered themselves for lifetime religious vocations. Candidates must meet these criteria: they must be willing volunteers, have family approval, be unmarried, and be under age thirty, with senior-high-school education. In lieu of an examination, they must write an article explaining what they know about Daoism. After moving into the temple for three months of study, labor, and community life (paying for their own board), they are examined by the head priests.

The young novices who have been admitted are wearing Daoist clerical robes. Master Zhang Zhilin teaches their Chinese class, while Master Zhang Zhiyi teaches *Wugong*. They chant the scriptures morning and evening, accompanied by drums and gongs. During the day they work at various jobs. Ten students have been sent to Beijing to study under sponsorship of the Chinese Daoist Association. The first graduates have returned and are in charge of daily routines at Guchang Temple.

One young nun had been orphaned during the "cultural revolution" when her mother, a teacher, died from unbearable insults. With no means of livelihood, she despaired of life in the outside world and decided to become a nun.

Another nun, originally a junior-high-school teacher of Chinese language and literature, came to the mountain for rest and therapy after falling ill. After recovering her health, she became a nun.

When asked why they had become Daoist believers, the young novices said they did so to provide successors to the older generation. Of course, there were other reasons. Some liked the freedom and quiet of the mountain, some wanted to become skilled in *Taiji wugong,* while others came to find a livelihood.

There are two kinds of income-producing projects at Qingchengshan, production and services. They produce wine, soda water, and tea, and offer services to visitors and tourists. ... Services for visitors include admission tickets, a restaurant, overnight accommodations, etc. With a million visitors a year, the admission tickets alone, at 20 *fen* each, provide 200,000 *yuan.* Overnight lodging also brings in significant revenues.

These solutions for the problem of self-support offer great potential for development. Fu Tianyuan, chairman of the Qingchengshan Daoist Association, said, "After Liberation, Daoism could no longer rely upon donations and fees for casting lots based on classic scriptures as before. Daoism must be self-supporting and create ways to sustain itself."

Zhou Enlai, Zhu De, Chen Yi, Deng Xiaoping, and other Chinese leaders have visited the mountain since Liberation. Foreign friends, such as the king and queen of Sweden, and friends from Canada, Australia, France, and West Germany have visited this scenic spot. Premier Zhao Ziyang came to the Qingchengshan Tianshi Cave on 21 June 1985 and showed great interest in its scenery, historical relics, and recent development.

With the help of the People's Government, the lingering problems of Qingchengshan were solved at the end of 1985 when responsibilities were allocated as follows: the government will take care of the mountain, the priests will manage the temples, and the tourist trade will be conducted outside the temples. By solving the problems in this way, the doubts of religious believers were effectively eliminated, their unity [with all the people] was strengthened, their patriotism was reinforced, and their support for the four modernizations was brought fully into play.

Document 56

White Cloud Temple Reopens in Beijing

By Li Yangzheng, member of the research staff, Chinese Daoist Association, in China Reconstructs *(in English) No. 7, 7 July 1984.*

The White Cloud Temple (*Baiyunguan*) in Beijing is the biggest Daoist temple in north China, and famous enough to be referred to in some literary works. Closed when the "cultural revolution" began in 1966, it is now training monks again and receiving pilgrims as well as other visitors, who come to see its ancient architecture and interesting relics. . . .

The temple has a number of important cultural relics. One is an original 5,503-volume copy of the Ming dynasty edition of the Daoist canon, a gift from Emperor Ying Zong in 1448. The books, stored in one of the temple's pavilions, were traditionally taken out to be sunned during the first seven days of the sixth lunar month. During that period many scholars and Daoist monks would come to read them.

The fifty-eight hundred characters of the *Dao De Jing* inscribed on the side wall of the Hall of Ancestral Worship are in the handwriting of an earlier inscription made for the temple by the famous Yuan dynasty painter and calligrapher Zhao Mengfu. The original blocks were lost, so this nineteenth-century replacement was done from a rubbing of the original carvings, and is thus able to reproduce Zhao's hand quite accurately.

The Temple Today

Today some thirty Daoists are resident in the temple, the oldest of whom is over eighty, and most of whom are novices who were taken on following 1980. Many come from areas in China where Daoism has always been strong. They wear the robe and leggings of ancient times and wear their hair long and tied in a knot. Rising in the predawn hours, they clean the temple before morning services. Another scriptural service is held in the evening and in between they attend classes on the Daoist canons. Daoist rites are performed at major festivals. They live mainly on donations received in the course of religious activities, although as a national cultural relic the temple receives a subsidy for its upkeep from the People's Government.

The temple houses the office of the Chinese Daoist Association, which was established in 1957. In addition to administering religious affairs and doing research on the Daoist canons, it operates a Daoist school in the

temple and has trained nearly a hundred students from various parts of
the country.

Document 57

Religion Returns as a Way of Life

South China Morning Post, *15 March 1985.*

During the "cultural revolution" a 1,670-year-old Daoist temple in Canton was turned into a plastics factory during an antireligion orgy.

Yet, that very same temple last Wednesday week—the fifteenth day of
the first lunar month—had to close its gates at 2 P.M. after a record crowd
of 110,000 worshipers had crammed in for Lantern Festival celebrations.

The intensity of religious feelings shown at San Yuan Temple is just one
example of how religion once again plays a daily part in the lives of millions
in Canton and elsewhere in China.

It surfaces most clearly during religious festivals such as Christmas and
last week's Lantern Festival.

"It was the first time we have had to close the gates," said Mr. Wu
Xinda, head Daoist priest of the temple.

The gracious building's brief career as a plastics factory happened during
the notorious reign of the "gang of four" who condemned religion as feudalistic.

The temple was reopened in July 1982.

Mr. Wu, who has been a priest for forty years, said San Yuan Temple
is the most popular in the province and one of the most well-known in the
mainland—attracting worshipers from all over the country and overseas.

Six more priests will be enlisted this year to cope with everincreasing
demand.

Currently the temple has about fifty staff, including nine priests. Mr. Wu
said the enormous Lantern Festival turnout was partly due to an opportune
relief from the past two months' misty weather.

He added: "It's a bit strange, we had the first fine day making it a perfect
occasion for worshiping at the Lantern Festival."

The temple is usually open from 4 A.M. until 5 P.M. for normal festivals.

But by early afternoon that Wednesday literally every inch of ground
was packed and the air was filled with smoke from burning joss sticks.

Said Mr. Wu: "Our staff complained about the stifling atmosphere and
thick smoke which reddened their eyes after many hours of work.

"It would have been dangerous for worshipers if we had not closed the
gates."

The festival is considered to be the Chinese version of Valentine's Day, and a large proportion of worshipers were young.

Thousands clutched windmills of fortune on the streets as a symbol of good luck.

Inside the temple worshipers had to fight their way up stairs, treading on half-burnt joss sticks and lucky papers to reach the main altar.

Document 58

Over 100 Daoist Temples Reopened

NCNA, in English, 17 September 1986 (excerpts). FE 8360, 10 September 1986, reprinted in China Study Project Journal 2:2, p. 74.

Xi Zhongxun, member of the Political Bureau of the CCP Central Committee, has called for further study of the Daoist canon and the training of more young Daoist professionals. The Daoist scriptures are valuable to the study of the country's ideological, literal (as received), and scientific development, he said at a meeting of delegates attending the fourth national conference of the China Daoist Association. . . .

More than one hundred Daoist temples have reopened since the association restored its religious activities in 1979. In the past few years, more than one hundred younger Daoist priests have been trained. The Daoist Association's fourth national conference, which ended today (17 September—report datelined Beijing), reelected Li Yuhang chairman of the association, and Wang Jiaohua, Liu Zhiwei, and Fu Zhitian vice-chairmen.

Document 59

Mao's Philosophy Influenced by Daoism

China Daily, 25 April 1988 (excerpts); from a review of the book, Mao Zedong Thought and the Chinese Cultural Tradition, *a collection of essays by Wang Shubai.*

Mao's philosophy also was influenced by Daoism. For instance, his principle of "one divides into two" can be traced back to the Daoist theory about *yin* and *yang*, and the roots of his belief that things may change into the reverse are found in Daoist philosopher Laozi's conception that fortune and misfortune may transform into each other.

The author also points out that the Daoist interpretation of historical development as a movement in endless cycles exerted its influence on Mao.

During the "cultural revolution" (1966-76) Mao went to such extremes as to conclude that nationwide turbulence like that needed for the country's order, was bound to happen every seven or eight years.

His firm belief in the principle of "one divides into two" led to a conclusion about absolute conflict and made him reject any possibility of compromise. . . .

Islam in China Today

Introduction

As the dominant religion and culture of ten ethnic minorities in China, Islam has survived and thrived since it was first brought in as early as the eighth century by Arab traders who came by land and by sea. While most Muslims are concentrated in the northwest, thriving communities exist in Beijing, Yunnan, and other parts of China, while other small communities stubbornly maintain their religion and customs in such isolated areas as Hainan Island, where, according to a U.S. anthropologist from UCLA whom I met in Hongkong, two Muslim villages have survived for centuries.

Indeed, in visits with imams and laypersons in Xi'an, Beijing, Hangzhou, Quanzhou, Fuzhou, Yunnan, Sichuan, and Tibet, I learned how tenaciously the Chinese Muslims hold onto their faith and life-style, even in places where the Han population is overwhelmingly dominant. Because of their strategic importance, both in numbers and in their geographical locations, the Muslims and their religion did not suffer the same degree of assault and depredation during the "cultural revolution" as did other religions. Some of the mosques I saw had been placed off limits to marauding Red Guards by government order. Moreover, Islam in China is so dispersed and localized, with no provincial or national hierarchy, that there is nothing, other than the mosque itself, to attack.

Islam in China has survived almost as a hermetic community within the larger population, replacing its numbers and growing largely from within the community itself. Yet, despite the total inculturation of Islam in China, the "acids of modernity" appear to be eating into this seemingly monolithic religious-culture group, and many of today's young people, marrying outside the faith and moving away from the Muslim neighborhoods, are moving away from the faith as well.

Islam at Local and Provincial Levels

As with other religions, estimates of total adherents of Islam in China vary widely, from as low as 12 million to 30 million or more. When interviewed in May 1988 the general secretary of the Yunnan Islamic Association said there are 14 million Muslims in China, with four hundred thousand in Yunnan Province and twenty thousand in Kunming City, which has only six mosques. Muslims in Yunnan trace back to the Yuan dynasty, when a Mongol general disbanded his army and the former soldiers settled there.

In other parts of China, particularly the northwest, whole districts and regions are overwhelmingly Muslim, although the in-migration of Han Chinese has dramatically changed the demographic patterns. Writing in the 1970s, Owen Lattimore, a U.S. specialist on Inner Asia, said that the number of Uyghurs in the Uyghur Autonomous Region of Xinjiang had fallen from 80 percent of the population in 1949 to 50 percent in 1973, while the number of Chinese had risen from two hundred thousand to 2.8 million.

It was reported to the 1987 National Congress of the Chinese Islamic Association that twenty thousand mosques were open, and that most Muslims could now worship in mosques close to their homes. The same report said that more than two thousand Muslims from China had gone on pilgrimage to Mecca in 1986. In several interviews I asked imams and Muslim laypersons about mosque attendance, new clergy vocations, and other indications of religious vitality. Mosque attendance varies, but in the Friday services I witnessed the worshipers were all men, middle-aged and older. Only sixty men, from a citywide community of seven to eight thousand Muslims, attended the Friday service at the last remaining mosque in Chengdu the day I was there. Young workers, men and women members of a class in Arabic at the Chengdu mosque, explained how the Muslim community had been forced to scatter due to the dispersion of jobs and housing, making it difficult to come to the mosque. In former days Muslims lived in their own communities surrounding the mosques.

An imam in Xiaguan, a town on the famous Burma Road in southern Yunnan, said that young people are "lured away from religion" by material things and other temptations of modern life. "Now they want money and things. It's too bad, after years of 'cultural revolution' and deprivation of religious rights, and now the government and the Party guarantee freedom of religious belief, but many young people don't care. They aren't interested in religion."

Young members of the Arabic class at the Huang Cheng Mosque in Chengdu, when asked about the faith of young Muslims, said, "It's not good here; it's better in the northwest. . . . Youth don't understand the Muslim faith, because they have little opportunity to come to the mosque.

"It's a very mixed up situation. Some believe and some don't. Some believe in Buddhism, some in Islam, some in Jesus Christ or Marx, or simply in themselves. . . . Young people today are pessimistic. They've given up believing in anything."

Another reason given was the language of the *zuma* (Friday service), which, except for the sermon, is all in Arabic, primarily readings from the Qur'an. "But the *ahong* seldom preaches a sermon. That's one reason there are few young Muslims at worship; they don't understand the doctrine."

According to a 1984 report (Document 63), the 29,000 mosques and 54,000 imams in Xinjiang in the 1950s had been reduced to 14,000 mosques, with 29,000 imams, by 1966. Only 1,400 mosques stayed open during the "cultural revolution." By 1983 the Regional Islamic Association said there were 14,000 mosques, with 15,000 imams, a significant recovery but still a serious decline from earlier years.

Reports from the National Islamic Association

As with the annual report of the Chinese Buddhist Association cited above, the main tasks listed in the report to the 1987 conference of the Chinese Islamic Association are limited, leaving much to the local *ahong* and his mosque committee. The Association's tasks are: to cooperate with the government in carrying out religious policy; to organize clergy-training programs; to continue publishing Islamic scriptures and the national periodical; and to continue friendly international exchanges. The main functions of religious administration are carried on at the level of the local mosque. Aside from the provincial Islamic Association, which is viewed as an arm of the government, the local mosque is autonomous. There is no religious hierarchy.

Islam in China, Religion and State

The author of "Notes of a Visit to Mainland China" (Document 68), a member of a Muslim delegation which visited China in 1985, gives his perceptions of the role and functions of the China Islamic Association, its relations with the Religious Affairs Bureau, and the limited authority of a local Association. According to his report, there were no Islamic clergy-training schools as recently as 1985.

Islam and Socialism

An additional task named in the 1987 annual report was "To enhance unity among the various [ethnic] nationalities," a situation especially complex in dealing with the Muslim community in China, with its ten ethnic minorities.

The article by John Voll (Document 69) compares the experience of Muslim minorities in China and the Soviet Union. Both countries have special policies for dealing with ethnic minorities, and the Muslims, with their tradition of *jihad* (holy war or crusade), and fierce sense of identity, pose particular problems. However, the author concludes that Muslim minority communities can survive in strong Communist states, which, in fact, is the case in both China and the Soviet Union. "They are not disappearing . . . . [and] it may be possible to discern the outlines of a nonmajoritarian but permanent style of Muslim community emerging . . . in a manner that insures continued, relatively untroubled survival."

PROBLEMS ADAPTING ISLAM TO CHINESE SOCIALISM

Document 70 presents the results of field studies in two Uyghur villages involving 207 households in summer, 1983. In addition to demographic and other information, the researcher divides his essay into three sections, each a thesis in itself: Islam is closely connected with the national [ethnic] character of the believers; Islam has a profound social and ideological foundation among its believers, and all national minorities in the past thirty years have traveled the same rough road in their religious activities.

His detailed analysis leads to the conclusion, in which he seeks to demonstrate how Marxists can form a united front with religious believers from such ethnic minority groups as the Muslims, giving political, economic, cultural, and socioethical reasons why this can be done. "The past thirty years," he writes, "have proven that it is fully possible for Islam in Xinjiang to adapt to the practice of Socialism in China and to play the role that it should."

THE DUAL FUNCTIONS OF ISLAM

Another scholarly article (Document 71) analyzes what the author calls the "dual functions" of Islam in a district of Xinjiang Province. His thesis, put in the form of a question, asks: What are the actual functions of Islamic activities in building the two civilizations [material and spiritual], and how do they relate to the building of the Socialist spiritual civilization? Since Islam is a religion, with dual functions, both positive and negative, does one function outweigh the other, and how is this situation best handled?

The positive functions are described and analyzed, with examples from field research in Xiji District, Ningxia: Islamic teachings and moral principles are consonant with those of Socialism; Islamic districts have a low crime rate; Muslims follow principles of equality, tolerance, compassion, honesty, and moderation; Muslims cooperate in promoting family planning and other government policies; the Muslim life-style fosters self-restraint rather than self-indulgence; Muslim teachings are opposed to idol worship and superstition; and Muslims have friendly exchanges with Muslims abroad.

The next section describes the negative influences, including what the authors call fatalism, feudal dross, interference with public schools, pressure on nonbelievers, and the economic burden of supporting the religious establishment. However, they conclude that "religion can play a positive role and make its special contribution when patriotism is combined with love of Islam," and that the focus of attention should be on the reform of society itself, rather than religion. It is wrong for some officials to "use religion as an excuse for every error, and cover up their own mistakes" by directing attention to the negative influences of religion. Religion and Socialism can work together for common goals.

Clergy Education

The training of clergy takes place at four levels, I was told by Ahong Zhang in Chengdu. First is the tutorial system, where a *tudi* (novice) studies under a local *ahong*. The next is a mosque school, where classes are organized and taught by the local *ahong*. At the provincial level, there may be an Islamic college, as there is in Kunming. Finally, there is the National Islamic Institute in Beijing.

Ahong Zhang told me that China has eight or nine Islamic colleges or academies, but many of the graduates do not become *ahongs*. They may become translators or take other jobs. The result, he said, is a shortage of well-educated clergy, and most young *ahongs* are still trained in their local mosque.

The article in *China Daily* (Document 73) confirms Ahong Zhang's observation about the Beijing Islamic College graduates: "Most of the students do not want to be ordained imams. They have a thirst for knowledge and want to see more of the world. One of their aspirations is going abroad to study." In fact, 8 had already gone to Egypt for further studies. With only 106 students from the whole country in 1985, the Beijing Islamic College would not supply many *ahongs* in any case.

Section I

Islam at Local and Provincial Levels

Document 60

Islam in Yunnan Province

Interviews by Donald MacInnis at four mosques in Kunming, Xiaguan, and Dali, 1988.

The Nancheng and Xuncheng Mosques in Kunming

THE PROVINCIAL ISLAMIC ASSOCIATION LEADER

I visited the Nancheng Mosque in Kunming in May 1988 and talked with the general secretary of the provincial Islamic Association, Mr. Ma. He was busy preparing for the Kaizaijie festival the following day—the end of Ramadan.

Q. How many Muslims are there in Kunming?

A. Kunming Municipality, which includes four districts and five counties, has 50,000 Muslims. We trace back to the *Yuan* [Mongol] dynasty. There are 14 million Muslims in all of China. Kunming City has six mosques, twenty thousand Muslims and an average of five imams for each mosque.

Q. How many persons come for weekly worship?

A. Tomorrow about half of the Muslims will come for the festival.

Q. Do you have any mosque schools here?

A. There are three mosque schools in Kunming. Nancheng Mosque has over forty students, Xuncheng Mosque over thirty, and Yongning Mosque about the same.

There is also an Islamic College [*jinxueyuan*] here, a government-registered school which serves three provinces, Yunnan, Guizhou and Sichuan. Graduates become imams at the "jiaozhang" level, which is higher than ordinary imams. They must be high-school graduates, pass the entrance examination, and study for three years.

The mosque schools accept students as low as primary-school level. They study for three or four years under the imam. Some study at home, using a correspondence course.

Q. Is there any problem finding young candidates willing to prepare for the life of a clergyman?

A. No, we have plenty of young men studying to be imams; in fact we have a surplus. Some must wait for job openings.

There are five hundred mosques in Yunnan, and quite a few have mosque schools. There are one hundred to two hundred graduates a year, but not all become imams immediately; they may have to wait for a job opening. We still have plenty of older imams. The students can "wear the hat" of an imam after completing their studies.

Q. How are new imams placed in jobs?

A. A local mosque invites the new imam. They may ask the Islamic Association to help by suggesting names.

Q. Are Islamic young people faithful to their religion?

A. That depends on the individual. Most of them are conscientious [*renzhen*].

Q. Are there ethnic minorities in Yunnan who are Muslims?

A. No, Yunnan Muslims are all Han [Hui]. But there are Muslims among ten national minorities in China.

Q. What happens when a Han Muslim marries, for example, a Uyghur?

A. When children are born, the parents decide whether the children will be Han or Uyghur. If the father is Han, the child will be Han.

Q. Tomorrow is Kaizaijie festival. What will you do?

A. Last night the government observatory telephoned us at the first sight of the moon, which marked the end of Ramadan. Today we will gather in the mosque for a two-hour worship service. This is one of our three annual festivals.

After that the families will travel by bus to the Muslim cemetery, to read the Qur'an and honor the ancestors. Then we will return to our homes for dinner, usually inviting friends or relatives to join us. After that we will go visiting.

Q. Was your cemetery destroyed?

A. Yes, the graves were destroyed and the cemetery land is occupied by others now. The government gave us funds to buy land for a new cemetery.

Q. Have any Muslims from Yunnan gone on pilgrimage to Mecca [*hajj*]?

A. Very few can afford it, since the individual has to pay his own travel costs. Nevertheless, forty Muslims from Yunnan applied to go this year, but we were only allowed to send fifteen. Fifteen went last year, among over a thousand from China. So people wait their turn.

The Local Mosque School

I spoke with a young student in the mosque school, which is taught by the imams.

Q. What do you study?

A. The Qur'an, interpretations of the teachings of Muhammad, and the Arabic language. We have some textbooks. We learn to translate Chinese into Arabic. Our curriculum includes religion classes and a language class, using lessons sent from Beijing written by elderly scholars who studied in Egypt in the 1930s. We also have the option of elective study, taking classes on our own in the local Chinese school. We study and use the Qur'an in Arabic, but have a recent Chinese translation which we use for reference.

Two Islamic Schools in the Xuncheng Mosque

I visited the Xuncheng mosque and was introduced to two elderly imams, one ninety-two and the other seventy-one, who were playing with their grandchildren. Families with children were relaxing in the courtyard in the early evening, a nice family atmosphere. We had the impression here, and at the mosques elsewhere, that the mosque is a center of social life. They were all waiting for sunset, so they could eat supper, since Ramadan had not yet ended.

Six or eight men came to pray aloud and read from the Qur'an at about 6 P.M. One woman prayed, kneeling behind a screen. They read aloud from an Arabic Qur'an, but I was told that "they can read the sounds, but not the meaning."

I talked with the two imams, and with some students and teachers from the two schools in the mosque compound. One is the usual mosque school, taught by the imams. The other, the Islamic college run by the government which opened the previous year, offers a three-year course to qualified high-school graduates.

The government school has thirty-five students, all young men. Half of the budget comes from the government, and half from the Muslim faithful. All expenses are paid for the students.

I asked the students about their future work. They were a bit vague, saying they would work for the government and serve the Muslim people.

The curriculum includes the Arabic language, study of the Qur'an, Muslim doctrine and theology, history, politics, economics, and Chinese.

The mosque school has a five-year course that includes Arabic, Persian, Qur'an studies, Chinese, Islamic doctrine, history, politics, economics, and natural science. The students all come from Muslim families. In Yunnan, Muslims are all *Hui*, "mixed blood," I was told, tracing back to the early Arab traders who came across Central Asia on the old Silk Road, or by sea to the China coastal ports, particularly Quanzhou in Fujian Province.

The Local Mosque

About 250 attend the weekly services [*zuma*] on Friday. During Ramadan they take no food or drink for as long as fourteen hours, depending on the time between sunrise and sunset. "We are accustomed to it," they said.

I asked one man, who worked in a factory, if he said prayers five times daily.

Not five times, he said, "It's not convenient to pray at work." He prays at home three times daily, in the morning, at noon, and in the evening.

At the Islamic college students assemble five times daily and pray together for twenty minutes. The prayers are actually readings from the Qur'an.

I asked about the survival of Muslim customs and life style. They observe Muslim dietary laws, and the government makes special provisions for them in State-operated dining rooms, restaurants and markets.

They do not drink alcoholic beverages (although one man, the owner of a small restaurant in Dali, told me he drinks beer; "stronger liquors make my mind fuzzy, which would displease Allah").

I asked the students about smoking. "We don't smoke, but some Muslim sects allow smoking."

Q. Can you have four wives?
A. Not in China. We obey the laws of China.

Q. Do non-Muslims convert to your faith, other than by marriage?
A. Very few, but anyone is welcome to become a Muslim. We belong to the Sunni branch of Islam. Our philosophy is peace among all people. We are a religion of peace. The whole world is a family. We want the world to be like that. Ours is a free religion. Anyone can join if they wish, without any pressure — unlike Christians [who aggressively evangelize, is the implication].

Q. Can imams marry?
A. We encourage them to marry. We have no nuns; women should marry and have families. We oppose birth control. [Mr. Ma, the restaurant owner in Dali, has four grown children, born during the time when the government imposed no limits on ethnic minorities. Now, he told me, the government limits them to two, by law. Formerly they only urged them to limit the number, but now they are fined if they have more than two.]

Q. How would you compare Muslims and Buddhists in China?
A. Buddhists aren't organized. They have no Buddhist community as we do. They aren't trained in doctrine. They go to the temple only when they want to ask for something from Buddha, or on special festivals. They burn incense and *bai bai* [kneeling and incantations]. Christians do the same.

Q. What Muslim publications do you have?
A. We have the Qur'an in Arabic and Chinese, but there are very few Qur'ans published in China. We have only one or two copies of the Chinese Qur'an. Only sixty-eight thousand copies were printed in the first printing.

Q. Is there a Muslim magazine?

A. Yes, it is published by the government. But it is very thin [*danbo*], nothing worth reading. There is no local or provincial publication.

The Mosque in Xiaguan and Dali

I visited the mosque in Xiaguan, near Dali in southwestern Yunnan, one evening about 8:00 P.M. The imam, seventy-six, is tall, thin, and distinguished-looking, with a wispy white beard and an energetic stride. He was friendly and talked freely, answering my questions without hesitation. He said he had no "school education," but had studied under the former imam. The previous evening about three hundred adults had spent the whole night here together in worship, celebrating the near end of Ramadan. First they had supper together, then they spent the night reading from the Qur'an and praying together, and finally eating breakfast together. There would be a big festival in two days, the end of Ramadan.

There are two thousand Muslims in Xiaguan, ten thousand in Dali Prefecture, and fifteen mosques, all served by imams.

The imam of Xiaguan Mosque was persecuted for his faith and "wore a cap" (suffered ridicule as a "bad element") for eighteen years, from 1958 to 1976. All imams were taken to a certain town in 1958 for four months of political study, then "capped."

I asked if there was a problem finding candidates to take the places of older clergy. This triggered a flow of words. "This is a big question here and everywhere, for all religions," he said. "The Catholic situation is even worse. Fr. Liu in Dali is all alone; there is no other priest." (That was true. Fr. Liu, who is the bishop, was the only priest in the entire diocese.)

"Because of the material progress in our country, young people are lured away from religion. They want more money and things. It's too bad, after years of 'cultural revolution' and deprivation of religious rights, now the government and the Party guarantee freedom of religious belief, but many young people don't care. They aren't interested in religion. Some young Muslims marry a non-Muslim and give up the dietary laws and stop coming to religious services. Or the husband and wife will fight about these things. They should not marry outside the faith. It's a big problem."

He said the Muslims in the northwest provinces, where the majority of the people are Muslims, have a problem. Some of them say, as his imam teacher had said to him, that it's better not to go to an Islamic school, only study Arabic and the Qur'an under a local imam. But he disagrees: it's better to go to a regular school, like the school in Kunming, and study Arabic, Persian, Chinese, even English. (But he had some doubts about the government-run Islamic college.)

Dali, nearby, had four mosques before the "cultural revolution" but has only two now. One burned and one was torn down. Xiaguan has one mosque in town and one in the nearby rural region. Wenshan, thirty kilometers from Dali, has twenty mosques.

Dali has ten imams, in their sixties and older, and two young imams who studied in a mosque school in Wenshan.

Document 61

Islam in Sichuan Province

Interviews by Donald MacInnis with the imam, students, and staff of a Muslim community and school, 1988.

I visited the Huang Cheng Mosque twice during a two-week trip to Sichuan and Tibet in July 1988. This is the only functioning mosque for the city of Chengdu, although I was told there are seven to eight thousand Muslims in the city and one hundred thousand in the province. Before Liberation there were thirteen mosques in the city and three hundred in the province, of which one hundred have been reopened. Ten older imams remain in Chengdu, six over eighty and three over ninety: "imams never retire." They have no young imams because they don't have a regular mosque school, only an after-work, spare-time Arabic class for about twenty young people, mostly men, all in their twenties.

I interviewed the general secretary of the municipal Islamic Association, Mr. Ma, sixty-seven, an energetic and committed layman who serves as a volunteer, taking no salary. (The provincial Islamic Asociation office was located across the courtyard, but is staffed by non-Muslims, I was told.) The Arabic class had just finished, and I talked with four young men, all factory workers, who were heading homeward.

Youth and Religion

I asked them about the faith of young Muslims today.

"It's not good here; it's better in the northwestern provinces. Formerly we all lived in a Muslim community near the mosque. Now we are dispersed, too far from the mosque. We have to work, even on Fridays. We travel by bicycle. [He showed me on a map where he worked, where he lived with his parents, and the location of the mosque, all widely separated.] Youth don't understand the Muslim faith. Why? Because they have little opportunity to come to the mosque.

"It's a very mixed-up situation [*hen fuza*]. Some believe and some don't. Some believe in Buddhism, some in Islam, some in Jesus Christ or Marx or simply in themselves. In China everyone has freedom to believe what they wish. The young people today are pessimistic. They've given up believing in anything. In the northwest, Muslims grow up in a religious culture; they learn the faith from childhood, and there are plenty of imams. Not here. There is no opportunity for young people to learn about religion. They don't live in a Muslim community any more. They are too dispersed. Our only hope is the new property [being discussed with the government], to build a new mosque and Muslims can move to that district and live together."

I asked a young man why he came to the mosque. He cited the "three cleans" [*san gan*]: *difang, i-fu,* and *shen-xin* [place, clothing, and person, i.e., body and heart]. "I feel an inner comfort [*shufu*] here. We are very busy at work, and come here to be quiet." Indeed, the shaded mosque courtyard was a quiet retreat from the busy city outside its gates.

Children

I asked them about children and religion. Formerly, they said, all children were brought to the mosque for dedication (*qimeng*) at the age of four years and four months, but no more. Why? Does the government prohibit it? They weren't sure. Maybe parents are too busy or live too far away.

There was also a *qimeng* ceremony at age twelve for boys and nine for girls, when they were allowed to begin study of Arabic, "because that is the age when they can understand," but they no longer do this. Muslims are too widely dispersed now.

"Are children taught the faith by their parents?" I asked. "What about mixed marriages?"

"That depends on the Muslim parent. We have freedom of religious belief. We can't force religion on anyone."

They asked me, "Do you believe in religion?"

I replied, "Yes, I am a Christian."

"Oh, we are very close then, we are really brothers in faith."

I asked why they are studying Arabic. Do they wish to become imams? They laughed, "No, just to be better Muslims."

One young man in his early thirties had come here from the northwest to take a job after completing a degree in electrical engineering. He works in a factory, but doesn't like his work. He plans to take an examination, hoping to be accepted for graduate study in Muslim cultural history at the National Minorities Institute in Beijing. He answered my questions as follows.

THE MUSLIM CEMETERY

Their cemetery was destroyed by the government in the 1950s, "when the government did not respect religion. Our cemeteries are very sacred to Muslims." Buildings now cover the site, so the government has given them new land for their cemetery.

MARRIAGE

Muslims are not required to be married in the mosque. But *xili* must be performed by an imam. *Xili* is administered for new converts, but not for children of the Hui Muslims. They don't celebrate the Qingming festival, but do go to the graves on the birth and death days of family members, and on the first day after Ramadan. Funerals are conducted in the mosque.

Formerly, any non-Muslim who married into the faith must become a Muslim (Hui), and the children are also Hui. Now things are not so strict; as a result, they are losing members.

MOSQUE ADMINISTRATION

Formerly there was a managing committee (*lishihui*), but not now, not since Liberation. Now the local Islamic Association manages everything, even the finances. "And they [the provincial-association staff] aren't even Muslims!" The imam never touches the money. All he does is lead worship and teach the Arabic class.

SABBATH WORSHIP

The sabbath worship service is all in Arabic (readings from the Qur'an), except the preaching, which is in Chinese. "But now the imam seldom preaches a sermon. That's one reason there are few young Muslims at worship, they don't understand the doctrine." (In fact there were about fifty persons at the *zuma* service that day, all older men. All came in clean white clothing, and all washed in a special bathroom prior to the service. There were no women.)

The Islamic Association

Mr. Ma, the association secretary, described the functions of his office. The Islamic Association has only a loose connection with the mosques, he said. Each local mosque is autonomous. There is no hierarchy, either in the province or nationwide. Each mosque is financially independent. Right now he is helping the mosque leaders negotiate with the government for a new place to build a larger mosque.

Q. Is there no accreditation process for new imams? Is it left up to the local mosque?

A. Yes and no. There is no examination, no criteria set by the Muslim Association. The local mosque invites any candidate they choose, investing him in a solemn ceremony. The association may help, by recommending qualified persons.

Q. Can you get permission to build new mosques?

A. Yes, if we can prove we need them. But the government doesn't like the people to waste money on excessive religious construction. Now farmers have more money, so they are building shrines and temples.

Q. What is your financial situation?

A. Money is no problem. We have all we need. Imams, even the oldest ones, are paid about 90 *yuan* a month, in addition to personal gifts from the faithful.

An Interview with Ahong Zhang

In a second visit I talked with the chief imam, Ahong Zhang. He spoke of the lack of new imams to replace those now over age.

"Formerly there were thirteen mosques in Chengdu, each with its own mosque school. There were ten thousand Hui in 1982, some of them non-believers, of course. Now, with a larger population, we have only one mosque and no clergy-training class.

"There are two other mosques that could be used, but they have been taken over by factories. The government can't get them out. This district alone had eight mosques. The Drum Tower Mosque is the oldest, with the most unique architecture in the city, but it now serves as a warehouse, and non-Muslim families have moved into the courtyard and built homes. We can't get them out."

"Won't the Religious Affairs Bureau help?" I asked.

"No, we have to do it ourselves, otherwise the Religious Affairs Bureau will manage everything we do. We are trying to get back the West Gate Mosque, but it's dragging along, because we Muslims aren't well organized, and we have differences with the Islamic Association."

Clergy Training

Ahong Zhang explained the four levels of training for Muslim clergy. The first is one-on-one, a tutorial system under the local imam. The next is a mosque school, also taught by the imam. At the provincial level, there may be an Islamic college, as in Kunming. And finally there is the National Islamic Institute in Beijing.

China has eight or nine Islamic schools, but many of the graduates do not become imams. They may become translators or take other jobs. So there is a shortage of educated imams, and most young imams are still trained by their local imam. "Before Liberation we had a very good mosque school here, operated by ourselves."

Women

I asked about women. Only men can become imams. In some places women can become deacons (*zhishi*); they can lead prayers, but for women only. While all Muslims are expected to say prayers and perform other requirements of the faith, women can be excused because of responsibilities at home, menstruation, pregnancy, or for health or other reasons. In this mosque the women all pray at home, except for one or two old women who come now "because things are lax, compared to the old days."

Document 62

Islam in One Province: Revival in Xinjiang

Excerpted from "Islam in China," China Study Project Bulletin, *No. 25, August 1984, p. 14.*

In the 1950s there were about 29,000 mosques in Xinjiang and 54,000 imams. By 1966 there were said to be 14,000 mosques with 29,000 imams. In the "cultural revolution" only 1,400 mosques stayed open (or, according to another report 1,040). Today the figure is back to 14,000 and may be higher. In August 1983 the Regional Islamic Association gave the figure of 14,000 and indicated that in Muslim areas each production team of 200-300 persons had its own mosque. The number of religious professionals was, however, only 15,000 — a clear indication of the process of decimation over the years of the "cultural revolution." A Qur'anic college has been established in Urumqi, and the leading members of the Islamic Association are permitted to take on two or three *manlas* — Islamic students.

Some recent reports from Kashgar have revealed the strength of Islam in this part of China. In this prefecture there are 6,180 mosques, 260 more than in 1966. In the city of Kashgar, with its population of 120,000, there are 99 mosques, including the huge Aitika Mosque, which holds 10,000 worshipers. About 10,000 attend daily prayers at the mosque and 50,000 on Fridays. During the "cultural revolution" the Red Guards were Uyghurs from Muslim families, but this did not prevent the burning of the Qur'an and the persecution of believers. A visiting group of Western journalists was told by the muezzin at the Aitika Mosque that now "the old Red Guards come and pray for forgiveness. Allah welcomes the people who have corrected their mistakes."

Another sign of the revival of Islamic fortunes in Xinjiang and of the increased official toleration is the upsurge in numbers of those going on the *hajj* pilgrimage. In 1982 the Regional Association sent 31 people to Mecca, and a further 8 went on their own. In 1983 the number rose to 313, most going at their own expense, the highest figure in Xinjiang's history. According to NCNA (27 March 1984) before 1949 only 20 or 30 wealthy Muslims could afford to go. Now in 1984 1,000 people have applied. Pilgrims will now be able to travel from Kashgar to Karachi direct instead of having to go to Beijing, thus halving travel expenses.

Document 63

Rural Muslims: Prayer and Progress, the Changying Mosque, Beijing

By Lu Yun, Beijing Review *(in English) No. 33, 18 August 1986, pp. 19-20.*

Most of China's ten Muslim minorities live in the northwestern part of the country. The Huis, one of these minorities, have a population of about 7.2 million, widely scattered around the country. In Beijing alone there are about 185,000. According to historical records, the Huis date back over one thousand years to the Tang dynasty. In the seventh century, Persians, Arabs, and people of Central Asia came to settle in China, where they gradually formed an independent ethnic minority. Though most Huis have adopted Mandarin as their spoken and written language, they have retained their particular religious belief and customs.

With a population of 8,500, of whom 5,400 are Huis and the rest Hans, the township of Changying, 20 km east of Beijing proper, offers visitors an interesting insight into the way of life and religion of the Huis.

The Changying Mosque

Life for the Huis in Changying has changed considerably since 1976, said sixty-seven-year-old Imam Qin Yuwen. During the "cultural revolution," the Red Guards criticized the imams and made it impossible for the Huis to carry our their normal religious activities. The Red Guards even installed a foundry in their mosque. Each production team, including Muslim ones, was required to run a pig farm. "Since 1976, however, all of these wrongs have been put right," Qin noted. The mosque has been reopened. The imams' religious rights have been restored and the pig farms have been demolished. Out of deference to the Huis' customs, the Hans in Changying do not now eat pork, even at weddings.

The Changying Mosque was built in the early seventeenth century and is one of the largest in Beijing. Now about one hundred Muslims, mostly old men and women, go to the mosque regularly to be led in prayer by the imam. On Fridays, about four hundred Muslims gather at the mosque for a special service, and on the holidays of the Prophet's Birthday, the Lesser Bairam, and the Corban Festival, more than seven hundred Muslims attend the mosque to attend the birth of Muhammad (c. 570-632), the founder of Islam. On the Prophet's Birthday last year, the Changying Muslims held elaborate celebrations involving the slaughter of cattle and sheep, making a special porridge, and preparing more than seventy tables for a dinner party attended by Changying's residents. Changying's two imams said they were satisfied with the availability of Qur'ans in Chinese. They said they were also satisfied with their work of presiding over festivals, weddings, and funerals was all carried out according to Islamic law. They gave money raised at such gatherings to the mosque management committee, which then paid them a monthly salary.

They also said the township had worked to repair the men's mosque, rebuild the women's mosque, build a women's washroom and garden walkway, and to expand the men's washroom. They said these projects were financed by the mosque and the local government. Part of the expenses were covered with donations from the Muslim community.

The mosque management committee, which is made up of the two imams and twenty other Muslims, oversees the mosques' religious functions, financial affairs, and sideline production. In 1981 it opened a mill for making noodles and husking rice. The mill now has seven machines and brings in an average monthly profit of 1,000 *yuan*.

The mosque has spent much of its income serving the Muslim community. In the last two years it has spent 10,000 *yuan* building a bridge, paving a section of asphalt road, and installing lamps along a 300-meter drive.

At the mosque, four young men are studying Arabic and the Qur'an with the imams. The four, who were recruited last October, have graduated from middle school and will study Islam for two years. They will then take the entrance examination to study at Beijing's Islamic College for another two years, after which they will become imams. One of the four, Mu Huaisong, eighteen, said he chose religious work after reading *A Brief History of Islam* and the Qur'an. Imam Qin, who teaches the young men, often says, "I am happy that we now have successors who will carry on Islamic beliefs in Changying."

Document 64

A Visitor Reports on Mosques in Tianjin and Xilinhot, Inner Mongolia

Peter Humphrey, "Islam in China" (excerpts), in Religion in Communist Dominated Lands, *Autumn 1982, pp. 174-76.*

Two mosques in Tianjin which the writer visited in 1981 have now been restored and are open for worship. There are 120,000 Muslims in Tianjin, concentrated mainly around the Great Mosque in the northwest corner of the old Chinese city and in the mosque in the suburb of Tianmucun. The

Great Mosque, built in the very conventional temple style of the Qing dynasty (1644-1911), with tiled roofs, red woodwork, and coffered ceilings, is also the headquarters of the Tianjin Islamic Association. The central and local governments provided 400,000 *yuan* for its restoration. A local Muslim claimed that the mosque has several tens of priests (*akhuns*), the youngest of whom is forty-six. This seems a rather excessive number, but some of them may originate from other mosques, now closed. (There were fifteen functioning mosques in Tianjin in 1936.)

The situation at Tianmucun falls far behind this. The mosque, also dating from the Qing dynasty, was closed at the advent of the "cultural revolution" in 1966. The mosque and its surrounding land became a factory and storage depot. The local and central governments have jointly provided 100,000 *yuan* for its renovation. The street-committee deputy told me that there were seven *akhuns* in Tianmucun with an average age of fifty, the oldest being eighty years old.

In Peking's Dong Si Mosque I saw a thousand worshipers attending the most important ceremonies, young and old, all wearing Muslim caps. After Ox Street Mosque reopened in 1980 some of the ten thousand Muslims who live in its vicinity but had been worshiping at the Dong Si Mosque returned to Ox Street for their prayers. But the overall total of Peking Muslims attending the two mosques has increased since the Islamic congress, and the local Muslims were extremely jubilant and proud at this development.

Yet there is evidence of restriction even so. A visit to a minuscule mosque in Xilinhot, Inner Mongolia, revealed a different story. Xilinhot opened to foreigners in 1979. It is a small town of mud-brick houses with very little attraction for the tourist but an overnight stay in a simulated Mongolian tent. Along one of its muddy lanes, the town hides its only mosque, also a shabby mud-brick building, totally unadorned. The inside walls are whitewashed, with two wooden pillars. The floors are covered with rough straw mats and a single strip of Koranic calligraphy occupies the center of the wall. The *akhun* lives next door in a spartan dwelling with chickens scratching around his doorway. He is sixty years old, retired, and lives on a pension of 40 to 50 *yuan* a month. He is in poor health and constantly bronchitic, but he beams with friendship and benevolence. There are two thousand Hui Muslims in Xilinhot, he said. They were originally small peddlers. The mosque was established after the Liberation. During the 1950s the Muslims worshipped freely every day. "I even gave scripture classes to the children, and in those days the mosque was decorated, not just bare walls as today," he said. But in 1958 the "religious reform" forbade the participation of children. He added that from 1958 to 1966 about thirty to forty adults continued to worship daily, and on Fridays they were up to one hundred.

"But in 1966 the 'cultural revolution' began, and the mosque was vandalized. It was occupied first by a school and later by a production brigade. Worship stopped completely except in the home."

He said he was away sick when this happened, euphemistically hinting he was in hiding. Although he suffered no bullying, he conceded that elsewhere *akhuns* were beaten. His own children, he said, were bullied in the street "because your daddy is an *akhun*." Some *akhuns* were paraded in the streets like common criminals and others were killed. The mosque reopened in 1979 under the new religious amnesty. But even today, with this reconstituted freedom of belief, they are permitted to open for worship only once a week.

"Now the gathering has dwindled to a dozen or so old men. Children and youths don't come." It seems they are pressured not to participate. "And I am not permitted to teach the children. Even the 'children' of the mosque school days haven't come back," he said sadly.

In spring 1982 in Canton, the writer found that the mosque there, which is celebrated as being the oldest in China, is only open once weekly on Fridays. The rest of the time it is locked.

In Lanzhou, the provincial capital of Kansu, and in Xinjiang the writer found literally scores of what were once mosques now being used as factories, albeit dilapidated ones. Admittedly, one or two mosques were under restoration there with local Muslim contributions, and Muslim traders and dough makers were back in free enterprise on the streets in accordance with the relaxation of economic policies for the ethnic minorities.

Section II

Reports from the National Islamic Association

Document 65

Resolution Adopted by the Fifth Conference of the Islamic Association of China, June 1987, in Beijing

In Journal of the Institute of Muslim Minority Affairs, *8:2, July 1987, p. 423.*

A resolution was unanimously adopted at the Conference, which declares that, after the conclusion of the Conference, the main tasks for the China Islamic Association are:

1. To further assist the government with the implementation of the policy of religious freedom.

2. To enhance unity among the various nationalities and that among the Muslims, on the basis of unity, run Islamic undertakings more effectively.

3. To bring about democratic management of mosques, establish and perfect rules and regulations, properly arrange religious affairs, and, according to the practical situation and possibility, organize production and social-welfare services to increase the income of mosques.

4. To conduct religious education well and train qualified young successors for the religion of Islam. Cooperation between the China Islamic Institute and the local Islamic institutes should be encouraged, experiences exchanged, and the ranks of teachers replenished so as to raise the teaching quality and train talented personnel who love the motherland and who have a comparatively high religious and cultural level.

5. To continue translating and publishing Islamic scriptures, run well *The Chinese Muslims* magazine, conduct researches in Islam, and study and carry forward the fine cultural and moral traditions of Chinese Muslims.

6. To continue international friendly contacts and cultural exchanges, further the existing friendship and cooperation with Muslims in other countries, oppose hegemonism, and defend world peace.

The resolution emphasizes that active efforts should be made to establish friendly ties with Muslims in Hongkong, Macau, and Taiwan and those residing in foreign lands and help realize the reunification of the motherland in line with the principle of "one country, two systems."

The Conference called on Muslims throughout the country to unite more closely and, under the leadership of the people's government, make concerted efforts and go all out to run well Islamic affairs and contribute to the rejuvenation of China.

Through democratic consultation, the Conference elected 211 members to the Fifth Committee of the China Islamic Association. And at the first meeting of the Fifth Committee, 80 were elected as standing-committee members, the tasks for the year of 1987 were fixed, and the leading body of the Fifth Committee was formed as follows:

Honorary President: Burhan Shahidi

Advisor: Mohammed Ali Zhang Jie

President: Ilias Shen Xiaxi

Vice Presidents: Kemaludin Bai Shouyi, Maulana Amuti, Salih An Shiwei, Godret Allah Ma Tengai, Abdul Rahim Ma Songting, Yahya Liu Pinyi, Hadji Husayn, Shamsudin Ma Jincheng, Sulaiman Zhang Bingduo, Nu'man Ma Xian, Ahmed Wajidi, Maulana Abdulah, Han Mansur, and Hadji Akbar

Secretary general: Nu'man Ma Xian (concurrently).

Document 66

Annual Work Report, June 1987, at the Fifth Conference of the Islamic Association of China, Beijing

Muslims in China, *June 1987, translated in China Study Project Journal 3:1, April 1988, pp. 85-86.*

Shen Xiaxi delivered a work report to the Fifth National Representative Conference of the China Islamic Association on 10 March 1987. His report was divided into two parts:

A. The work of the China Islamic Association done in the past few years:

1. Assisted the government in propagating and implementing the policy of freedom of religious belief. Since the Fourth Conference of the China Islamic Association, the Association has consistently paid great attention to studying, propagating, and implementing the policy of freedom of religious belief. Leading members and staff of the Association investigated and increased understanding of problems on implementing the policy of religion while they visited local Islamic Associations and attended meetings. They also raised suggestions and measures in order to solve problems. Over the past few years the Association received more than six hundred visitors and dealt with over three thousand letters.

2. Urged Islamic figures and the masses of Muslims to take part positively

in the construction of the two civilizations. The Association and the local Islamic Associations at various meetings positively guided the Islamic figures and Muslims of various nationalities to participate in the construction of the two civilizations. In addition, standing-committee members, committee members, and persons of Islamic circles also supported and advocated compulsory education in their remote home counties, raised money to set up schools, encouraged children to go to school and their family members to practice family planning, and planted trees and vegetables. Over the past two years mosques and Islamic Associations in some areas opened hotels, restaurants, shops, clinics, and nurseries, and other service enterprises which not only increased the incomes of the mosques, but also provided service to society.

3. Cultivated Islamic professionals. According to the resolution of the Fourth Conference of the Association, the China Islamic Theological College was reopened in 1982, and recruited the first batch of 42 students to attend the five-year regular course in September. The college now has 129 students of six nationalities. They come from twenty-seven provinces, cities, and autonomous regions in China. The students are divided into five grades and six classes to study Islamic scriptures, doctrine, the history of Islam, Arabic, and foundation courses of liberal arts at the university level. In the meantime, the China Islamic Theological College also gave its full support to the establishment of the Islamic Theological Colleges in Shenyang, Lanzhou, Ningxia, Zhengzhou, Kunming, Qinghai, Xinjiang, and other places by providing them with financial help, donating scriptures and books, teaching materials, recorders, Qur'an tapes, and Arabic typewriters. In recent years, Islamic Associations in some areas held refresher courses for *ahongs* and *mawlas*, and gave certificates to qualified *ahongs*. Moreover, with the support of government departments concerned, the China Islamic Association sent ten students to study in Egypt in 1982 for the first time since Liberation. In 1986 the second batch of students was sent to study abroad; three of them went to Libya. Last year the Islamic Associations of Xinjiang and Gansu also sent Muslim students to study in Pakistan.

4. Assisted in the reopening of mosques. At present more than twenty thousand mosques have been opened in China to meet the need of the masses of Muslims. Most mosques also set up democratic management committees so as to administer religious affairs and mosque properties. Some mosques' democratic management committees ran various collective production and service enterprises to reach a goal of being self-supporting.

5. Printed and published Islamic scriptures and books, conducted academic research on Islam, and published the periodical *Muslims in China*. The China Islamic Association printed and published more than eight hundred thousand copies of ten kinds of Islamic scriptures and books. The Association also participated in the editorial work of the Islamic section of the religious volume of the *Chinese Encyclopedia*. The periodical *Muslims*

in China in the Han and Uyghur languages resumed publication in 1981 and 1983.

It produced twenty-two issues of the Han edition and fourteen issues of the Uyghur edition. The Islamic Scriptures and Books Circulating Office was set up by the China Islamic Association. Since 1984 the circulating office was set up by the China Islamic Association. Since 1984 the circulating office also sells goods so as to provide service for Muslims of various nationalities.

6. Organized Muslim pilgrimages to Mecca. Since the Fourth Conference of the Association, the Association has organized seven Chinese Muslim pilgrimages to Mecca, with 187 pilgrims of ten nationalities taking part. Last year the number of Chinese pilgrims reached over 2,000. In 1986 the Association also edited and printed the "Notices of Pilgrimage" and set up the "pilgrimage reception team."

7. Developed friendly international relations and academic exchanges. The China Islamic Association invited and received thirty-six groups from more than twenty countries and regions, totaling 126 people. In the last seven years, the Association also organized twenty-five delegations of 73 members to Islamic countries, paying goodwill visits or attending academic conferences.

B. The tasks for the future.

1. To carry forward the traditions of Islam, to positively lead Islamic figures and the broad masses of Muslims to strengthen unity, and to contribute to the construction of the two civilizations of the motherland.

2. To assist the government in implementing the policy of freedom of religious belief and to strengthen the democratic management of mosques.

3. To run Islamic education well and to develop Islamic academic research.

4. To run theological education well and to nurture the young generation of patriotic imams.

5. To continue the publication of Islamic scriptures and books and to run the periodical *Muslims in China* well.

6. To collect and sort out Islamic relics and records and to develop academic research in Islam.

7. To do a good job of organizing pilgrimages.

8. To promote the unification of the motherland, and the maintenance of world peace.

Document 67

The Role of the China Islamic Association

By Ibrahim Ma Zhao-chun, Journal of the Institute of Muslim Minority Affairs *7:2, July 1986, pp. 382-83 (excerpt).*

All that has been said above points to one conclusion: the present situation is quite favorable to Chinese Muslims, who are capable of carrying forward the excellent traditions of Islam to fulfill the needs of national development under the "four modernizations." In this respect we have to acknowledge the cementing role played by the China Islamic Association and the local Islamic Associations at all levels. Through it the demands of Muslims are made known to the government and the policy of freedom of religious belief is implemented and carried through. In this way many mosques were repaired with financial aid from the government and protected as cultural places of historic value. In addition, the China Islamic Association and local Islamic Associations at all levels have played an especially important role in organizing pilgrimage missions, developing friendly relations with foreign Muslims, establishing the China Islamic Institute, printing and publishing Islamic books, etc. The three important undertakings recently accomplished by the China Islamic Association are worth noting again. The writing and compiling of the Islamic part of the religious volume of the *Chinese Encyclopedia*; organizing Muslims all over China to pray for world peace; collecting and, after putting on display, publishing *Collections of Chinese Muslim Calligraphy and Paintings* in aid of welfare for the disabled.

Nevertheless, the China Islamic Association is now confronting many urgent problems. These are: how to raise the working efficiency of their membership to meet the needs of the government policy of opening up to the world and of enlivening the national economy; how to train successors to the cause of Islam in China; and how to set up a comparatively large-scale Islamic Cultural Center in Beijing, and so on.

The Chinese Muslims firmly support Palestinian and Afghan Muslim brothers in their just struggle to restore their lost territories and safeguard their sovereignties. . . .

We are particularly concerned about peace and solidarity among Muslims, and maintain that all disputes among Muslims should be settled by consultation, according to the teaching of the Holy Qur'an: "Hold fast to the rope of Allah and do not split."

Section III

Islam in China: Religion and State

Document 68

Notes of a Visit to Mainland China

Ahmad Salah Jamjoon, Journal of the Institute of Muslim Minority Affairs *6:1, January 1985, pp. 215-17 (excerpt).*

It is quite evident that the Islamic Association in China is an official organization that serves to coordinate Islamic activities in conformity with official rules and laws of the country. Our inquiries revealed that the office bearers of the Islamic Association in Peking were government servants; so were some others working in the branches of the Islamic Association outside Peking. The activities of the Association were confined to regulating and fulfilling the wishes of the Muslims within the limits prescribed by the laws of the land. It could not on its own take any decision without referring to the Religious Affairs Department of the government. This was quite clear during our visit to the province of Eastern Turkestan. The delegation wanted to offer some copies of the Qur'an and other books, as well as some financial help, to the local branch of the Association. The office bearers of the Association accepted the books and copies of the Qur'an but refused to accept any financial help except through the Central Islamic Association of China based in Peking. This left the delegation with no choice but to give the amount, half a million dollars, to the central association, based in Peking.

On inquiring about the Islamic activities of the Islamic Association, the delegation came to know that these did not extend beyond the Islamic Institute that was established by it for training imams and teaching the Arabic language. We were told that this institute had been closed for quite a long time and was reopened only that very year. During our visit to the Institute we did not come across any of its students, but the management of the Institute told us that the Institute was closed for the vacation and the students had gone away to their homes after completing a full course. They told us that the Institute was to reopen next August.

The Islamic Association also undertook the printing of the Holy Qur'an.

It printed thirty thousand copies of good quality of the holy book in 1400 A.H. (1980 A.D.). This edition was already out of stock, and at the time they were preparing to bring out a second edition. As to the Association's magazine *Al-Muslimun*, they told us they were thinking of restarting its publication in the beginning of the coming year. These were the only important practical activities of the Association.

We also came to know through our inquiries that there were many Muslims in other cities who adhered to the teachings of Islam and taught Qur'an to their children, but in homes only. The government had completely forbidden its teaching in mosques. The number of such people among the Chinese Muslims was, however, very small, and that was one reason why there were no Islamic schools.

Section IV

Islam and Socialism

Document 69

Islam in China and the Soviet Union

*An excerpt from "Muslim Minority Alternatives in China and the
Soviet Union," by John O. Voll,* Journal of the Institute of
Muslim Minority Affairs *6:2, July 1985, pp. 349-52.*

Official Establishments. In addition to the informal Muslim organizations
and the indirectly Islamic nationalities, there is an important third dimension of Islamic minority life in China and the Soviet Union. In both countries there is some form of an officially organized Muslim establishment.
These are often criticized as simply being mouthpieces for government
policies. However, the simple but startling fact that these are government-
supported Islamic organizations in a political system which is officially atheistic is often overlooked.

The government-supported Islamic leaders clearly operate under many
restrictions. At the same time, they give at least some visibility to the continued existence of Muslim communities in China and the Soviet Union.
The revival of the Chinese Islamic Association and the reopening of the
Chinese Institute of Theology in 1980 represent continued public presentation of Islam, regardless of how circumscribed the conditions. . . .

These Muslim organizations are not directly tied to the officially recognized nationalities. They cross the boundaries of the nationalities and
become a different level of Islamic action. The Soviet muftis and Chinese
leaders have played a role in articulating Muslim ideas in the context of
Communist ideology. Majoritarian Muslims might not accept the pro-
nouncements of the official Muslim leaders in Communist states, but these
states do represent an expression of explicitly Islamic views, from within a
Communist regime.

The mediating role of the official establishments is clear. It provides a
link between the governing political system and the Muslim communities.
This religious establishment is not regime-threatening and does not insist
on an autonomous-type program. However, at the same time, it helps to

support the continued existence of the Muslim communities in a basically non-Muslim society. This establishment provides acceptable ways of articulating Muslim sentiments while remaining within the framework of Communist policies. The existence of this mediation provides the argument from the existing institutions that Muslim communities can survive within a Communist society, again, without having to live with only the alternatives of *hijrah, jihad,* or hidden, secret belief. . . .

Certain basic assumptions about Muslim minority life deserve to be reexamined in the light of the contemporary Muslim experience in China and the Soviet Union. In particular, the basic assumption of the clear or absolute incompatibility of Islam and Communism needs to be reconsidered. In concrete terms of social and religious life, it appears that mediating structures have emerged which make Muslim minority life in a Communist society possible without resort to the classically defined options of *jihad, hijrah,* or secret belief. Public belief and practice appear to be possible within the Soviet Union and China.

The informal devotional groups and *tariqahs,* the nationalities, and the formal "official" establishments with the government-approved mosques and administrations all provide a framework of institutions supporting the continuing life of Muslim communities in the Soviet Union and China. While under certain conditions any of these structures might be vehicles for autonomist movements, this does not, at present, seem to represent their primary function. Rather than acting as a focus for opposition to the existing political system and social order of which the Muslim communities are a part, these structures appear to be performing a significant mediating function. This makes it possible to be, in many significant ways, an individual with those characteristics which — in the Communist theory, majoritarian Muslim teaching, and much Western analysis — appear to be contradictory and impossible to combine: being a Muslim and being a Communist.

It may be necessary to develop a set of assumptions relating to Muslim life that recognizes more clearly the realities of the Muslim minority condition. In particular, the cases of the Soviet Union and China make it clear that there are large Muslim communities (in fact, the fourth and twelfth largest in the world) which are minorities now and will not gain majority control for the long-term forseeable future. These communities are living in a context where *jihad* has been tried by parts of the community, but such actions have not been successful. It is difficult to conceive of a Muslim revolt being able to defeat the armed forces of the central governments of either China or the Soviet Union. In addition, it seems quite clear that most Muslims in these two countries do not have a great desire to engage in a *jihad* against their own government.

Similarly, there seems to be remarkably little desire in these communities to emigrate to regions where they could live under the circumstances of being a part of a Muslim majority. It seems clear from many studies that

Central Asian Muslims are tied to their homelands and, even with substantial material incentives, have little inclination to move from them. . . .

The special cases of the Muslim communities in the Soviet Union and China may not provide people with firm conclusions about the modern Islamic experience. However, it seems clear that whatever may be the contradictions in terms of logical analysis, in terms of actual life Muslim minority communities can and are surviving in strong Communist states. They are not disappearing, nor are the only viable survival strategies those of *hijrah* or *jihad*. Instead, it may be possible to discern the outlines of a nonmajoritarian but permanent style of Muslim community emerging. This is a community with both formal-official structures and informal organizations. These mediate between the Muslim communities and the larger societies, not always in a manner that is free from tension but apparently, at least, in a manner that insures continued, relatively untroubled survival.

Document 70

Problems Adapting Islam to Chinese Socialist Practice in Xinjiang Province

He Yanji in Religious Questions under Socialism in China *(Shanghai Academy of Social Sciences, 1987), pp. 247-56; translated by Zheng Xi'an and Donald MacInnis.*

Religion is a complex social phenomenon. In old China it was under the control of the ruling classes, who used it for their own purposes with serious negative effects on social progress. Since Liberation, after the profound transformation of the economy and society, and major reforms in the religious systems, religion in China has experienced fundamental changes. Contradictions related to religion are mainly contradictions among the people [nonantagonistic contradictions]. Religion, as a social ideology and as a belief held by a portion of our people, will continue to exist for a long time. Religious believers are only a minority of the people of China. But in Xinjiang more than half the people are Muslims. Therefore, both in theory and practice, it is important to study the relationship between religion and Socialist practice, and, in Xinjiang Province, to study the relationship between Islam and the developing construction of Xinjiang.

There are ten Muslim national minorities in China, and all ten can be found in Xinjiang. Three of the ten, that is, the Dongxiang, Sala, and Bao'an, moved to Xinjiang from the eastern provinces after Liberation. Based on the size of their populations, beginning with the largest, these ten groups are: Uyghur, Kazakh, Hui, Kirgiz, Dongxiang, Tajik, Uzbek,

Tartar, Sala, and Bao'an. These ten peoples are all Muslims, but, owing to differences in their way of life, environment, social influences, ways of economic production, and religious history and customs, there are differences in the depth of their religious belief and religious practices. Even members of the same national minority are influenced in the way they practice their faith by where they live, whether in cities or the countryside, near cities and towns with convenient communications, or in remote mountainous areas, as well as by their occupations, whether farmers, workers, intellectuals, or cadres.

From May to July 1983, we carried out a sample survey of 207 Uyghur households in two compact rural communities in the Kashi area. In villages A and B, 92.1 percent of the adults surveyed took part in religious services. Of these, (1) there were more women than men, (2) more elderly than middle-aged, and even fewer among the young. There were fewer Uyghur workers living in Kashi City going to services than the Uyghur villagers. The results of our survey can be compared with those of an earlier one made by our Nationalities Research Institute. It is easy to see from these statistics that fewer urban workers take part in religious activities than people in the countryside.

From May to July 1984, we conducted field research on Islam among residents of two Kazakh villages in Yili, made up of both farmers and herdsmen. I visited every person and every household, with the following results. 21.55 percent of the adults regularly participated in religious activities, of whom (1) there were more men than women, (2) they were mainly people over 50, with very few middle-aged or younger. Among the 102 Uyghur, Kazakh, and Hui Muslim workers of the Yili woolen textile factory surveyed by the Nationalities Research Institute, 50.99 percent took part in regular worship services. Of those surveyed, 30.39 percent could recite from the Qur'an, and 26.4 percent observed the Islamic rules on fasting, either fully or in part. Most of this group were Uyghur, and very few Kazakh, therefore it is difficult to compare their situation with data obtained from the two Kazakh villages. The number of workers from the Kashi cotton textile factory is different from those of the Yili woolen textile factory, as well.

Although these Muslim nationality groups surveyed all believe in the same religion, they show differences in many respects, yet they do have common factors which derive from their religious faith. These are:

Islam is closely connected with the national [ethnic] character of the believers, and shows strong national [ethnic] features.

Islam was introduced into Xinjiang more than a thousand years ago, and Islamic customs have long been absorbed into the national [ethnic] culture of these believers. In a Muslim family, people take part unconsciously, from birth to death, in the various religious activities that come along, such as the giving of an Islamic name, circumcision, funerals, etc. Some religious activities must be observed according to the ethnic custom, such as the special reading [*nika*] at weddings, and worship services for festivals, which must be observed by all the males, even children as young as five or six. They have several meals a day, and after each meal they will say "*duwa*" to thank Khuda [Persian for Allah] for his beneficence. Usually these people, particularly the elderly, connect Khuda with whatever happens to them in their daily life and work, including their successes and failures. Every one of these people, even those who do not read the scriptures, and those under age eighteen, never cease to praise the True Lord. This is a powerful social force, and many people accept the Islamic faith under these subtle influences.

Except for the Yi-chang sect, no other sect in Xinjiang has formal requirements for membership. It can be said that when a Muslim child is born, he is a Muslim. This is why some people consider the term Muslim to be equivalent to the Islamic national minorities.

Islam has a profound social and ideological foundation among its believers.

Muslims believe that, besides the real society of this world, there is a supernatural heavenly garden [paradise] and a fiery hell. They believe that the real world is temporary, and the heavenly garden on the other shore is everlasting. In the village of Kashi, when we made a sample survey of 100 Uyghur high-school students, asking whether a person's soul lives on after death, 95 of them answered yes. In the village of Yili we put the same question to 159 Kazakh junior-high-school students, and 128 of them, that is, 80.5 percent, answered, yes. The foundation of their religious epistemology is belief in the everlasting soul. The replies of the junior high school students represent their own thinking, but also reflect the minds of the adults in those villages.

At present, most people above the age of fifty or sixty, including activists, model workers and basic-level cadres who worked on land reform and the movement to organize cooperatives in the period after Liberation, take part in religious activities. A number of basic-level cadres who have not yet reached the retirement age say that they will live a religious life after they retire. In their hearts they are constantly concerned with the problem of whether their souls will go up to heaven or down into a fiery hell after their death. While young and full of sap they ill-treated people and handled some things in a wrong way under the misguided influence of the "leftists." Now they are old and demoted to the level of ordinary people, old folks living at home with no work to do. They have relaxed their self-imposed strict ideological demands. Looking back on their past in a repentant mood, they do not review their past record in a correct way, but spend their time hoping for a final "good result," that is, to go to heaven. These people are most regular in worship, and are highly influential.

In the past thirty years, all national minorities, in their religious activities, have traveled the same rough road.

Our Party has always practiced the policy of religious freedom. But in the course of carrying it out, problems have occurred. From the year of Liberation [1949] to 1957 we abolished the religious system of exploitation and carried out religious reforms while upholding the Party's policy of freedom of religious belief. Religious activities were carried on in a normal way during those years. In 1958, during the "great leap forward," places of worship [*libaisi*] were severely damaged. In the ten years of domestic turmoil, almost all places of worship were destroyed, and imams were denounced. Since the Third Plenary Session of the Eleventh Party Congress, people's hearts have been won over by the Party's implementing of all policies, including the policy on religion. According to surveys made in three successive years, Muslims from all national minorities are quite satisfied with the Party's policy on freedom of religious belief. Since 1979, the number of people attending Islamic activities has greatly increased, for many reasons.

First, religious believers have revived normal religious activities because the policy on religion is being carried out. Religious feelings which were suppressed for many years were suddenly released. The number of people attending religious services has increased with a rush, just as a spring will stretch beyond its normal length when pressure on it is released.

Second, their attendance at religious services since the inauguration of the responsibility system in agriculture is protected in a material way, because the standard of living for rural people has greatly improved, giving them more flexibility in arranging their time. Man's first need is to fill his stomach. With his stomach rumbling with hunger, who can think about attending worship services? When people all "eat from the same big pot" their time also belongs to the collective, and there is little time left at one's own disposal. Nowadays people are much freer than before to decide whether they will work in the fields, attend religious activities, or take a rest. The flourishing of the Mali Muslim sect in southern Xinjiang is directly related to the improved economic situation. In the past, only one member of the family could ride the donkey to the mosque for services. Now every family has a vehicle drawn by a donkey, horse, or ox, and the whole family can ride to worship. Some even go by cars or tractors, with several families riding together.

Third, political and ideological work in the villages has weakened, due to its failure to keep up with the changing situation. Some people turn to religion because their spirit is unsteady.

Fourth, religion in this area is spread widely in hundreds of thousands of homes, and religious activities are thriving. Religious policy restricts the propagation of religion to temples, churches, and mosques, but it cannot be so sharply limited when an entire people group is religious. In certain places in recent years, nonbelievers were put under spiritual pressures. For example, religious believers would not shake hands when they met them, they would not pay neighborly visits to non-Muslims on holidays, nor would they attend their funerals. In certain areas, where there are large population movements, imams would appear without having a residence registration and without proper occupations; they moved from place to place, setting up small meeting points for reading scriptures and in general stirring up a religious atmosphere.

The Marxist worldview is opposed to any kind of theism; but in political action it is fully possible, in fact it is absolutely necessary, for Marxists to form a united front with religious believers in the common struggle for building Socialist modernization. Our field surveys show that Islam can coordinate with Socialist practice and play its role as long as we can implement the Party's policy on religion and do our work well.

1. From the political viewpoint, Socialism represents the basic interests of all of China's people, including the Muslim minority nationalities. The intrinsic difference in comparing Socialist society with slave-holding, feudalist, and capitalist societies, is that the social phenomenon whereby some people oppress and exploit other people is wiped out. In the process of carrying out land reform and cutting rents and opposing local tyrants after Liberation, we seized the land which had been taken over by people in the feudal upper ranks of religious circles and redistributed it to the peasants who had little or no land. We abolished religious taxes [wushouer] and [zaket], enabling 550,000 households with more than 1,900,000 peasants to acquire 7,200,000 mu of land, 70,265 head of livestock, more than 390,000 farm tools, more than 190,000 houses, and 9,340,000 catties of grain. These people stood up and began to live a new life.

As a result, Socialism and the Communist Party were loved and supported by the broad masses of the Muslim national minorities. One liberated peasant, Kurban Tulumu, expressed the class feeling in a vivid way by wishing to go to Beijing on his donkey to see Chairman Mao.

What is this "heavenly garden" [paradise] that Moslems talk about? They say that it is larger than this real world, a seven-story heaven. There are two rivers running through it, with water whiter than milk and the fragrance of musk. The people there use household utensils made of gold and silver, and the food they eat is something we have never tasted. This heavenly garden is not beyond the imagination of real people. Muslim comrades from the Xinjiang national minorities have seen that only the Communist Party could make them masters of the land, only the Socialist system could give them a comfortable living and create a "heavenly garden" on earth where fragrant flowers bloom in all directions. Elderly persons recall how people were filled with political enthusiasm in the early days after Liberation, and attendance at Islamic services decreased.

2. From an economic point of view, the interests of believers and non-believers coincide. The eagerness of all the people to get rich, including Xinjiang Moslems, is seen in the way they take part in Socialist construction and the struggle to achieve the four modernizations. The favorable turn in the Xinjiang economy, particularly economic progress in northern and southern Xinjiang, is without question due to the cooperation of believers and non-believers under the leadership of the Party.

In 1983 we gave an examination to 100 Uyghur third- to fifth-graders, and this year we examined 225 Kazakh students from the same grades. Their answers to the question "How can one have a happy life?" are as follows:

CHART 1

Primary Students from Two Villages Reply to the Question "How Can One Have a Happy Life?"

	No. of Persons Interviewed	How Can One Have a Happy Life?							
		By One's Own Labor		Rely on Allah		Mainly Rely on Allah but Also on One's Own Labor		Mainly Rely on One's Own Labor, but Partly on Allah	
		No. of Persons	Percent	No. of Persons	Percent	No. of Persons	Percent	No. of Persons	Percent
Village #1	100	7	7	7	7	36	36	50	50
Village #2	225	17	7.56	31	13.78	112	48.78	79	35.11

The children's answers correspond very closely to those of their parents and other adults. In our surveys we discovered that 90 percent of the Muslims assume that a happy life depends on both one's own labor and on *Khuda* [Allah]. On this point, where we take the view that one can get rich by one's own labor, most Muslims will agree, at least in part.

3. With regard to the relationship between Muslims and non-Muslims, we assume that they will stand shoulder to shoulder and unite in the cause of progress. Relationships between most national minorities in Xinjiang and the Han people are the same as relationships between Muslims and non-Muslims. . . .

Since its introduction into China, Islam has been influenced by Chinese culture and historical and ethnic traditions, and from the beginning Muslims in China have come from the national minorities. Therefore the usual hostility of Muslims to non-believers has undergone basic changes in China.

The unity and cooperation of Muslim and Han workers have always been good throughout the history of Xinjiang. They have gone through thick and thin together, sweating together on the farms and shedding blood together to protect their territory. During the thirty years since Liberation this sharing of weal and woe has further developed through the education and practice of national unity. Now the idea that the Han people and the national minorities cannot be separated is deeply embedded in their hearts.

4. There is nothing contradictory between the Socialist code of conduct and certain Muslim moral norms. Although the starting points and the connotations are different, the end result can be the same. For example, in dealing with person-to-person relationships, the Islamic faith requires that its believers speak the truth, do good deeds, respect the elderly, give alms to the poor, aid the victims of natural calamities, care for orphans and widows, help each other, etc. As for themselves, Muslims are required to observe strict self-discipline, avoid doing bad things, refrain from smoking, drinking, gambling, stealing, etc. Objectively, this certainly is beneficial for social stability and order and for building Socialist spiritual civilization.

According to our surveys in Kashi, 78.8 percent of male adults in the two Uyghur villages did not smoke, and 99.6 percent did not drink alcoholic beverages. In the two places studied in Yili, 67.2 percent of the adults did not smoke (although women in the Xingyan pastureland region do smoke), and 87.8 percent did not drink. The people and cadres of the two Kashi villages said there had never been a case of drunkenness in recent years, and there was rarely a case of children failing to respect parents. What does it matter if religious believers do not understand the norms of Socialist morality from the Communist viewpoint, when their behavior conforms with the requirements of Socialist material and spiritual civilization, even though it is based on Islamic teachings and traditions?

The past thirty years of history have proven that it is fully possible for Islam in Xinjiang to adapt to the practice of Socialism in our country and to play the role that it should.

Document 71

A Study and Analysis of the "Dual Functions" of Islam in Xiji District (Ningxia Province) and Their Relation To Building a Spiritual Civilization

By Zhang Tongji and Zhang Yongqing, in Journal of Ningxia Social Sciences *No. 2, February 1986, reprinted in* Zongjiao *(Religion), Nanjing, February 1986. Translated by Tam Waiyi and Donald MacInnis.*

We live in a nationalities autonomous district where most of the people are members of the Hui minority. Our question is: What are the actual functions of Islamic activities in building the two civilizations [material and spiritual]; and how do they relate to the building of the Socialist spiritual civilization? It is extremely important both in theory and practice for us to clarify this question by seeking truth through facts. This study and analysis will not only help bring about a correct understanding and thus a correct handling of the nationalities religious question in our district, but it is essential for building a Socialist spiritual civilization in the district.

In our study of this problem over the past year, we have visited places where the majority of the people are members of the Hui minority, asking many people for their opinions and suggestions. Based on these surveys, we have formed our own views, which are set forth in this essay. . . .

Do Islamic Activities Have Only Negative Functions in the Building of Spiritual Civilization?

There are three dramatically different opinions regarding the relationship between Islamic activities in our district and the building of the two civilizations, especially spiritual civilization. The first view holds that the two are diametrically opposed, like fire and water, and if Islamic activities do not cease the building of a spiritual civilization in the Hui districts will be impossible. Supporters of the second view believe that there is no contradiction between the two. If religious activities are properly carried out, spiritual civilization will not be [adversely] affected. There is a third view which holds that Islamic activities under Socialist conditions have dual influences and functions, both positive and negative, and whether positive functions can be brought into play or not depends on correct and appropriate policies and measures.

Through our investigations of the current situation of Islamic activities in the Hui districts, we think that the first two opinions are too extreme and therefore not in line with reality. We support the third view because it reflects the new changes and characteristics of Islam under Socialist conditions in our district. If we respect facts, and do not base our fears on what we read in books or hear from officials, we cannot ignore the positive points of religion.

The positive functions of Islam in building a Socialist spiritual civilization are demonstrated by the following evidence.

First, some Islamic teachings, directly or indirectly, can serve the building of a Socialist spiritual civilization. For example, the moral principles of Islam which urge people to give up bad habits and practice good behavior are, objectively speaking, helpful, regardless of the motive of the speaker, in bringing bad social norms under control. Good social norms teach people to be good citizens and abide by the law. While the obvious improvement in social order in the Hui districts in recent years is due mainly to correct political and economic leadership, the positive functions of Islamic moral teaching should not be ignored.

The Hui villages of Jingxing in Wuzhong and Taizi in Lingwu are examples where the imams have added their teaching against stealing and gambling, based on the Qur'an and other sacred teachings, to the local governments' education of the masses about the civil law. The result is that many persons who were guilty of offenses have repented, some even returning stolen goods to the rightful owners. Now, not only are bad habits in these two villages under control, but there are many other persons who perform good deeds, such as not pocketing money found on the street, respecting the aged, and helping persons in need. In other Hui villages those "village customs and regulations" which conform to secular moral standards have been transformed into Socialist moral standards; this is very helpful in the movement for building "civilized villages" [model villages].

The positive functions of Islam are also demonstrated by the crime rate in Hui districts in recent years. Statistics published in a survey report on Hui criminals by Comrade Wang Xiren of the Ningxia Social Science Academy's Legal Research Institute show that only 0.06 percent of the entire Hui population had been charged with crimes even during the period of "strict justice" [*yen da*], while the rate was 0.1 percent in the Han districts.

Although the principle of "All Muslims are brothers," which promotes equality, tolerance, obedience, compassion, honesty, moderation, etc., was used by the reactionary rulers as a means to befuddle people's minds in the old capitalist society, it is an important factor today for strengthening unity and love within the Hui people, mediating differences among the people and giving full play to Socialist humanism. For example, after the responsibility system was inaugurated in the rural areas, there were quite a few conflicts caused by struggles over water rights and farmland. Religious teachings, supplementing [the government's] positive education, could double the results with half the effort in solving these problems.

Many conflicts among neighbors and families were resolved after principles such as respect for parents and concern for neighbors were promoted.

Second, some religious professionals became special propagandists, to a certain extent, for promoting and implementing the Party's policies and measures. The elders and imams in many mosques have combined the teaching of religious principles with promoting State matters in a new preaching form called *chuanjiang* (combination talks), which take place during the weekly *zuma* (Friday worship service) and other religious festivals. These "combination talks" are very effective because they can touch what is actually on the minds of the Muslim listeners.

Promoting family planning had been considered a difficult job in the Hui districts in recent years. Now, compared with other districts, this district has taken the lead, due mainly to the efforts of people in religious circles. Many imams who are skilled theological scholars have discovered teachings on birth control and contraception in the Qur'an, explaining in their sabbath day [*zuma*] preaching that family planning does not violate the principles of Islam. Some imams even take the lead, asking their own relatives and children to undergo tubal ligations to ease their anxieties about birth control.

Dongfeng Village, Wuzhong County, where more than 98 percent of the people are Hui, has one of the best family-planning programs in the county. Many religious professionals are no longer satisfied with keeping hands off these matters, as can be seen by the great contributions made by the imams of twenty-four mosques in Wuzhong County to promotion of state teachings; instead, they have organized on their own the "Hui Nationality Education Promotion Association" in Tongxing, Haiyuan, and Wuzhong counties. They want to use their influence to promote education. Some imams use the teachings on education in the Qur'an and other sacred teachings to convince Muslims they should send their children to public schools; some even donate money for the running of the schools. Some imams themselves teach children the importance of study, and urge them not to fast [during Ramadan] while attending school.

The positive functions of Islam mentioned above have been fully affirmed and highly praised by people at all levels in the district. More than twenty-five religious organizations and sixty-three persons were honored in the Meeting Praising the Services of Islam in Building the Four Modernizations held by the district in 1984.

Third, in life-style, Islam requires its people to strictly follow the habits and customs of their [minority] nationality, to practice self-restraint in matters of morality, and to avoid luxury and self-indulgence. Under the current open-door policy such constraints can help hold back the corrosive influences of capitalist culture and life-styles imported from abroad. Unhealthy books, magazines, audiotapes, and videocassettes widely circulated elsewhere in China are seldom seen in Hui villages. One of the most important reasons for this is the opposition of Muslim people themselves, who put up strong resistance to them as soon as they began to appear in Hui districts.

Fourth, because it does not condone worship of idols or nature worship, Islam also opposes superstitious activities which are harmful to people and swindle them of their money. For example, activities that are common in the Han districts, such as using witchcraft to heal illness, exorcising demons and fortune-telling, are seldom seen in the Hui districts. Some comrades hold the opinion that this is nothing more than "using a greater superstition to oppose smaller ones," or "combating poison with poison," while serving neither a positive or negative function. This is a kind of one-sided view of Islam which is unacceptable, for it lacks concrete analysis.

Moreover the Islamic world [in China] is helpful in promoting friendship and cooperation between China and Middle Eastern countries, and serves as a channel for cultural exchanges. This is of particular importance for opening to the outside world in the areas of cultural and economic exchanges with Islamic countries, which in turn will advance the building of the two civilizations in our region.

After making this survey and analysis, we are in basic agreement with those comrades who believe that, generally speaking, the contributions of Islam and Islamic activities to the building of Socialist spiritual civilization in this district certainly outweigh, objectively and subjectively, their negative effects. Islam can be turned into a positive force for the building of the two civilizations. We should encourage people in Islamic circles to thoroughly study the teachings of their sacred classics so as to utilize those that can serve the four modernizations, and come up with creative explanations of the teachings according to the spirit of the new era and the will of the majority of Muslims. Religion can play a positive role and make its special contribution when patriotism is combined with love of Islam. . . .

Negative Influences Should Not Be Ignored

It is not right to consider Islam under Socialism as a purely negative force; neither is it correct to think that religion is completely compatible with building a Socialist spiritual civilization, with no contradictions whatsoever.

We should clearly understand that the worldview of any religion is antagonistic to Communism. The explanations given by any religious worldview to the basic questions of the world are unscientific and contradictory to the objective laws of nature and the development of human society. Their predictions about the final ending of the world, which run counter to the faith and ideals of Communists, are ridiculous. Their theism is obscurantic and controls people's minds. It is not accurate to say that religion is in complete accord with Socialist spiritual civilization, with no negative impact on real life, on people's thinking, or on the two civilizations. Our investigation shows that Islam has several negative functions and influences on the two civilizations in our district:

1. The fatalism advocated by Islam is in direct opposition to the contemporary reform spirit. It makes some people with strong religious thinking believe that everything is decided by Allah [*zhen zhu*], causing them to take a negative attitude toward life. In rural reform these people are conservative-minded, easily satisfied with the status quo, and not interested in progress.

2. The feudal dross within Islam can easily link up with traditional ideas from the feudal society, strengthening some old customs, bad habits, and feudal superstitions that should be eliminated, and obstructing the correct implementation of the Party's policies and measures.

3. In a few places religion is still interfering with education and other social affairs, influencing the popularization and upgrading of science and culture, and weakening the receptivity of religious people to new things.

4. Some nonbelievers do not feel free under the psychological pressures of a suffocating religious atmosphere which prevails particularly in the Hui-nationality rural areas, where it brings a negative influence which is not helpful for the building of Party organization and ideology at the grassroots level. According to estimates of comrades in the United Front Department, about 70 to 80 percent of the Party members in Hui villages have, in varying degrees, taken part in religious activities; about 10 percent have even become faithful religious believers. We discovered a similar situation in some of the Hui villages where we conducted surveys.

5. Conflicts and contradictions among different religious sects still exist. Although they have eased up now, in some minority areas these unexpected incidents still flare up, damaging unity among the different nationalities and stability within the Hui people.

6. The economic burden on Muslims is growing heavier. Several million dollars have been spent for construction of mosques in various places over the past few years. Although this religious burden has eased up a bit now, it is still the heaviest expense borne by Muslim farmers in many places. According to a sample survey of 113 families in Najiahu, the "*mietie*" religious tax in 1984 was 8.4 *yuan* per person, a sum which exceeded the amount people gave to the government or put into collective savings. That was harmful not only to the Hui people but also to the development of the commodity economy and the cause of education and culture in the Hui districts.

However, the degree and extent of negative religious influences varies from place to place according to different conditions. In places where Party organization, Party style, and ideological work are in good shape, the influence of religion is less and can soon be overcome.

As a matter of fact, the "dual functions" of Islamic activities always overlap. When Islam is exercising positive functions, it will usually produce certain side effects. For example, during "chuanjiang" [combined talks in the Friday service], some imams mix Party policies in with religious teachings, thereby confusing the people. When teaching young people to resist unhealthy Western ideas and to be law-abiding, they also advocate certain feudal moral principles and old habits and customs which run counter to modernization concepts and life-style. We should have a clear understanding of these problems, insisting on using dialectical materialism for understanding the social functions of religion, and recognizing the unity of opposites. To neglect or exaggerate the influence or social functions of either one will be harmful to social practice.

Based on the above understanding and the precondition of freedom of religious belief, we believe that we should take a correct and vigorous attitude in dealing with religious questions in our district so as to bring into full play, insofar as possible, the positive functions of Islam and restrain its negative functions. We should face reality, acknowledge the protracted nature and mass character of religion, and protect the people's rightful freedom of belief. But this is not equivalent to accepting the negative effects of religion as reasonable. It is not in the fundamental interests and wishes of the great majority of the people, including religious believers, to take a *laissez-faire* attitude toward religion or to fail to give proper guidance.

Of course, to speak of putting limits on the negative effects of religion is not to advocate direct criticism of religion, for that will lead to "leftist" errors again. What we mean is to firmly carry out the religious and other social, political, and economic policies of the Party, and to raise the scientific and cultural levels and cognitive ability of the people through building the two civilizations. From the point of view of historical materialism, the negative influences of religion come from backward social and economic conditions rather than from religion itself. Facts prove that under the Socialist system, the more advanced the social and economic conditions are, the less the negative influences of religion will be. The reverse of that is that the more backward the social conditions, the greater the impact of such negative influences will be. Thus the focus of our attention should be on the reform of society itself, rather than on religion. The thinking and methods of those [officials] who use religion as an excuse for every error, and cover up mistakes in their own work by exaggerating the negative influences of religion, are unacceptable, while those who stop doing their part in economic production or other important work, but continue to criticize religion in order to demonstrate their "strong Marxist standpoint," are, in fact, widening the distance between themselves and Marxism.

These are some basic opinions and conclusions derived from our first-stage investigation and analysis. Some of our opinions have not yet matured. We sincerely hope that other comrades who also are interested in this problem will offer their help.

Section V

Clergy Education

Document 72

The Islamic Theology Institute, Ningxia

Xinhua, translated in JPRS-CPS-85-097, 19 September 1985, p. 112.

The first institute of Islamic theology in the Ningxia Hui autonomous region will enroll twenty students from senior middle schools and Muslim groups this month. Over five years, they will study Arabic, Han, and English languages, the Qur'an and other religious works, Islamic and other histories, law, and Chinese and world geography. After graduation, religious degrees will be awarded, according to the Regional Religious Affairs Bureau. Teachers will be invited from Beijing University and selected from local experts, the bureau said. Hui Muslims comprise one-third of the four million Ningxia residents. Over the past few years, 1,600 mosques have been built or restored in the region, 2,500 imams trained or invited, and more than 10,000 copies of the Qur'an printed and distributed. China now has six Islamic theology institutes and is planning to establish two more in Henan and Yunnan provinces.

Document 73

Beijing Islamic College

China Daily *(in English), 6 May 1985.*

Beijing Islamic College, opened in 1955, is the highest institution for Islamic education in China.

Run by the China Islamic Association, the college aims at turning out another generation of imams. Its first batch of graduates left the school in 1985.

When the "cultural revolution" started in 1966, the college was closed in the leftist frenzy that suppressed religious life. It opened again after the leftist turmoil and began to enroll students in 1982.

Through exams in Arabic, the Islamic creed, Chinese language, history, and geography, the college chooses students among applicants recommended by provincial Islamic institutions. The applicants must be under twenty-five, with high-school education, and, of course, they must be Muslims.

They have written and oral exams, which relate to their personality, appearance, and manners.

Upon graduation, the students will go back to the places they came from and be posted by local Islamic institutions as imams.

For the year 1984, the college enrolled 21 students, expanding the student body to three grades and the total number to 106. All of the students are men. The students come from all the provinces and regions of the country except Tibet, Taiwan, and Jiangxi, and belong to the national minority groups of Hui, Uyghur, Kazakh, Dongxiang, Bonan, and Salar.

In their five-year schooling, the students take courses in history, geography, the creed, the Chinese language, physical training, and Arabic. Religious courses make up 70 percent of the lessons.

Most of the students do not want to be ordained imams. They have a thirst for knowledge and want to see more of the world. One of their aspirations is going abroad to study.

The college has sent eight students to study the Islamic creed in Egypt. The rest long to be offered the same opportunity.

The Catholic Church in China Today

Introduction

The first Roman Catholic church in China, planted by Franciscan missionaries from Italy during the Yuan dynasty, did not survive dynastic change. Today's Catholic church dates back to the Jesuit missionaries who first came in the sixteenth century. They and their successors, with a century-long hiatus following the Rites Controversy, served the church in China until the early 1950s, when all foreign missionaries were forced to leave. Yet, as will be seen in the story of the Catholic fishermen of Qingpu District [Document 76], Chinese Catholics kept the faith even during times of persecution. Today's Catholic seminarians, almost to a man, come from Catholic families, some of them dating back many generations.

A visitor comes away from talks with Catholic bishops, priests, seminarians, and laypersons with a number of impressions. First, Chinese Catholics, despite grievous suffering endured by many during the "cultural revolution," are fiercely loyal to their church, and, the break in relationships that began in 1957 notwithstanding, the great majority are loyal to the Holy See and the universal church.

Along with this unyielding loyalty to their church, Chinese Catholics in positions of authority have repeatedly affirmed their support for the policy of Three-Self autonomy (self-support, self-government, self-propagation) which was adopted by both Protestant and Catholic leaders in the 1950s. No missionaries serve the church in China today.

The Catholic church faces problems common to all religions in contemporary China, stemming from the "lost years" when no new clergy or women religious were being trained. The agonizing leadership problem is evident when one meets the aging priests and bishops who continue to staff the churches and dioceses and learns how few there are in relation to total Catholic members. Many of the Chinese nuns were laicized in the 1950s, the others are elderly or infirm, and almost no trained catechists are serving the church today.

Although budgets are tight, and bishops complain that older Catholics (unlike Protestants) were not trained to give generously to their church, money is not the major problem. The churches receive rental income from properties used by other units, and the government provides subsidies for restoring damaged churches and training seminarians.

A problem unique to the Catholic church in China, however, is the break with the Vatican, a situation which divides the Chinese Catholics and causes discord in every parish and diocese. Many Catholics, out of loyalty to the Holy See, refuse to attend services at the reopened churches, all of which are under the supervision of the Chinese Catholic Patriotic Association (CCPA), with the result that there is what many call an "underground church" served by so-called loyal priests. In fact, there is only one Catholic church in China, and this terminology is unfair to those bishops, priests, and religious who serve the church but remain loyal to the Holy See, pending a resolution of this problem.

Local Church Life (Section I)

In the course of field research I talked with Catholic clergy and laity and visited churches and seminaries in Chongming and Qingpu (in the Shanghai diocese), Fuzhou, Xiamen, Kunming, Xiaguang, Dali, Chengdu, Beijing, Nanjing, and Shanghai City. As with other religions in China, even local membership statistics are unreliable. The figure usually given for all Catholics nationwide is 3.3 million, the same as in 1949. In fact, the bishops admit that they have no way of knowing how many practicing Catholics there are in their own dioceses, including those attending services led by the so-called underground priests.

Attendance at church services varies from place to place. In some dioceses, such as the Korean-language churches in the provinces bordering North Korea, there is a vigorous church life and the churches are packed. In other places, remote and understaffed, the church barely survives. This was evident in Dali, for example, where the bishop, eighty-six, is the only priest in a diocese that had 60 churches and 5,038 Catholics in 1957 [Document 77], and where barely a dozen attended mass on a Sunday in May 1988.

In an interview published in *Asia Focus* (January 7, 1989), Bishop Zong Huaide, president of the CCPA and acting head of the Chinese Catholic Church Administrative Commission and the Chinese Catholic Bishops' College, said there were 1,100 priests, (including nearly 90 ordained since 1983), 630 seminarians in twelve seminaries, 1,500 religious sisters, 300 novice sisters, 57 bishops (four of them Vatican-appointed), more than 1,000 churches and 2,300 chapels opened, and an average of 40,000 baptisms each year. However, while great progress has been made, with only 57 bishops to serve 112 dioceses, (most of them over 70 and many over 80), and 1,100 priests, most of them equally aged, the shortage of ordained clergy and other trained leaders remains a critical problem.

The first two sections below describe the local church in various parts of China based on firsthand interviews. Theresa Chu, a Catholic nun born in China but living in Canada, reports on her five months visiting with Catholic communities in central China in 1986. A reporter from *Yi*, an independent Catholic periodical published in Hongkong, reports on a visit to a Catholic diocese in Inner Mongolia where 32 churches had been reopened to serve 200,000 Catholics. The report on the religious faith of Catholic fishing families in Qingpu County, an abridged version of a scholarly study published in 1987 by the Shanghai Academy of Social Sciences [*Religious Questions under Socialism in China*, Shanghai, 1987] helps explain the constancy and survival of China's Catholics through the vicissitudes of history.

Interviews (Section II)

The three documents in Section II are all excerpted from notes taken during interviews with Catholic bishops, priests, nuns and laypersons from four dioceses in Yunnan and Fujian provinces.

These divisions have eroded church attendance. Not only do some "loyalists" stay away from church, but others boycott Masses celebrated by priests said to be married. Because of bitter experience, some Christians employed in government jobs stay away from public religious services until they retire to avoid problems on the job. Some are busy working on Sundays in this secularized nation. Others, such as the residents of a Bai village in Yunnan which once was completely Catholic, refused the bishop's offer to restore Catholic services because of fearful memories: their former lay leader, a woman, had been killed by the Red Guards, the Catholics terrorized, and the church destroyed.

Statements by National Catholic Leaders (Section III)

Three published interviews and a speech by Catholic bishops have been selected as representative of the views of China's Catholic leaders. Bishop Tu's speech, delivered at the ecumenical conference in Montreal in 1981, is the most stringent, a scriptural and historical review of the reasons supporting the present policy of autonomy of the Chinese church, and an unsparing recital of cases describing what the Chinese call missionary imperialism. Bishop Tu reminds his listeners that there were only 29 Chinese bishops out of 137 dioceses in 1949, and that 121 out of 145 dioceses, unfilled by the Holy See, remained vacant up to 1958, when China began electing and ordaining its own bishops.

An excerpt from the 1984 interview in *Beijing Review* with Bishop Fu Tieshan summarizes the usual reasons given by Chinese Catholics for the broken relations with the Holy See, while Bishop Jin, in another interview, discusses the church in Shanghai, the seminary of which he is rector, and the strained relations between the Chinese church and the Vatican.

Seminarians and Novice Nuns, A New Generation (Section IV)

According to Bishop Zong Huaide (Document 82), there were 11 Catholic seminaries and a dozen convents in China in 1987, a total of about 600 seminarians, and perhaps 300 novice nuns. In addition, some priests and bishops have taken on preseminarians in local tutorial programs, preparing them for the seminaries. Two documents have been selected for this section, one a series of four interviews conducted at the Sheshan Regional Seminary, Shanghai, and the other an interview with a Catholic Sister from Hongkong who spent three months visiting novitiates in three cities in Guangxi Province.

SEMINARIANS

Although the seminarians were interviewed separately, there is a striking consistency in their answers to the same questions. All come from families that have been Catholic for generations, and family influence led to their decision to study for the priesthood. All were motivated by the need to help the overworked and aging priests, and to fill the gaps left by priests already dead or retired for health reasons. All confirmed that they have felt no hostility, rather an openness to religion, even a reaching out, a search for religious faith among their age peers. The biggest problem facing the church is to make up for the "ten lost years" of the "cultural revolution."

One of them spoke of the generation gap, particularly in the matter of rites and liturgy. Whereas older Catholics prefer the pre-Vatican II Latin rites, they are unintelligible to young people today. (I was told that seminarians in another seminary had complained about elderly priests who served as professors, using the same pre-Vatican II lessons and methods they were trained in.) Today's seminarians don't want to spend time learning Latin, but want to move to a vernacular mass.

Finally, when asked about the problem of relations with the Vatican, they said this was basically a political matter related to the Taiwan question. "We hope that the church in China can have friendly relations with [the church in] every country. We are all of the same faith. We believe in one Christ. We all worship in the same way. If the political factors could be resolved, everything would be all right."

NOVICES IN GUANGXI

With three vicariates in Wuzhou, Guilin and Liuzhou in 1940, the Catholic church in Guangxi Province had 13 churches, 124 chapels, 54 missionary priests, 13 Chinese priests, 21 missionary Sisters, 48 Chinese Sisters, and a total communicant membership of 21,560.

With only 5 priests, all over seventy in the entire province today, the report from Guangxi makes starkly clear the need for new priests and nuns. The city of Guilin, for example, has two seminarians studying in the Wuhan seminary but no resident priest. Three former Sisters who married and retired from secular work now help the church and teach six novices, all seventeen years old, and all from Catholic families. Why do they want to become nuns? "Because they want to follow Jesus and help other people to become Christians."

Two other newly established novitiates, one in Wuzhou, with 21 novices, and one in Liuzhou, with 11 novices, are taught by three former Sisters, all over sixty, and two old "virgins" (lay Sisters). Because of the desperate need in their home parishes, some of them have been called back to help before finishing their spiritual formation.

People are just beginning to come back to the churches. Some are still afraid. How did Catholics maintain their faith during the hard years? The older generation passed the faith on to the next, parents baptizing their infants, and aunts, grandparents and parents teaching the prayers to children.

Section I

Local Church Life

Document 74

Learning from Christians in Wuxi

"Learning from Christians in Wuxi" is a thirty-six page report written by Dr. Theresa Chu, director of the Canada China Programme (Toronto), after spending five months visiting Catholic communities in China in 1986. These excerpts (published in 1988) were selected because they offer insights into the faith and life of Chinese Catholics in a rural church. However, the entire report should be read, for the author presents her report as a response to questions about Catholic relationships in Socialist China raised in the preface.

While staying in the city of Wuxi, I spent my days visiting one or another of the many Catholic villages in the vicinity. Usually, a family would invite me to a midday meal, after which we sat and talked. The following is an attempt to recapture one of those occasions on which I learned much about Catholic life in a village. . . .

After the briefing, the village leaders took me around to visit the metal factory, the school, and a fish farm. We ended the tour in one of the Catholic homes for dinner. At table with me were Mr. Yang Fu-quan, owner of the house; Mr. Yang Fu-gen, his cousin; Mr. Wang Ji-gen, director of the AICU; Lao Wang (Old Wang) [this is a familiar yet respectful way of addressing an elderly person or a person in authority]; Ji-gen's father; Lao Yin (Old Yin), Jigen's uncle; Mr. Xu Xing-bao, secretary of the CCPA of Wuxiprefecture; Mr. Yuan He-guan, director of the CCPA of Wuxi City; Ms. Xue Wen-qin, head of the Wuxi suburban district United Front Department; and Ms. Cao He-fen, head of the Wuxi suburban district Women's League.

Yang Fu-quan (F.Q.) is the lay leader of the Catholic community in Miao Zhuang. Although to date there is no church in the township—the nearest church is one and one-half hour's walk away—the people have kept together as a faith community. As I learned later, the people follow a traditional way of praying together. F.Q. and his family go to St. Joseph's parish in Wuxi whenever they can, and certainly on big feasts. The family has contracted 20 *mu* of pond for shrimp farming and has succeeded in attaining an annual income of 10,000 *yuan*. People seemed to take pleasure in speaking of *"wan yuan hu"* (literally, "10,000-*yuan* households"). This was unthinkable during the "cultural revolution." At that time, to get rich was considered reactionary and shameful. In this context, it is easy to understand how praising the rich who enjoy the fruit of their labor becomes an expression of freedom.

Yang Fu-gen (F.G.) is in his late fifties. Married twenty-five years ago, his wife and two sons are all devout Catholics. Having no daughter, they have adopted a niece who is also a Catholic. In 1983, the niece-daughter married a man who had received instruction and became a Catholic before the marriage. They all live in the same house, which was built in 1982 at a total cost of 6,000 *yuan*. The family is proud of their spacious two-story house and even more proud of the fact it has been blessed by the parish-priest from Wuxi. A crucifix hangs on the wall in the living/dining room. Similarly, a holy picture, a liturgical calendar, or a statue of Mary can be found in all the other rooms.

Wang Ji-gen is thirty-one years old. He used to lead a work brigade, but for four years now he has been the director of the AICU. He works with a team of three vice-directors. Wang did not talk much but everything he said was to the point. Looking at him, his Uncle Lao Yin remarked, "We, the older generation, could not be cadres because we are all illiterate."

Lao Wang is of Lao Yin's generation. He has never been a cadre. But he had been in a leadership position for many years. When cooperatives were organized all over China in 1957, the village became a production team, and he was the first team leader. On 18 November 1959, a project to reclaim land along the shores of Lake Tai was launched. Lao Wang and thirteen others were the first group of people who went to a small island and started the work. Much of the high-yielding fisheries that Wuxi boasts of is a direct result of work done in those days.

Different from Lao Wang, his brother-in-law, Lao Yin seemed less interested in fishing and more attracted to prayer. He loves to serve Mass and claims to know all the parishioners. After talking with him for a while, I realized he is a catechist, that is, a lay Catholic who, in areas where priests only go occasionally or regularly once a month, performs pastoral duties short of giving the sacraments.

Mr. Xu Xing-bao is fortunate in that he lives in a township where there is a chapel dedicated to the Holy Rosary. Although the priest only visits them once a month, the people consider themselves fortunate. Mr. Xu told me that plans are underway for two more churches to be reopened in Wuxi Prefecture. Given the fact that the prefecture has thirty-five Catholic villages and two Catholic fish farms, three chapels seem far from being sufficient. But perhaps this is a good beginning.

Mr. Yuan He-guan lives in Wuxi. He is a daily communicant in St.

Joseph's parish. As director of the CCPA, he has a full-time job assisting the two priests in the parish—Fr. Chen and Fr. Jiang—in works that involve civil authorities. That includes claiming churches back for worship, supervising repairs in those churches, purchasing equipment in big quantities that require special permissions, making sure that sick priests or Sisters receive proper hospital care, that units occupying church properties pay rent at appointed times, etc.

Xue Wen-qin, a woman in her forties, only returned to her work in the United Front Department (UFD) in 1984. The UFD is a Party organ dealing with questions of minority races and religion in China. It is the organ of which the counterpart in the government is the Religious Affairs Bureau (RAB). During the "cultural revolution," both the UFD and the RAB were disbanded. Some of the workers were severely criticized for being too lenient toward religion. In 1980, the UFD was reestablished, but in the Wuxi suburban district implementation only came four years later. . . .

At one moment the conversation turned toward the contribution of Catholics to society. Xue mentioned that the hamlet of Guang Yi in the neighboring area has been emulated as a model village. Since the foundation of new China, no one there ever had a police record. Forty out of a total of forty-three households in the hamlet being Catholic, Xue concluded that Catholics are contributing much to society at large. More examples were cited by others on Catholics being people who positively contribute to the common good.

Toward the end of the meal, I asked Lao Yin by what means had the Catholics kept their faith throughout the "cultural revolution." He explained to me that people in rural areas love praying together. First of all, they are fishermen and cannot attend Mass regularly. Second, there has not been any resident priest for as long as he can remember. The believers depend on the prayer meetings for mutual encouragement. A tradition evolved out of this situation. It is still faithfully kept. He added that this was done even during the "cultural revolution," except that people recited their prayers less loudly during those days.

According to that tradition, the prayer season begins on December 8th and continues till the end of the year. Lay leaders or catechists would be asked by individuals to go to their respective homes for an afternoon of prayers. Two or three catechists would go together to a designated home. Neighbors were informed of the schedule beforehand. They drop in to pray with the host family. Some prayer-lovers go to all the sessions. They end up spending every afternoon in prayer throughout the season.

The following format is usually followed. When people have gathered after lunch, they begin with prayers for the deceased. The catechists recite the prayers aloud. Others follow. Those who have forgotten gradually remember them through sheer repetition. Even though they may not be able to recite the prayers by heart on their own, they have no difficulty doing so when people do it together. After the prayers for the deceased, they take a break. Then the catechists preach for a couple of hours. People can ask questions and make comments. They end their session by saying prayers of thanksgiving together. It would be supper time by then.

The topic of conversation then turned to Catholics who have gained public recognition as exemplary citizens. In the greater Wuxi area in 1985, two hundred Catholics were among citizens receiving the honor. . . .

Talking with Catholics in China, in Wuxi and beyond, I have the impression that there is a new reality in China concerning church-society relationships. The role of Christians as salt, yeast, and light has been greatly stressed by both Protestants and Catholics. This suggests an understanding of "church in society" rather than "church as a perfect entity above society." On this point, Catholic and Protestant theologies seem to converge toward the same direction. There are both similarities and differences between the Chinese attitude to society epitomized by the "model citizens" and the approach of justice groups in Western societies that work toward social change. . . .

Document 75

A Visit to Inner Mongolia

In Yi (Hongkong), December 1986.

The Catholic Church has existed in Inner Mongolia for over 120 years. The present bishop, Wang Xue-ming is the third bishop of Inner Mongolia and also the first Chinese bishop since the first beginnings of the Catholic church there. The first bishop was Bishop Dyk Ludovicus Van from 1924 to 1937, and the second was Bishop Morel Ludovicus from 1938 to 1951. Bishop Wang was ordained bishop in 1951, thirty-five years ago.

Situation of Diocese

Bishop Wang said that there are about two hundred thousand Catholics in Inner Mongolia and they are mainly concentrated in the villages. There are at present four dioceses (Ulanqale Meng, Baotou City, Bayannur Meng, and Hohhot City) but with only one bishop. The other dioceses have diocesan leaders in charge of church matters. The bishop said that many of the faithful have not seen a bishop for over forty years.

You will have to travel 4,000 kilometers to go from east to west of Inner Mongolia. Though transportation is better than before, there is still a lack of manpower in the Church and so a more comprehensive contact and development have not been achieved yet. Bishop Wang said that thirty-two churches have been reopened, as well as a hundred activity points or places in remoter areas where churches have not yet been reopened. In Otog Oi there are two thousand Mongolian Catholics and two Mongolian priests. They have their own prayer books and the Bible in Mongolian, the latter having already been available in pre-Liberation days. But as people of the Han nationality are numerous in the western part, there is more communication between the Mongolians and the Hans, and many Mongolians do not know how to speak the Mongolian language. On the other hand, in the eastern part, they can speak Mongolian and Chinese.

There are a total of seventy-seven priests in Inner Mongolia. It was relatively early, on 4 May 1980, that the first church was reopened there.

Formation

"We started up a theological and philosophical seminary on 15 June 1985," said Bishop Wang. It is for the formation of priests. Most of the seminarians have had some years of working experience, some of whom had even been earning 80 to 120 *yuan* a month—a high salary for the place. What motivated them to enter the seminary, according to Bishop Wang, was often the needs of the church and the fact that many priests were very old.

Document 76

A Study of the Religious Faith of Fishing People in Qingpu County

In Religious Questions under Socialism in China *(Shanghai Academy of Social Sciences, 1987). Translated by Zheng Xi'an and Donald MacInnis (abridged).*

On 2 May, 1983 the most impressive groups among the Catholic pilgrims going to the church on Sheshan near Shanghai for religious services were the fishing people from Qingpu County. At about 5:00 A.M. over two thousand believers came in groups from various fishing brigades of Qingpu county. After assembling at the foot of the hill, they formed a line and slowly walked to the top of the hill while chanting the prayers, entered the church, which was still under repair, and took part in the Mass. When the Mass was ended, they descended halfway, to the "Pavilion of the Three Saints" and the "Pavilion of the Holy Mother." There they knelt in groups, again chanting prayers in unison. Some of them walked prayerfully along the newly repaired "Way of the Cross" [the fourteen stations of the cross].

For the entire morning they immersed themselves in a strong religious atmosphere.

Ours is a Socialist country. New China was founded over thirty years ago, and the fishing people still devoutly hold to their religious faith. Why is this? Is it beneficial or not for the cause of Socialism that they maintain such a pious faith and carry on religious activities such as "pilgrimages"? This essay is an inquiry into these two questions.

Believers for Many Generations

Qingpu Catholics, of whom most are fishermen, numbered between nine thousand and ten thousand shortly after Liberation. About one-third of those have died in the past thirty years. Those who were thirty years old then are now over sixty, and one-time teenagers are now in their forties. These believers, in their forties, fifties, and sixties, now form the main body of Catholics.

Before Liberation, Chinese Catholic churches were controlled by foreign forces. The church considered all who had joined the church as "church members" [jiao min — people of the church], and required all parents of newborn children to take them to the church to be baptized by the priest within three to eight days after their birth.

The Catholic fishing people of Qingpu are also called "net-boat Catholics." Their boats are their homes. They make their living from aquatic products such as fish, shrimp, and crabs, wandering about on the rivers of Qingpu County. Because their nomadic way of life sometimes prevented parents from taking their newborn children to the church for baptism within the time prescribed, the church required that they take the child in such cases to a lay Catholic who had been examined and authorized by the priest to administer baptism. Later, the parents would take the child to the priest for formal baptism. Catholics today who are middle-aged or older joined the church in this way, by baptism soon after their birth. . . .

From Youthful to Adult Believers

In the old society, two and even three generations of "net-boat Catholics" lived together on a small boat in a cabin not big enough for a four-foot bed. In ordinary times these "multi-generation believers" [shidai jiaotu] had their own family worship on their boats, such as "morning lessons" and "evening lessons." On Sundays, called "the Lord's Day" by Catholics, they "read the special Sunday prayers" on their boats when they could not go to church. These religious activities carried out on their boats were only a part of their religious life.

At that time most of the fishing people were members of the churches in Tailaiqiao, Yangyuyu and Zhujiajiao. The same "parish priest" was in charge of the churches in Yangyuyu, and Tailaiqiao, and the Zhujiajiao church had its own "parish priest" beginning in 1945. Any church which had its own "parish priest" was called a "parish church" [huikou]. The principal activities of a parish church were to "fulfill the four precepts": Mass on Sunday, and on important festivals such as Christmas; fasting on Friday; "confession" and "holy communion" at least once a year; and contributing money for the support of the church.

Dates for special church services were fixed by the "parish priest," and on those occasions the fishing families traveled by boat to the point nearest the "parish church" to which they belonged to take part in the special activities, which took from a few days to more than a week.

In addition to "fulfilling the four precepts," these churches also had their "major" and "minor" festivals. The major festivals were Christmas, Easter, the "Assumption of Mary," and the "Local Church's Special Festival." The "minor festivals" were "Lent," the "Month of our Lady" [May], "Pentecost," "Birthday of Our Lady," "All Saints' Day," and "All Souls' Day." On those occasions all fishing families were expected to row their boats to the churches and attend the religious activities.

May was the "Month of Our Lady" [literally, "Holy Mother"], the month for Catholics of the Shanghai region to go on pilgrimage to Sheshan. The parish priest required that the Catholic fishing families of Qingpu attend the "Day of Pilgrimage to Worship Our Lady," and hundreds of boats docked at the foot of Sheshan Hill. Family after family climbed the hill to take part in worship.

The middle-aged and older Catholics have learned from their parents through the years the prayers, Bible readings, kneelings, and forms of worship, so they know the rites and ceremonies from habit.

In the old society most children of "net-boat Catholics" never went to school, but went instead to "Bible class." Even before they joined a "Bible class," they had already heard the "Six Daily Prayers" and the "Questions and Answers on Doctrine" [Catechism], so in two or three months, or, at most six months, they could recite everything from memory after attending the "Bible class."

When they had completed the class, they were interviewed and tested by the "parish priest." They could recite the "Six Daily Prayers," but they couldn't understand them very well because they were written in classical Chinese language. The "Catechism" was written in modern Chinese language, so at least they could recite and understand the questions and answers about doctrine after completing the "Bible class," and the chief Catholic doctrines were rooted in their minds.

After the "Six Daily Prayers" and the "Catechism" came the "First Confession" (confessing their sins to the "parish priest") and "First Holy Communion" (the first time they could receive the "sacred host" from the "parish priest" during the Mass). Before these two "first" occasions, they could not take part in the holy ceremonies with their parents. After "First

Confession" and "First Communion" these children became complete young Catholics.

These children returned to their boats after "First Confession" and "First Communion" and lived a life just as they did before the "Bible class." Only those whose families were better off could study at the Catholic Wangdao Primary School, which was run by the Tailaiqiao Catholic Church, the seat of the parish priest in charge of all the Qingpu Catholics. Students at the Wangdao Primary School all lived in the school and had to attend frequent religious functions at the local church. In addition, the class on religion was one of the main courses offered at the school. The children were even more influenced by what they saw and heard in the Catholic classes, rites, and services there.

Both the children who returned to their boats after they finished the "Bible class" and those who studied at the Wangdao Primary School had to be "confirmed" when the bishop came to inspect the church. At that time, the bishop came to Tailaiqiao every four years. When he came, all the Catholics who belonged to those churches came by boat to the place where the bishop would lead the church functions. Children who had not been "confirmed" following "First Confession" and "First Communion" had to be confirmed by the bishop. According to the "catechism," "confirmation has the purpose of assuring that those who are confirmed have a 'firm belief', will be 'brave soldiers of Jesus', and will 'prove their faith by their words and deeds, and even by the sacrifice of their lives.' " Thus it can be seen that "confirmation" is really a "vow" by these children to show their firm belief in the religious doctrines. Today's Qingpu Catholics who are middle-aged and older all were "confirmed" while teenagers as proof of their "firm belief."

The influences of family, society, and education in one's childhood are very important for one's growth in later years. Qingpu's Catholic fishermen who are now over forty have lived on boats since childhood, having little contact with the outside world. They only went to the churches, and the main influences in their lives were religious. Religious ideas were deeply embedded in their minds and became the norm for their words and deeds.

When the children of "net-boat Catholics" wanted to marry, they had to go to the church and ask the priest to perform the ceremony of marriage. Before the wedding they had to be interviewed and examined by the "parish priest," just as they did after the "Bible class." Today's Qingpu Catholics who are over fifty have all passed this "examination" and have moved through the stages from "young Catholics" to "adult Catholics."

Examples of Religious Ideology

The religious experience described above makes devout believers of the Qingpu Catholics, with the result that their way of looking at everything comes under this religious influence.

In the past hundred years, imperialism used the Catholic church in its invasion of China. Qingpu's Catholic fishermen knew nothing of this fact of history. They only knew that Catholicism was the "true religion," not that it was being used by the imperialists. In facing the problems of wealth and poverty, happiness and suffering, the Catholic "teaching" wanted Catholics to believe that everything was arranged by God, and so this is what they believed.

For example, following this Catholic "teaching," they looked on the real world as a place of misery because God made it that way. People suffered because of their sins, and their misery was God's punishment. The only way out was to submit to what God had arranged, and endure suffering in this world so as to acquire everlasting happiness in the next world.

Before Liberation there was nothing to safeguard the life of a fisherman, wandering about the rivers and lakes in a small boat under constant threat of accidents. They believed the Catholic doctrines because, on the one hand, it helped them to endure the temporary sufferings of this world, while, on the other hand, they believed that "praying for blessings and protection from God, Jesus, and the Blessed Mother" was efficacious. . . .

In the old society Qingpu Catholics, under strong religious influence, endured their sufferings because they believed that "God had arranged things" that way. On the other hand, they prayed for "protection from God, Jesus, and the Blessed Mother" to save them from sufferings. Day after day and year after year it was like this. For many of them, their faith grew even deeper and more pious as time went by.

From Liberation to the Eve of the "Cultural Revolution"

After Liberation, the Catholic fishing people of Qingpu moved from the old to the new society, taking their devout religious faith with them. Many Catholics did not dare to show their patriotism or draw close to the government and Party, because there were people inside the church who spread fabricated rumors that the Communist Party wanted to wipe out religion; moreover, leaders of the church in Shanghai, acting on instructions from the Vatican, gave orders to Catholics not to endorse the Party.

In 1953 and again in 1955, struggle campaigns in the Catholic churches cleaned out the imperialist and counterrevolutionary elements, removing the heavy weight of stone that had pressed down on the Catholics. But a number of the Qingpu Catholics still did not know that the purpose of the struggle against the imperialists and counterrevolutionaries was to protect proper religious belief. They mistakenly thought that the imperialists and counterrevolutionaries using the guise of religion were their "church elders" [shen zhang], and dared not draw a line of demarcation between themselves and these enemies.

They gradually came to know that the acts of these imperialists and counterrevolutionaries using the guise of religion were illegal and harmful to the people of China and were unacceptable because they were contrary to the doctrines and regulations of the church as well. Only then, following the Christian teaching of love for others, and the fourth of the "Ten Commandments," which says that one should love one's country, did they denounce the evildoings of the imperialists and counterrevolutionaries using the guise of religion. Having drawn a sharp line between themselves and their enemies, their consciences were clear.

However, just when the Qingpu Catholics began to follow the patriotic road, "leftist" influences began to appear, and proper religious activities were confused with superstitious activities in the process of implementing the religious policy. On the pretext that religious activities would "hamper production," measures were taken to reduce the number of churches and religious activities. The fishing people dared not go to church for fear of being despised. They carried on their religious practice and Bible reading on their boats. After 1958 one could "catch sparrows on the doorstep" of the Catholic church in Tailaiqiao.

On Christmas 1964, the church at Zhujiajiao, with less than one hundred believers attending Mass, was desolate. This did not mean that the Catholic fishermen had given up their faith; it showed that they were again doubtful about the religious policy, and that there was a barrier between them and the Party and government. During the period of the campaigns to wipe out the imperialists and counter-revolutionaries using the guise of religion, it had not been easy to bring the Catholic fishing people around to loving both religion and country, even using patient education. Now "leftist" influences were pushing them back away from the road of loving their country and their religion, causing heavy losses in the work of uniting with Catholic believers.

Catholic Faith Holds Firm during the "Cultural Revolution"

At the beginning of the "cultural revolution" in 1966, Catholic churches in Qingpu County were closed or destroyed. Catholics consider their churches to be "holy sanctuaries" [*sheng tang*], that is, sacred places. After 1958, due to "leftist" influences, the Catholics had already come to suspect the religious policy. When the "cultural revolution" broke out and they saw their "holy sanctuaries" destroyed, what would they think? At the time of Liberation they had feared that the party and government would "exterminate religion," and now, with all the churches closed, was it not true that religion was being exterminated? That would be a bitter disaster for Catholics, and now it finally was happening.

At the same time that churches were being destroyed, religious believers were deprived of their civil rights: they were not allowed to read the Bible, to wear "holy medals," to place "holy pictures" in their boats, or to have rosary beads or religious publications. All "holy pictures," "holy medals," and "rosary beads" had to be "handed over." Moreover, some devout Catholics were publicly criticized and denounced, even imprisoned. . . .

The "ultra-leftists" believed that China had become a "country without religion." They did not know that it is precisely times like this, when churches are destroyed and Christians assaulted, that the faith of devout believers is strengthened. Their firm faith gave the Catholic fishing people of Qingpu courage when they were wrongly attacked. Now they are all saying that they followed the example of "Jesus, who was nailed to the cross and died," and that their sufferings were their "gift to God," believing that God would compensate them. When they were not allowed to read the Bible, many of them resorted to silent reading in their hearts. Others, together with their whole families, and even groups of boat families, read aloud while sailing out of earshot of the shore. They used every means to hide the few "rosary beads" and "holy medals" which had escaped detection. Thus it turned out that while the "ultra-leftists" attempted to stifle religion by administrative methods, the final results were exactly opposite to what they had intended. This proves that banning religion by administrative decree will not work.

Violating the Policy on Religion Gave Opposition Forces an Opportunity

The post-Liberation patriotic anti-imperialist movement among the Catholics was carried out unevenly. Some of the Qingpu fishing people had their awareness raised in varying degrees, while others received no education in patriotism and anti-imperialism. There were Catholics among those who were assaulted during the "cultural revolution" who, indeed, had taken the road of loving the motherland and loving religion after the patriotic anti-imperialist movement. To assault these Catholics was to assault core members of the patriotic forces. The Catholic situation was complicated; religion was often used as a front for evildoings. Qingpu fishing people who had not received patriotic anti-imperialist education usually had only a vague understanding of the difference between proper religious functions and illegal activities using the guise of religion. They were easily cheated, and after the religious policy was trampled [by the ultra-leftists] the core group of patriotic Qingpu Catholics collapsed, making it even easier for someone to deceive them.

In March 1980, before any of the Shanghai district churches had reopened, Qingpu Catholics heard the rumor that the "Blessed Mother" would show her power and presence by appearing on Sheshan hill surrounded by a halo. For over ten years they had not gone to Sheshan to worship the "Blessed Mother," so, when they heard the rumor passed around by some people, they quit working and went to Sheshan to see the "apparition and radiance of the Blessed Mother." When they arrived at Sheshan, the people who had spread the rumor, hiding themselves among the crowd, shouted reactionary slogans, breaking, smashing, and abusing the government.

This happened just at the time when the policy on religion had been restored at the Third Plenary Session of the Eleventh Party Congress, but chaos and instability prevailed among the Catholic fishermen. Illegal activities under the guise of religion carried on in the dark, together with the circulating of rumors, split the Shanghai churches just when they were striving for independence and self-government.

Unite Devout Catholics by Carrying Out a Workable Religious Policy

The "ultra-left" line violated the religious policy and caused religious believers to completely lose trust in it. The only way to gain their confidence was to truly carry out the policy and make believers see the actual implementation. By doing this, the questions caused by their ignorance, such as the illegal activities carried on under the cover of religion, could be more easily resolved.

As a result of the sincere implementing of the religious policy by the Qingpu government and Party committee, the Qingpu Catholics saw the following actions take place: sixty-five cases of unjust and false verdicts were corrected after reexamination; cadres visited them time after time, making friends with them and talking earnestly heart-to-heart in order to untie the knots in their thinking; Catholics who had once taken the road of loving the motherland and religion, but who were scattered during the "cultural revolution," were located and welcomed home; a number of priests, nuns, and lay Catholics were elected as people's representatives to the Qingpu and Zhujiajiao CPPCC; some Catholics were taken on trips by relevant [government and work] units; and, before the Zhujiajiao church reopened, local Catholics were allowed to go to Shanghai to attend Mass in reopened churches, provided that it did not interfere with productive labor. Not only was this done without condescension by the leaders of relevant units, but with their support.

In addition they [the Catholics] saw that relevant units made a clear distinction between the two contradictions [antagonistic and nonantagonistic] with regard to those Catholics who had been deceived by rumors of "the apparition and halo of the Blessed Mother," and had gone to Sheshan. Ideological work was patiently, sincerely, and painstakingly carried out, helping Catholics draw lessons from their wrong actions and encouraging them when they made a little change or progress. Believers were deeply moved, uniting and educating many of them. Some Catholics who had been fooled told of their bitter experiences after gaining a better understanding, while others even exposed some who had engaged in illegal activities, struggling with them face to face. The chaotic situation among Qingpu fishing people rapidly changed and negative factors became positive ones.

The decisive factor in regaining the confidence of the Qingpu fishing people in the religious policy was the return to them of the Zhujiajiao Catholic church, its repair and reopening, and the restoration of normal religious activities. In December 1980, with strong support from the Religious Affairs Offices of Shanghai and Qingpu County, and with the help of the Shanghai Catholic Patriotic Association, the first meeting of the Qingpu Catholics Representatives' Committee was convened, and Qingpu Catholics announced the founding of the Qingpu Catholic Patriotic Association, formed by Catholic laypersons, priests, and nuns. Before the opening of the meeting, the broad masses of Catholic fishing people (in response to their insistent demands) had already been given back the Zhujiajiao Catholic church, which had been taken over by a work unit, and had begun to make repairs.

After its founding, the Qingpu Catholic Patriotic Association worked actively with the government to carry out the religious policy and speed up repairs. They chose 25 December, Christmas Day, 1980, the biggest festival of the Catholic year, as the reopening day. On that day more than a thousand Catholics came to the first church in the Shanghai suburban districts to celebrate Christmas after reopening. Catholics who had not been able to attend Mass for more than ten, some even twenty years, and felt "uneasy in their conscience," attended "midnight Mass," and "dawn Mass" as well. They were so happy that they thanked the government, Party, Religious Affairs cadres and the Patriotic Association from their hearts. Many believers shed hot tears as they expressed their thanks to cadres and members of the Patriotic Association.

In the wake of this, the Qingpu Catholics' understanding of the Party's and government's implementing of the religious policy deepened, their patriotic awareness was raised, and their relations with cadres became more and more intimate and friendly.

Some Catholics had been doubtful about the religious policy, and, under the influence of the Vatican's sabotage activities, harboring misgivings about loving the motherland, loving religion, and self-government and independence of the church, had not been willing to attend religious services in the churches. But now, more and more, they began to shed their doubts and misgivings and take part in the activities of the Patriotic Association, attending meetings and study sessions, and going to church for normal religious activities. After the reopening of the Zhujiajiao church, churchgoers have numbered between two thousand and three thousand on the big Catholic festivals, and over four thousand for the annual Sheshan pilgrimage. . . .

After Gaining a Better Life

In the old society most Qingpu Catholics suffered hardships. They were called "fisher beggars." Every year at Spring Festival time, they usually went ashore to "beg for New Year's cakes." They were also called "thief boats" because, when they had nothing to live on, they had no choice but to go ashore and steal vegetables and squash from the fields to ease their hunger. With no provisions in the boats and only rags to wear, they drifted on the waters the year around. Neither girls nor boys on the boats could marry someone who lived ashore. While the peasants suffered then, the fishing people suffered even more.

After Liberation, the Catholic fishing people stood up. Now the majority of fishing families have moved ashore into new villages prepared for them. Following the development of mariculture projects, the aquatic production brigades, where fishing people are concentrated, can spare some of their labor force and unemployed youths to work in industries operated by the brigades. For example, some fishermen from the Baihe Aquatic Brigade are working in the leather-shoe factory, the box factory, and the sand-washing plant run by the brigade. In recent years, the income of every household has increased. Many have bank deposits of more than a thousand *yuan*. Bicycles and sewing machines are very popular, and many have TV sets and tape players. Take the Zhaoxian Aquatic Brigade for example: in 1981 they bought twenty TV sets at one time. Their living standard is steadily rising, and they like to describe it as "a sesame plant which puts forth blossoms joint by joint, higher and higher."

Qingpu fishing people clearly know that they owe all the benefits gained since Liberation to the leadership of the Communist Party. They remember the kindness of the Communist Party as their production output grows and their living standard rises. But, at the same time, they remember that they are "multigeneration Catholics," and that man has a "soul" as well as a physical body. They believe that their "soul" will rise to "paradise" after the death of their physical bodies. Devout believers have no doubts about the "soul" and "paradise"; all is contained in one word, "faith." In the old society they lived a hard life and yearned for "everlasting blessings in the next world," while on the other hand they asked for the "protection of God, Jesus, and the Blessed Mother." Today, as they live a better life, they still yearn for "everlasting blessings in the next world." Thirty years after liberation, with their lives much better, Catholics still judge good and bad on the basis of whether it will help or hinder their "soul" to go to "paradise." They think it is really good if it is good for their "soul"; if it is contrary, they worry that their "soul" will go to a frightful "hell. . . ."

Today, the main activities of the Zhujiajiao church are the celebration of Christmas and Easter and the "pilgrimage" to Sheshan in May. These activities are well-organized; they don't just drift along without leadership. Those who are at work generally do not attend religious services until they have worked overtime to fulfill their duties. In the past three years they have always fulfilled or exceeded the production quota. One devout Catholic, an expert at catching fish and prawns, said he was "more diligent in his work than before" after his demands [to authorities] to go to church were met. He is taking the lead in his work, studying new fish technology and getting higher and higher yields.

As Qingpu Catholics have come to understand from their personal experience that a better life does not keep their "soul" from going to "paradise," they are making big strides forward on the road of loving both the motherland and the church, and of running the church independently. Today they are no longer "jiaomin" [church people] like the Catholics of before, under the control and direction of foreign forces. In the past they thought that religious faith meant obeying the pope and the Vatican. Now, after political study [xuexi], many Catholics hold that the pope is also a human being, and pure religion for them is to believe in God, not the Vatican. They are vigilant against infiltration by hostile foreign religious influences and the few persons who use religion to carry out illegal activities. In the past they did not dare to come close to the Party and the government, while today they know that religious believers are one component of the Chinese people, and all people must support the Party's leadership, obey the government, love the country and abide by the law. . . .

New Believers in the Past Three Years

In this article we have mainly described Qingpu Catholics over age forty. The religious situation of their children and grandchildren between the ages of eighteen and forty is quite different from theirs. Children born into fishing families before 1955, the year when Catholic counterrevolutionaries were rooted out, were baptized and joined the church soon after their birth just like their parents. But they have not attended "Bible classes." Of the children born after that year, some were not baptized immediately, while others were only given conditional baptism. Children born in the fifties and early sixties are now twenty to thirty years old. They generally fall into two types: one, those whose parents taught them to read the Bible privately; the others, those who never studied the Bible at all. After the reopening of the Zhujiajiao church, those who had been conditionally baptized went to the church to be formally baptized by the parish priest and thus become full church members. Those who had not been conditionally baptized but had learned something about the Catholic faith, went to the church, were baptized, and became church members.

In the past three years, there have been fifteen hundred new Catholics baptized or re-baptized by the parish priest. These new Catholics did not know very much about the hows and whys of Catholicism, and some knew nothing at all. Some of them said that they were willing to be baptized and join the church through the influence of their families, particularly their mothers. They think that the "Ten Commandments" are helpful, teaching people to do good and guard against evil, so they joined the church because they wanted to observe the "Ten Commandments." The demands of these new Catholics for a religious life are much less strong than their parents'. Every evening when they read the "evening lesson" at home, the middle-aged and older Catholics want to finish the reading, but the young ones hope they don't have to read that long a time, and they soon disappear from the family gathering. They have no heart for "Bible reading" when there is a particularly good TV program. During the year, they mainly attend services on Christmas and Easter, and go on pilgrimage to Sheshan. They are very interested in these activities, and do all kinds of service work then, particularly singing in the choir, which is composed mainly of young people.

In our survey of new Catholics in the past three years, we discovered that the depth of piety of Qingpu Catholic fishing people is changing. In the past, the whole family read the Bible together and went to church together. Today it is not rare to see that in a given family some take part in religious activities, while others do something else. This tendency will continue.

In China today there are now about three million Catholics scattered in different places and circumstances all over China. Judging by Catholic history before Liberation, there must be many "multigeneration Catholics" like those in Qingpu County. These "multigeneration Catholics," just like the Qingpu fishing people, devoutly hold to their religious faith while at the same time playing an active and useful part in Socialist construction. The important thing for us to do is to earnestly carry out the policy of religious freedom, to be completely forthright with them, to do a good job in educating and uniting with them, and to make them feel that they can be both "good-for-the-body" and "good-for-the-soul" in their daily life and thus take love for the country and love for their religion as the motive force for contributing to Socialist construction.

Section II

Local Church Life: Interviews with Provincial and Diocesan Church Leaders

Document 77

The Catholic Church in Yunnan Province

Excerpts from interviews by Donald MacInnis and John Cioppa, May 1988, in Kunming, Dali, and Xiaguan, Yunnan Province.

History

The Kunming Diocese was under the Paris Foreign Missions. In 1957 there were 10,025 Catholics and forty-four Catholic churches, a main Catholic center, a major and a minor seminary, and three religious congregations, including lay Sisters, convents, novitiates, schools, and a hospital. Today only one church remains in Kunming City. There are six seminarians, no convent, and no novice nuns. Only a small minority of the estimated 3,000 Catholics in Kunming attend weekly Mass.

Dali was an apostolic vicariate of the Congregation of the Sacred Heart of Jesus (Bettharam). In 1957 there were 5,038 Catholics and sixty churches in Dali. Today there is one open church and one priest, Fr. Liu Hancheng, eighty-six, who also serves as bishop. Only a handful attend Sunday Mass. There are no catechists, nuns or "virgins" (lay Sisters). Two seminarians will graduate and return to Dali in 1988.

There are three bishops in Yunnan, two eighty-three years old and the third eighty-six, dividing this province of 380,000 square kilometers and 24 million people into three dioceses. As is the case in Fujian, the scarcity of priests is worsened by the refusal of some priests to serve the official church. The roster of active priests in the province includes two in Kunming, one in Wenshan, one in Zhaotun (who also serves as bishop), two in Mi-le, and one in Weixi.

The brightest spot in the church in Yunnan is Weixi, where Fr. Shi Guangrong ministers to an extensive parish of Zang (Tibetan) people. Fr. Shi, a seminarian before Liberation, was ordained last year. His mother was a Zang, his father a Han. It is said there are 80,000 Catholics in his parish, where he baptized 880 persons in seven months in 1987. Over 30 young men and 40 young women want to pursue religious vocations, but the men can't go to the seminaries because of their inadequate schooling, and there is no convent for training novice nuns.

The Bishop of Dali

We talked with Bishop Liu Hancheng, eighty-six, in his church in Dali, the only priest in this vast diocese. A former seminarian, Mr. Li Quan, sixty-nine, is a great help to Bishop Liu. He graduated from seminary in 1946, but was not ordained, and was later married. When we asked if he would be ordained, he laughed and said, "I have to ask my wife's permission first." He has three grown children.

Only a handful attended Sunday Mass, two men and two women at the first Mass, three men and six women at the second.

Many people are afraid to publicly attend religious services, the bishop said. He has twice visited the Bai minority village near Xiaguan which was once all Catholic. They suffered grievous persecution during the "cultural revolution," when their lay preacher, a woman, was killed. Now they are afraid to come to church.

They have had no baptisms recently in Dali, but thirty were baptized at Christmas, all villagers from across the mountain who have no priest now.

We asked the seminarian, who was home on leave from the Chengdu seminary, where he would work after graduation.

"I don't know," he replied. "The government will decide."

"What department of the government?" we asked.

"The United Front office [the Religious Affairs Bureau]. I will probably be assigned to Dali, which is my hometown."

We asked if there were any Catholic nuns in the Dali region. "Formerly there were many nuns, both Chinese and foreign, and 'virgins' [lay Sisters], too. They ran the orphanages, schools, clinics, etc. Today there are only four 'virgins' left, all very old, and not serving the church. One elderly nun lives in the Xiaguan church with her nephew and his family. There are no 'virgins' or catechists in the Dali diocese."

The Cemetery Desecrated

We asked about the depredations and suffering during the "cultural revolution." The Catholic cemetery had been destroyed in 1958, the fate of all Christian and Muslim cemeteries. Now the government has given land for new cemeteries.

The grave desecraters were led by a local bully who was the Communist leader of the workers' group at the time. He stole gold rings and jade bracelets from the graves and sold them on the black market. He also stole anything valuable from the Dali and Xiaguan churches. Later he was punished and now lives in a small village.

The Faithful

We asked if there are any lapsed Catholics.

"That is difficult to answer," said Mr. Li. "We cannot know for sure about people who stay away from church. Some are afraid because of persecution during the 'cultural revolution.' Many are busy working, even on Sunday. They come on Easter and Christmas. My son, a carpenter, is like this. He is very busy."

Document 78

An Interview with Bishop Huang Ziyu, Xiamen

By Donald MacInnis, May 1988 (excerpts).

I interviewed Bishop Huang Ziyu, seventy-eight, in the rectory adjoining the church on Gulangyu Island, Xiamen in April 1988. The church reopened in 1981, and is completely renovated, with large new sacred paintings throughout the interior, painted by a local Catholic in traditional European style. A small hotel has been built on the property with the hope of earning income for the church.

Catholics in South Fujian

There are twenty thousand to thirty thousand Catholics in southern Fujian, mostly in the rural areas. Putian County alone has nearly twenty thousand. Although once there were two churches, now only one is open in Xiamen. Two priests, sixty-eight and seventy-five, both in poor health, minister to about five hundred Catholics. A new graduate of the Shanghai seminary will come on 3 May and another, also from Xiamen, will graduate and return next year.

His Views on Rome and the Sacraments

"The church should change the regulations, requiring a priest for only two sacraments, confession and Mass. This will give lay leaders more opportunities to serve the church and relieve the overworked priests."

"Rome should not fear schism. This will never happen." *Tianzhujiao* means 'holy Catholic Church' [he said, *ecclesia catholica*]. Vatican II opened up great opportunities for innovation and renewal in our church. Our Catholics have nothing to fear. We should act, not just talk. Rome shouldn't listen to the church in Taiwan. We are one Church, and the purpose of the Church is to serve, that's all. Don't confuse things [*fuza*]; we should serve the people [*wei renmin fuwu*]."

He celebrates his fiftieth year of ordination this year. He was invited to Rome to celebrate, but declined.

The Future

How does he view the future for the church in China?

"It will be very difficult. It is hard to get young people to give their lives to the priesthood. We can't see the future. We didn't have faith before [*meiyu xin xin*], and as a result did not raise up enough priests. There are plenty of people who want to believe, but we don't have priests to teach them."

"There is also another problem, the past actions of the government. For years the government criticized religion, so that most young people now have that attitude. They can't suddenly change course like this. The government doesn't bother us now. They see that Christians have better moral behavior than others; they don't cause trouble."

Document 79

An Interview with Bishop Joseph Lin Quan, Fuzhou

By Donald MacInnis, April 1988 (excerpts).

I interviewed Bishop Joseph Lin Quan at the Catholic rectory in Fuzhou on 4 April 1988. Bishop Lin, sixty-nine, studied at the major seminaries in Shanghai and Hongkong, and was rector of the Fujian Seminary until it was closed down. There is no seminary in Fujian at present.

Fujian originally had six dioceses, each with its own bishop. Today there are only three bishops, each with an enlarged diocese. Bishop Lin's area includes sixteen counties covering all of northern Fujian. He has no car, and must use public transportation when he makes episcopal visits.

Priests, Seminarians, Nuns and Catechists

Fujian Province has about one hundred open churches now. While they have no accurate statistics, Bishop Lin thinks that the total number of Catholics is about the same as before Liberation, 150,000. However, he has no contact with Catholics who stay away from the open churches, which are affiliated with the Catholic Patriotic Association, but acknowledges that there are three "underground" bishops and a number of priests who minister to those Catholics, perhaps more priests than he has under his jurisdiction. In the district surrounding the Fuzhou cathedral, he said, there are 10,000 Catholics, but only half come to church.

Before Liberation there were seven churches in Fuzhou. Only three are open now, but a fourth will open soon. There are four priests in Fuzhou, two over eighty, and the others sixty-eight and sixty-nine, and only ten elderly nuns.

The church in Fujian Province has twenty seminarians studying in Beijing and Shanghai. The first graduate will return in two years. Pre-seminarians usually study for two years under their local priest before going on for the six-year course at the major seminary. A convent with about twelve novices will open in Fuzhou later this year under the leadership of an elderly nun.

Bishop Lin has taught three training classes for catechists since 1980, about thirty each time, but only ten catechists from these classes are now serving the churches.

Church Finances

Priests, nuns, and catechists are supported from members' contributions and rents from church properties. The government gives partial subsidies for church repairs only. The local church pays for the tuition and living costs of seminarians, about 1,000 *yuan* a year.

Bishop Lin spoke of the old days, when missionaries provided financial subsidies which are no longer available. "The French priests purchased land and created Catholic villages," he said, "and the missionaries set up orphanages, buying babies in order to increase membership. Of course this was a good work and it saved many young girls. But we don't need this any more. Now all we have to do is preach the gospel. We don't rely on the foreigners now. The church has no special privileges. Yes, we do receive money from the government for repairing the churches, but this is simply paying back what is owed to the church. Members of the cathedral gave over 100,000 *yuan* for repairs. Now we believe in God and rely only on him."

The Church in China and the Holy See

"Rome need not fear that we will break away from the Catholic church, after what we endured in order to stand up for our Catholic faith, wearing the 'hat' [symbol of ridicule] which they forced on us. We will not break away, either old or new Catholics. China is not the same as other Socialist countries in Eastern Europe. China is changing now, opening up. But the Communist Party still worries about the church, fearing that the church wants to reestablish foreign ties and to rely on money and personnel from abroad. We don't need that now. . . . There is a new climate now in China. China and Rome can resolve their differences. It is not possible now for the pope to be *primatus pontifex* here, but our loyalty to the pope remains as always. When we say Mass we pray for John Paul II by name; but the former papal authority over the Chinese church cannot be restored as it was.

"The Chinese Catholic Church is not like the church in other semicolonial nations, as we once were but no longer are. We are not dependent on outside help. Our members and our young people are proud of their own contributions for repairing and rebuilding our churches, some of them built from the ground up. Some Catholics are so moved by this that they come to the church to pray daily.

"The Vatican is changing a bit. But the Catholic Church absolutely cannot go back to the old system. Now we have taken off the foreign hat, but some here still have the old thinking. 'You have no head of the church,' they say. 'The church has to obey the pope.' But we have a head, Jesus Christ; he is the head of the church. The Vatican still controls behind the scenes, no matter what they say about a new attitude."

Disunity Among Catholics

"Some priests 'stay at home' [*zai jiali*]. They won't have anything to do with the official church. There is an underground church in parts of Fujian that is quite strong [*lihai*]. In the whole province, less than fifteen of the older priests 'came out from home' to serve the churches. Only about ten able-bodied priests now serve the churches in the entire province. There are more priests 'at home' than those serving the churches. We try to persuade them to come and help. Some are old and ill, but others lead underground services in the countryside. They do all right financially. The local Catholics, and some Hongkong Catholics, give them money. What with mass stipends, some of them earn far more than we do each month."

One reason that the underground church seems to flourish is that some Catholics don't want to be seen publicly going to church. "They feel freer, more at ease in the underground church. They don't want to get in trouble, so they keep a low profile until after they retire."

Can the underground church be found elsewhere? Yes, in several provinces. "For several years the government has been arresting them. Now they don't arrest them unless they actually break the law. In fact, they *do* disturb the peace. But now the security police [*gonganbu*] say they have freedom of religious belief. Religious *activities* are under government control, not religious belief. So if they arrest them, they soon release them. It's no use to arrest them. Arrests just lead to more hostility and opposition to the local bishop. In fact, we had nothing to do with the arrests."

Catholic Seminarians

Bishop Lin commented on some problems described by seminarians during his visits to the Chengdu and Wuhan seminaries. The religion courses are taught by elderly priests who themselves were trained in the pre-Vatican II tradition. Today's seminarians are frustrated by the requirement to study Latin, to use Latin in the Mass, and to limit the use of the vernacular in church services. So church leaders are now discussing how and when to change the language and the rituals. This reflects a generation gap, he said; the older Catholics want things just the same as they were before, while the younger Catholics say that this will not attract new believers, particularly young people.

Another problem is mandatory celibacy for priests, he said. "The seminarians are not happy [*bu an*] about this. You can't tie up the priests and seminarians like this. The Protestant seminaries don't have problems finding students; they have far more candidates than we do. Most of our seminarians come from the countryside; we don't have a single one from the two largest cities, Fuzhou and Xiamen. There are too many job opportunities for young people now."

Q. What about the Buddhists? They require celibacy. Why do they have novice monks and nuns? They are even more isolated from society than Catholic priests.

A. Yes, eight hundred to nine hundred have taken vows, both men and women, in Fujian. Most come from Putian County, but some from Fuzhou too. Buddhism in this province gets plenty of money from overseas Chinese. One person gave 100,000 *yuan* to the Drum Mountain Temple. The Guanghua Temple in Putian has received contributions of over 1.2 million.

In contrast, Catholic and Protestant churches are not allowed to accept gifts of money from foreign visitors. The salary and living allowances of a Protestant pastor are about the same as other professionals in society, but Catholic priests can't receive a salary.

Q. Why are there fewer Catholic than Protestant churches open now in Fujian?

A. There are five hundred to six hundred Protestant churches and one hundred Catholic. Formerly there were more Catholics and more churches. Why is this? One reason is the rapid growth in Protestant membership. Another is that some Catholics don't come to church. They either stay away altogether or attend underground services.

Q. What about the future?

A. We follow God's leading. We rely on God. I am optimistic. Many people want to learn the truth of Christianity. There is a thirst for doctrinal truth [*daoli*], much more than before. Our greatest need is for trained persons to teach them.

Section III

Statements by National Church Leaders

Document 80

We Want Communion as Brothers, Not Subjects

An interview with Bishop Aloysius Jin Luxian, published in English in Asia Focus, *Hongkong, 24 May 1985.*

SHANGHAI—Aloysius Jin Luxian, a Jesuit, was ordained a Chinese appointed auxiliary bishop of Shanghai 27 Jan. Rector of the regional seminary at Sheshan, Bishop Jin spoke with *Asia Focus* 13 May, the day after the cornerstone for a new seminary building was laid.

Q. Is it unusual for the government to allow the opening of a new Catholic seminary?
A. I think it is a milestone, because we now truly have religious freedom. This is not only for a while, it is permanent.

Q. Is it possible that the religious freedom we see today will be gone tomorrow?
A. No! We have learned from our experiences. Too much change in policy is not good for the welfare of our country. So we are confident that in the future there will be no change in politics, especially in religious politics.

Q. Many hope the Catholic church in China will reunite with the Catholic church outside. What is your view?
A. We are Catholics, we want to have good relations with Catholics all over the world. Earlier, we concentrated on building Catholicism inside China. Now, it is time to go abroad and have good relations with the whole Church all over the world, especially with those who treat us as friends and in a brotherly way.

Q. Do you want to be related with those who accept you in this way?
A. That is right. We want communion—as brothers, not as subjects.

291

Q. What about the Catholic church in China and its relation with Rome?

A. Our relationship with the Vatican is a complex problem. The complexity comes from history. At the beginning of Liberation, foreign missionaries, especially the Roman Curia, treated us as colonial subjects. That was not good for us, nor for the church.

In the church, we are brothers. I always think the local church and universal Church must be united in the love of Christ. We are created in the image of the Holy Trinity. In the Trinity are three persons, and every person is fully God. They are united in love. I think that every local church is fully Church. Every local church has full rights. They must be united in one Church, but equally as the Holy Trinity.

The preface of the Mass of the Trinity says: In person, different; in substance, the same, equal in glory. The relationship between local church and universal Church in my concept is like the Holy Trinity.

Q. You feel the church in China was not treated as an adult in the past?

A. Yes! We should be autonomous, independent, but united with the whole Church. That is my concept.

Q. What is most important about the relationship of the church in China with that of the rest of the world?

A. Brotherly love! We are brothers in Christ: *Ubi caritas et amor, Deus ibi est* ["Where charity and love are found, there is God."]

Q. Are Catholic religious orders allowed to function in China today?

A. That is a delicate question. In the past, religious orders did very well for the Chinese church. Without them, we would not even know God's name. But religious orders have also had bad effects.

China was once divided into influence zones by religious orders. For instance, Jiangsu and Anhui provinces were run by Jesuits; Beijing, Jiangxi, and Zhejiang by Lazarists (Vincentians). Disputes among the orders were known in China. The dispute between Dominicans and Jesuits and the Chinese-rites problem were catastrophes for the Chinese church. So, now we have a fear if religious orders emerged again.

There are only a thousand priests in all of China, and half had been religious. If every religious order from abroad wanted to control us there would be confusion in China.

We now want union among Chinese priests, so it is better that the religious orders do not interfere in Chinese religious affairs. We must acknowledge that religious orders have done very well in some areas in China. I am a Jesuit, and I still want to keep my Jesuit observance, if possible. But if every religious order existed in our country it would bring much harm. I hope you understand our position.

Q. Bishop, how old are you?

A. I am sixty-nine years old. The average age of priests in the Shanghai diocese is seventy-three.

Q. In contrast, you are a youngster! What are you doing to overcome the problem of lack of young priests?
A. Our focus is on our new seminary. We hope to have new priests very soon. This year, seven deacons will be ordained before Christmas.

Q. How old are they?
A. Three are already in their sixties, the other four are about forty. They kept their vocations during the "cultural revolution" and remained celibate till now. They wanted to become priests and their dream will be realized very soon.

Q. How many seminarians are in your regional seminary?
A. There are now ninety-three, coming from the twenty dioceses we serve in east China. There are not enough for the twenty dioceses, but we are short of housing. We are building a new seminary this year—we just laid our foundation stone. Next year, we will be able to receive more seminarians here.

Q. Do men have to join the Chinese Catholic Patriotic Association before entering the seminary?
A. Absolutely not! I myself am not a member of the Patriotic Association. As long as they are in the seminary, they do not belong to the Patriotic Association. Later, they can decide as they like, to join or not.

Q. Must seminarians be celibate?
A. We want them to be celibate their full lives. To be priests, they must be celibate.

Q. We hear there are married priests and bishops in some provinces of China. What happens if a seminarian from one of those provinces comes here to study for the priesthood?
A. In some provinces some bishops and priests are married. This is a by-product of the "cultural revolution." These priests regret it, but it is a de facto situation. In the future, our priests will not marry.

Q. Your seminarians all wear black. Do they stand out and feel strange here in China?
A. Our seminarians go outside seminary grounds wearing ordinary clothing. The media in China are very favorable to Catholics today.

Q. How do the seminarians today in your regional seminary compare with the seminarians when you were younger?

A. In some aspects, they are equal. Seminarians of thirty or forty years ago were more pious, more obedient, more docile. Today's young generation came after the "cultural revolution." They are very clever, but don't like discipline very much. We have some difficulty keeping them under strict discipline, but they are making progress. They are more clever than we were forty years ago, more active, more quick to catch things, but in discipline, they are not very good.

Q. What will the new seminary cost?
A. Our new seminary will cost about 2,000,000 *yuan* [about US $705,000], just for the buildings. The furnishings will be extra.

Q. Where does the money come from?
A. Shanghai diocese will pay half, the other dioceses contribute some. The money of Shanghai diocese comes from two sources: we collect rent from Church-owned property, the rest comes from the gifts and offerings of Christians. There are more than 100,000 Christians in Shanghai, and they are very generous.

Q. May people outside China send you money?
A. Certainly, they are welcome! I need their help.

Q. Are there conditions to send you money from abroad?
A. It must be given without political conditions or involvement.

Q. We understand there is a relationship between the church and the government. Does the government run the church?
A. The government helps us in religious life. For instance, we want to build a new seminary. Without its help, it would be unthinkable. If we want the land or even construction materials at official prices, it would be impossible without the help of the government.

For instance, a ton of cement on the free market costs double the official market price. So, with the help of the Bureau of Religious Affairs, we can get the materials at the official price. We could do almost nothing without them.

In purely religious affairs we are perfectly free. The government gives us a free hand. For instance, in the education of seminarians, we follow traditional education and in preaching we are very free.

Now, I am preparing to publish books. I have ten ready and the government leaves me absolutely free.

Q. In the past, the government was suspicious of Catholics and feared they would undermine the government. Are Catholics trusted today?
A. Yes. At the beginning of Liberation, the government was afraid that Catholics were manipulated from outside. Now they see that good Catholics

are good citizens, especially in the observance of law. Two years ago, there was a government drive to punish criminals. Among all those arrested, there were no Catholics.

Q. Does the government notice this?

A. Yes. The government especially notices that in professions like medicine and teaching, Catholics are very ardent in their work. They are not interested in money. They work better because they work for God.

Q. As one Catholic bishop in China, what message would you like to give to Catholics around the world?

A. My respect! My admiration! My love to all the brothers of the world. Because we are Christians, we are all brothers. Every day, in my Mass, I pray for the whole Church. I say the Mass in the name of the Church. In saying Mass, I am not alone, I am with the whole Church. We are one in the Mystical Body of Christ. I hope that my brothers abroad pray for us.

Document 81

Key to Rapprochement Lies in Vatican

An Interview with Bishop Fu Tieshan in Beijing Review *(in English) No. 6, 30 January 1984 (excerpts).*

Bishop Fu Tieshan was born into a Catholic family in 1931. He studied philosophy and theology in various seminaries and became a priest in 1956 when he began teaching Latin at a seminary and preaching in a church. He was elected bishop of the Beijing parish in mid-1979 and consecrated later that year. In a recent interview with *Beijing Review* correspondent Zhang Zeyu, he discussed Chinese Catholicism.

Q. As far as I know, foreign churches and Catholics are concerned about the relationship between Chinese Catholicism and the Vatican, hoping for a reconciliation between the two sides. What are your opinions about this, Bishop Fu?

A. Regarding this question, the feelings of foreign Catholics are understandable. But this question is very complicated, for it involves not just the relationships between churches. For several hundred years, the Vatican has treated Chinese Catholic churches like colonies under its control. Collaborating with the forces of aggression against China, the Vatican has in the past one hundred years taken advantage of Chinese Catholic churches to do things both against the will of Christ and detrimental to the interests of the Chinese people. After new China was founded in 1949, the Vatican continued to pursue a policy of hostility toward China, engaging in activities intended to subvert new China through the churches. In this way, it set itself against the Chinese people, including Chinese priests and Catholics. During the 1950s, 90 percent of Chinese parishes were without bishops. Considering the interests of the parish members' souls and the development of church affairs, the Wuchang and Hankou parishes democratically elected new bishops in 1958 and reported this to the Vatican. The Vatican, however, unreasonably refused to recognize these bishops, thus bringing its relationship with the Chinese Catholic church to an impasse. To date, the Vatican has not ceased its interference in the sovereignty of Chinese Catholic churches in an attempt to change the structure of Chinese society by regaining its control over Chinese Catholic churches. That being the case, it is very difficult to change the situation.

In recent years, the Vatican has assumed the posture of rapprochement with Chinese Catholic churches, but at the same time it has tried to use every possible opportunity to carry out divisive and subversive activities, both overt and covert, against Chinese Catholic churches. This inevitably makes people doubt its sincerity in seeking a rapprochement. The Bible teaches us that a tree is judged by its fruit and a person by his actions. Future developments in our relationship with the Vatican depend on how the Vatican acts. The key to a reconciliation lies in its hands.

Q. Some foreign churches and Catholics have asked whether a dialogue is possible if the Vatican is willing to change its policy of hostility toward China and treat Chinese Catholic churches equally and with friendship.

A. The Chinese Catholic church has not authorized me to comment on this. In my opinion, there is still no sign that the Vatican has fundamentally changed its policy toward China. Whether it can genuinely respect the independence of Chinese Catholic churches and treat them equally and in a friendly manner remains uncertain. The time is not yet ripe to consider a dialogue. Moreover, the Vatican still maintains "diplomatic relations" with Taiwan province. There is no basis for dialogue when the Vatican disregards China's sovereignty and interferes in its internal affairs. As a patriotic citizen, I firmly oppose the policy of "one China, one Taiwan," or "two Chinas."

According to the Constitution, the Chinese Catholic Church and church affairs are not to be controlled by foreign forces. In April of last year the joint conference of the National Administrative Commission of the Chinese Catholic Church and the Chinese Patriotic Catholic Association adopted an important resolution setting forth the principle of letting spiritual brethren around the world share the love of Christ. Chinese Catholicism adheres to the principle of running its churches independently and at the same time it actively develops friendly exchanges with foreign churches. In making contacts, it is necessary to follow the principle of equality and friendship, mutual respect for the sovereignty of each other's churches, and noninterference in each other's church affairs. For many years, we have been following this principle in our contacts and exchanges with foreign churches and Catholics.

I think that Catholic churches in China and their counterparts abroad enjoy equal status. Running Chinese churches independently is not a closed-door policy, nor is it antiforeign. We are willing to establish relations of genuine equality and friendship with foreign Catholics and on this basis continue to expand exchanges with all Catholic brothers and sisters to jointly enjoy the love of Christ and acquire useful foreign experience in order to run our own churches well.

Document 82

Chinese Catholics: More Religious Freedom

An interview with Bishop Zong Huaide in Beijing Review *No. 25, 22 June 1987.*

Joseph Zong Huaide is the bishop of the Jinan area in Shandong Province. He was elected president of the Chinese Catholic Patriotic Association in 1980 and is vice-president of the administrative commission of the Catholic Church in China and of the Bishops' Conference of the Chinese Catholic Church.

He recently spoke with *Beijing Review* about Chinese Catholicism.

Q. In the past few years, many of China's Catholic churches have been restored and membership has been growing rapidly. Why?

A. The past five years could be called the most encouraging period in the history of the Catholic church in China.

During the "cultural revolution," churches of all denominations were closed and all the priests, bishops, ministers, and nuns were sent out to the countryside to do manual labor, even though China's constitution said the nation's citizens enjoyed freedom of religious belief.

Now, almost 2,000 churches and meeting places for church services have been restored and reopened. We have also elected and ordained 22 bishops in 20 dioceses. China now has 3.3 million Catholics, including 140,000 converts in the past five years.

Q. Is the increase due to the open policy and the influence of Western culture?

A. The open policy has certainly created a favorable atmosphere for people to choose their own religious beliefs. The influence of Western culture has also had its effect. But neither of these is the most important factor. The existence of the Catholic church in China and the example set by practicing Catholics here are the major attractions to converts.

Most Chinese Catholics are serious, decent, law-abiding, and industrious. More than 1,600 of our church members have received national recognition as model workers, and 950 have been elected to national or local People's Congresses or to the Chinese People's Political Consultative Conferences.

Many Chinese Catholics are farmers. Those in the cities are to be found in all walks of life, including doctors, lawyers, teachers, administrators, and workers. Most are middle-aged or older; only about a quarter of our Catholics are young, and they come mostly from Catholic families.

Q. You say Chinese Catholics are active in the modernization drive. How do they combine their love for God with their love for the motherland?

A. We are all children of God. When we love God, we must follow God's teachings to love our parents, our brothers and sisters, our neighbors, all the people, and our country. Achieving China's four modernizations means creating a society in which everyone lives a happy life. This is also the ideal of Chinese Catholics.

We Chinese Catholics appreciate highly the Communist Party's resolution on principles for promoting ethics and culture. I believe that the resolution bears a close resemblance to the Ten Commandments.

Q. What do Chinese Catholics think of China's birth-control program? And what about abortion?

A. Chinese Catholics are patriots. They accept the birth control policy willingly because they understand that it is intended to benefit the interest of the nation and because China's population situation affects the rest of the world as well.

At this point, birth control is not contradictory to God's teaching because God says we should live for others' happiness. If we don't control China's population, we will all suffer from the shortage of resources as basic as water, and from a lack of development. But as for abortion, I would say it's better to do our best to avoid pregnancies.

Q. What church services are offered?

A. We have morning and evening prayers, Masses, holiday celebrations, and all the other services a Catholic church is supposed to provide, including confession and baptism.

Q. Most of China's bishops are quite old. Who will succeed them?

A. This is one of our greatest concerns. We have established eleven seminaries and a dozen convents throughout the country.

The National Seminary in Beijing now has seventy students. All the recruits were recommended by their dioceses and then chosen by examination. Since the students are expected not to marry, we also require their parents' consent. The dioceses pay for their studies. During their six years in college, the students take courses in dogmatics, moral theology, the Bible, church history, philosophy and the history of philosophy, spiritual practice, church music, and foreign languages, including Latin. After they graduate, they will return to their home dioceses to serve in their local churches.

Q. The Chinese Patriotic Catholic Association has no contact with the Vatican, but Pope John Paul II seems to have shown interest in China.

A. The Vatican has adopted an unfriendly policy toward China ever since Liberation in 1949. It refuses to recognize the People's Republic as the only legal government of China and maintains diplomatic relations with Taiwan. Nor has the Vatican shown enough respect for the sovereignty of the Chinese Catholic Church.

It is true that the pope recently called China a beautiful country with a long history of civilization. This might be interpreted as an overture, but what we need is action, not words.

Unless the Vatican changes its basic policy toward China and the Chinese Catholic church, any improvement in the relationship between the Vatican and our church is out of the question.

Still, we Chinese Catholics are not isolated from our brothers and sisters in other countries. In the past few years more than 70,000 Catholics from ninety countries have visited China. Among them have been India's Mother Teresa and a delegation from Canada. We want to maintain equal and friendly contacts with Catholics from all nations.

Q. The church's growing role in China must mean that its financial needs are increasing. What support do you get from the government?

A. Very little. Our churches are basically self-supporting and receive most of their income from donations and from renting out houses they own. We sometimes apply for government funds for big projects such as renovating major churches, but we try to avoid this because we know China's financial resources are scarce and must be spread over many areas.

Document 83

To Have an Independent, Self-Ruled, and Self-Managed Church Is Our Sacred Right

By Bishop Tu Shihua in A New Beginning, *the collected papers of an ecumenical conference in Montreal in 1981, the first such conference attended by Chinese church leaders in many years. (A New Beginning,* Theresa Chu and Christopher Lind, editors, the Canada China Programme, Toronto, 1983, pp. 99–103.)

According to the account of Matthew 28: 18-20, "But Jesus came near and spoke to them: 'All authority in heaven and on earth,' he said, 'has been given to me; you, therefore, must go out, making disciples of all nations, and baptizing them in the name of the Father, and of the Son, and of the Holy Ghost, teaching them to observe all the commandments which I have given you. And behold I am with you all through the days that are coming, until the consummation of the world.' " Here Jesus awarded the whole authority of teaching the peoples, administering the sacraments, and governing the churches to the apostles. He also promised his continuous presence in the churches to assure the accomplishment of the tasks entrusted to them. One may conclude, therefore, that there must be successors to continue the ministry and mission of the apostles. As soon as the apostles received the Holy Ghost, they founded churches everywhere, beginning with Jerusalem. Their successors, or bishops of the local churches, have the power in the full sense to govern independently the local churches respectively entrusted to them. Thus the local churches, with the bishop as head, have the power of independent self-rule and self-management.

As far as the dogma is concerned, bishops of various local churches, as a college of bishops, are successors of the apostles' college. Since they are the successors of the apostles, the powers of teaching, sanctifying, and governing that the apostles received from God are immediately accorded to them. Each bishop, after he has been elected by the clergy and laity in the respective local church, immediately receives the power to govern his church through episcopal consecration. This power of the bishop in a local church is an ordinary power associated with the ministry of the bishop, an immediate or proper power that is exercised in the bishop's own name; a power invested by God. The bishop of a local church neither receives his powers by the appointment or ratification of the pope, nor exercises them as his delegate. Therefore, the authority of the bishop in his local church possesses by itself the characteristic of independence; the local church headed by the bishop possesses the right of independent self-rule and self-management in line with the apostolic tradition of collective leadership and democratic administration. No other bishop is allowed to interfere, to restrict, still less to deprive a bishop of this ordinary, immediate, proper power awarded by God. On the contrary, it must be respected.

Various local churches practice independence and self-government while belonging to the same church of God. "The same hope, the same Lord, the same belief, the same baptism, and the same Holy Ghost" unite the local churches within the mystical body of Christ, rendering them the unique, holy, catholic, apostolic Church. The Chinese Catholic church is one of the members of Jesus Christ. Christ is the head while we are brothers within it.

In view of the early tradition of the Church, the apostolic father St. Ignatius of Antioch, in the beginning of the second century, spoke of the unparalleled, sublime position of bishops in their own local churches. He said, "No one must act in anything concerning the church without the bishop. Only the eucharist celebrated by the bishop, or by those appointed by him, counts as valid. Wherever the bishop appears, his people are there too, just as where Jesus Christ is, so also is the Catholic Church" (Smyrna 8:1). This is the true portrayal of tradition in the era of the apostolic fathers, in which the bishop is the center of the independent, self-ruled, and self-managed churches.

From the fact that the bishops of the second and third centuries were elected by the clergy and laity themselves, one can see the precious tradition that prevailed at that time in the independent self-ruling and self-managing local churches. For instance, in referring to the election of bishops, the early church father Tertullian said: "Everybody will pass through tests. Not those who rely on the power and influence, but the senior who acquired dignity by his virtue will preside over the church" (Apologetics 39). St. Cyprian has told us in detail about how the new bishop Cornelius was elected by the whole clergy and peoples (Epistles 10). He has also remarked: "They [clergy and people] have the right to elect a well-suited bishop or to reject an unsuited one" (Epistles 68). All these reflect the original tradition of the early period of the Church.

In the fourth century, the Catholic church became the state church of the Roman Empire and the emperors began to control the church. It was at this time that the metropolitan episcopate appeared. But in the fifth century the choice of people for bishop and even for pope was controlled by the secular powers. Finally, with the Worms Concordat of the twelfth century, a turning point was reached in the matter of the installation of bishops. As John Dolan remarked in his *History of the Reformation*, [John P. Dolan, *History of the Reformation: A Conciliatory Assessment of Opposite Views*, New York: The American Library, A Mentor-Omega Book, 1964, pp. 201-202.] "It was, in fact, a final triumph of feudal principles over the Church. Henceforth, bishops were chosen from cathedral chapters composed exclusively of the nobility. Their chief qualifications lay in their ability to carry out affairs of state." After the Worms Concordat, a series of such concordats were signed by the Vatican with various countries all over the world: Italy, France, Germany, Spain, Guatemala, Honduras, Nicaragua, and so on. All of these concordats have affirmed the rights of the countries and their respective churches over the matter of the installation of bishops. This is a well-known fact.

The pity is that the rights of the colonial or semicolonial countries and their churches have never been given the respect that is their due. This was also the case for our church. Four hundred years have now passed since the founding of the church in China. Matteo Ricci first came to China in 1582, but it was 103 years before the first bishop for China was appointed — Gregario Lopez in 1685. It took another 241 years for this event to be repeated. In 1926 six more indigenous bishops were appointed. After the victory of the anti-Japanese war in 1946, the Vatican claimed that a normal hierarchy was founded in the Chinese church. Yet, at that time, there were only twenty-nine indigenous bishops in 137 Chinese dioceses. The rate of indigenization was only 21.1 percent. The number of indigenous bishops was small to begin with, and after Liberation, under the influence of the Vatican's anti-Communist and anti-Chinese position, some of these left China. Up to 1958, 120 out of 145 dioceses remained vacant. The great majority of clergy and laity, on account of the basic interests of the church, launched a just call for the election of bishops by the Chinese Christians themselves. In the meantime, the bishops of Hankou and Wuchang dioceses were elected and reported to the Vatican in accordance with the conventional practice of the church. Yet, in response, these people were attacked with the unjustifiable punishment of "excommunication." Earlier in 1956, Father Chang Shilang had been elected by the Shanghai diocese as vicar *capitulaire* and his name was submitted to Rome for approbation. Yet, again, the response was nothing but unreasonable disapproval. In fact, the Vatican praised Gong Pinmei, who had been convicted of serious offenses and sentenced according to China's law, as "the most competent bishop." At the same time, the measure of "transferring pastoral powers to the lower level" had been taken so that a few *pax et communio*[1] elements could come to power in the affairs of the church, throwing it into confusion. After the departure of Cardinal Tien Geng-hsing (Tian Gengxing) from Beijing diocese in 1948, that see remained vacant for ten years. Bishop Yao Guangyu was elected in 1959 to fill the position, but after his death in 1964 the Beijing see remained vacant until 1978, a further fifteen years. It was under these circumstances that on 25 July 1979 Fu Tieshan was unanimously elected bishop by the clergy and laity of Beijing diocese — but even this was censured by the Vatican as "illegal." These activities of the Vatican concerning the church of China are in conflict not only with the instructions of the Gospel but also with the original traditions of the church. Regarding the rights due to the church of China, the conventional practices of the church have not been considered in the least. Instead, the Vatican has put its political prejudices above all the interests of the church and the faithful. Nothing is more intolerable than this! The clergy and laity of the Chinese church have learned some painful lessons from these experiences and have gradually recognized the real intentions of the Vatican with regard to the installation of bishops in the Chinese church. The intention of the Vatican has been to continue to place the Chinese church in a colonial situation. They have insisted on appointing bishops who would faithfully carry out revolutionary government. The Vatican wants to mislead the Chinese church so that it will stand against the great majority of the Chinese people.

Nevertheless, in the course of more than twenty years our Chinese church has remained faithful to the instructions of the Gospel and to the original traditions of the church. It has upheld the principle of the independent self-rule and self-management of the church. It has stood up against the interference and the acts of sabotage by the Vatican so that the Chinese church is now flourishing—full of vim and vigor. In these circumstances, the Vatican now hides in a pose of reconciliation but it continues to sabotage our sacred cause of independent self-rule and self-management. A living example of this was the way Deng Yiming was illegally appointed, behind the back of the Chinese church. On account of this, our Chinese church has issued a solemn statement of protest, describing how the Vatican disregarded the sovereignty of our country, interfered ruthlessly in the internal affairs of the Chinese church, and went against the instructions of the Gospel and ancient ecclesiastical traditions. We will by no means tolerate it.

What we will do is to persevere in the independent self-rule of the Chinese church, according to the instructions of the Gospel and ancient ecclesiastical traditions. Our task is the sacred task that Jesus Christ trusted to us. He will be with us forever—until the consummation of the world.

Note

1. The term was used by the Sacred Congregation for the Propagation of Faith (SCPF) in its two letters to the Diocese of Shanghai dated 17 March and 10 July 1957, respectively. By *pax et communio* or "peace and communion" (PC) elements, were meant those priests who, like Gong Pinmei, kept contact with the See of Rome and carried out its directives in opposition to new China and to the Socialist system. In both letters, the SCPF stated that faculties and "the privilege of administering the diocese" were to be given to PC elements only, that "none other may be granted such faculties and privileges."

Section IV

Seminarians and Novices, a New Generation

Document 84

Interviews with Four Seminarians from Sheshan Regional Seminary, Shanghai

By Donald MacInnis, in Tripod *(Hongkong) No. 46, August 1988, pp. 47-55.*

On 13 November 1987 I interviewed five fifth- and sixth-year students at the Sheshan Regional Seminary, which is located an hour's drive from Shanghai on a low mountain near the restored Basilica of Our Lady. In a year or two these men will complete their theological studies and be assigned to parishes in the East China Region of the Catholic church in China. Sheshan Seminary, with 127 students, is one of the seven major seminaries in China. In addition there are four minor seminaries and several one-year preparatory courses, actually tutorials, taught by local priests.

The first student interviewed in the main classroom of the seminary was Ni Guoxiang, twenty-three, a sixth-year student.

When asked about his ordination, he explained that the priest of the parish where he will serve as curate will decide on the time, but it would probably take place within two or three years.

Q. When did you decide to study for the priesthood?
A. In 1981 our government reinstated the policy of freedom of religious belief. The church in our town, Nantong in Jiangsu Province, was reopened and I began to attend church each Sunday. I also began to study the church's doctrine. One day our priest gave a talk on the situation of the church in China today, pointing out the shortage of priests. I reflected on this for a time and came to realize that our church is in a time of crisis; there is an urgent need for young men to replace the elderly priests. I saw my generation's responsibility to carry on God's work as something that we cannot neglect. The best way to do this is to become one of his represen-

tatives, to minister to his people. So I decided to enter the seminary.

Q. Are any members of your family Christian?

A. All of them are. My family has been Catholic for many generations. I am a fifth-generation Catholic.

Q. After ordination, how would you most like to serve the church?

A. I would like to serve in the parish. Many of our priests are old and do not have the time or physical strength to teach our people. They simply do not have the strength to do all the pastoral tasks that face them. Many of the Christians, especially the young, lack proper religious instruction. I also wish to help people outside the church to become believers. So in order that the church may grow, I want to be in the parish and do God's work there. That is how I am thinking about the future now.

Q. What do you think are the greatest problems facing the church in China in the near future?

A. As I see it, our greatest problem is how to reach out and help those outside the church, especially the many young people who want to know more about the Christian faith. They know a little bit about our church and are interested in learning more. But we still lack sufficient avenues of approach in presenting the church to them. They want us to talk with them about our faith, but our biggest problem is that we do not know how to help them understand and accept the church's teaching. They don't think of religion in the same way as we do. How can we convey to them the understanding of the faith which we have?

Q. Are people antagonistic to religion? Or are they merely indifferent?

A. Most people are not hostile toward religion. Many of them have studied secular [Marxist] philosophy and are in fact searching for the truth, especially young people. They see us, like themselves, as fellow searchers, but as those who have found the truth. They say to us, "Ah, you have found the truth, we would like to find it also." So they come to us in their search. Of course, we ourselves are not the source of truth; we are merely bearers of the truth of Jesus to people. Most people are not opposed to Christianity. If they were hostile to religion, they wouldn't be talking with us in the first place. Those who really want to know more about our faith talk with us. Then there are people who talk with us about religion simply out of idle curiosity. But others are sincerely searching for some kind of faith and meaning in their lives. These are the ones who will eventually come into the church.

Q. Marxism teaches that all religions are superstition. How do most people feel about this?

A. Most people feel that Marxism cannot answer the basic questions of our human lives. Marxism is taught in all the schools of China today. We began studying Marxist philosophy in senior middle school. But even after attending these classes we still felt that Marxist explanations are inadequate. Others outside our circle felt the same way. They say, "Ai-ya, this ever-changing world is full of questions that we still cannot understand." As Christians we are able to talk with them and help them to understand that this is God's world, and since the world is His creation then all human concerns come under His care.

Yuan Guozhan comes from Fuan diocese in northern Fujian Province and is twenty-four years old.

Q. When did you feel in your heart that God wanted you to study for the priesthood?
A. I felt God's call to the priesthood when I was in middle school.

Q. Did this happen as a result of praying about it, or due to other influences?
A. It was due to my family training and environment. My family has been Catholic for over three hundred years. My two elder brothers also studied for the priesthood.

Q. When was your parish church reopened after the "cultural revolution"?
A. In 1982.

Q. Did you have a priest in residence at that time?
A. Yes, we did. There are several priests in our diocese, all of them elderly. They were allowed to come back to us at that time. Our diocese once had thirty to forty churches, but now there are just a few old priests left.

Q. What foreign missionaries served your area in the past?
A. The Spanish Dominicans. Of course, they had to leave in the early 1950s.

Q. How old are your priests now?
A. Mostly in their seventies, one or two in their sixties.

Q. Were you influenced by these priests in making your decision?
A. I was mainly influenced by my family. I first thought about it back in junior middle school, right after the "cultural revolution" when the situation for Christians was still very tense. There was no priest to say Mass at that time. In our family we continued to read the Bible, to say the rosary, and to pray together. My father and mother led the prayers. Also, I have

two aunts who never married, but remained at home and led a religious life. While they never had any formal religious training, they remained celibate and served the church. Our church calls these women who devote their lives to the church "virgins."

Q. Did they serve the church before the "cultural revolution"?
A. Yes, they taught us the catechism. Even though we were not allowed to have public worship during those years, we did have catechism classes in our homes, and preaching was done by lay men and women. We had no priests then. Later an old priest came to our village and once again we had Mass and received Holy Communion.

Q. Do you live in a town or village?
A. We live in a village of three hundred people, of whom about two-thirds are Catholic.

Q. Did you have any difficulties during the "cultural revolution"?
A. Yes, our church was taken over and used by the village government. We could not use it for religious services. All our prayerbooks, missals, and Bibles were burned. But our parents and the older Christians carried on religious activities in our homes. They would recite from memory whole sections of the Bible and the catechism books.

Q. Does your village have a church now?
A. Yes, our church has been returned to us.

Q. How do you hope to serve the church in the future?
A. We should be like servants in the church, preaching the Gospel in the spirit of Christ so that it enters the hearts of those who hear it. I can't simply rely on my own strength, that's not enough. I must rely on God for His help and guidance—that is the most important thing.

Fu Jianrong is twenty-four, and he is from Hangzhou diocese, Zhejiang Province.

Q. In what year are you here at the seminary?
A. I am in my sixth and last year. I hope to be ordained in about two more years.

Q. How did you come to your decision to study for the priesthood?
A. I was fortunate to be brought up in a Christian environment. My whole family is Catholic, and, even though our church was closed, we had prayers and doctrine classes in my home. My aunt taught me about the Bible. We had no Bibles. They had all been burned during the "cultural revolution." But I did have a copy of the four Gospels and the Acts of the

Apostles which our parish priest had copied by hand. This was when I was in junior middle school. From that time I began to understand the teachings of the church and to develop my own faith and understanding of the Bible. Of course, my understanding was not very deep. Given this kind of background, when I heard that our diocese would open a seminary, I made the decision to begin to study for the priesthood.

I came here to study for two reasons. First, I felt my own faith was too superficial. I wanted to study theology in order to deepen my faith and my understanding of it. The second reason was that I wanted to become a priest. From an early age, I admired priests and was deeply moved by the example of their lives.

Q. How do you hope to serve the church after finishing theological studies?

A. I wish to preach the Gospel. There are still comparatively few Christians in China, very few. When I return home for vacations many of my former classmates and friends whom I know, and others whom I do not, look me up. They want to learn about our Christian faith and its teachings. I enjoy these opportunities to talk with them.

Q. Are you saying that the Chinese people, especially the young people, are not antagonistic toward religion?

A. That's right. They are not hostile to religion. There are some people who are prejudiced. This was especially evident during the "cultural revolution," and was directed mainly toward older Christians and priests, not toward us younger believers. Yes, I hope to be able to preach and teach our faith to those outside the church. . . . I also like the study of theology very much.

Q. What do you believe is the biggest problem facing the church in the future?

A. I believe that the biggest and most immediate problem for our church is to make up for the "ten lost years" of the "cultural revolution." All activities of the Chinese church were suppressed for over a decade and now the church has to catch up. Just catching up is not enough, however. The church also has to move ahead if it is to grow. This means that my generation must make great efforts to help the church go forward.

We also have a generation gap. For example, in the matter of rites and liturgy, there are differences of opinion between older and younger church members. The younger Catholics are outnumbered by the older ones, who prefer the old rites and liturgy, while the young people want the newer ones. We still use Latin in the Mass, even though none of us young people understand it. But the older Catholics still cling to the old forms. These contradictions are still to be worked out.

Q. Can these questions be resolved?

A. I can't really answer that. We are only students, and we only now are becoming conscious of these difficulties. I think it will take time. I also believe that indigenization is very important for our church. We must develop our own theology and our own liturgies.

Q. What are your feelings about relations between the Catholic church in China and the Vatican?

A. As I see it, this is basically a political matter, related to the Taiwan question. We hope that the church in China can have friendly relations with every country. We are all the same in our faith.

Q. Tell me something about your family.

A. We are all Christians. My mother and father, four brothers, and a sister are all living. I also have two sisters-in-law and a brother-in-law who are believers. During the years when we did not have freedom of religion, we carried on regularly with worship in the family at home.

Q. You had no Bible or other religious books at that time?

A. No, we had nothing. They had all been taken from us and burned.

Dou Xuexiao is twenty-four years old and comes from Shandong Province.

Q. When did you begin studying for the priesthood?

A. I came here to begin my studies in 1983. Before that I spent a year studying basic doctrine and Latin with a priest in Jinan in our province. This is part of a preparatory course we have there.

Q. Please tell me about your family.

A. I am from an old Catholic family. I am a fifth-generation Catholic. Each generation has had a priest. If I succeed, I will be the fifth generation to become a priest in our family.

Q. Are there any nuns in your family?

A. No, but two of my aunts were "virgins." They never married and gave their lives to serving the church.

Q. Did you have any difficulties during the "cultural revolution"?

A. I was too young then to remember much about it. I was only three years old when it began. But I do remember our family had prayers at home when the churches were closed. I just followed along with the prayers they were saying, but I was too young to understand their significance.

Q. When did you begin to understand?

A. After graduation from senior middle school.

Q. How did you come to your decision to study for the priesthood?
A. I saw how overworked our two priests were. Both are quite old and I realized the need for young priests in our diocese. As a consequence I applied to enter the seminary.

Q. How do you hope to serve the church in the future?
A. The standard of living of our church members, both in material and cultural areas, has been raised. But they still need help in their spiritual lives and this is where I hope to assist our people.

Q. Today over half the population of China, about 60 percent, are young people under thirty. What is their attitude toward religion?
A. Many of China's young people are interested in religion, but they have had few opportunities to learn much about it. They have studied atheism in school, but haven't had a chance to learn about theism. They are really searching for this kind of knowledge.

Q. How do they feel about atheism? You had to study it in school, didn't you?
A. Yes, I did. I'm a Christian. I believe in God. Studying atheism was just another required course for me.

Q. What do you believe is the biggest problem facing the church in China?
A. The biggest problem for our church is the shortage of clergy. We younger men must be ready to take over the work of the older priests. We need to raise up a new generation of young priests.

Document 85

Catholic Novitiates in Guangxi Province

Excerpts from an interview with a Catholic Sister by Donald MacInnis, 1988.

In early 1988 I interviewed a Catholic Sister, born in Guangxi, shortly after she returned to Hongkong from a three-month visit in Guangxi Province. She had stayed in three cities, Guilin, Wuzhou, and Liuzhou.

Guilin: Priests, Sisters, and Novices

In former days there were only missionary priests in Guilin, some seminarians, but no Chinese priests. Today the entire province of Guangxi has only five priests, all over seventy, and, of course, no missionaries. Guilin has two seminarians in the Wuhan seminary, but no resident priest.

There had been fourteen Chinese Sisters in Guilin, trained by missionaries, but today only two aged Sisters, ninety-one and ninety-three, remain in Guilin. Three former Sisters, married and now retired from secular work, are helping the church. They lead prayers, teach catechism, visit in the homes, and, in the absence of a resident priest, provide pastoral care.

On 14 December 1987, the Guilin novitiate was reopened. Three former Chinese Sisters will teach and guide the novices in spiritual formation, while a layman in charge of the church will teach politics. They hope to find a priest to teach scripture. Until they get the old convent back, they will live in the church.

The six novices, all from Catholic families, are all seventeen years old. Why do they want to become nuns? Because they want to follow Jesus and help other people to become Christians. The older Sisters are an example to them. Most of them have completed junior middle school.

The Catholic Church in Guangxi Province

There are churches and outlying chapels in five cities: Wuzhou, Guilin, Nanning, Liuzhou, and Bantian.

Q. Are there any catechists?

A. Only in Bantian, which was a Catholic village, and is still over half Catholic. The young Christians were all baptized as infants by their parents when they had no priest. Now the priest rebaptizes them.

The first Catholic marriage in Bantian in many years was conducted by a visiting priest from Liuzhou on 1 January this year.

As for baptisms, there were ten on Christmas day. Eight are from Catholic families and two are young women factory workers.

Two New Novitiates in Liuzhou and Wuzhou

There is a new novitiate in Liuzhou with eleven novices, twenty-three to twenty-seven years old. Two old "virgins" [lay Sisters] are teaching. The novices earn their subsistence by doing sewing subcontracted from a factory.

There are twenty-one novices in the Wuzhou novitiate, all in their early twenties. Three former Sisters, all over sixty, and the aging parish priest serve as teachers. They follow the same daily schedule as missionary sisters did in former years: rise at 5:15; morning prayers and meditation; Mass; breakfast; household duties; classes; noon prayers; one hour of rest; sewing work in the afternoon; visit the Blessed Sacrament at 5:00; prepare and eat supper; free time in the evening; evening prayers; and bedtime at 9:30. Silence is observed at mealtime, while selections from the Bible and other religious books are read aloud. They use old Latin hymnals, because, as the old Sisters said, "That's all we know."

Some of the girls have been called back from the novitiate by their parish priest, because he desperately needs help in the parish.

The Future of the Church

Q. How do you view the future of the church?

A. I am very hopeful. Young people are coming to the church. Yes, we are short on clergy, but that is why we opened the novitiates.

Q. Is there any training of lay leaders?

A. Not yet. People are just beginning to come back to church. Some are still afraid. The Sisters say to the Catholics, "Come back, it's safe now," but many are still afraid to come.

The former Sisters who now help the church, and their families, suffered much. Their children couldn't get jobs, so now they are reluctant to see their mothers go back to the church.

The government now is being good to the church. Government officials came to the Christmas program and made speeches. They also came to the church annual meeting and made speeches.

Q. Does the government control the church?

A. Yes. For example, they must get permission from the Religious Affairs Bureau to accept and use any gift over 1,000 *yuan*. They need the help of the government to get back the use of buildings, such as the former convent. A priest from outside the district must get permission to say Mass. Of course the church committee makes decisions about the internal affairs of the church, but the leader reports to the Religious Affairs Bureau. The government is harder on the Catholics than Protestants because of the Vatican connection.

Q. Is there freedom of religious belief?

A. The government says we cannot offer prayers outside the church, except for last rites administered in the home. Older Catholics do not have to refrain from expressing loyalty to the pope in the Mass prayers. They still pray for the pope without naming him.

Q. How did Catholics maintain their faith during the difficult years?

A. Often they were baptized by their parents, usually their mother. Sometimes they weren't told of this until they became adults.

The Protestant Church in China Today

Introduction

Protestant missionaries did not arrive in China until after the Treaty of Nanking (1842). Conversions came slowly in the early decades, but by 1949 there were 936,000 baptized members and 2,963 clergy, 68 percent of them Chinese and the rest foreign missionaries. (Of the 4,788 Catholic priests, 56 percent were Chinese.)

Protestant clergy and laity, like the Catholics, suffered persecution, repression, and banishment to prison or work camps during the "cultural revolution." Unlike the Catholics, they were not dependent on ordained clergy, and congregational worship was sustained in clandestine house meetings organized by lay leaders. Today those house meetings have multiplied into the thousands, providing spiritual nurture for perhaps millions of Christians, new and old, often in situations where no ordained clergyman is available. Because these groups spring up spontaneously, no one knows how many persons attend in total, or how many of them are baptized Christians. As a result, estimates of Protestant Christian numbers range from five million, the latest figure accepted by church leaders of the China Christian Council, to one hundred million, an estimate put forth by a mission research center based in Hongkong, but unsubstantiated by any reliable sources or analysis.

Like the Catholics, Chinese Protestants are devoted to their church, many of them testifying to their faith as the spiritual anchor (*jingshen jituo*) that kept them from foundering during the storms and buffeting of the "cultural revolution." Today that experience binds them together in the tasks of rebuilding the shattered work of the church and in reaching out to non-Christians. With the shortage of able-bodied clergy, much of that work now is carried on by lay volunteers, many of them trained in local classes that run for as long as six months. This dedicated lay leadership, it seems, is the main reason for the explosive growth in numbers of Protestant Christians and the construction of many new churches paid for and built by local Christians.

Church Growth

Statistics issued by the China Christian Council in 1987 (*Tian Feng*, November 1987) report 4,044 churches, of which 1,067 are newly built, 16,868 meeting points, 151,062 newly baptized adult Christians, 4,575 professional

313

church workers (the 1986 figure was 6,000 clergymen, but this must include retired persons), 26,336 lay church workers, 14,891 volunteers participating in lay-workers' training programs, and 594 theological students enrolled in seminaries.

Volunteer Lay Workers

The most significant figures here are those referring to volunteer lay workers, who outnumber the professional workers (pastors and others) ten to one. In addition, one learns from visiting in homes that many Christians, particularly women, whose names would not appear in these rolls, give a great deal of time to such church work as calling in homes of the sick and elderly and leading home prayer and Bible study meetings (Documents 90 through 93).

The Church in One Province

Three provinces lead all others in total numbers of Protestant Christians: Henan with 830,000; Zhejiang, 800,000; and Fujian, 600,000 (statistics from an interview with Bishop K.H.Ting in October 1988). According to a report in *Tian Feng* (August 1987), the church in Fujian Province had ordained 57 pastors, none of them young, in five ordination ceremonies since 1982. In the same period there had been 400,000 baptisms and 500 churches reopened or newly built.

Figures from the provincial Religious Affairs Office dated April 1988 show 224 full pastors and 398 unordained pastors for the province. The same report shows 26 Catholic priests and 104 unordained deacons provincewide.

Problems Facing the Church

Church leaders do not hesitate to speak of problems facing the church. In a lecture at the Luther-Northwestern Theological Seminary, St. Paul, Minnesota, in April 1988, Bishop K. H. Ting spoke of six problem areas: aging church leadership; shortage of pastors and insufficient pastoral care; shortage of seminary teachers; inadequate theological guidance for house-meeting leaders; continued restrictions on religious freedom in some places; and the urgent need for an organized united church in China. On other occasions Bishop Ting and others have spoken of the lack of content in preaching and worship services, and the danger of heretical or eccentric teachings fostered by untrained local evangelists, charismatics, and faith healers. Finally, despite the emphasis on "mutual respect," old denominational loyalties and customs referred to in Documents 87 and 91 still cause dissension and disunity in some places.

Local Church Life (Section I)

Local church life is described in three reports, one an interview with the pastor of *Sanyi* (Trinity) Church in Xiamen, one an abridged translation of a paper based on field research in Anhui Province, and one a report in the Protestant journal, *Tian Feng*.

The pastor of Trinity Church sketches a picture of his large and active church, which reopened in 1982 and is growing so fast that he can't say how many members there are, has a weekly youth meeting attended by 170, and takes in enough money in the Christmas offering to run the church for a whole year. Other offerings are used to support three seminarians, help struggling new churches and give aid to widows, orphans, and other needy people.

He explains how three pastors from different denominational backgrounds cooperate, the problems in dealing with sects and heresy, and ends with an account of his own bitter experiences during the hard times and a statement of his personal faith.

"Building on a Rock" tells a story, repeated many times in recent years, of the members of one congregation building a new church themselves, in this case carrying seventy thousand bricks, five thousand tiles, cement, and other materials to the top of a low mountain, where even old men of eighty helped build the church.

In their study of a rapidly growing Christian community in Anhui Province (Document 88), the Shanghai social scientists set out to answer the questions, who are these people and why have they become Christians? They analyze the content of the preaching, the beneficial social effects of Christianity in the lives of the converts, the reasons for its rapid growth, and finally they suggest ways in which local Party and civic leaders can deal with this matter.

Having just made the observation, substantiated by case stories, that "people from all walks of life, including numerous cadres . . . all speak well of these people," they conclude, incongruously, with this advice:

"The basic measures needed to free them from . . . the fetters of religion are to diligently promote Socialist modernization, to increase the speed of social productive forces and to actively raise the level of their material and cultural life, . . . and to popularize scientific knowledge."

Clergy and Lay Leadership in the Local Church (Section II)

Because it so important to the ongoing life of the local church, five documents on lay leadership in the local church have been selected. Two of these were taken from interviews conducted in 1988 in Fujian Province, one with a woman lay leader and one with the two pastors of a large church in Putian, while the others are translated from *Tian Feng*.

The Flower Lane Church in Fuzhou is divided into fourteen districts, with four deacons and deaconesses responsible for each district. In addition, there are thirty neighborhood groups which meet during the week in homes. Mrs. Lin, the widow of a pastor, meets with two of these and leads a third group which meets in her home on Wednesday evenings "to nurture spiritual life through prayer and Bible study . . . [and] discuss the work of the church, and which persons we should go to visit."

The two Putian pastors, both in their seventies, could never minister to their large parish without lay volunteers. As many as sixty laypersons come to Putian city from outlying districts for two-month training classes, living at a nearby church and providing their own food, then returning to take leadership in local churches without pastors. Putian City and County, with 32 churches and ten meeting points, has only seven experienced pastors, all over seventy, and six others recently ordained. Each pastor serves several churches, assisted by lay volunteers.

Like Flower Lane Church, the Shantou church has divided its members into dozens of neighborhood and district groups. Each group has a liaison person, also called a group leader, whose duties include calling on the sick, visiting families having problems, helping with weddings and funerals, offering prayers when needed, counseling inquirers, and generally offering pastoral care and outreach.

Cao Shengjie's account of the church in Wenzhou, Zhejiang, describes a county with thirty thousand Christians and over a hundred churches and meeting points where there are only five pastors. Preaching and pastoral care is largely in the hands of lay volunteers. This article describes both the pros and cons of such dependence on lay volunteers.

Why They Become Christians (Section III)

Two articles by Chinese social scientists, translated from *Zongjiao* (Religion) magazine, describe the spread of Christian faith among specific groups, one in Shanghai, the other in Anhui Province. As with similar field studies cited elsewhere in this volume, the researchers, using methods of social analysis based on the Marxist materialist assumption that religion will wither away under the social and economic conditions of the new age, seem almost bewildered as they search for answers to the question: Why do they become Christians? Their findings, so far as they go, seem accurate enough; but they do not go beyond the limits of dialectical and social determinism (which would be entering the realm of idealism) to acknowledge what they, themselves, report — that religious adherents believe in spiritual truths that have made a very real, (that is, material) impact on their lives and others'.

The Shanghai case-study group consists of elderly, retired persons who had suffered in the old society, but "under the leadership of the Party have been able to lead a happy life." If that is true, the writers ask, then why have they turned to religion?

First, as the end of life approaches, they fear death and hope for a future life. The reason for their religious faith "is to make sure they have a final home." Although science and materialism "have already answered the questions about life and death," death still remains a mystery.

Another reason for turning to religion is the search for healing of illness. "God," they write, "cannot cure illness, yet some patients do get better after becoming Christians," and the news of these cases spreads, attracting others.

Loneliness is another factor leading older people to religion. In retirement their life patterns change, their family may move away, and their spouse may die.

The Christians in the second essay, rural women of all ages, are a different kind of group. The writers attribute their religious conversions to several factors. First, with an illiteracy rate of 67 percent, they have always been easily influenced by superstition, and they don't distinguish between the gods and "God."

Further, these women have observed that family relations improve after Christian conversions. This is a way to achieve peace in the family.

Third, the circumscribed lives of rural women often lead to depression. Joining a church provides a new and active social life, including hymn singing and various meetings. Depression and other illnesses are often cured.

County leaders, searching for ways to deal with this situation, opened up rural cultural centers, created contests for "cultural villages" and "five-good families," and tried ways to improve the political-thought work among women, but still there were insufficient recreational and cultural activities in the villages, and the women were too busy to attend political-study classes. And so Christianity continues to fill a need, attracting both older and younger women who believe that their Christian faith not only helps themselves, but "will raise the productivity of the brigade."

Interviews with Provincial and National Leaders (Section IV)

The final three documents consist of interviews with two church leaders, one the eighty-six-year-old leader of the church in Fujian, Bishop Moses Xie, the other the president of the national China Christian Council, Bishop K. H. Ting.

Bishop Xie answers questions about the provincial administrative organs of the church, the training of new clergy, the relations among Protestant denominations now working and worshiping together, lay volunteers, and problems facing the church.

In two interviews, one in 1987 and one a year later, Bishop Ting answers questions about church growth, church and state relations, printing and distribution of Bibles, and criticism by outsiders leveled at the Protestant Three-Self Movement and China Christian Council leadership. Bishop Ting's response to outside critics is, "As long as God is using us in some small way for the cause of the gospel of Jesus Christ, our hearts are at peace."

He also describes the functions of the China Christian Council and the Three-Self Movement, progress in church growth and clergy training, and reports that local cadres had illegally interfered in the Christians' freedom of worship in certain places. The national church leadership interceded, he said, advising the government cadres not to curtail the rights of Christians.

Section I

Local Church Life

Document 86

Building on a Rock

Translated from Tian Feng *(July 1986) in China Study Project*
Journal *1:3, November 1986, p. 61.*

The building of Mingshan Church in Nanxian County, Hunan, was officially completed on 4 February 1986. The church is situated at the top of
Mingshan mountain. The church building is a magnificent sight. Inside,
there are golden rainbow-colored lamps hanging from the ceiling, and there
are bright lights at each of the four corners. On the platform there is a
loudspeaker, a record player and a tape recorder, together with roses and
chrysanthemums. There are new benches, blue windows, and white cur-
tains, very pleasing to the eye. There is a quiet room at the back for church
workers, together with an office, a reception room, and a large kitchen.

To begin with, Mingshan Church met in the home of one of the members.
The place was too small for the large number who came, and when it rained
there wasn't even room for those who were standing. So the members
needed a larger place in which to meet for worship. But there were difficulties in the way of building something suitable, such as finding suitable
ground and getting the money required. All the Christians could do was
pray earnestly to God and put their trust in him. But thanks to our Savior
and to the concern and support of the government, we were given 200
square meters of land on the top of Mingshan on 25 November 1985.

Building on top of a mountain is much more difficult than on level
ground. All the building materials had to be transported to the foot of the
hill, which was a quarter of a mile away from the building site. We required
more than seventy thousand bricks, and more than five thousand tiles, not
to mention cement and other materials, all of which had to be taken to the
top of the hill. Because of the great love which the Christians had for the
Lord, they all worked together with a will, forming two teams to do various
tasks. There were even old men of eighty working on the hillside for four
or five hours at a stretch. The work continued like this for five successive

319

Sundays, and by then all the materials had been carried up to the building site. It would be difficult to forget the last such occasion. It snowed hard early that morning, and when the morning service ended the preacher, in his concern for the health of the workers, said, "Don't do any work today. Leave it till next Sunday." But the Christians were determined to get the building completed by Chinese New Year, and they took no notice of his advice. The preacher was so moved by this evidence of their faith and love that he himself joined in, working side-by-side with them in the snow. They had not been working an hour when the snow stopped and the sun came out, so everybody joined in praising the Lord and giving thanks to our heavenly Father. The total cost of the building was 10,200 *yuan*, all given by local church members. Some gave 10 or 20 *yuan*, some gave 100, 200, or 300 *yuan*, each in accordance with his resources. Some were like the widow who gave her mite, which God willingly accepted. You are all asked to pray for the newly built church at Mingshan, that God will bless us and enable us to bring forth more fruit.

Document 87

An Interview with Pastor Chen Yiping, Sanyi Church, Xiamen

Donald MacInnis interviewed Pastor Chen Yiping, fifty-nine, pastor of Sanyi (Trinity) Church on the island of Gulangyu, Xiamen, Fujian Province, in April 1988. Pastor Chen talked readily and with enthusiasm, answering questions for nearly three hours. He is an ebullient man, full of energy, a man who obviously loves his work and his people. Judging by the rampant growth of his church since its revival in 1981, he is also a very effective pastor.

Gulangyu, an island, is a five-minute ferry ride from Xiamen City, also an island, but much larger. Before 1949 there were fifteen churches and preaching points belonging to four denominations: the Church of Christ in China, the Seventh-Day Adventist, the True Jesus, and the Little Flock (*Juhuiso*), the latter two being indigenous Chinese sects. Today there are three open churches, including Sanyi, and nine others in the Xiamen district, only two with ordained pastors, both over seventy. Pastor Chen preaches four to five sermons a week, rotating among three churches.

Seminarians

Sanyi Church alone has sent three young people on for seminary training, one of whom has graduated and is teaching in the Fuzhou seminary. The local church provides all expenses for these students, including travel. One, now studying in the Shanghai seminary, receives an additional 110 *yuan* per month from this church, which is the salary he had to forfeit when he gave up his former factory job.

Membership

Sanyi Church has about twelve hundred members, some not yet baptized. Since the number grows daily, he said, they can't keep accurate statistics. Attendance averages seven hundred to eight hundred on ordinary Sundays. He felt that he had to explain why (in his view) so many were absent.

1. Some have to work on Sunday, because the government sets a rotation schedule for workers' days off, not just Sunday.

2. A number of church members have been forced to move to a distant housing project. Sanyi Church plans to open a branch church there.

3. Some older Christians who suffered during the "cultural revolution" are afraid to publicly attend church services, so they don't come. Recently, some schools have warned students and teachers not to go to church, although, said Pastor Chen, this is against the government's policy of freedom of religious belief. "This instills fear, and keeps people away from church."

"Is this directed only against Christians?" I asked. "Yes," he said, "because the cadres are most heavily prejudiced against Christianity; this is a carryover from former days when Christianity was linked with foreign imperialism. They have even more antipathy toward the Catholics because of the Vatican."

Church Finances

Sanyi Church receives enough money in one major offering, like Christmas, to run the local church for a year, including salaries and all expenses. There are two major offerings a year, Christmas and Thanksgiving (*ganen*), the first Sunday of the lunar new year. Last year these offerings totalled 16,000 *yuan*. Special offerings are taken to help widows, orphans and needy people, for special church repairs, or to help other churches repair and rebuild. "This church is entirely self-sufficient; we receive nothing from the government, the Protestant Three-Self Committee, or any other source," he said.

Youth

In response to my question about young people, Pastor Chen told me how he had started a weekly evening meeting three years earlier with a handful of young people. Today about 170, ranging in age from fifteen to thirty, come each Sunday night.

"Why do you think they come?" I asked.

"They come to church searching for answers to questions about faith and meaning in life. These are intellectuals [with at least high-school education]. Today's young people are better educated; they have higher expectations than their predecessors. I have to help them, so I try to provide answers to real questions about religion and life. I try to expound on one basic theological question each time I lead the meeting. They don't know church teachings and they don't know the Bible, so that is what we teach them."

House Meetings

I asked Pastor Chen his opinion of "house meetings." Are they divisive in the Christian community?

"There are several ways to look at the house meetings," he replied. "Small family meetings are all right. The government won't interfere. But when several families with many people get together, as many as one hundred or even two hundred persons, that is illegal. The government used to try to force them to quit, but now they only cajole. So far they don't dare to use force. They are very polite, just urging them to attend church instead."

Denominational Loyalties

I asked about present loyalties to former denominations. Sanyi Church has three denominations now, he said: the former Church of Christ in China (which was formed by the union of three mission-founded denominations), the Little Flock, and the Seventh-Day Adventists, each with its own pastor but using the same church building. The three pastors cooperate well, he said, using a common word for baptism (xili), instead of the different old terms which imply immersion or sprinkling. Each new member chooses his own mode of baptism.

The Adventists worship on Saturday. They are vegetarians, so special vegetarian cuisine is prepared for them at general church meetings. "We show mutual respect for each other's customs," he said. A visiting Adventist pastor who had joined us during our talk said that they no longer baptized secretly in the river at night, as I had heard. They do not require a tithe, but many Adventists still give at least 10 percent of their income to the church. He assured me that they cooperated with the other pastors and Christians, which they did not do in former days.

Problems: Sects and Heresy

I asked if there are any sectarian Christians who opposed the so-called official church. Yes, Pastor Chen replied, there are some Little Flock people from an older generation who are critical of the Three-Self leadership.

"Many of them went to prison in the 1950s. Some of them continue to preach to groups outside the churches. People respect their courage. Some have given this up and come to church, but others refuse. Recently some of us have discussed how to deal with them. This is what we decided:

"First, to use love only. Second, to use patience. Don't be hard on them. We Chinese all have freedom of religious belief. If they are preaching the true gospel, and do nothing against the government, they are not breaking the law. It's a religious question, not a political question. We have carefully avoided using forceful measures against them. However, they should not steal our members; we call that sheep stealing."

Pastor Chen said that heretical groups like the "Children of God" (now banned from China) and the "Yellers" (*huhanpai*) had caused trouble. Why are some Christians led astray by such groups? "New Christians have only a shallow foundation in Christian doctrine, and we don't have enough trained pastors to teach them. Moreover, many of the new Christians, especially in the rural areas, have little education. Because we require six months of training in basic doctrine before baptizing new Christians in Sanyi Church, we have had no problem with sects in this church."

Pastor Chen and the "Cultural Revolution"

Pastor Chen graduated from Yenching, China's leading seminary, in 1956, and served a church for less than two years before he was declared a "rightist" in 1958. He spent over twenty years in various jobs, none of them as pastor.

"I spent over twenty years 'eating bitterness,' but now I only thank God, for my experience has strengthened both my body and spirit. I'm much stronger than before! Now I rely completely on God, and I understand the Bible far better as well. God has cared for me, safeguarding me up to the present moment, and he gives me twenty-four hours a day to serve him."

Document 88

A Look at the Rich Soil on Which Christianity in a County in Anhui Province Is Growing

By Zheng Kaitang; translated from Religious Questions under Socialism in China *(Shanghai Academy of Social Sciences, 1987), pp. 257-268, by Zheng Xi'an and Donald MacInnis (excerpts).*

In recent years [Protestant] Christianity has been growing and spreading in the region around my native town in a certain county of Anhui Province. This is a phenomenon which deserves study.

A General Survey

Before Liberation there were only two Protestant churches and one Catholic church in the county seat (which became the prefectural center after liberation), and a few small churches scattered in nearby small towns. The influence of Christianity was neither great nor deep-seated.

After Liberation, members of the clergy took other jobs, churches closed down, and residential church properties were turned over for other uses. Today, most people under forty do not know what Christianity is.

Following the "cultural revolution" in the early 1970s, Christianity began to revive, but not in the open. Believers were few, mostly older women. In the years 1976 and 1977 during the "[Party] line education" movement, Christian activities were attacked and Christians, guarded by local militia, were assigned to "study classes" or placed in solitary confinement to confess their crimes. Those in "study classes" were deprived of their personal freedom, and, in addition to bringing their own food, were forced to pay an extra 1 or 2 *yuan* each day for the guards' expenses. People greatly feared being sent to these "study classes", because while they were there they had no gainful employment and so could not afford to pay for the expenses of the "classes." Some even lost their family savings.

In the spring of 1977 a certain "work team" engaged in "[Party] line education" discovered some Christians praying in secret. Viewing this as a counterrevolutionary activity, the deputy team leader, after launching an armed attack at night, found that the group consisted entirely of elderly women who had scattered in fright upon their attack.

After the fall of the "gang of four" and the implementing of the Party's religious policy, formerly clandestine Christian activities came into the open and more and more people became Christians. In some places whole families and villages converted.

I have visited their religious services. One visit was made on 1 March (January 15 of the lunar calendar). That was the local market day, and many Christians gathered in the market square in the morning for a preaching service. Because of the size of the crowd they had to break into groups, dividing over eight hundred persons among the homes and courtyards of three of the Christian families. Moreover, it was evident that this was not the total number of Christians in that locality, for some of the Christian men did not attend public services, and some families only sent one person as a representative. All these religious activities were voluntary, with no [church] organization whatsoever.

In villages where there are no churches or special places for services, Christians from a small area often gather in one of the Christian homes for services, thus forming a Christian meeting point. There are many such meeting places. A number of Christians who do not attend congregational worship, but only pray at home, are considered to be the same as long as they are faithful to the Lord.

There are still no resident full-time pastors here. The preachers are volunteers or persons with some status locally. Very few of those who preach have been Christians for more than ten years, while the majority are newly converted middle-aged persons who have had only a smattering of education.

Of the above-mentioned eight hundred people who attended the worship service, only one had a "Bible", printed long ago, which was considered a treasure. A few had notebooks in which were copied some verses or chapters from the Bible and some hymns (in fact some had been clumsily set to popular tunes and melodies). I have seen a small two-thousand-word pamphlet about 3 inches by 4 called "Questions and Answers About Christianity" [a catechism], which is circulated among the Christians and copied by many. Only one Christian had a picture of "the crucified Jesus," which had been woven from silk in a Hangzhou factory. As for their form and content, it must be said that these religious activities, despite the fact that Christianity came from abroad and has been a man-made religion from early times, were quite natural and spontaneous.

Who Are These Christians?

Some of the Christians are workers, a very few are cadres and teachers, while the vast majority are peasants. There are more women than men. I have compiled statistics for one meeting place, where 73.8 percent are women and 26.2 percent men, but these figures are not very precise, because many men who are unwilling to be publicly known as Christians do not attend public religious activities.

As for the age range of Christians, there are more elderly than middle-aged or young people. At the above-mentioned meeting place, women over 50 numbered 53 percent, middle-aged women from 30 to 50 were 25.9 percent, and young people 21.1 percent.

I once put two questions to a group of 29 men at a meeting place: 1) When were you converted? and 2) Why do you believe in Christianity? Five of them replied that they came just to have a look (it's possible that some did not reply honestly). Of the other 24, only one had been a Christian for more than ten years, while 95.8 percent had converted within the past four years.

When asked about their motive for becoming Christians, 13, that is 54.2 percent of the men [who said they were Christians], replied that they accepted the Christian faith in order to ask the Lord to bless and care for persons suffering from illness — their wives, parents, themselves, or other family members.

Two answered that they became believers in order to get the Lord's help in controlling a bad temper. Five of them replied "peaceful belief," meaning there was no illness or suffering in their families, but they felt that it was good to have religious faith, so they followed others and became Christians. Three became Christians because Christianity teaches people to do good. One answered that he came to believe through reading the Bible. These last 11 men made up 45.8 percent of the group.

As for education, the great majority of the middle-aged and elderly were illiterate or barely knew a few words without true reading ability. Quite a few of the young Christians were primary or junior middle school graduates, while 3 of those I met had graduated from senior middle school.

How the Christians Worship

Worship services are generally held on Sunday mornings when the weather is good. After breakfast Christians come one after another to the [open-air] meeting place. Some come early to arrange benches and planks as seats. They do this without pay. Some elderly Christians who cannot walk are taken in carts (wheelbarrows or small cargo carts) by their children or grandchildren. Those few who are too sick to get down from the carts lie there listening to the preaching. . . .

The most frequent sermon topic is filial piety. Originally a moral precept of the Confucian school, filial piety has been given great emphasis in Christian preaching. This is clearly linked with the failure of sons and daughters to care for their parents and to poor relationships between mothers-in-law and daughters-in-law, phenomena which can be blamed on the sabotage and interference of the counterrevolutionary clique of Jiang Qing and Lin Biao. At the outdoor preaching place the preacher sang this [rhymed] "holy hymn" which brought a strong response from the congregation:

We exhort you to be filial; it is not easy to repay parents for their kindness.

They cleaned your dirty bottom and held you out to urinate. Who knows how often they lay [with you] in your wet bed?

When her son was ill, your mother feared for you; she neither slept nor ate, but prayed day and night. Only after she nearly died of worry did her son recover.

When he was four or five, she was always watching out for him, afraid he would swim in the river or climb a tree in search of birds' nests.

When he reached the age of 15 or 16, he became impolite, neither respecting the elderly nor loving the young, and forgetting his parents' kindness.

When her son married and prospered, he indulged himself in eating and drinking.

When he had a baby son, he embraced him and provided him with beautiful clothes and hats, calling him pet names while taking walks with him. You love your own children, why do you forget how much your parents loved you?

Sweet water cannot be taken from a bitter well; brambles will not grow grapes, nor pumpkin vines grow yellow silk.

There is reward for evil and reward for good; the moving cart leaves its tracks, and the unfilial parent will have unfilial progeny.

The content, language and tune of this song all come from local folk tradition. It is a perfect popular art which arouses such strong response from the Christian congregations because it strikes at a social problem which has long concerned the Christians. About half of the "holy poems" and "holy hymns" which I have seen are like this.

Another frequent topic for preaching is forbearance, forgiveness and obedience. Here are the words of a certain song, called "Keep One's Way":

> When struck, I do not strike back;
> When abused, I do not retort,
>   nor do I get upset or sulk.
> I smile when rebuked.

Forbearance and obedience are Christian teachings, and forgiveness is [also] advocated by the Confucian school. The Christians offer new explanations when they preach. The Bible [they say] tells people to obey those in power because they represent God's will; thus the preacher offers a new reason for obedience to the cadres.

Other doctrines are preached apart from these. In the words of its followers, Christianity advocates that one should "Show filial piety to parents, respect to the elderly, and love to the young; do not believe in superstition; do not worship idols or burn paper money as offering to the dead; do not steal; do not profit at others' expense; do not strike others nor abuse them; give up evil and return to good; eliminate the false and keep the true; hold firmly to the truth."

Naturally, "Do not believe in superstition" means the feudal superstition that has long prevailed in the countryside, such as belief in geomancy, ghosts and monsters, celestial beings, and fortune telling and divination. "Do not worship idols" means to worship only Christ, not idols such as the God of Wealth, the Earth God, Buddha, the Heavenly Lord, the Dragon King, and other heretical idols. By "Hold firmly to the truth" they mean to hold firmly to the religious position of Christianity. . . .

Its Influence on Social Life

The popularity of Christianity has produced certain social effects. These are seen not only in the increasing number of Christians, but also in the influence of Christian teachings on the actions of Christians and the impact of its spiritual force on social life.

1. Since Christianity preaches against "superstition" and "worshiping idols," many Christians have given up belief in traditional gods and spirits of heaven and earth; they no longer kow-tow in the lunar-new-year ceremony, shoot off fireworks, pray to the gods for healing, or solicit help from witches and shamans. They no longer give homage to the god of the planet Jupiter when breaking ground for a new house, nor believe in geomancy at the time of death, or in sackcloth and images of gods. The spread of Christianity has weakened the influence of feudal superstition.

2. It is said that Christians, on several occasions, returned money on their own initiative when shop clerks gave them too much change. They said, "We believe in our Lord and must not profit at the expense of others. If I hadn't returned the money I would have committed a sin." Numerous Christians have given up smoking and drinking.

3. The greatest influence of Christianity is on family relations. Many sons and their wives who had ill-treated their parents have behaved well after their conversion. A man nicknamed "Second Crazy Fellow" had struck and abused his parents many times, but has become filial after his conversion. Relationships greatly improved after the conversion of a young woman who, for a long time, had paid no attention to her mother-in-law.

Two sisters-in-law had not provided food for their parents-in-law. When the elderly couple came to ask for food, they not only refused to feed them, but verbally abused them. After their religious conversion they have completely changed, showing full courtesy to their in-laws, and always serving them first when the meals are prepared. Now the old couple always tell others, "Our daughters-in-law have changed for the good."

I saw with my own eyes a woman, about to strike her daughter, who drew back her hand when other Christians admonished her, saying that would be a sin. After first defending herself with an alibi, she then confessed her sin.

People from all walks of life, including numerous cadres (despite the fact that they are nonbelievers), all speak well of these people. On the other hand, I have also heard of an incident where a certain house caught fire. The husband was out and the woman, a Christian, knelt and prayed for God's protection and blessing instead of putting out the fire. The fire, of course, became even worse. This is an example where religious conversion made a person act foolishly.

A cadre in a certain brigade who was addicted to smoking and drinking fell ill with apoplexy. He spent a great deal of money for prolonged treatments without result. After conversion to Christianity he confessed his sins before God, such as embezzling relief funds, attacking others, taking revenge, etc. He was ridiculed near and far.

Of course we have to be alert, for the current style of Christianity can easily be used by evildoers, but I have not heard of such things.

Questions on Faith Healing

Contemporary Christianity does not now advocate using religion to heal illness without medical treatment. Christians believe that doctors are needed to heal illness, and those who should go to hospitals should be taken there. Christianity teaches simply that one can be blessed and protected by the Lord if he is free from sin and has a sincere heart. However, many recent converts came to believe in religion because they themselves or their family members had fallen ill and failed to recover. . . .

Two brothers, whose mother, a long-time invalid, recovered her health after converting to Christianity, are now key volunteers for Christianity, and their home in the county seat has become a small chapel.

Another young man, who came down with bronchial asthma in his childhood, had undergone lengthy medical treatment, including surgery and acupuncture. After marrying, his condition worsened, and he was cheated by a sorcerer, losing one hundred *yuan*. It is said that his mother converted, and the whole family became Christians, with the result that the young man's condition has greatly improved.

Christians thoroughly believe in cases like these, never doubting them. After careful analysis we find that most of these examples supplied by the Christians are mental illness, or pathological changes of organic functions closely connected with the nervous system such as schizophrenia, psychosis, arthritis, functional disorders of the stomach and intestines, etc. . . . It is possible for patients to get better or recover completely when, after religious conversion, they shed their spiritual burden, believing that they are now under the watch and care of God. There is nothing strange about this. . . .

Causes for the Rapid Growth of Christianity

The fact that Christianity is growing in a number of areas shows that in our country and society, particularly in the vast countryside, there is soil on which religion can grow.

For a long period of time after Liberation, religious activities had "disappeared" in these areas. To most people religion is a brand-new thing, despite its long history, and people are always curious about new things. Comrade Mao Zedong said that Marxism-Leninism is sure to develop, but if it remains the same old stuff it will be ineffective. Due to the interference and sabotage of the Lin Biao-Jiang Qing counterrevolutionary clique, the prestige of our Party and of Socialism has declined. Not only did they bring the social economy of our country to the edge of bankruptcy, they also caused a vacuum to form in the minds of many people, giving an opportunity for religion, which takes advantage of this weak point. This tells us how important it is to educate people to hold firmly to the four basic principles, to enforce ideological work, and to establish a Socialist spiritual civilization.

Statistical data show that most new Christians came to this faith to ask God for protection of health or healing of illness, either their own or their family members'. Health problems are undoubtedly the most important inducement for conversion. This situation, that is, the hope that people can free themselves from suffering caused by ill health, poses a serious challenge to our medical and health work and the level of medical treatment offered. Religion seems to have succeeded in freeing them from their suffering, where society has failed. Hospitals did not cure their illnesses, while God seems to have done so. How could they possibly be led to give up their belief in religion and their worship of God!

Statistics also show that among the Christians there are more elderly people than young, more female than male, more illiterate than literate, and more with low culture [little education] than high culture. All the statistics show that the number of Christians in different categories is in inverse ratio to the amount of cultural and scientific knowledge they have, and in direct ratio to their degree of backwardness, ignorance, and benightedness.

This shows that it is most easy for religion to form firm ties with people who possess no knowledge and know nothing of science. Religion is silently competing with our work in education, culture, and universal science for the masses of our people.

Apart from freeing themselves from the physical suffering of this world, people also need spiritual comfort, encouragement, strength, hope, and ideals. Religion satisfies their curiosity, broadens their social relationships, and, what is more important, fills in their spiritual vacuum. Christ has not asked them for a cent, but freed them from misfortune and calamity, giving them well-being in this world, while promising them happiness in the next.

All people are pragmatic, and peasants even more so. Religion is also pragmatic. Peasants can begin to leave religion only when the pace of Socialist modernization has greatly quickened, when their material and cultural life has risen to a sufficient level, when the knowledge of science has become universal, and when they can quickly free themselves from the ills and pains of their real life. Only when their spirit is fulfilled can they consciously place their hope in Socialism. Therefore, the basic measures needed to free them from suffering and the fetters of religion are to diligently promote Socialist modernization, to increase the speed of social productive forces, and to actively raise the level of their material and cultural life. Another important means to liberate them is to rapidly improve and raise the level of medical and health work. Finally, an even better way to open up a direct route for their liberation is to develop education and culture and to popularize scientific knowledge.

Section II

Local Church: Clergy and Lay Leadership

Document 89

Clergy Training: Theological Education Conference at Moganshan

Translated from Tian Feng, *November 1985, in China Study Project* Journal *1:1, April 1986, p. 61 (excerpt).*

In a great many places, prior to the opening of theological colleges, the local Christian organizations had been holding short training courses of one kind or another. This had the great advantage of providing important experience for the setting up of a college. There were certain distinctive features of these training courses. They were not excessively concerned with "standardization," they were content to make do with simple necessities, and they were practical and down-to-earth, and these features were undoubtedly given expression in the newly opened theological colleges. The Fujian and Zhejiang colleges laid great emphasis on the preaching and pastoral abilities of the students, since such skills were urgently needed in the present situation of the churches in those areas. We cannot, of course, be content with turning a theological college into a center for training and preaching. This would not be true of either of the colleges I have just mentioned, and still less would be true of them in the future. The staff at Beijing take the view that those whom they are training will be engaged in serving the church in its pastoral work. Consequently, they are kept in close touch with the local churches during their period of training. Arrangements are made for the students to go to the churches to lead the singing, to teach Sunday school, to make contact with house churches, to have practice in preaching, and to become familiar with the various features of the churches' life. The Sichuan college has bought ten harmoniums and teaches the students to play hymns, and this too arises from the practical needs of the church. Of course, we hope that sometime or other the Sichuan college will be able to buy ten pianos and will be able to provide even better courses in music. The Sichuan college provides yet another example of the principle of making do with simple necessities and being practical and down-to-earth, namely, in the realm of physical training. Theological students need to be in good physical shape, but the Sichuan students have no suitable sports ground, and can only be provided with the equipment for a few simple ball games. So they make the journey every morning from their hostel to the classrooms at a run. This is quite a fair distance, so what might be considered a disadvantage has been turned to good advantage, and there has been an improvement in the physique of the students.

Document 90

An Interview with a Lay Leader of the Flower Lane Church, Fuzhou

On 10 June 1988, Donald MacInnis interviewed Mrs. Lin Qinyi, a senior lay leader of the Flower Lane Church of Fuzhou, the widow of a former pastor of the Church of Christ in China. She is an elected deacon of the church, elderly, but very active in church service and a leader of her neighborhood group.

Flower Lane Church has an average Sunday attendance of one thousand, a congregation that overflows the main sanctuary, requiring the use of loudspeakers in an overflow room. A Wednesday evening congregation also fills the church.

Baptisms of new adult Christians average four hundred to five hundred a year. Two hundred were baptized the day prior to our interview, including eleven from Mrs. Lin's neighborhood group, all women, ranging in age from twenty to seventy-five.

I asked about the neighborhood groups, having heard that they were, at times, a divisive influence in the parish. She said they were not divisive, but a natural response to the shortage of ordained pastors. She attends two meetings, one on Friday and one on Sunday afternoon, which average over one hundred in attendance. In addition, a group of twenty meets in her home each Wednesday evening, one of about thirty such groups among Flower Lane Church members. What is the purpose of these meetings? "To nurture spiritual life through prayer and Bible study. We have no differences with the church; in fact we pray for sick church members, for the pastors, for the new Christians. We discuss the work of the church, and which persons we should go to visit."

Mrs. Lin gave me a monthly work-report form for the neighborhood group members. The form has three columns, the first describing the work activity, the second the number of persons involved, and the third, remarks. The activities were new believers enrolled, home visits, hospital visits, letters sent, assistance to the needy, deaths, and aid to the sick. A second form lists the name, sex, age, and address of new believers — a primary and effective form of evangelism.

Volunteer Lay Leaders and Denominational Loyalties

In addition to three pastors (one about sixty, the others over seventy), numerous volunteers serve the church. The parish is divided into fourteen groups, with four deacons in each group. They meet monthly at the church to discuss and plan the work of the church, finances, persons with problems, etc. The pastors and members come from four denominational backgrounds, but they work well together. "Only the True Jesus people and the Adventists meet for separate worship services, but they cooperate in general church work. However, they don't join the deacon meetings."

Church Finances and Property

Flower Lane Church is financially self-sufficient. They provide full support for eight or nine seminary students from their church each year, pay all staff salaries and church expenses, and collect about 8,000 *yuan* a year for the needy. Recently, 80,000 *yuan* was raised in a special offering for church repairs, and 6,000 *yuan* in another offering for a new piano. Regular quarterly receipts average 18,000 *yuan*.

Document 91

An Interview with Pastors Zheng Yupei and Huang Jinghua at the Putian Protestant Church, Fujian Province

By Donald MacInnis, January 1988.

The local Christians regained possession of the Putian church in 1979. Five work units had occupied it at different times during and since the "cultural revolution." In addition to volunteer labor, the costs of replacing 110 missing pews, repairing the leaky roof, and general refurbishing were borne by the church members. The church, said to be the largest in China, seats three thousand. Capacity crowds fill the church on Christmas and other special days, with the main floor filled on normal Sundays.

Lay Volunteer Workers

When I asked how two elderly pastors, both in their seventies, could minister to such a large parish, they said it would be impossible without lay volunteers. As many as sixty volunteers meet for two-month training classes here in Putian, returning to their home churches where many of them, lacking a local pastor, carry on the pastoral work. During the two-month training class they live in the two Putian churches, providing their own food and receiving no pay or subsidy.

The curriculum, prepared specifically for such lay-training classes, is sent periodically from the major seminary in Nanjing and includes basic catechism, the life of Jesus, homiletics, pastoral care, church history, and church administration. There are examinations, including preaching a sermon. The volunteers, men and women of all ages, prepare their own meals, organize their own schedule, and conduct evening meetings in the Putian churches. After returning to their home parishes, they assist the pastors, teach catechism classes, organize choirs, visit church members and help with preaching. (Classes of any kind for children under eighteen are not allowed.)

Putian City and County have thirty-two churches and ten meeting points. Twenty-one of these churches are new, built from the ground up, either because the old buildings had been destroyed or were too dilapidated or too small to meet the needs of the people. The ten largest seat up to five hundred each. Although there was some compensation money received from the government, and back-rental money from work units which had occupied the churches, most of the money for construction and restoration was given by church members. All told, 189 buildings, including residences and other structures, have been turned over to the church in Putian district.

There are only thirteen ordained pastors, six of them recently ordained and the rest over seventy, one of them eighty-nine. Each pastor serves several churches, assisted by lay volunteers. Since 1985 this district has selected nineteen young people from many applicants for the two-year course in the Fuzhou seminary; three have gone on to the major seminaries in Nanjing and Shanghai.

There are meetings in the Putian church every night of the week except Monday: Tuesday, young people; Wednesday, prayer meeting and Bible study; Thursday, choir practice (mainly young people); Friday, spiritual revival meeting (*peilinghui*), for Christians affiliated with the True Jesus sect; Saturday morning and afternoon, sabbath worship for the True Jesus members; Sunday morning, sabbath services for Methodists and Anglicans; and Sunday afternoon, sabbath services for Little Flock (*juhuiso*) followers.

Denominational Loyalties

Surprised at the casual reference to denominations, I asked if, indeed, denominations still exist, despite the fact that they had been officially abolished years earlier. "Yes and no," was the reply. "We all belong to one church here, use the same building and contribute for its support, and send our young people to the same seminaries for training. But denominational loyalties live on in the people's hearts, and the True Jesus members have always worshipped on Saturday instead of Sunday. So we have worked out a modus vivendi. We practice mutual respect."

What about "house meetings"? Are they a divisive influence, taking people away from regular church services?

No, these are attended mainly by older people who find it difficult to walk to church. There are about two hundred in Putian district, in the cities often led by pastors, but in the rural areas by lay members.

I asked the two pastors what, in their opinion, was the reason for the strong revival of Christianity in Putian district, for they had told me that church attendance and new conversions were far ahead of the old days. "The main reason is that Christian faith is passed on from one generation to the next. Also, the Holy Spirit brings people to church. Superstition is widespread. People waste a lot of money. Christianity provides answers to life's problems, and doesn't waste their money with no results."

Document 92

Church Life in Shantou

Translated from Tian Feng, *May 1986, in China Study Project* Journal *1:3, November 1986, pp. 52-53 (excerpts).*

Here in Shantou all the Christians in the city have been divided into dozens of small groups based on their places of residence. The smallest consist of thirty or forty families, and the largest of seventy or eighty families. Each group includes one or two devoted Christians who act as liaison officers. Some people call them "group leaders," but we prefer to use the term "liaison officers," as they serve as bridges between the church and its members and are very effective in linking Christians together.

The pastors here in Shantou are few in number and well on in years, so how can they keep in effective touch with so many church members? However hard we try, we can do no more than visit them once a year, and cannot get to know the circumstances of every Christian family. We cannot get to know whether they are regular in attendance at worship, so how can we be familiar with their individual needs and give them pastoral care?

Fortunately these liaison officers are loyal in their devotion to the church and to the Lord. Even though they are busy with domestic duties and have children or grandchildren to look after, and even though some of them are busy in factories or in other various spheres of work, they manage to spare the time to pay regular visits to every family in their group. They have at their fingertips a knowledge of the Christian convictions, the conduct, and the way of life of every Christian household in their group. They are deeply concerned when any member falls ill, and whenever any go into hospital, they go at once to visit them, and when a family is in difficulties, they ensure that the church gives them help. They are always ready to help when there is a wedding, a funeral, a removal, an occasion for rejoicing, or any matter requiring prayer.

The liaison officers are generally able to cope with everyday problems and pour oil on troubled waters, but if there are more serious matters requiring the attention of the pastor the liaison officer can promptly ensure that he is aware of it.

We have also been able to link smaller groups into larger units. In this way the individual liaison officers can cooperate and join forces. When some important matter arises for the whole church to deal with, the leaders of the larger units are informed, and they communicate in turn with the liaison officers, who in turn pass on the information to the individual families; in this way, everyone is prepared in advance.

Every month there is a prayer meeting attended by all the liaison officers. There is a united prayer, mutual encouragement, and exchange of information between the various units. They learn of family removals, marriages, deaths, and families in special need. They are informed of families in which there is an indication that friends or relations are about to make up their minds to become believers, and of inquirers who are prepared to enter a class for instruction in the faith. They find out if there is some church member who could encourage such an inquirer to join a Bible class or a choir, and who may be prepared to undertake some voluntary work within the church. After each monthly prayer meeting there is evidence of mutual concern and encouragement to love one another and to perform good deeds (Heb. 10.24).

There is a proverb that is current in these parts: "A crab has to have feet to be able to walk." Thanks be to God! Under the direction of the Holy Spirit we have been provided with an abundance of voluntary workers (of whom the liaison officers form a part) by whose help the Church here in the city of Shantou has made progress. Without them, the pastors would be like a crab without feet, incapable of effectively administering the Church of God!

Document 93

Volunteer Lay Leaders in the Wenzhou Church

By Cao Shengjie, "Learning from Grass-Roots Churches" (excerpts), Tian Feng, March 1988; translated in China Study Project Journal 3:2, August 1988, pp. 69-70.

In the past, the establishing of churches depended almost entirely on the work of the pastors. But in recent years, the situation has altered. There are some places where in the past they had their own pastor, but in due course they became old or infirm and were unable to continue their work, or else after their death no successor could be found, and the church had to rely on voluntary workers. For example, I visited Anqing, a large city in Anhui, where the church had been founded a long time ago. But for the last two years or more, after the aged pastor had died, there was no one to take his place. Fortunately there were some senior church members who were willing to undertake responsibility in a voluntary capacity, and they worked hard at restoring the church property. During the "cultural revolution," pastors were forced to relinquish their duties, and in some areas voluntary workers would lead the scattered congregations. When I was in Wenzhou I was told that in some of the villages this practice has continued more or less ever since. After normal relations had been restored, and churches were able to resume their activities, there was a great scarcity of pastors. For instance in Pingyang county, where there are more than thirty thousand Christians, there are only five pastors. Preaching in the hundred or more churches and meeting points is largely undertaken by a "task force" of voluntary workers appointed by the two Christian organizations, so that these volunteers are in effect responsible for these local churches. This situation provides evidence that churches throughout the country include many sincere Christians who love the Lord, and who wish to devote themselves to the service of the Church. In fact, if there had not been this army of volunteers during these past years, the church would not be enjoying its present success. . . .

In general it may be said that the advantages of voluntary workers include the following: they do not increase the burdens imposed on other Christians by being paid a salary; as they have a secular employment, they are more sensitive to the situation prevailing in society, and to the policy of the government; and as they themselves belong to the local Christian community, they understand the needs of that community. As they have not undergone a formal training, they suffer from the following disadvantages: they have an inadequate knowledge of the Bible; they have an insufficient understanding of the Three-Self principles; and they may have no more than a superficial comprehension of the Government's religious policy. In view of this situation, the two Christian organizations in the various provinces and cities have in recent years been providing on a large scale training classes for volunteer workers, which have been proving effective. When I was in Pingyang I was told that the county had been running a successful training class with the support of the two Christian organizations in Wenzhou City. Those who attended willingly forewent their normal income and studied hard in the intense heat of summer. They were given a firm foundation of biblical doctrine and went forward with determination along the path of love for the country and love for the church. At one time Pingyang was one of the areas in which the "Yellers" were rampant, but nowadays the Christians meet in an orderly manner and among them there are many advanced workers, changes which are in no small measure due to the efforts of the voluntary workers.

In consequence of my tour, I became more and more convinced that for quite a long time in the future there is likely to be no change in the situation facing the church, in which there will be an interval between the departure of the older workers and the rise of new ones to take their place, and so the need for voluntary workers will become more and more urgent. Pastors must give full recognition to this situation, and must as soon as possible train up these workers and give full play to the tasks which they can perform. The voluntary workers also need to see their position and their calling in its proper light, that is to say, raising under the leadership of the regular pastors the awareness of the place of patriotism and love for the church, and so enabling the church to strive wholeheartedly to follow the Three-Self policy. . . .

Section III

Why They Become Christians

Document 94

An Attempt To Explain the Reasons Why Older People Believe in Religion: The Psychological Factors of Religious Faith among Elderly Believers

By Luo Weihong in Zongjiao *No. 3, 1984; translated by Tam Waiyi and Donald MacInnis.*

We recently conducted a field study of the religious faith of elderly people living in a certain neighborhood district of Shanghai where the residents are mainly workers. In recent years the number of older religious believers, mostly Christian, has been increasing, along with religious activities. These older people, most of them women, are mainly retired workers, half of whom were believers in their youth, while the other half had no contacts with religion before; they were attracted to religion only after retirement.

These people suffered bitterly in the old society, and only under the leadership of the Party have they been able to lead a happy life. Since Liberation they have been working hard in their jobs for the Socialist construction of our country. Even after they become religious believers, they still love the Party, support the Socialist system, and actively take part in various civic and social activities. Many people find it hard to understand why they have turned to religion. What dissatisfactions do they feel that push them toward God? Our investigation shows that, in addition to cognitive reasons, psychological changes caused by various factors are the direct reason why they turn to religion.

Seeking a "Happy Home" After Death

Life and death have always been a major problem for human beings. They experience the joys and troubles of daily life, the fear of death, and the hope for a future life. No one can avoid death, and older people, approaching the end of their lives, think more about death than others.

Under the influence of ideas handed down to them, they look for a home after death where they can feel secure and at ease. One seventy-six-year-old woman in this district has had no major problems all her life, is still in good health, and is respected by the younger generation. Everyone says that she is fortunate, and she, herself, is quite satisfied with her life. Yet she became a Christian in 1979, and since then has become actively involved in Christian house meetings. Why did she become a Christian? She is satisfied with her life in this world, yet she seems to be searching for something "at a distance." She hopes that her life in the "next world" will be as happy as this one, so she became a Christian. Moreover, she invites other older women to join her so that they, too, can go to "heaven." The reason for her religious faith is to make sure she has a final home.

Science and materialism have already answered the questions about life and death. Marx said, "Life, first of all, means that an organism is, at the same moment, both itself and something else. Life exists within matter, and the process by which new life comes from within itself spontaneously resolves its own contradictions; when contradictions cease, so does life, and death takes over" (*Anti-Duhring*, p. 118). Life and death form a unity of opposites, and when the movement of life ceases, that is death; there is no other world.

However, death is always a world of mystery for living people. The other worlds described by the various religions, such as the Christian heaven and hell, Buddhist reincarnation, Daoist immortality, transfiguration into a celestial being—all have great appeal for people who lack scientific education and are deeply influenced by traditional, superstitious ideas which, of course, are idealistic. Many older people will turn to religion when they think about a final home. The seventy-six-year-old woman mentioned above turned to God for this reason. Belief in a specific God is not very important to her. What she cares about most is God's gift of a happy life in the next world. She is a Christian because there happens to be a Christian house meeting near her residence. If it had been a Daoist or Buddhist temple, she would now be burning incense, asking for the protection of a bodhisattva.

If we say that the exploited class in the old society put their hope for a happier life in life after death because they were unable to fight against their exploiters, then their reason for religious faith in a Socialist society, where they have found happiness in real life, is not to fight against the realities of this world, but is based in their hope to extend their present happiness on into "the other world."

It Is Hard To Free Oneself from the Fear of "Death"

Although the laws of biological development tell us that where there is life there will also be death, that still cannot banish people's fear of death. The search for happiness after death is a negative reflection of this psychology, and people's efforts to extend life are one positive way they go about it. Since ancient times, people have never stopped searching for longevity. Many feudal rulers of ancient China, such as the Qinshi Emperor and the Wu Emperor of the Han dynasty, sent people to look for magic elixirs to prolong life. Of course, none of them succeeded in escaping death.

In today's society the greatest threat to human life is illness, which is always linked to death. People suffering from chronic illness have a stronger fear of death, and are more susceptible to religion, than other people. In our field surveys, about 70 percent of the new Christians among the elderly were medical patients. Illness is the main reason leading older people to become religious.

In old age one's health deteriorates because of organic changes in the body, and illness, especially chronic illness, can set in. Elderly people are usually especially careful about their health, taking regular exercise and going to the doctor for very minor problems. When these measures prove unsuccessful, they are disappointed and become depressed, still hoping that some famous doctor or magic medicine can cure their illness. This psychology easily opens them to belief in "magic" propaganda, making them targets for the elderly Christians looking to "harvest fruit" for their religion. When they are chatting with each other about family news or their health after exercising in the park, these elderly people are approached by Christians who tell them about the healing "miracles" that come to people who believe in Jesus. Jesus thus becomes the magic medicine which can rescue them from their suffering. Some medical patients then turn to Christianity with the psychological attitude of "Try it out, if it doesn't cost any money."

"God," of course, cannot cure illness, yet some patients do get better after becoming Christians. Such cases are taken as "evidence," and the news spreads rapidly, which in turn attracts others to religion. Why is this? Several factors contribute. Some patients improve anyway, having taken medicine for some time; if it happens after they became Christians, then God gets all the credit. Some people with chronic illness have ups and downs, sometimes feeling better, sometimes worse; it's quite understandable that they may emphasize the influence of God in order to promote their religious faith.

We cannot neglect another important factor—mental influences in curing illness. After becoming Christians, some sick people place their hope in Jesus, praying daily and believing that Jesus will heal them. This reduces their fears and worries, they increasingly come to believe that their health will improve, and their feelings of pessimism and despair turn into optimism and joy. Many medical experiments have shown that one's emotional state is closely connected to one's illness. A mood of depression will worsen illness, while a positive mood can ease it. Medication may not produce the same effect. In some countries, psychologists use the method of "auto-suggestion" to heal illness. They cause the patient to accept certain hints or suggestions, which the patient then carries out. Many patients have improved by using this method, which works especially well with mental illness. Daily prayer is similar, that is, it heals illness by using one's own mind. But religious people do not understand this point. They think it is Jesus who saves them when they feel better. In return, their faith is strengthened. However, mental powers are not magic after all; they cannot heal all illnesses. Some people don't feel better after believing in God; some even feel worse. But they think "Since we believe in God, we should thank God if we feel better; if we die, we die in the arms of God." This spiritual consolation thus eases their fear of death.

The Psychology of Incurable Loneliness

Another major psychological factor leading older people to religion is loneliness, which evolves from the following three changes in their lives.

First, physiological changes, like the imbalance of hormones, or the hardening of arteries, bring psychological changes, which bring personality changes, such as loneliness.

Second, people's social status changes. Retirement is a turning point in their lives which will greatly influence their psychology. They are now free from their active life and regular schedule, and the arena for their social activities now turns from the factory to the street. Some people will feel that society has abandoned or neglected them. While some retired cadres, intellectuals, and skilled workers can still perform services and fill their empty hours while serving society with their knowledge and skills, others, whose educational and skill levels are low, and who are not interested in doing ordinary manual labor, feel bored, with nothing to do. This is especially true for those who still have plenty of energy with few household tasks (some people retire at around fifty, giving their jobs to their children), and don't know how to fill their time. Some indulge in playing chess or poker, and some get together with their families for recreation and personal satisfaction.

Third, their status in the family also changes. In Chinese traditional extended families, the senior man is the head of the whole family. Old people, parents and the senior generation, are respected by children and have great authority. But this kind of family structure is changing now. The number of small families is increasing, which means that more old people have to live alone. Even those who live with their children have a generation gap, because of different levels of education, culture, and interests. There are no common topics for discussion, even less so when it comes to discussing feelings. Family relations are loosened. There are also family disputes over money and housing problems. Moreover, losing a spouse in old age also increases the stress and loneliness of the elderly.

Some of the elderly who cannot get used to these changes in their lives, especially those without a spouse or children, or whose children are elsewhere, will feel incurably lonely. Lonely people who feel they have nothing to lean on are especially attracted to religion. They are happier when taking part in prayers or listening to sermons. Frequent religious activities can enrich their lives as well as strengthen their relations with other believers. They treat other people with Christian "love," taking care of lonely old people, visiting sick people, and bringing warmth to their lonely neighbors, which in turn strengthens their relationship to their religion.

As mentioned above, loneliness, fear of death, and the search for a happy life in the next world are the main psychological reasons why elderly people become religious believers. When analyzing these psychological causes, we should also pay attention to other factors, such as physiological, personality, and family changes that also contribute to psychological changes in older people. But most important are the social factors. According to Marxism, social existence determines people's ideology, which is the product of human social activities and is formed when people take part in social activities. Thousands of years of old traditions are, on the one hand, still influencing the minds of people, while on the other hand, our Socialist system is still not perfect, and people still meet up with frustrations. Our economy, culture, and science (including medicine) are still not very advanced, nor have the cultural needs of the people been fully satisfied. Not enough care is given to the special needs and interests of older people. These factors, too, will drive some people, in their search for some source of hope, toward religion. Because these social factors cannot be solved within a short period of time, the phenomenon of some people turning to religion will not soon go away. We should not feel surprised by this. As Marx pointed out in his "Theses on Feuerbach," "religious feeling is itself the product of society." The above analysis proves this to be a truth that is in accord with the laws of religious development.

Document 95

A Field Study of Women Who Became Christians in Lai'an County, Anhui Province

In Zongjiao No. 1, 1987, by He Junying and Liu Shuxian; translated by Tam Waiyi and Donald MacInnis.

We have recently made a social investigation of women Christians in Lai'an County, Anhui. Just prior to Liberation there were 11 Christians in Lai'an County. By 1976 the number of Christians had grown to only 77 persons. Since 1976 the number of Christians has grown rapidly, now totaling 989. Before 1983 there was inadequate supervision of religion due to lack of understanding of the religious policy by the local Party, resulting in such things as spirit healing, demon exorcism, cheating, swindling, and incidents of some Party members becoming religious believers, etc. Beginning in 1983 supervision of religious work was strengthened and the Party's policy on religion, based on the spirit of relevant documents issued by the Party's center, was carried out. The Protestant Three-Self Committee of the county and five local Three-Self Committees were organized. Five central meeting places were opened in Shuangtang, Yangxiang, Shiguan, Yanchan, and Wuji, and the Protestant Three-Self Committee of Lai'an County established a charter and supervisory system. At present the Protestant Christian activities of Lai'an County are quite normal.

The Christians of Lai'an County can be divided into four categories according to sex, age, cultural level, and length of time since becoming Christians.

1. Female members are the majority, with a total of 820 in the entire county, 82.9 percent of the total church membership.

2. A total of 394 persons, 39.8 percent, are older members over age 50; 19.4 percent of the Christians are between 40 and 50, a total of 192 persons.

3. Overall, they have a low cultural [educational] level: 9 persons with senior-middle-school education, 59 with junior-middle-school, and 105 with primary-school education; 716, 72.3 percent of the whole, are illiterate [wen mang — "culturally blind"].

4. Most members have joined the church since 1976, a total of 912 persons, 92.2 percent of the whole.

Three out of 7 members of the Protestant Three-Self Committee for the country are women. Fifty-four-year-old Wu Lanying is the leader of the Yangxiang meeting point; 41-year-old Yan Maohua is the leader of the Shiguan meeting point, and 31-year-old Cheng Yuhua is treasurer [bao-guanyuan] for the Protestant Three-Self Committee of the county. We conducted a social investigation of Yangxian Township. This remote mountain community has 356 Christians, of whom 319 are women, 89.6 percent of the local Christians; 6.7 percent of all the village women over age 18 are Christians.

Jingbo Village of Yangxian Township has 61 Christians of whom 56 are women, or 91.8 percent, making up 13.5 percent of all village women. We also surveyed the Shuangtang Christian meeting point, and found many Christian women carrying umbrellas converging on the church from over a dozen streets and lanes to attend services, despite a drizzling rain. Over 200 persons, more than 80 percent of them women, were singing hymns of praise inside the church with full voice.

I

Why does Christianity have such attraction for rural women? We will explore the social, historical, cultural and personality factors of rural women in seeking the answer to this question.

1. During thousands of years of feudal society the traditional psychology of China's rural people was to place their hopes for changing their environment on an idol, a savior [*jiushi zhu*]. They once worshiped Buddha, the god of wealth, and Zhao Gongming ["General Zhao"]. Now Christianity preaches that God in heaven will protect them from disaster and turn bad luck into good, a teaching they readily accept. Moreover, the cultural level of rural women is lower than the men's; thus more women than men believe in God. There are 4,916 women in Yangxian Township over age eighteen, of whom 67.7 percent are illiterate. Aside from a few with primary-school education, the Christian women are illiterate. When discussing the good things in rural life at the present time, a Christian woman said, "Reliance on the Party and reliance on God's protection."

2. Before Liberation the economic and social status of Chinese women was low. According to the strictures of the [Confucian] "three obediences and four virtues," the daughter-in-law is always subordinate to the mother-in-law. After Liberation, when women joined the labor force and took on many tasks in society as a result of a succession of laws and policies carried out by the Party and government for the benefit of women, they became an important force in building a Socialist nation. But, in dealing with the consequences for families, a contrary social phenomenon has appeared: many mothers-in-law are abused, and sons and daughters are not taking care of their parents. However, the Christian message regarding family relations is love your parents, love your children, and love everyone; don't get into arguments, don't pick fights, reform your bad habits, etc. Catering to the psychology of rural women, who want peace in their families and peace with their neighbors and stable family relations, Christianity is warmly received.

Thirty-four-year-old Zhang Shaohua of Jingbo Village, Yangxian Township, formerly had a vile temper and frequently argued with her mother-in-law and the brigade leader. She was called "Red-Hot Pepper" by her neighbors. After becoming a Christian her temperament changed, as she herself says: "God's word changed me from a bad person to good, one who can now truly and wholeheartedly be good to her mother-in-law." There are many examples like this one in Yang Xiang. The women all say, "It's good to become a Christian. It will bring peace to your family, respect for mothers-in-law, and love for daughters-in-law." The leader of the Yangxiang Chapel, Wu Lanying, makes use of this slogan to promote the good points of Christianity: "Christianity preaches civilized manners."

3. Rural women, being confined to small social circles, are not very active socially, which limits their range of activities. They often think they cannot solve their daily living problems and become depressed. Since doctors cannot treat this problem without using psychotherapy, and the rural areas lack such medical facilities, some who suffer from depression turn to Christianity in their search for a cure.

The wife of the leader of the Shiguan Chapel was a worker in the county waterworks, but was dropped from the production brigade because of family demands on her time. Work in the fields was strenuous, and because she took care of her family in addition to the farm chores, and the family had economic difficulties, she fell ill and went everywhere searching for a cure. Later, a Christian neighbor urged her, "If you become a Christian and join our church and sing songs of praise it will solve your depression." She has been a Christian since 1976, and because she now has a spiritual basis of hope, and the rural economy took a turn for the better after the third session of the Central Committee, her health has gradually improved and she is now the responsible person for the chapel.

The leader of the Protestant Three-Self Committee of the county, Cheng Yuhua, was graduated from senior-middle-school in Shuangtang Township in 1976. She was recommended for university after graduation, but when the system of mandatory entrance examinations was reinstated, she was turned down and had to go to Wang Boyang farm as a worker, where she was married. She fell ill some time after her marriage because of heavy household responsibilities, economic difficulties, and the death of her father-in-law. The doctors could not cure her illness. Responding to an invitation from church members to attend services, she accepted the teaching "patience will bring peace," and felt she now had spiritual sustenance on which to place her hope. Her physical health was gradually restored after she prayed for peace in her heart and soul.

There are many examples like this of people with health problems who sought healing from the Christian religion, about 50 percent of the women Christians, according to statistics of the Religious Affairs Office of the county. Xu Mingxiu, a Christian woman in Yangxian Township, said, "It's not true that religious belief will cure illness; but it is true that singing hymns will dispel boredom and make one feel happy inside." This is the spiritual healing that doctors speak of.

II

Why did Christianity in Lai'an County experience this rather large growth after 1976? It reflects, on the one hand, the restoration of freedom of religious belief after the clearing away of "leftist" pernicious influences on religious questions, and the return of the Party from disorder to normalcy after the smashing of the "gang of four." But on the other hand, it reflects the relatively weak work on political thinking in rural areas, and particularly among rural women.

1. After the Third Plenary Session of the Eleventh Central Committee, Lai'an County and other places searched for ways to carry on the work on political thinking under the [new] rural responsibility system. They initiated the "Party members' responsibility system" [baocun lianhu — a Party member assumes responsibility for a group of families], opened rural cultural centers in towns and villages, created movements for "cultured towns" and

"cultured villages," "five-good families", etc. But all the research and efforts by Party committees on the work on political thinking in rural areas was inadequate, when compared to the progress on economic work. The "Party members' responsibility system" was not carried out in some villages, and the establishment of competitions for "cultured villages" and "five-good families" was only short-lived. Some villages and brigades, especially those in remote mountain areas, became forgotten corners for the work on political thinking, and rural women, an important class stratum, were neglected in this work.

Take the reflections of a village cadre in Yangxiang Village as an example. Our heads were filled, he said, with hard targets for grain, oil, cotton, family planning, and other township enterprises, so that we could not take on other work. After launching the rural responsibility system, the party policies were announced in the villages and we had to rely on cadre meetings rather than on mass meetings for the allocation of tasks; or we had to call "family-heads" meetings, that is, one person from each family, and most of them were men. No matter how many or how few came, we held the meetings. Four women Christians in Jingbo Village said that since the inauguration of the responsibility system they had not attended a single meeting. When asked if they knew who the president of China was, they replied: "Don't talk about what we don't know; even the men don't know."

This village has an old meeting hall which seats 480 persons, a cultural center with 800 books, a village radio-broadcasting station, and an amateur drama group, but besides showing films and other activities during the spring [lunar new year] festival, there are no other regular activities that would attract the people.

2. At the grass-roots level, although the Party center gave responsibility for children's and youth work to the Women's League, the local Leagues had already taken on the heavy burdens of organizing women for building the two civilizations and for participating in the reform of the economic system; they were also responsible for protecting the legal rights and interests of women and children, etc. But most of them are also members of the leadership groups for family-planning work at the village level and below, and all take part in the allocation of family-planning work among teams and brigades. They are responsible for the accomplishment of eight big goals. They have little to say about establishing work among women regarding [political] thinking, ethics, or culture.

In order to lighten the burdens of rural people, beginning in 1981 the production brigades of Lai'an County no longer appointed leaders of women's work, and women's work mainly devolved on the Women's Leagues, but their qualifications are not high. For example, in Yangxiang Village, among the eleven women members of the Women's Leagues, two have senior-middle-school education, two have junior-middle-school, and two primary-school; the others are illiterate. Because of their low level of education, it is already hard for them to handle the family-planning work and the center; they just can't take care of other women's affairs as well.

Christianity is booming in the rural areas, while work among women and political-thought work is quite weak. Since the Third Plenary Session of the Eleventh Central Committee, the first stage of rural reform has been successfully completed, and the second stage is in progress. The Party's policy of bringing prosperity to the people has been popular among the rural masses because they have actually benefited. But improving material life does not necessarily mean that spiritual life is enriched. On the contrary, if the demands of the rural people for a Socialist, civilized, and healthy spiritual life are not fulfilled after the improvement of their material life, religion will pull in even more rural people.

When everyone was shouting slogans in Yangxiang County, it was the women, tied to work in the fields by day and working half the night on household tasks, who were most miserable. Now, under the responsibility system, when there is not enough farm work following the autumn harvest, the women make cloth shoes at home. Aside from the minority of women with special skills, and women who can get ahead by making some product for sale, most of the women who now have a "refined rice and white flour" standard of living spend their extra time and energy searching for some place to find spiritual sustenance. They say: In the years just after Liberation we still had the Women's Self-Salvation Association, which organized cultural and study activities for women such as singing and establishing women's rights in marriage. Now what activities do the women's organizations provide?

Just at this time Christianity fills a need, offering a weekly worship service and attracting women by teaching hymn singing, helping people to be good, etc. In the beginning it was mostly older women who joined the church, but later younger women began to come as well. All of the eighty-four Christian women under thirty-five have joined the church since 1980. Not only do the Christians believe that they will benefit personally from their Christian faith, but "belief in religion will raise the productivity of the brigade, so that the Grain Ministry will nod its head in approval, and will surely not take measures to wipe out Christianity. . . ."

Section IV

The Protestant Church in China: Interviews

Document 96

An Interview with Bishop Moses Xie, Fuzhou

On 21 January 1988, Donald MacInnis interviewed Bishop Moses Xie, 85, at his home in Fuzhou. Bishop Xie is chairman of the provincial Christian Council, the provincial Protestant Three-Self Movement, rector of the Fuzhou seminary, and member of the executive committee of the national China Christian Council. Although there is no national church in China today with power to consecrate new bishops, since he was consecrated bishop in the Anglican church, he carries the title and office for life.

Q. What is the function of the provincial China Christian Council (CCC) and the Protestant Three-Self Movement (PTSM)?

A. The PTSM deals with general affairs outside the church, while the CCC deals with internal matters of the church.

Q. Does South Fujian have separate PTSM and CCC committees?

A. No, they send delegates to the provincial committees here in Fuzhou.

Q. In your opinion, will there be a genuine united church of China in the future?

A. At present we are really one church, showing mutual respect for the differences [doctrine and practice] among us. We have already begun one church, but we allow adherents of different traditions to practice different forms of worship.

Among the seminarians there are no differences. By and by we can all become one. The Christians don't care about denominational differences, especially the younger ones, and the new Christians.

Q. Are there divisive sects, like the Little Flock (*juhuiso*)?

A. No, the younger Christians don't care about these differences.

Q. What about the shortage of trained clergy?

349

A. We have graduated three groups from our seminary in Fuzhou already. Most of the graduates come from the Methodist, Anglican, and Congregational traditions, while about twenty graduates came from the Little Flock background. All are equally accredited and are appointed elders pending their trial period and final ordination.

The Fuzhou Seminary

We began a two-year seminary course in 1983 and graduated the first class two years later. The old seminary buildings are occupied by a military unit, so we first used the Flower Lane Church. Recently we moved to the former YMCA, but that is crowded, since we have to share it with the Thirteenth Middle School. We hope to move into the former Methodist office building, which has been returned to the church by the government unit which had occupied it. Our library is too small. The old library was lost, burned by the Red Guards.

The present class, which will graduate soon, has fifty-five students, and the new class, fifty. There are sixteen Fujian students in the Shanghai seminary and nineteen in Nanjing. Sixty-four graduated in the first class and eighty-one in the second.

We have ordained fifty-four persons in recent years, including twelve women, mostly unmarried or widows. Their average age is sixty, mostly drawn from older catechists and Bible women. The committee reviews candidates for ordination. Were they loyal to the faith during the difficult times? Yes, all have some former theological education.

Q. What are the sources of income for the seminary?

A. The local churches support their own students, and there is an annual church offering for the seminary. Church members are very generous. They even give their family ration coupons for food, oil, and coal. They gave twenty quilts to the first class. There is also a government subsidy of 10,000 *yuan* a year. Our total annual budget is 70,000 *yuan*.

We have five full-time teachers, all of them elderly, only two of them with full theological education, and some part-time teachers, including three recent graduates from the Nanjing seminary who also serve local churches. The five part-time teachers, all pastors, get no extra pay. Thirty percent of the curriculum is secular, such as Chinese language and literature, politics and world history.

Q. Is it true that the Little Flock do not ordain?

A. Yes, they have elders only, but we still have seminarians from their groups.

Q. What are the provisions for salary, housing, pension, and so on for pastors?

A. These differ from place to place. Some churches have income from rental properties, or have more church members and higher income than others.

Take Fuzhou for example. We suggest a minimum of 47 *yuan* per month for a seminary graduate. Some churches only give 40, some 50 or 60.

Housing is quite different. In Fuzhou we pastors, including myself, pay rent to the Three-Self office for a parsonage. I pay 15 *yuan* a month. After retirement we continue to pay rent. Some church workers live in the church, but they, too, pay rent. This presents a problem for pastors who have to care for aging parents, since most children have government housing and can take their parents in.

Pension allowances also vary from place to place. The Fuzhou Three-Self office pays 3 *yuan* a month. The local parish may also pay something, but not smaller churches.

Church Statistics

Q. Can you tell me the Protestant Church statistics for Fujian Province?

A. Over seven hundred churches are now open. Two hundred were opened in 1987. Thirty new churches have been built since the "cultural revolution," all paid for by the local members. For example, in Funing all the Christians, who are largely boat people, carried stones and built the church, which seats seven hundred, themselves.

In Fuzhou there are four churches now open, but we need more, because these are often filled to overflowing. They are trying to open a former Church of Christ in China church, but too many squatter families are living in the church; it's hard to get them out.

Q. What about house meetings?

A. We estimate there were over one thousand house meetings in the province in 1987. The house-meeting Christians are not against us. They are good Christians, many come to our churches.

Q. What about the future?

A. Fuzhou now has only four open churches. Formerly there were ten. We need at least seven or eight right now. Formerly each church had less than one hundred members, some only thirty or forty, but now they are all full. Before Liberation we had less than a hundred in the Church of England cathedral, but now seven hundred to eight hundred come each Sunday.

The same was true of the Methodist Tian'antang church. Before Liberation they had perhaps three or four hundred, most of them students and staff members from the nearby mission schools and hospitals. Now they average nearly a thousand on normal Sundays and over three thousand on big days, like Christmas. Moreover, all are devout Christians.

Today all Christians are evangelists, all give witness to their faith, not just the clergy.

Church Problems

Q. What problems does the church face?

A. Our number-one problem is shortage of trained church workers. In 1952 all the seminaries in China were merged into one, in Nanjing. That closed in 1966 and didn't reopen until the early 1980s. We can't do all the things we want and need to do without trained leaders. Plenty of people want to study to become Christians, but we just don't have proper teachers for them.

Q. What about women's and children's work? Are you prohibited from teaching religion to children?

A. Yes, religious education for children now depends on the parents. There are no Sunday schools. Children are too busy in school, doing homework. Parents should teach them the Christian faith. We have a lay training class for mothers.

We do have women's work, but we need more women pastors and church workers to visit women, because most of the active church members are women.

Lay Volunteer Workers

Q. What about lay volunteer workers?

A. Trained leadership is our biggest need. Seminary education is of first importance. After the "cultural revolution" we realized the scope of our problem. In 1981 we began lay training classes. We chose good Christians. They study the Bible and are trained to lead home meetings. We had three classes, three months for each. Now each church district conducts its own lay training classes. We send people to help.

In some districts they train for one or two months. In Fuqing county they have had nine classes already, averaging thirty to forty in each class.

In Linjiang County they have a training class every month. They have twenty-seven churches and only two pastors, both over sixty.

Minxing City has over ten churches but only one pastor, a woman, and four recent graduates from the Fuzhou seminary. We believe that Christians should be the light of the world in their daily life and witness.

The big Methodist church in Putian opened last year. One elder pastor is an invalid, the second pastor has lung trouble, and the third, who is younger, is in good shape. They have a young graduate from the Fuzhou seminary, not yet ordained. He will be ordained in a few years, after we see if he is fit to be a pastor.

Q. Are there restrictions on teaching religion to people under eighteen?

A. Age eighteen is the voting age. Baptism is all right at any age, if one can understand the teaching and attend the preparatory class. Not infants, of course. We have baptized about five hundred a year in Fuzhou in recent years.

Reluctance Among Christians

Q. How many Christians are there in the province?

A. We don't know how many there are. It's impossible to do a tally, because some persons believe in their hearts, but don't dare to show it openly. At Fujian Teachers' University, for example, there are quite a few Christians on the faculty, but they are careful not to show it publicly as long as they continue to work. They don't come to church services. They remember what happened to Christians a few years ago. After retirement they don't care. One retired professor spends all his time visiting potential members, leading house meetings, and doing church work quite openly.

In some rural areas even today some local cadres are obstructive to the Christians and try to prevent them from meeting for worship. The government has conducted several classes for these officials to come and learn how to carry out the official policy on religion. Now it is quite different from the 1950s and 1960s.

The Future

Q. What about the future?

A. I am optimistic. At eighty-five, people say you should retire, but I can't do that. We are still needed. I am optimistic about the future, because I know that we are instruments in the hands of the Holy Spirit. He can't do anything without us. We do our best, placing ourselves in the hands of God.

Document 97

An Interview with Bishop K. H. Ting on the Growth of the Church in China

By Rev. Ewing W. Carroll, Jr., (16 October 1987), published in China Study Project Journal 2:3, December 1987. Rev. Carroll is Executive Secretary for China-Related Areas, General Board of Global Ministries, and Director of the United Methodist China Program, New York.

Q. How many Protestant Christians are there in China today?

A. There are three to four million. They include baptized Protestants, who worship in over four thousand church buildings and tens of thousands of homes or meeting points — frequently inaccurately referred to abroad as "house churches."

Q. How have these figures been derived?
A. The National China Christian Council office receives figures from provincial Christian councils, who in turn collect their figures from local councils. Some local figures also include inquirers.

Q. How does this total compare with that of 1949, when the People's Republic of China was founded?
A. A growth at least twice as fast as our nation's population growth. But we are still fewer than half of one percent of the total population.

Q. What does this growth indicate with regard to evangelism in China?
A. Let me share several things. First, the gospel of salvation in Jesus Christ is just as valid and needed in a Socialist society as in any other. Second, more people are open to and willing to hear and accept what the gospel has to say to them when the church ceases to be an appendage from abroad and speaks the Word of God in its local context. Third, it is sufficient if a government will just recognize the right of religion to exist and to organize its own work. Fourth, Chinese Christians are responding actively to the call that they bear witness to Christ by word and deed wherever they are.

Q. Some critics suggest that the China Christian Council and the Three-Self Movement represent only what they call "government-registered churches." Is this true?
A. Certainly not. Our work includes and serves all non-Roman Catholic Christians in China no matter where they meet and worship. Church buildings and ordinary houses are different only in locality, without spiritual, theological, or political significance. The structure and style of Chinese government and society neither requires nor provides any process whereby Christian groups must be registered.

Q. What then is the task of the government's Religious Affairs Bureau?
A. It handles only state affairs regarding religion. Mainly, the implementation of the principle of religious freedom. It is not permissible for the Religious Affairs Bureau to meddle in our church affairs. As I have just said, China has no system whereby Christians must register with any government agency or any other organization.

Q. Are there not many Christian groups and individuals within China who oppose the Protestant Three-Self Patriotic Movement?
A. Three-Self (self-government, self-support, and self-propagation) is

such an obviously good and right principle that those who oppose it are bound to be few in number. When established in the early 1950s it was a new thing in China, and not everything it did was good or welcomed by all Chinese Christians. I suspect that is true of all human organizations. But Chinese Christians are not so unloving and so unforgiving as to want to stand against Three-Self, even to this day. Of course, there are those who are very active in the movement and others not particularly enthusiastic over it. That, to me, seems quite normal.

Q. How do you react to the label "government-approved churches"?

A. Our churches in China are certainly not any more government approved than churches in North America or many other places. The church's work aims at the proper maintenance of Christian worship and witness and the nurturing of the spirituality of its members in the Body of Christ. It is not our aim either to win the government's approval or its disapproval. I find it highly dangerous to use government approval or disapproval as a criterion for the nature and existence of the church of Jesus Christ.

Q. What comments have you regarding those abroad who claim that there are from thirty million to one hundred million Protestant Christians who form an underground force in China?

A. Our work of Christian witness tells us that a gospel that convicts women and men of sin and demands their repentance is not so easy to be accepted as people watching a TV program. An increase at least twice that of our nation's population growth is already a huge miracle for which we humbly thank God.

It is highly unlikely for one looking at China through a distant telescope to do accurate accounting. These big figures must have been derived by choosing a small area with a large concentration of Protestants and then projecting this high proportion to the whole of China.

If there are indeed one hundred million Protestants in China, it means their numbers have been doubling every four or five years for thirty-eight consecutive years. If the total is fifty million, it means the numbers doubling every six years over the same period.

I find it interesting that those statisticians from afar stick to using the same old figures for so many years. Why? In giving figures, I think we should be sober, honest, resist sensationalism and exaggeration, and shun all political and other considerations.

Q. Can Bibles be secured by Christians not actively supportive of the China Christian Council and the Three-Self Movement?

A. Certainly. We are serving all Christians. Why should we discriminate on the ground of the place where Christians meet? We Chinese Christians know better than anyone the problem of insufficient availability of God's written Word. We are pleased that in addition to 2.5 million copies of scripture we have printed over the past few years, the recent opening of the Amity Printing Press in Nanjing will enable approximately two hundred thousand more copies of the Bible to be printed by the end of 1987.

Q. Some critics outside China claim you are "playing favorites" with various evangelical groups abroad. Is this so?

A. We have friends all over the world, including many warmly evangelical individuals and groups. Observant China visitors know the church in China is predominately evangelical in nature and spirit. At the same time, to be evangelical in China is not to be anti-Three-Self or anti-Socialist. We urge evangelicals and others abroad to grasp this uniqueness of China's religious people.

Q. The Three-Self Movement, the China Christian Council and you personally are frequently vilely attacked by certain groups abroad. How do you take this?

A. As I mentioned to you in an earlier interview, the history of the church in China since 1949 has shown how important self-government, self-support, and self-propagation are to church growth. The church is alive and well in China. Under God's care it has grown phenomenally over the past thirty-eight years without outside help and is more united than ever before.

As long as God is using us in some small way for the cause of the gospel of Jesus Christ, our hearts are at peace. We pray for God's gift of love so that we can also say to those who attack us, "Father, forgive them, for they know not what they do."

Document 98

An Interview with Bishop K. H. Ting

By Rev. Ewing W. Carroll, Jr., 1 November 1988, published in China Talk *14:1, January 1989.*

Q. How do the China Christian Council and the Three-Self Movement view their main task today?

A. Our main task is to build up the life of the church and to strengthen our witness to Jesus Christ and the spiritual nurture of our constituencies. For this reason we need to defend the principle of religious freedom and the rights of the church, and do a good job of self-government, self-support, and self-propagation.

Q. How large is the Three-Self Movement?

A. Any movement, not being an organization, has no membership and is always looser, and likely broader, than an organization. People neither join it nor leave it. We may say that the Three-Self Movement includes all Protestant Christians who are not opposed to, but practice the principles of self-government, self-support, and self-propagation, no matter where they worship or meet, or whether they are regularly or directly related to Three-Self organizations.

Q. What has been the Chinese Christians' attitude toward the State since the formation of the People's Republic of China in 1949?

A. In the early years after the establishment of the PRC, Protestant leaders made an all-important choice. That choice, based on faith and a study of facts, was that the new government should be supported through goodwill and participation, not confrontation and combat. In new China, we have found that the State enables people to live and work in peace. It does not assume the position of God and tell Christians what to believe and how to run the church. We welcome the State's policy of stressing common grounds and preserving differences. This provides a good enough environment in which the church is to be the church and to bear witness to the saving gospel of Jesus Christ. History teaches us that it is not good, but dangerous, for a church to expect favors. As long as ways are open for dialogue, mutual criticism, and mutual give-and-take, it would be irresponsible, and possibly vain, for Christians to speak easily the language of martyrdom. Herein lies the essence of our difference with certain "China watchers" outside of China, some of whom have never even lived in China.

Q. What strides have been made in recent years regarding the implementation of the principle of religious freedom?

A. Taking China as a whole, it is moving ahead. There are now over five thousand renovated and newly constructed church buildings used for Protestant public worship, thanks to the hard work put in by both fellow Christians and government cadres. Then, there are tens of thousands of groups of Christians meeting in homes. The number of Protestant Christians today is six times that of 1949 (from seven hundred thousand to four or five million). Protestants now have twelve theological training centers with over seven hundred fulltime students. We are also publishing a number of journals. But, unfortunately, we still find persons here and there, mostly lower government cadres, who lack respect for the principle. There is much work yet to be done.

Q. In a previous interview you said that it was not the practice in China to require places for religious activities to be registered with the government. Recent reports have indicated to the contrary in Guangdong Province. Can you comment on this?

A. Some time ago government agencies in Guangdong Province asked that places for religious activities apply for registration. If this is a measure aimed at eliminating meetings of Christians in homes without first providing more suitable places for them, it is an infringement on religious freedom. At least, for the sake of openness and public supervision, the appropriate government agencies should make public the grounds for permission to be granted or denied. We are watching developments in Guangdong carefully and have already written to the Religious Affairs Bureau of the State Council and other related bodies about our concern and views.

Q. Last year, the Shanxi Provincial Three-Self Movement Committee and Christian Council issued regulations which also seemed aimed at limiting the freedom of Christians to exercise their religious beliefs. What had happened there?

A. From our inquiries we learned that our colleagues in Shanxi felt they were forced to lay down those strict regulations in the face of the infiltration of elements from Hongkong and elsewhere, preaching with strong political innuendoes, distributing anti-government "religious" literature, and getting people to attend midnight meetings which could easily lead people around them to suspect all Christians. We can understand this concern of these Christian colleagues and government cadres in Shanxi, but we have advised them not to use methods that curtail Christians' right to practice their religion and alienate them from the church.

Q. There is the notion abroad that ministers, evangelists, and worshipers are required by a so-called three-designates policy to stick to their assigned churches and meeting points and are not allowed to attend other churches and meeting points without permission from the government. Is there any truth in this?

A. I am aware that there are local government cadres who, out of their desire to maintain order in society, simplistically lay down such rules without giving regard to Christians' traditional practices and their freedom to move about. The Three-Self Movement and the China Christian Council have never discussed laying down such rules as "three designates." We are working for their removal.

Q. The front page of the July/August 1988 issue of the Chinese-language *China and the Church*, published in Hongkong, reproduces what appears to be an official statement issued by the United Front Work Department of an undisclosed county Communist Party committee requiring Protestant churches and meeting places to be controlled by the local Party organ. If you have seen this, could you please comment on it?

A. I received a copy of this particular issue directly from the publisher. The stipulations laid down in the statement are in such gross violation of national policy, and the whole tone is so harsh and unfriendly, that I am fairly certain the document, together with the chop affixed to it, are composed by anti-China elements in Hongkong or elsewhere. We have requested and are still waiting to see if the publisher is willing to disclose the name of the county, so that we can bring the matter up with the proper authorities. We want to do all we can to address any infractions of religious freedom.

Q. Some foreign friends consider Wang Mingdao among China's greatest evangelists. Others find him antagonistic to the Three-Self Movement. How do you view him?

A. I have met persons who speak highly of the spiritual help they received from Wang Mingdao's preaching. I thank God for that. I can understand his strong opposition to and condemnation of the Three-Self Movement because I have read his book on his fifty years of service to God and found that he continually opposed and condemned other Christians who did not agree with his theological and other views. In the 1950s, some articles did appear in *Tian Feng* monthly which answered some of Mr. Wang's attacks and urged him to support Three-Self. But opposition to Three-Self is not a crime and could not have brought about his later imprisonment. We have made inquiries as to what he was accused of, but have not got a clear answer. Mr. Wang himself does not give a clear answer either. I know that many of his friends are writing and visiting him to urge him to be humbler and more forgiving. We often pray for him when we have meetings.

The Russian Orthodox Church
in China Today

Introduction

The first Russian Orthodox Christians entered China in 1685, a cleric and thirty-one prisoners of the Emperor Kangxi's forces captured in the battle of Albazin. They were incorporated into the imperial troops, and through the years priests and clerics were sent from Russia to minister to the Albazinians. It was not until the eve of 1900, however, that the Russian church began to reach out to the Chinese. In 1916, with twenty foreign missionaries and sixty-one churches and chapels in north China and Mongolia, the church had reached its apogee, with 5,000 baptized Chinese members. Mission support was cut off after the Russian revolution, and the church barely survived, mainly ministering to the White Russian refugees who settled in some of the main cities. Today, two churches have been reopened, one in Harbin and one in Urumqi.

Document 99

Orthodox Church Reopens in Harbin

Xinhua, in English, 17 October 1984; in China Study Project Documentation, Vol. 16, April 1985, p. 5.

An Eastern Orthodox church reopened to worshippers in Harbin this week after being closed for eighteen years. The church was damaged during the "cultural revolution." Renovation work started in 1982 with the help of the local government.

Document 100

Orthodox Church Reopens in Urumqi

China Daily, *1 October 1985.*

The Russian Orthodox church in Urumqi, capital of northwest China's Xinjiang Uyghur Autonomous Region, has reopened after being closed for twenty years, a Xinhua report said.

The agency disclosed that there are 2,600 Russian inhabitants among the 13 million people in the 640,000-square-kilometer region of central Asia, which borders the Soviet Union and lies on the ancient silk route through China.

The report said 640 Russians live in Urumqi and 100 of them gathered for the church opening on Saturday.

The revival of the Orthodox church's activities came as Chinese leaders were preparing to mark the thirtieth anniversary of the founding of the autonomous region.

The newly elected head of the Orthodox religious community was identified by Xinhua only as Seyniya, a seventy-six-year-old woman who has a daughter in the Soviet Union and a son in Australia.

She told Saturday's gathering that local authorities have allocated 15,000 *yuan* to build a new church in the capital next year.

The ceremony was also attended by representatives of the Islamic, Protestant, Catholic, and Buddhist faiths in the city.

"The Orthodox church in Urumqi was badly damaged during the 'cultural revolution' [1966-76]," Xinhua said.

Apart from reopening the church, Xinhua said Urumqi authorities have granted the city's Russian inhabitants the right to observe Christmas and Easter holidays, and have allocated a plot of land for a Russian Orthodox cemetery.

The city also plans to set up a Russian boarding school and a Russian restaurant.

Document 101

Orthodox Church Being Built in Urumqi

Xinhua, in English, 30 May 1988, in FE 0169.

Work on the first Orthodox church in Urumqi, capital of the Xinjiang Uyghur Autonomous Region, is well under way and is expected to be completed by the end of the year. The church, located in the southeastern part of the city, will cost an estimated 130,000 *yuan*, part of which is being covered by the government and part by donations from local religious believers. There are a thousand residents of the Russian ethnic group in the city, of whom more than one-tenth are Orthodox Christians. In addition, a Buddhist temple is also being built for some thousand Buddhist believers in the city.

Judaism in China Today

Introduction

Although there has been no practicing Chinese Jewish community since the last rabbi in Kaifeng died in the nineteenth century, there are still Chinese families who trace back to the Jewish community centered in Kaifeng, where the first synagogue was built in 1164 and the last synagogue was destroyed by a flood in 1852. It is these who do not want the memory, at least, to die.

Document 102

China's Jews Found Harmony

From Baike Zhishi *(Encyclopedia of Knowledge); reprinted in China Study Project* Documentation, *Vol. 18, December 1985, p. 10.*

As early as the beginning of the twelfth century, large numbers of Jews had settled in Kaifeng, Henan Province (China's capital during the Northern Song dynasty, 960-1127).

In contrast to the Jews in other countries, Chinese Jews, who have lived in China for more than seven centuries, are in perfect harmony with the Chinese nation. In 1867 a British bishop visited Kaifeng and said that all of the Jews in China had forgotten their religious belief and were now no different from the Chinese.

After Jews moved to China, they underwent a long process of settling in. The community grew and prospered and soon blended in with the Chinese.

In the first fifty years of the twelfth century, most of China's Jews were in the cotton and silk trade with the West, and many of them became rich.

During the following seven hundred years, the Chinese Jews continued to multiply and their religious activities developed. Some members of the Jewish upper strata gradually took their place among the ruling class. Marco Polo recorded, "In the late thirteenth century, Jews in the south of China were held in esteem in business and politics." At that time the Jewish population in Kaifeng alone had reached four thousand.

With the passage of time, the sense of religion among the Jews became dim, and their religious activities stopped completely by the mid 1800s. By 1910 there were only two hundred identifiable Jewish descendants, and their religious beliefs and dietary customs were indistinguishable from those of the Han population.

Why did they practically disappear? According to Chinese scholars, Chinese Jews began to intermarry with other ethnic Chinese groups in violation of Jewish law no later than the mid-fourteenth century. With the polarization of the rich and the poor, Chinese Jews gave more priority to a spouse's social and economic status than to his or her nationality and religion.

Another reason for the disintegration of Jewish customs is that some well-to-do Jews became literati to the imperial court and were deeply influenced by Confucianism. In the meantime, Chinese culture and ethics made their way into Jewish religious activities. By the mid 1800s, no Jews were left who could read or recite the Five Books of Moses in Hebrew, and some Chinese Jews began to profess Buddhism, Islam, and Christianity.

The Jewish descendants had also dropped their food taboos against eating pork. Especially those Jews who had taken official posts found it difficult to obey Jewish dietary laws. Intermarriage with the Hans also brought changes in food habits and life-styles. Of course, an important reason why the Jews blended so well with the Chinese was that China never discriminated against the Jews. Chinese governments through the ages adopted a policy of equal treatment without discrimination. As American writer Michael Pollack pointed out in his book *Mandarins, Jews, and Missionaries* (1980), "In China no rulers have chosen Jews as the targets of discrimination. They have never been enslaved."

Document 103

Writer Aims To Spread the Word of Judaism

By Victor Su, in South China Morning Post, *23 June 1985.*

A young woman writer from China whose 28-year-old husband is currently an international affairs reporter with the *People's Daily* in Beijing has received a full scholarship to attend the University of Judaism in Los Angeles this autumn.

Miss Qu Yinan, twenty-five, who arrived in the United States last year to study English and American culture at the Community College in Portland, Oregon, has learned to read Hebrew from Rabbi Joshua Stampfer.

She now plans to return home to write a book about Judaic traditions, because such books are not available in China.

Miss Qu said Mr. Stampfer discovered she was among the several hundred surviving Chinese Jews after her mother, Miss Jin Ziaojing, a journalist and anthropologist, learned of the Jews of Kaifeng, eight hundred miles south of Beijing, at a conference on minorities in 1981.

Last year, her mother wrote an article entitled "I Am a Chinese Jew" for national publication, outlining the history of Chinese Jews and her own memories, particularly from her own family.

Miss Qu demonstrated that she could expertly pour water first over her right hand, then her left, and again over both hands from a two-handled pewter jug the rabbi uses for the ritual to prepare for a Jewish Sabbath meal. She said she learned the ritual from her grandfather in China.

Mr. Stampfer, who visited China in 1983, met both Miss Jin and Miss Qu and sponsored the latter's study trip to the United States. Miss Qu is now living with Mr. Stampfer and his wife, Goldie.

She now reads Hebrew, attends Sabbath services at Mr. Stampfer's synagogue in Portland (the Congregation Neveh Shalom), helps with the Sabbath school, sings grace at meals, and will soon be called on to recite the Torah blessing at the Saturday morning religious services.

Miss Qu said records show the first Jews arrived in China more than two thousand years ago. A large number later arrived via the Silk Road and settled in Kaifeng, the imperial capital during the Song dynasty.

The Kaifeng Jews built their own synagogue, which they called the Temple of Purity and Goodness, in 1164. Destroyed by fire and flood and rebuilt several times, it was finally allowed to fall into disrepair after a flood in 1852.

By that time, the Kaifeng Jews were a declining community. The town's last rabbi died in the middle of the nineteenth century, and the Torah scrolls were acquired by an Anglican missionary who later donated them to the Royal Ontario Museum in Canada.

Miss Jin's family is one of the seven clans of Jews who have lived in Kaifeng for centuries. Her family maintains many Jewish practices. They do not eat pork or shellfish, and she recalls that her grandfather always wore a blue skullcap.

Mr. Stampfer said Miss Qu is now the only Kaifeng Jew with the ability to read Hebrew and take part in basic Jewish rituals. He also revealed that the Jews of Kaifeng are planning to convert a house into a museum and community center—making it the first meeting center for Jews there since the last synagogue was destroyed.

Both the rabbi and Miss Qu say they do not know whether the move will spark a revival of interest in the Chinese Jewish community, but Mr. Stampfer said it represents "the first faint light of a renaissance of an ancient community."

Document 104

Kaifeng Jews Reopen Synagogue

Translated by Ian Ward in China Study Project Documentation
Vol. 18, December 1985, p. 9.

In east central China, Kaifeng (pop. 450,000) has seen unexpected changes: in the back streets of the religious quarter the "Peaceful Economic Development Company" has started business, but this enterprise, with its nine employees licensed by the State, makes no profit, nor does it seek customers; its plans are to open a museum commemorating one of China's least-known but most distinctive minorities, the Jews.

Company director and founding member, sixty-year-old Zhou Pingmao, does not hesitate to call the Jews a nationality. "I naturally feel affinity with Jews from abroad," he said.

He is one of only a few hundred in Kaifeng, where once there was a community of several thousand, mostly merchants. As far back as the early Tang dynasty in the seventh century, they came from Persia and India, and Marco Polo, in the thirteenth century during the Yuan dynasty, knew of thriving groups of Jews in Beijing, Hangzhou, Suzhou, and to a lesser extent in Guangzhou and Kunming; but it was not really until the Song dynasty that they became established in the capital, Kaifeng, as it then was, and received the emperor's favor. Although cut off from Israelites elsewhere in the world, they continued to observe the same customs and sanctions, having kosher meals and running their own schools, teaching the Talmud and keeping the Sabbath holy.

The temple was destroyed in 1642 when the Yellow River overflowed its banks. The members of the synagogue rebuilt it, only for it to be washed away again in 1850. In the meantime the community itself had undergone great changes: not persecuted, as elsewhere, its sons and daughters had married into the upper class literati, and its teachers had followed civil-service careers. Some even converted to that other monotheistic religion, Islam (whose white caps, covering themselves before God, contrast with the dark skullcaps of the Jews). When the synagogue had to be rebuilt, funds were lacking, the wood and bricks having been sold to buy provisions. To step into the modern three-story building—the word "museum" is not entirely a misnomer—is, despite the boiler imported from a neighboring hospital, to immerse oneself in the Judaic tradition, and it is only a pity that many of the most precious artifacts and scrolls were removed by Christians during the nineteenth century. (Some have gone to Israel, others to private collections in the U.S. and Canada.)

Popular Religion in China Today

Introduction

Popular religion in China is alive and thriving, as any visitor to rural areas discovers. Whereas government policymakers and theoreticians draw a clear distinction between religion and superstition, they have chosen to ignore the fine line which separates popular (or folk) religion from officially recognized religion on the one hand, and superstition on the other. Since popular or folk religions are not included in the five religions officially protected by Article 36 of the constitution, this poses a problem for local officials charged with preserving public order. If they try to stop popular religious practice the people will protest against government interference with what they view as their legitimate right. If they ignore cult practices that, in their view, are more superstition than religion, they may be charged with failure to implement the laws. In fact, recent visitors have observed popular religious practice taking place unhindered in many places.

C. K. Yang, in his field studies of traditional popular cults in eight localities of Guangdong Province (*Religion in Chinese Society*, Berkeley, University of California Press, 1967), identified, using local gazetteers, three groups of what he calls ethicopolitical cults: those related to Heaven, Earth, and the underworld; cults of deified personalities; and the cults of Confucius and literary deities. For the ordinary person, the first group, "the dominant religious belief in Heaven, Earth and the underworld, which represented a hierarchy of supernatural beings possessing the power to determine the fate of every man on the basis of his moral conduct" (p.150), was most important.

There is no recent study of popular religions in China comparable to C. K. Yang's, but two American anthropologists have begun such studies, and their observations are included in this section.

While the location of Professor Siu's work is not disclosed, it also is in Guangdong Province. She was surprised at the "aggressive public display" of religious rituals and festivals, and suggests that the government, as in former days, could find ways to utilize these in an ethicopolitical way (to use her terminology) to promote social and ethical discipline.

Do today's young people, participating in these ritual practices, have the same understanding of them, in a religious sense, as their elders? Professor Siu has her doubts: "Make offerings and go through the ceremonies when one has the free time. Who cares if there are spirits or not, but one casts a wide net just in case."

367

With the loss of faith in current ideologies and the demise of old hierarchies of power, the pilgrimages of today's youth to the old temples and deities attest to their search for something to believe in: "The random ritual maneuvers of the young unveil to me a generation actively and desperately trying to anchor itself in a supernatural and a corporeal world they have little faith in."

Document 105

Popular Religion in Guangdong Province

Excerpted, with permission, from "Reforming Tradition: Politics and Popular Rituals in Contemporary China," by Helen F. Siu, an anthropologist on the faculty of Yale University. Professor Siu carried out field research in a market town in the heart of the Pearl River delta in Nanxi (a pseudonym) in 1986. The entire paper will be published in a forthcoming anthology.

... There is ample evidence that what appear to be traditional ritual practices have reemerged in China, especially in the rural areas.[1] During the year I spent in Nanxi, I was struck by the ritual intensity that was displayed. Eight years into the reforms, one would not have been surprised if the market town, traditionally known for its 393 ancestral halls and 139 temples and monasteries which had been the scenes of rituals throughout the year, had resumed at least some of its customary ways.[2] Such usual religious items as paper money and incense were sold not only in the markets by peddlers, but also in individually owned shops that conducted a prosperous business. Moreover, contrary to observations elsewhere that public rituals are lacking (Whyte, 1988), community temples and secular festivals that were linked to the interests of overseas compatriots were actively promoted by the town government.[3] Even when the residents eagerly pursued rituals related to the life cycle of individuals, there was an aggressive touch of public display that implicitly acknowledged the limits set by the officials. The primacy of performance in these rituals, as similarly observed by James Watson (1988) in those of the late imperial period, is significant here, especially with regard to the complicity of both the State and the practitioners. If the Socialist government today actively appropriates tradition in order to make cultural communications suit its political priorities, as the imperial state had done, and if local society actively pursues them with such understanding, will the consequences be a unifying culture of "reritualization," to use Watson's term, in which the state and society continue to give each other recognition? ...

Traditional Rituals in Nanxi

... The lineage and temple networks [in old China] partly merged in community-wide festivities that centered on the five large temples and major ancestral halls in town. Through taking part in the rituals, the inhabitants sought affiliations that confirmed status and differentiated access to resources, claimed rights of settlement and tenure, forged political alliances, arbitrated conflicts, and secured social mobility. ... [4] The wealth and scholarship flaunted by the elites, and the social networks organizers employed, revealed political agendas by which the language of imperial authority percolated downward and negotiated with local initiatives in the ritual arena. The process reproduced the values of kin, community, class, and politics among the town residents to guide social life both in the domestic and public realms. ... [5]

Rituals and the Socialist Revolution

... During the high tide of the "great leap forward" in 1958, the ancestral halls were dismantled and their bricks and stones transported to the surrounding villages under the Party slogan to aid agricultural production. Notions of kin continued to exist but were weakened when the material evidence and the instrumentality of lineage solidarity were replaced by the priorities of the Socialist government. In the late 1950s, old trees that stood above neighborhood shrines were also cut down to fuel the backyard furnaces; the disappearance of the physical symbols of the former *she* [shrine neighborhoods] coincided with their reorganization under the fifteen neighborhood committees. ...

The temples were spared at the time because they were physically rather small-scale compared to the halls. With the 1960s even these remnants of cultural tradition were destroyed: during the "cultural revolution," young students were mobilized to attack the "four olds": classic texts and genealogies were burned, and the images of deities were smashed. A former Daoist priest recalled that out of fear he voluntarily took most of his ritual texts and tools to the brigade headquarters to be burned and promised not to recruit apprentices for his trade. However, he managed to hide some of the ritual scrolls and a geomancy compass, and preserved a large copper bowl used for funeral rites by storing pig feed in it. The Buddhist monastery and two convents in the area were closed down. The monks were sent away and the building converted to private living quarters. The nuns were made to return to secular life. With the religious specialists prohibited from their trades, the annual communal exorcism and the temple festivals that were tied to the agricultural cycle, together with the more personal funeral rituals, gradually faded from people's memories. Though there were rumors that the destroyers of the Chengwang temple had turned mad, which preserved the fear of the gods among the elderly, young skeptics who could not tell one deity from another regarded these tales as hearsay.

The suppression of popular rituals extended to the domestic realm as well. With the demise of the ancestral halls and the prohibition of burial, rituals related to individual life cycles such as births, weddings, funerals, and memorial rites to ancestors were stripped of their wider social linkages and increasingly confined within the household. During the "cultural revolution," not only was cremation strictly enforced, but also the large mound on the edge of the town which had served as the community's graveyard for centuries was appropriated for agricultural use. Some villagers grew crops in the midst of the tombstones. Most often, graves were dug up and the land converted to fish ponds and vegetable gardens. . . . Furthermore, every street committee saw to the burning of domestic altars and ancestral tablets, fueled in part by the efforts of young students who were mobilized by the radical faction of the town government. . . .

An Intensified Ritual Landscape

Today the ancestral halls in town remain closed. Cadres in the town government are adamant that "superstitious practices" in this former "fortress of feudalism" such as Nanxi should not be publicly condoned or revived. . . . The cadres . . . look the other way when faced with a flourishing of ritual practices related to individual life cycles. In fact, practically every household has restored its domestic altar, including several of the homes of leading cadres. In the central part of many sitting rooms, the tablet that used to represent the nine popular deities has been replaced by a large word *shen* (deity), written in gold against a red background. . . .

Funerals, like weddings, have been widely conducted with ever-increasing extravagance to the point that some of the old "literati" in the town complain about their vulgarization. Gifts of condolence accompany the shiny wood coffins that are taken in procession through the main street, and the passersby, instead of avoiding them as they customarily would have in the past, eagerly stand around to comment on the number of wreaths and the size of the funeral bands playing their noisy tunes. For families who have thrived in the decade of reforms or who have overseas connections, funerals are followed by a dinner of up to thirty or more banquet tables. Some even hire Daoist priests and nuns to perform the funeral rites which can extend for seven weeks. Taken together, the expenses easily amount to 10,000 *yuan* or more. For the market town where the average worker only earns 200 *yuan* a month, the sum is extraordinary. . . .

While subscribing to the ceremonies is expensive and difficult, especially when ritual specialists do not operate altogether publicly,[6] they are nonetheless eagerly pursued by young and old alike. The involvement of the youthful generation is unexpected, especially since they are taking an active part both in organizing and financing the rituals. Young entrepreneurs are most concerned about geomancy, about which they know little, and are diligent in their offerings to Guandi (regarded as the god of fortune). A majority of those young people I interviewed had also gone on pilgrimage trips with friends and coworkers to the Longmu Temple up the Xi River in order to make personal appeals ranging from passing examinations to gaining a fortune and finding a spouse.[7] One can also see old trees covered with red paper on which are names of young children linked with tree spirits believed to be efficacious. At neighborhood entrances and street corners there are a variety of offerings to small stone slabs. The indiscriminate fervor leads one to wonder what meanings popular rituals are taking on for their practitioners today.

Furthermore, a singularly talismanic concern underlying the ritual behavior of the younger generation was brought home to me most vividly on a visit to a major Buddhist temple that has recently been reopened for tourists. In late 1986, I took a trip there with several former nuns to perform a *yangkou* ceremony for their religious master, who had died during the "cultural revolution." For three days I was lodged at the temple and watched them perform their rituals in the evenings after the temple closed its doors to the public. In the quiet chilling nights of the mountain, they chanted with the monks to reach out to their deceased master. They wept quietly, communicating their regret that they had yielded to adverse political realities and had not come to relieve their master sooner.

The world these nuns unveiled to me could not have been more different from that of the young visitors who occupied the temple during the busy hours of the day. The latter came in hordes, indiscriminating in the ways they placed their incense and in their ritual performances. They crowded the gift shops looking for an "efficacious" souvenir, and patronized the temple canteen for a good vegetarian meal. After posing for pictures at the grand entrance of the temple, they hurried off as noisily as they had come. They and the old nuns share the same social space, but they seemed worlds apart. Granted that rituals mean different things to different people, the divergent meanings they have assumed today are noteworthy. The prevalent attitude toward rituals for the generation is: "Make offerings and go through the ceremonies when one has the free time. Who cares if there are spirits or not, but one casts a wide net just in case. If there are spirits, it is too easy to offend one unknowingly and may lead to misfortune. If the spirits in one's path are happy, they may even bring pleasant surprises. . . ."

The practitioners of these rituals [weddings, funerals, etc.] are not entirely utilitarian in their motivation. Certain talismanic qualities of the rituals are particularly appealing to the young, who are uncharacteristically eager about practicing and financing the rituals. They believe that the umbrella, the sugar cane, and the lettuce in a wedding are objects invoking efficacy by association, but these views differ fundamentally from those of their elders, who appreciate the legends concerning the power of the spiritual forces in the form of the white tiger and the potential harm of the golden rooster. The intellectual justifications for these rituals by the Daoist priest, in terms of the contradiction embedded in the forces of nature, are even less relevant for them. A similar assumption lies behind their pilgrimages to deities about whose legendary power they are largely ignorant, but with whom they nevertheless are eager to associate. It appears that when traditional hierarchies of power are no longer relevant and when the Socialist power structure that replaced it ceases to inspire confidence, social as well as moral existence becomes very much in flux. The ideological crisis of the Socialist system affects the younger generation more than the old because they have no alternative worldview for comparison. In three decades of political vicissitudes, the gods, about whom they know little, and many of the Party leaders, whose power they know all too well, have not been able to save themselves. The random ritual maneuvers of the young unveil to me a generation actively and desperately trying to anchor itself in a supernatural and a corporeal world they have little faith in. . . .

Notes

1. See chapter 9 by Martin Whyte, in Watson and Rawski, *Death Rituals in Late Imperial China*. Watson has similar observations in his fieldwork in rural Guangdong in 1985.

2. A manuscript written by He Yanggao in 1946 that I was shown during fieldwork lists the local temples, the lineage halls, and some of the neighborhood shrines. A draft of the Nanxi gazetteer compiled by a group of local historians (manuscript) also contains similar information. There are also the published genealogies of the He, Li, and Mai surnames in Nanxi.

3. See Helen Siu, "Recycling Tradition: Culture, History and Political Economy in the Chrysanthemum Festivals of South China" (unpublished paper).

4. The connection between notions of community and the rituals of community exorcism (*jiao*) is described vividly by scholars who conducted fieldwork in Hongkong. See the works of David Faure, James Hayes, and Tanaka Issei.

5. See my paper on the chrysanthemum festivals of Nanxi in a Chinese volume on Ming-Qing regional economic history (forthcoming, Zhonghua Shuju, Beijing).

6. I interviewed a 68-year-old Daoist priest who was forced to give up his practice during the Siqing movement in 1964, but who resumed semi-publicly in the early 1980s. He said that he would only perform rituals for individual households because he was unsure of the political winds.

7. The temple used to be popular among local residents, not only for personal appeals, but also because it was an important center where rituals were performed for calming the floodwaters of the Xi River. Today, the town provides a special bus service that leaves once a week to cover the ten-hour trip. One can also take an overnight boat up the river to the town of Yuecheng where the temple stood.

Document 106

Popular Religion in Sichuan Province

Professor Stevan Harrell, an anthropologist at the University of Washington, Seattle, conducted ethnographic fieldwork studies among ethnic groups in southern Sichuan Province from January to April, 1988.[1] *While religion was not his primary research topic, he did make observations of current religious practice, which he shared in a letter to me. Excerpts from that letter are reprinted here (with permission).*

In Yishala village, Pingdi Township, Renhe District, Panzhihua City, which is a Yi village that is culturally almost totally Han, traditional Han folk religion is flourishing. We didn't count, but I would estimate that at least 80 percent of the households had traditional four-part altars, dedicated to (in order of seniority) Heaven and Country, the Stove God, the Ancestors of the Lineage (worshipped collectively), and the Lord of the Earth. They don't have tablets for their ancestors, but just have a red paper pasted on the wall. They seem not to burn incense daily, but only on holiday occasions. We didn't observe this, but they say they visit the ancestral graves on the Qingming Festival as well.

We did see activities conducted by a ritual specialist, a Daoshi. He presided at one ritual in the weddings we saw, directing the bride and groom in worshiping a "Horse and Chariot Spirit" outside the groom's house before entering. At the one funeral we witnessed, he played a very important part, spending a whole evening and the next morning reading Buddhist canons of absolution from hand-copied books, assisted by three village laymen playing drums and cymbals. He also directed the geomantic placement of the grave. He currently has no disciples. Both the weddings and the funerals were, as far as I could tell, done in almost wholly traditional style; for weddings, this doesn't involve much religious ritual; for the funerals, of course, it does.

My overall impression is that folk religion in this village is a normal, matter-of-fact part of people's lives. It was, of course, suppressed in the 1960s and 1970s, but I don't have any accurate idea of how much activity there might have been before Liberation. There is no temple in the village at present.

In Renhe, a wealthy Han community, and Zhuangshang, a poor Shuitian [an ethnic group] community, traditional altars are also in evidence, but my impression is that only half or fewer of the families have them. One very knowledgeable schoolteacher had all sorts of charms in addition to his altar, and told us he thought there was scientific proof that they worked, especially for healing purposes.

We lived, for a time, in the Catholic church in Jingtang village. All Jingtang villagers are Catholic, tracing back to the French missionaries who first came there in the mid-nineteenth century. The villagers kept up their faith at home during the years when religion was suppressed, and have practiced it openly again since 1981. All are baptized and have been christened with the names of saints, which are inscribed on the tombstones of the deceased. We were told that they use the sign of the cross as a form of recognition when going to religious meetings.

When I asked people if they were Catholic, they were very emphatic about it, and seemed to consider even the question rather surprising. When I asked what this meant, they seemed less clear, with the exception of the church caretakers (admittedly, this was only a small sample, since we weren't conducting research in Jingtang village). I think that it is a part of life for them in the same way as folk religion is a natural part of life for most villagers in other communities.

Note

1. I learned of Professor Harrell's fieldwork studies from his scholarly report, "Joint Ethnographic Fieldwork in Southern Sichuan," *China Exchange News,* 16:3, September 1988.

Confucius in China Today

Introduction

While there were religious elements in traditional Confucianism, such as the belief in heaven and fate, practice of sacrifice and ancestor worship, condoning of divination and acceptance of a spiritual world, Confucius was not a theist, and his teachings developed into a sociopolitical doctrine more ethical than religious, even when infused with elements of Buddhism. But this did not protect it from the assault on the "four olds," which included an all-out attack on the Confucian heritage that reached a fever pitch in the 1970s during the "Anti-Lin Biao, Anti-Confucius" campaign. Even scholarly discussion of the Confucian legacy ceased after the Forum of Confucian Scholars in 1962.

While Confucius has not been entirely rehabilitated, it is now safe for scholars to suggest that some of his teachings, at least, can contribute to building a Socialist civilization. As for the religious aspects of Confucianism, the news item "Children Cheer Up Old Temple" (Document 110) tells that story: the Confucian temple in Quanzhou has become a recreational center for children and youth.

A Confucius Foundation and a Confucian Study Society were organized following the Symposium on Confucius's Educational Thinking held in Qufu, his hometown, in 1985. For six days one hundred delegates heard papers and discussed the views of scholars on his thinking and teaching. It is now acceptable, as the opening speaker said, to find that Confucius is "neither a god nor a devil." He was, rather, "a great educator, thinker, and statesman" who lived twenty-five hundred years ago, some of whose teachings supported the feudal overlords, but whose legacy is not entirely bad.

The main task, as expressed by the well-known scholar Kuang Yaming, is not to ignore him; "He was a great thinker, educator and politician who had a profound influence over the past 2,000 years. . . . [We should] carry out scientific research . . . to clear away the miasma, assign Confucius to a proper place in history, make a rational assessment of him, and inherit this precious legacy."

Document 107

A Summary of the Symposium on Confucius's Educational Thinking

By Yuan Huanying, in Jiaoyu Yanjiu *(Educational Research) No. 11 (in Chinese), November 1984. Translated in JPRS, 1 March 1985, pp. 65-81 (excerpts).*

One hundred delegates from twenty-six provinces, cities, and autonomous regions attended a six-day symposium on Confucius in Qufu, his hometown, in September 1985. More than ninety papers were presented, mainly focusing on Confucius's educational thinking.

With the approval of the Central Committee of the Chinese Communist Party, a Confucius Foundation was established and a preparatory group for the formation of the Confucian Study Society was organized. The year 1989 is the 2,540th anniversary of Confucius's birth.

An Assessment of Confucianism

The delegates unanimously endorsed Comrade Zhang Jian's assessment of Confucius in his opening speech. "Neither a 'god,' nor a 'devil,' Confucius was a great educator, thinker, and statesman who lived twenty-five hundred years ago in ancient China." In conjunction with his own research, Zhang Jian explained the issue from diverse angles and proposed some distinct views in his concrete assessment.

According to one delegate, "Confucius was a thinker and a statesman, but even more an educator. This great man with a world impact is the pride of Queli, of Qufu, of Shandong, of the descendants of Shennong and Huangdi [legendary kings], and of the whole nation of China. He was neither the god extolled by the feudal rulers, nor the devil condemned by the 'gang of four,' but a man living in the era of the Warring States, a man of flesh and blood, aspirations and feelings, a dignified man of Shandong, and a learned and talented scholar and teacher." Like ordinary people, he was subject to joy and anger, sorrow and happiness. Hearing the *Shao* [music of the legendary emperor Shun], for instance, he was so overwhelmed that he could not taste meat for three months. Upon the death of Yan Hui, his best disciple, he wailed: "Heaven has deserted me! Heaven has deserted me!" In short, he was an ordinary man, not a god. The feudal rulers had an ulterior motive in dressing him up as a god. *The Analects*, a record of his words and acts, is a valuable legacy left by him to posterity, and the wealth of its contents was unprecedented. . . .

Raising the Study of Confucianism to a New Level

The delegates unanimously felt that after the downfall of the "gang of four," the study of Confucianism made great strides along with the progress of bringing order out of chaos in all aspects. However, to restudy and reassess Confucius, critically carry on the valuable historical legacy left to us, and serve the four modernizations and two civilizations, we must raise the study of Confucianism to a new level. On the issue of how to accomplish it, the delegates felt that we must strengthen the Party's leadership, uphold the guidance of Marxism, further implement the "dual hundred" policy, adhere to the principle of making the past serve the present, properly build the scientific and technical contingent, and reinforce data gathering. . . .

According to one delegate, the focus of Confucius's curriculum as a whole was on the moral issue.

According to another, Confucius's education covered the development of the moral, intellectual, and physical aspects. According to a third, rather than an education covering the development of the moral, intellectual, and physical aspects, one may say that Confucius stressed education in moral character and political expertise. His special emphasis on moral character and political expertise in personnel training was determined by his times and his life experience, and by his political outlook and philosophy. In addition, he also advocated education in music, military affairs, and health, but he opposed labor education. . . .

Confucius's Thinking on Politics, Economics, Philosophy, Literature and Art, and Ethics

On Confucius's philosophical thinking, according to one delegate, the most salient point was that he refused to discuss superstition, ghosts and gods, or life and death. It was stated in *The Analects* that "Confucius does not talk about strange forces and gods." When his disciples asked him about life and death, and ghosts and gods, he replied: "When we cannot serve humans, how can we serve ghosts?" "When we do not know life, how can we know death?" He also said: "What has it to do with Heaven? The four seasons follow one another and all things grow. What has it to do with Heaven?" Rather than by order from heaven, the revolution of the seasons and the multiplication of all things are governed by their own laws. Thus, it was felt that Confucianism contains elements of materialism and dialectics. But there were also some delegates who considered Confucius's philosophical thinking basically idealist. . . .

According to one delegate, ethical thinking is the basic part of Confucianism. In addition to its rich substance, it formed a system encompassing such fundamental theories as the origin and social impact of morals, their relations with interest and with knowledge, their class nature, their principles and norms, the methods of their performance, moral education, and self-cultivation. Occurring more than twenty-five hundred years ago, it is indeed worthy of esteem. . . .

Document 108

Restudy and Reassess Confucius

By Kuang Yaming, in Guangming Ribao, *Beijing, 13 September 1982. Translated in FBIS 351, 1982, pp. 93-99 (excerpts).*

Our attitude toward historical figures should be as follows: we must assign them to given historical conditions and study the degree to which they stimulate or hamper the advance of history; and based on the principle of "making the past serve the present," we must study the degree to which they are beneficial or harmful to the current cause of the people and to Socialism, while "making comments and assessments in a down-to-earth manner." We not only oppose the attitude of "stressing the past and not the present," but also oppose a nihilistic attitude toward history. This is especially true in our approach to a historical figure of great weight like Confucius. Since the Third Plenary Session of the Eleventh CPC Central Committee, academic circles have raised the question of reassessing Confucius and have held discussions. This is a pleasing phenomenon. But we still have a long way to go to meet the needs of the current situation. Therefore, to restudy and reassess this great historical figure, who carried great weight both at home and abroad, in ancient and in modern times, is a timely and necessary affair and a matter of great significance as well. This is closely related to the current effort in building material civilization, and Socialist spiritual civilization in particular. . . .

A significant question is about dealing with Confucian ideology from these aspects; that is, Confucian ideology should be studied and handled from the following aspects: First, Confucius's ideology and words, which obviously defended the rule of the feudal landlord class and its class ethics, were determined by the historical background of Confucian ideology. Our present task on the ideological front of eliminating the feudal remnants is, to a fairly large extent, directly or indirectly connected with all these. Therefore, we should severely criticize them and send them to a history museum to prevent them from spreading poison through society!

Second, although some of Confucius's views and words were outwardly feudal, they had affinity to the people and embodied progressive characteristics. After making an analysis we can derive rational content from them, which can be used for reference. For example:

First, the ideas of "the world is for all" and "great harmony" originated from Confucius's liking for the recollection of "things of the past." These were also his ideals. More than two thousand years ago, some enlightened thinkers like Confucius also had such a "lovely" fantasy. We all know that during the eighteenth and nineteenth centuries, the ideological trends of utopian socialism and communism occurred in France and England (represented by Saint Simon, Fourier, and Owen). Due to the restriction of social conditions (early period of capitalism), they considered themselves to be "persons of foresight" and regarded the "liberation" of the poor laboring people as their own task and dreamed of establishing an experimental "phalanstery" and "socialist territory" by not touching the existing social system but begging the capitalists for sympathy and donations. All of them failed to attain their objectives. The Confucian idea of "the world is for all," which occurred in feudal society two thousand years ago, was, of course, never aimed at changing the feudal system. Under the precondition of maintaining feudal order, Confucius begged the gentry and the feudal lords to realize his ideals. He traveled to various states but ran into snags and was foiled everywhere. Of course, he failed in his efforts. Although Hegel, a great German philosopher of the nineteenth century, proceeded from his revolutionary ideological method, he drew an extremely obedient and reactionary political conclusion and eventually became a royalist. Such being the case, it was not at all strange that Confucius, a great Chinese enlightened thinker of more than two thousand years ago, would come to the political conclusion of maintaining the rule and order of the feudal landlord class. Engels held that Hegelian philosophy, which was an extremely influential ideological trend, did play a great role in developing the intelligence of the nation and that we should not discard it simply on the grounds of its "fallacy and harmfulness." He stressed: "We should 'develop and discard' it in its own sense. In other words, while critically eliminating its form, we should derive new content from it" (*Selected Works of Marx and Engels*, Vol. 4, p. 219). This is also the way we should treat Confucian ideology, which played an important role in developing the intelligence of the Chinese nation. The idea of "the world is for all," which occurred in China more than two thousand years ago, should be regarded as a precious historical heritage. We should critically "develop and discard" it, that is, we should absorb its rational "nucleus" and use it as a reference. This is a matter of great significance.

Second, now let us discuss the concept of "benevolence." Confucius talked about the concept of "benevolence" in different ways. The main points can be summarized as follows: politically, Confucius regarded "benevolence" as the end result of his ideal "the world is for all"; ethically, Confucius regarded "benevolence" as the highest criterion determining the relations between people in his ideal society—"the world is for all" was not aimed at touching the feudal system itself. Therefore, his concept of "benevolence" naturally conformed with the feudal society. In the feudal society, people were rigidly stratified, and they did not receive equal treatment. Although Confucius stressed that "brotherly love and significant benevolence are shared alike," do equal love and benevolence actually exist between the monarch and his subjects, between father and sons, between brothers, between husbands and wives, as well as between the rich and the poor? Politically, Confucius's "benevolence" manifested itself in "the world is for all." At most, the principle of "benevolence" could only be pursued within a limited scope of "being concerned with inequality rather than meagerness and being concerned with instability rather than poverty." In other words, such "benevolence" was partial in nature. Ethically, "benevolence" was limited to a moral scope of loyalty, forgiveness, filial piety, brotherly manner, courtesy, and righteousness. The unequal relationships among people were permeated with the spirit of abiding by the law and behaving discreetly, aimed at maintaining the stability of society. Therefore, Confucius's concept of benevolence and brotherly love was nothing but consciously and unconsciously trying to harmonize and conceal the unequal relations between people in feudal society. However, after criticizing and "casting away" the feudal garb of the Confucian ideology on "benevolence," its rational factors can be used as reference. . . .

We should no longer treat Confucius coldly. He was a great thinker, educator, and politician, who had a profound influence over the past two thousand years. Instead of doing superficial work or making empty clamor, we should adopt a down-to-earth manner to carry out scientific research. This is a task for the academic circles and the unshirkable responsibility of Marxists to clear away the miasma, assign Confucius to a proper place in history, make a rational assessment of him, and inherit this precious legacy.

Document 109

Return of Confucian Virtues of Kindness and Restraint

By Yang Liuxie ("It Is Still Good To Be a Little More 'Temperate, Kind, Courteous, Restrained, and Magnanimous'") in Beijing Ribao, *16 January 1981. Translated in FBIS 175, 1981, pp. 22-24.*

It has been a long time since I last saw [the phrase] "temperate, kind, courteous, restrained, and magnanimous"! During the reign of terror of Lin Biao and Jiang Qing's antirevolutionary cliques, these splendid virtues handed down by our forefathers were drowned in the midst of the fervor of "ceaseless struggling" and "endless fighting" and blamed for "creating a predisposition to villainy," yet who dares come forward and make inquiries? Even in times like today I am afraid it is hard to avoid being suspicious of anyone preaching the Confucian philosophy of life. But I still have to cry out against the injustices inflicted on a few words.

These words originally came from a sentence in *The Analects* in which Zugong lauded Confucius. In its original context he said that Confucius, as a result of being "temperate, kind, courteous, restrained, and magnanimous" was able to attain the status to participate in the political administration of any state he went to. Whether or not Confucius really did possess these splendid virtues is irrelevant, but the fact is that these splendid virtues gained dissemination via *The Analects*. At that time the numerous princes who were embroiled in relentless dominations and struggles for hegemony ruled the people and defined their borders by virtue of leather whips and iron dagger-axes, and it was impossible for them to even take seriously, much less pursue, this sort of moral concept espoused by the Confucian shop. The reasons why later rulers took a fancy to these five words and preached them relentlessly were, for one thing, to keep the laboring people servile, to bear exploitation and suppression, and to use it to protect their feudal ruling system; for another, they wanted to use this sort of moral concept to keep the members of the ruling cliques in bounds, regulate internal contradictions, and prevent their own downfall. However, the natural instincts of the exploiting class to try to cheat or outwit each other made it virtually impossible for them to implement these splendid virtues, much less carry them out fully. From observing the few thousand years of recorded history, the general rule is that the only regard the exploiting class had for the laboring people was cruel oppression and exploitation. They never said anything about being "temperate, kind, courteous, restrained, and magnanimous," and even within the exploiting class these virtues were seldom observed; all one saw was even more mutual jostling and picking of fights, and they all resembled a pack of hungry animals ready to devour each other or be eaten themselves. With the arrival of the Socialist society, the situation underwent a basic change, and these virtues were given an even newer substance where they could and should flourish. We destroyed class exploitation and oppression and a basic change occurred in the relationships between people. A mutual affinity exists among the laboring people and among comrades because of their common interests and goals. This sort of new-model relationship has determined that people can get along with one another equally, treat each other like brethren, and be mutually understanding and accommodating. In other words, they can be "temperate, kind, courteous, restrained, and magnanimous."

However, another problem has surfaced: didn't Comrade Mao Zedong, in the "Report on an Investigation of the Peasant Movement in Hunan," clearly say that revolution cannot be so temperate, kind, courteous, restrained, and magnanimous, and that "[a] revolution is an insurrection, an act of violence by which one class overthrows another"? Some people frequently take this as a basis for treating these five moral qualities and the revolutionary outlook as something incompatible with each other, such as fire and water. Actually, what Comrade Mao Zedong said was that the struggle in which "the peasant class has the power to overthrow the feudal landlord class" is a violent revolution. If we take the conclusion that it is only applicable in a violent revolution and indiscriminately change it into a principle applicable to all areas, it is then a gross error. Could one imagine that after the end of a large-scale, tempestuous class struggle there would still be violent acts carried out among the people with one section overthrowing another section of the people, and that one could not be a little more "temperate, kind, courteous, restrained, and magnanimous"? As far as this extremely important point was concerned, the people in the past never gave it a thought, and when the "Great Proletarian Revolution" came it was too late to give it serious thought, so with feelings of kindness and hazy friendships the people accepted this "baptism of combat" against the unprecedented "red storm."

Lin Biao and the "gang of four," using the power they had usurped to fly the banner of "revolution," created ideological chaos and moved the violent measures reserved for the enemy on the people and in the Party. For a time roughness cloaked refinement, temperance was layered in dirt, fraudulence was sky-high, kindness reached an all-time low, boasts were crowned, and restraint was humiliated. Former comrades became opponents, and past leaders became the hated foe. Subordinates were against superiors, masses were against masses, staring angrily at one another and trading sarcasms to the point where fists flew, clubs were brandished, and brutal attacks ensued. Under the guise of various "revolutionary" slogans some old cadres tasted the bitterness of the flesh and some good comrades sacrificed their lives under the club. It only caused the moral climate to sink from bad to worse, and the perfectly good condition of Socialism was beset with endless disasters and ceaseless hatreds. The "revolutionary" theories promoted by Lin Biao and the "gang of four" severely contaminated the pure, kind hearts of a number of our Party members and the masses, and seriously damaged the Party style and social atmosphere. Even now some people still believe in "for me-ism," injuring other people's teeth and eyes scrambling for profit and power everywhere.

There are also others who still have not given up factionalism, who still recall past grievances, want an "eye for an eye" and are feverishly engaged in settling old scores; and there are even a number of youth who look down upon social morality, regard restraint as a weakness, treat "useful people" as pawns, conduct themselves as they please, and cause others to make a sidelong glance of indignation. Over ten years of lessons, and the present reality, clearly indicate the very necessity of recommending a swift infusion of these five moral qualities among the people. At present there are calls everywhere to readjust the Party style, with everyone hoping to study and establish Socialist moral standards, endeavoring to establish a Socialist spiritual civilization. I believe that guiding the people to gradually cultivate a good atmosphere in which kindness, restrained thoughtfulness, tempered thriftiness, and binding friendships between the people conform to the needs of the times and the people and should be very beneficial.

"In doing so do you not want the people to become modest gentlemen and keep on the right side of everyone?" This type of censure is a gross misapprehension. If one acts like a "good old boy" when confronting mistakes and consistently indulges in excessive leniency to the point where evildoers and evil deeds, mistaken ideological trends, and unhealthy trends are met with endless "courtesy," then our Socialist cause cannot forge ahead. But these five moral qualities we advocate should not be mutually excluded from criticism within the Party and among the people, because the struggle and the criticism we speak of can only be applied through methods that are reasonable, democratic, and are like gentle breezes and mild rains, which spring from the desire of unity, and undergo criticism and struggle to attain a united goal; yet they are never permitted to blow in a "twelfth-grade typhoon," where people are beaten to death with clubs. Speaking along the same lines, it is also desirable to be a little "temperate, kind, courteous, restrained, and magnanimous" when launching ideological struggles within the Party and among the people.

Li Ruzhen of the Ming dynasty fabricated *Jun-Zi Guo* [Land of Gentlemen] and toward the end of the Qing dynasty Kang Youwei wrote *Da Tong Shu* [Great Harmony]. They both felt the ups and downs of officialdom, the misfortunes and happiness of the troubled times, and composed an imaginary setting for the people which could be called a Chinese-styled utopia that was basically impossible to realize. Today it is a different age, for we have eliminated Lin Biao and the "gang of four," the prime culprits of the troubled times, and bestowed a new significance on the splendid virtues of being "temperate, kind, courteous, restrained, and magnanimous," so that they absolutely should be and can be realized among the people. I really believe that once these splendid virtues start to take effect among the people and masses throughout the country a stable unified Political Bureau will certainly be able to attain further consolidation and development.

Document 110

Children Cheer Up Old Temple

China Daily *(in English), 9 June 1988.*

FUZHOU (XINHUA) - A Confucian temple in Quanzhou City in south China's Fujian Province, a hometown of overseas Chinese, draws an increasing number of domestic and foreign visitors.

These visitors have come to witness the rich diversity of activities for children which has added new meaning to the one-thousand-year-old site, now converted into a youth and children's palace.

The young people bring a happy atmosphere to the otherwise solemn and grand ancient building surrounded by nodding willows, towering trees, and a rippling pond.

A team of girls is learning martial arts in the yard. Their coach told Xinhua that there are a total of fifty martial arts trainees at the center.

Deng Shimian, deputy director of the Youth and Children's Center, teaches children to play traditional Chinese two-stringed musical instruments.

He said that these pupils take normal courses in their respective schools in the morning, and in the afternoon they come to the center to study music. Other children learn dancing, painting, and calligraphy.

Religious Surrogates in China Today

Section I

Superstition and Religion in China Today

Introduction

While Communist Party members are, by definition, atheists, the current policy shows more tolerance toward religion than superstition, which raises this question: if the main reason for the policy of freedom of religious belief is to induce religious believers to cooperate with all the people in building a strong, modern, Socialist nation, then why are not superstitious practitioners tolerated for the same reason? The reasons, set forth in the documents selected for this section, are clear: normal religious practice, by improving social and personal morality, enhances rather than impedes Socialist nation building, while rampant superstition has the reverse effect.

By "propagating nonsense," superstitious practitioners counter efforts to spread scientific culture and knowledge, they harm social order and discipline, and, we are told, can go so far as to form reactionary secret societies. Superstitious practitioners, such as fortune tellers, sorcerers, and shamans, prey upon gullible and ignorant people, swindling them by charging high fees for conducting seances, divination, "ghost weddings," exorcism, and other sham rituals. The time and money wasted in these practices not only drains the meager savings of peasant families, it "damages agricultural production, pollutes the social atmosphere, and disturbs social order." Superstition can even endanger lives, when patients fruitlessly spend money on fake cures rather than going to a doctor, or jump in a pond and drown when a shaman tells them to [Document 122].

These writers ask, why have these activities resurfaced after years of education in modern science and culture? There are several reasons. First, modern education has not reached enough people, particularly in the rural areas. Moreover, some educated young people go in for fortune telling and divination, even if they don't believe such things, "because of a spiritual void" in their lives.

385

These practitioners, "the dregs of old society," had been outlawed for years, but now are quitting their regular jobs and returning to make an easy living by defrauding gullible people.

Finally, local Party and government cadres are to be blamed for failing to make clear distinctions between legitimate religion and superstition. "There are even many . . . cadres who do not interfere because they regard superstition and swindling as religious activities." One Party cadre said, "It's hard to be sure about this kind of thing, [so] it's better to close the eyes." Even worse, some Party officials take part in superstitious practices, such as ancestral sacrifices, wasting time and money, adversely affecting production, and inciting "a feudal, clannish mood among the masses" [Document 121].

How should the Party and government deal with superstition? Those practitioners who are defrauding gullible people should be dealt with according to Article 165 of the Criminal Code, which stipulates prison terms of up to seven years for people convicted of using superstitious practices to swindle people, while others should be admonished, educated, and helped to find work and earn an honest living. As for people who patronize them, they should be given "patient ideological education."

Ren Jiyu, the former director of the Institute for World Religions, writing in *China Daily* makes it clear that Marxism is the best way to cure feudal superstition, saying that religion and feudal superstition (which he calls "religion-superstition") are inimical to Socialism because they "seek the protection of God or some supernatural power, while [Marxism] relies on our own strength to transform the world."

Bishop Ting's letter in a subsequent issue of the same newspaper, a response to Ren Jiyu's article, protests against Ren Jiyu's lumping together of religion and superstition, pointing out that this gives a false impression of China's current religious policy, which separates religion from superstition.

What is the basic difference between religion and feudal superstition? Ya Hanzhang, a veteran theoretician who has written often on this subject [see MacInnis, *Religious Policy and Practice in Communist China*, New York: Macmillan, 1972, pp. 37-49], wrote this for the *Guangming Daily* in 1981: "Religion differs from feudal superstition in many aspects, but the most fundamental one is: Religion is a way of viewing the world, while feudal superstition is a means by which some people practice fraud."

Qigong

While *qigong*, one form of traditional Chinese slow motion exercises, would not be labeled a superstition in China, where members of the China Qigong Scientific Research Association have organized systematic studies of this mysterious phenomenon, some scientists are skeptical. In any case, *qigong* has experienced explosive growth in popularity in recent years. While it is said that its present-day practitioners, numbering as many as one in 20 Chinese of all ages [*Beijing Review*, 24 April 1989, p. 20], have divested *qigong* of any religious connotations, historical researchers have identified over 400 varieties divided among several schools, including Confucianist, Daoist, and Buddhist. The aim of all the schools is to bring the body and mind into balance and harmony with nature, concentrating one's *qi*, or elemental energy, for purposes of strengthening or healing oneself or, by transmission, another person. The Daoist school holds that *qigong* should be used to cultivate one's mind, character, and moral integrity as well as physical wellbeing.

Document 111

Why Are Superstitious Activities on the Rise Again?
An Investigation of Rural Superstitious Activities
in Chuansha County, Shanghai Municipality

By Gong Jianlong in Shehui *(Society) No. 3, 1982; reprinted (in English) in* Chinese Sociology and Anthropology, *No. 16, 1983, pp. 204-211.*

I

Since the founding of the People's Republic of China, as a result of the Party's and the Government's major efforts which propagated a materialistic ideology, spread scientific culture and knowledge, [and] cracked down on destructive activities of reactionary secret societies, superstitious ideas among the masses have been greatly reduced in comparison to before Liberation. But in recent years in some regions, especially in rural areas, superstitious activities have developed again, causing many problems in the public order which are extremely harmful to the "four modernizations" construction, thereby calling widespread attention of various social circles. To do away with superstitions is an important aspect of building a Socialist civilization. Thus, it is absolutely necessary to determine why superstitious activities are able to develop under the present circumstances so that countermeasures may be taken to solve the problems. For this reason, we made some investigations in Chuansha County in peri-urban Shanghai.

Located in peri-urban Shanghai, there are more than twenty people's communes and towns in Chuansha County where superstitious activities are widespread. The activities mentioned here refer to the specific seeking out of professionals [engaged] in superstition *(mixin zhiyezhe)*, in "fortune-telling," "divining by the Eight Diagrams" (*bagua*), "catching ghosts to cure sickness," etc. As for those who generally believe in ghosts and deities, in holding memorial ceremonies on New Year's Day or other festivals, they are even more common. Devout believers in ghosts and deities are not only limited to old folks and women; a sizable number consists of young people. For instance, among a total 461 members of the Qingsan Brigade in Cailu Commune, over 95 percent are believers, but less than 5 percent are non-believers. There is an old sorceress, Zhang so-and-so, in Jiangzhen Commune, self-proclaimed as being able "to call immortal celestial beings," "to capture demons," "to cure the terminally ill," who set up in her home four incense tables; every day a continuous flow of people go to her for "fortune telling" and healing, making her front door and courtyard like a market-place. At Lianqin Brigade in Cailu Commune, fortune teller Mr. Xu so-and-so at first charged two *jiao* [0.20 *yuan*] for fortune telling each time; later seeing that people wanting fortunes told came in droves and having more business than he could attend to, he raised the service fee to 1 *yuan* and still "the business is brisk." At one brigade in Huanglou Commune, where also in vogue was "arranging ghost marriages" (*pan guiqin*), eight couples were so arranged, of which surprisingly the parents of three couples were Party cadres. The so-called ghost-marriage arrangement consists of making a match, with the sorceress as the go-between, for a marriage in the netherworld, joining the deceased son of the Zhang family with the deceased daughter of the Li family. However, the occasion of their wedding is not inferior to that of the living, with bride price and dowry from both sides and invited relatives and friends for wine; the only difference is that the bride and groom have only memorial tablets instead. A cadre of Shiwan Commune made a computation about a peasant believer in superstitions; the latter's household was busy with superstitious activities the whole year round, with the new year welcoming of the God of Wealth, making sacrifices to ancestors at Spring Festival (Qinming), by the Seventh Lunar Month worshiping "Dizangwang" [a Buddha who saves souls], by the year end sending off the Kitchen God [on his way to report to the powers above about the doings of the year], and, in between, death [in the family] bringing monks to chant Buddhist scriptures for the deceased every seventh day for seven times, on the one-hundredth day, the anniversary, etc. Some other commune members climb over mountains and wade through rivers distant from their hometowns to burn incense and worship Buddhas at the Lingyin Temple in Hangzhou and the Putuo Mountain in Ningbo; these practices are on the increase.

II

The prevalence of superstitions not only has brought a heavy burden to peasant family life but also, with very serious damage, has affected agricultural production, polluted the social atmosphere, and disturbed social order.

First of all, superstition professionals get rich by foul means, but the burden is too heavy for the peasants to bear. Just in the three commune regions Jiangzhen, Chengzhen, and Cailu, there are six sorceresses and fortune tellers who have used the money they swindled to rebuild their houses. Some commune members said, "They move their lips a few times; we have to work at least ten days in the fields." Some members ordinarily live frugally, reluctant to spend even a single cent casually, but in order to "arrange ghost matches" for their children, and under pressure from relatives and friends, do not hesitate to stake one thousand pieces of gold on one throw [to spend money like water], to commit to flames whole batches of new clothes, beddings, mosquito nets, and even tables and chairs, etc., saying that this will let their children live a better life in the netherworld. Early this year, in the villages rumor had it that paper ingots made of sanitary/toilet paper were worth a lot of money in the netherworld. Consequently, many peasants rushed to purchase toilet paper to use as a substitute for paying condolences to the netherworld to be burned for deceased relatives. One peasant bought forty rolls of toilet paper at once; more than 10 *yuan* turned into ashes in an instant. Not only was money wasted but it exhausted the toilet-paper stock of some stores.

Second, [superstitious activities] adversely affect the sick, even endanger lives. Sorceress Diao Qiuju of Gaojiao Brigade, Chengzhen Commune, swindled the masses by claiming herself to be possessed by "Meng dalaoye" [Master Mencius]. Wang so-and-so, a young peasant ill with typhoid, sought her out for a cure. She talked nonsense about a person having been executed by shooting near the Wang home, the ghost of one who has suffered a wrong which has not been righted was making trouble; she wanted the Wang family to buy joss sticks and candles and toilet paper to beseech the deities to expel the ghost. Busied for three days, Wang spent more than 40 *yuan*. Finally, the illness became more serious; he died on the way to the hospital due to delaying of treatment. In Sanwang Brigade, a young woman had chronic nephritis; a sorceress said that she was pestered by a fox spirit and wanted her to beseech the deities to expel the fox. After suffering for more than one year, the woman's illness did not get better, but more than 1,000 *yuan* had been swindled from her and the house had to be sold.

Third, the activities affect production and undermine social values. In Wangyi Brigade, Shiwan Commune, member Yang left home after quarreling with a neighbor; unable to find him anywhere, his mother went to seek divination, which said that he threw himself into a body of water to the east. Consequently, his mother begged many commune members to borrow fishnets to drag for the body in every river and stream; dragging for three days without a trace, they then went to search in the marshland by the sea, but also to no avail. Later, he was found roving in Hangzhou. In the region of Tangzhen Commune, an old man of almost seventy had been very ill. He was already dead by the time he was transported to the home of a sorceress who, pretending to be imposing and awesome, told the over-sixty-year-old wife of the deceased to carry the corpse home to brood heart to heart for three days, saying that will revive him. The ignorant old lady did as she was told; after three days the corpse stank and only then did she know that she had been taken and already swindled out of 178 *yuan*.

Fourth, these activities lead to contradictions among fellow villagers, hindering solidarity. Last June a young woman of Bangyi Brigade, Shiwan Commune, was raped; her parents went to a sorceress to seek the where-abouts of the offender. The sorceress talked nonsense that he was in the southeast. Based on the direction given, the victim's parents suspected a commune member, Zhu, of the same brigade, and said to others that Zhu could be the rapist, which caused Zhu to be resentful. Later the matter was settled and the case solved as the Public Security Bureau investigated and caught the culprit. On 10 March this year in Jielong Brigade, Huanglou Commune, a Zhang family had suffered a loss by theft of 160 *yuan* in cash, and Mrs. Zhang sought advice from the sorceress. The sorceress said that the thief was tall and thin and wore gray cotton clothes. Thinking that the description was a bit like that of the production-team leader, Mrs. Zhang probed the team leader on the sly, which almost caused disputes.

There are exceptional cases where sorceresses and sorcerers even talk nonsense that they have been possessed by revolutionary leaders and mar-tyrs, engaging in swindles and bluffs which create a very negative impact politically.

III

More than thirty years after Shanghai was liberated, it is worth ponder-ing the surprising rapidity of the resurgence of superstitious activities in the rural outskirts of a large city with relatively developed culture and science. What really are the reasons? Viewed from the circumstances of the investigation, we believe there are the following four main points:

First, that peasants lack possession of scientific cultural knowledge and are ignorant and backward is still one of the main reasons. Not only is it that some young peasants have a low literacy, but also it is very difficult to eliminate deep-rooted superstitious ideas in their thinking. Moreover, as a result of the damage of ten years of internal disorder, many of the young peasants now have the mistaken idea that "schooling is useless," so that although they are high-school graduates in name, their actual cultural level and the knowledge they possess are very low. Under the influence of old folks and antiquated ideas and being swindled by superstition professionals, they are easily taken prisoner by what ghosts and deities say. Especially in recent years, some rural market towns' itinerant troupers perform and sing in vivid sound and color old dramas about the supernatural which propagate superstitious ideas among peasants and also serve the function of adding fuel to the fire.

Second, some young peasants who have more or less accepted scientific knowledge do not believe in ghosts, deities, or Buddha, but then why do they also go for fortune telling, divination, and also pray to deities and Buddha? According to our understanding, some, because of a spiritual void, and lacking lofty ideals and work aspirations, go for fortune telling in order to seek some stimulation. For example, in going to ask shamanesses about marriage, jobs, good or ill luck, and whether they can succeed in abandoning farming to engage in business, etc., some of the youth who sought shamanesses do not believe much in what they say; instead, feeling no spiritual sustenance, they only did those things just to console themselves. Not having lost anything, some youth deliberately spent some money to have sorcerers divine; when the fortune tellers said to search in the southeast or southwest direction, in an uproar they departed with their hearts contented.

Third, is the resurfacing of dregs of old society. Having been outlawed in the past, a majority of superstition professionals in shamanism, sorcery, fortune telling, and divination no longer engaged in those but already had [regular] work. But in recent years, seeing that their tricks of deception still have believers in society, and moreover that basic-level cadres do not interfere, they have taken up the old trades. Chuansha County originally had eighty-six superstition professionals; now fifty or sixty percent of them have resumed the fraudulent line of business.

Finally, serious shortcomings which exist in publicity work of our concerned departments are worthy of attention. With respect to peasants, basic-level cadres have not done sufficient work in publicizing extensively and in depth the distinctions between religion and superstition and fraud, and between permitting the freedom of religious beliefs and the necessity of carrying out education on atheism. There are even many commune and brigade cadres who do not interfere because they regard dealings in superstition and swindles as religious activities. A Party branch secretary of Huanglou Commune said, "Now, with the emphasis on emancipating the mind, it's hard to be sure about this kind of thing; it's better to close the eyes." Now that churches are open and the masses can be religious, some cadres even think preposterously that they can also believe in deities and worship the Buddha.

The emergence and existence of superstition have deep historical and social roots. The thorough elimination of this kind of social malady cannot be accomplished overnight; it is a long-term task. However, seeing the serious harm [superstitions] do to society, we must consider the elimination of feudal superstitions and pay attention to science as the long-term, arduous task of struggle, as a struggle against corrosion and for the construction of a Socialist spiritual civilization. It is necessary to strengthen propaganda and educational activities and to mobilize the broad masses to struggle against superstitious and unlawful activities. Concerned departments must do well the work of prohibition and distinguish circumstances and deal severely with those who engage in superstitious and fraudulent practices.

Document 112

Superstition Reemerges in China

Hong Kong Standard *(in English), 12 April 1986.*

BEIJING—Several newspapers yesterday carried stories about the re-emergence of superstition in China, including a lavish wedding for a dead couple, and two brothers who blew up a bridge when told it would bring them bad luck.

A newspaper in the northern city of Xian said a local family last month held a lavish two-day wedding for their son—who died three years ago—and a dead neighbor girl.

"The boy's parents wanted to find a bride for their dead son," the *Xian Evening News* said. "It turned out that a girl living in the same lane died, so the two families put urns containing the couple's ashes on a table and held a wedding ceremony that lasted for two days."

It said the dead boy's home was festooned with flowers, red paper, and colorful banners wishing the couple a long and happy marriage and urging them to "love one another until they grow old," the paper said.

"Lots of relatives were coming and going and many people gathered outside to talk," it said.

In central Sichuan province, two brothers were arrested for blowing up a bridge near their house after a geomancer advised them the structure was positioned wrong and would prevent them from ever getting rich.

"The geomancer said since the traffic and irrigation bridge was pointed at the middle hall of their home, the brothers would not make their fortune," the *Sichuan Daily News* reported.

"So on the morning of 31 March, the two brothers blew up the bridge with high explosives."

And in the coastal province of Fujian, scores of boat-dwellers refused to help a drowning girl because they feared "water spirits" would haunt them, the *Fujian Daily News* said.

"One afternoon in the middle of March, a girl slipped into the river," the paper said. "Another girl accompanying her was crying out for help. Several people in thirty or forty boats, all of them about 30 meters away, heard the screams but just looked at the girl and made no effort to rescue her as she sank beneath the surface."

When asked why they did not save the girl, one witness said: "We live on boats. Traditionally, we do not rescue people in the water because the spirits will haunt us."

Chinese officials have criticized the reemergence of superstition in many parts of rural China and last week urged people to trust in the Communist Party rather than "gods, witches, and wizards."

Document 113

Worshipers Are Cut Down to Size

South China Morning Post *(in English), 2 March 1986.*

BEIJING—More than one thousand worshipers, praying for good health and fortune, lit joss sticks and candles and prostrated themselves before an ancient gingko tree near Shanghai last week.

They believed the tree was the reincarnation of a goddess of mercy formerly worshipped in a dragon temple destroyed by Red Guards in the 1966-76 "cultural revolution."

A news report and photograph of Friday's folk-religion gathering appeared in the Shanghai newspaper *Xinmin Wanbao* (Xinmin Evening News), seen in Beijing yesterday.

A report in the national newspaper *Guangming Ribao* (Guangming Daily) carried a Communist Party condemnation of ancestor worship and other "superstitious and feudal practices" that have reappeared in Zhejiang Province, south of Shanghai.

The reports indicated Party concern that, thirty-seven years after the Communist revolution and the denunciation of religion as mere superstition, many Chinese still cling to beliefs handed down by their ancestors.

The countryside is punctuated by crude burial mounds, often covered with paper money, despite government directives to cremate the dead. Geomancy, folk cures, and even rain prayers remain popular.

The Shanghai report said the one-thousand-year-old gingko tree stands in Xinmong Township in Jinshan County, next to a school built on the site of the former dragon temple.

"Local people believe the goddess of mercy in the former temple could cure all illnesses," the newspaper report said. They lit firecrackers and made offerings before the hallowed tree.

In a report to Beijing, the Zhejiang Party Consolidation Guidance Committee blamed lax ideological work by local Party officials for the appearance of more than 500 illegal temples and monasteries in Wenling County, 256 of them erected since 1984.

"Some temples were put up right beside schools. Joss sticks and candles offered by worshippers burn all day long, disrupting children's study. Farmland has been occupied to build temples, spoiling plans for township construction," the report said.

"Witches, sorcerers, and other superstitious practitioners take advantage of people by swindling their money."

Local officials have begun educating the superstitious about "materialism," and more than four hundred of the illicit temples have been pulled down, the report said.

Such feudal and superstitious activities exceed the limits of religious freedom allowed under the Chinese constitution, the Party said.

"To build ancestral temples, establish family trees, and offer sacrifices to clan ancestors are feudal and patriarchal activities not permitted under the Socialist system," the paper said.

Provincial officials demanded an end to fortune telling, geomancy, praying for rain, and the exorcising of ghosts.

Document 114

Superstition Still Holds Sway among Cadres

Hong Kong Standard *(in English)*, 21 January 1988.

BEIJING — The Communist Party, purging members who break laws and cling to discredited radical policies, is confronting another problem in its ranks: superstition.

Letters to the Editor on Thursday in the *Workers' Daily* newspaper disclosed that one local Party leader participated in occult marriage rites for his dead sister, another threw a superstitious good-luck party for his young daughter, and a third invited monks to his home to mourn his dead father.

"How is it that Communist Party members still believe in superstition?" wrote Su Han and Yu Tian, residents of the Henan provincial city of Xin Xiang.

They explained about Hao Zhangyi, a Party leader in the city's Labor Department, whose father died last October.

"Hao complied with the superstitious ideas of his mother and uncle, like keeping the coffin at home for twenty-three days and erecting a mourning arch," the letter said. "He even called home monks to perform the death rites."

An editor's reply said the local Party disciplinary team had investigated the incident "and discovered that Comrade Hao only did the above things under pressure from his family." But it also said the Party "has strongly criticized the practice and people responsible."

Another letter, signed by "An Official of the Yangquan City General Store" in Shanxi Province, claimed the store's deputy Party Secretary Yu Zhanning conducted a wedding ceremony last November for his sister, who died in 1940.

The letter said Yu Zhanning was concerned that his sister could not be happy unless she had a mate, "so he found her a husband, someone who is also dead."

"The thing hardest to understand was that all the other leaders of the general store knew about these things but made no attempt to advise or dissuade Yu," the letter said. "Instead they even provided him with transport. In such circumstances people cannot help but ask, 'where are your Party principles?' "

An editor's reply said the Yangquan Party Disciplinary Committee investigated Yu Zhanning and found that the actual wedding rites were performed by his parents and brother.

"However, Yu, instead of stopping and opposing those activities, took no action and instead participated in them," the reply said. "For that he definitely is in the wrong."

It said that Yu Zhanning has gradually accepted his mistakes and he will be strictly supervised.

A third letter, signed by a worker at the Yuenan Coal Mine in Shanxi Province, disclosed that the mine's Party Secretary, Ying Heshang, threw a big birthday party for his five-year-old daughter last October 20 because of a local belief that it was good luck.

"He invited guests for the ceremony and even accepted gifts," the letter said. "The mine bus brought many leaders to his house."

The worker wrote that Ying Heshang "is a Party secretary but he believes in and propagates superstition. This is wrong."

Document 115

On Several Questions of Breaking Down Feudal Superstitions

By Ren Jiyu in Guangming Ribao, *Beijing, 2 May 1983; translated in FBIS 13 June 1983.*

Feudalism, which dominated China for several thousand years, must inevitably place superstitions in the service of its prerogatives and privileges. Feudalism was part of the superstructure of China's feudal society. To break down feudal superstitions, we must on the one hand rely on science, and on the other hand we must eliminate the social factors giving rise to superstitions. These two aspects should be included in the building of Socialism. With the development of science, people will have scientific minds, and superstitious and absurd ideas will lose their market. If social production is developed, people's livelihood is improved and people-to-people relations are established on the basis of mutual concern and mutual affection; there will no longer be the phenomenon of people oppressing people or people exploiting people in society, and this will contribute to the wiping out of superstitions.

There is no strict dividing line between superstition and religion. Some religious believers have made use of curing sickness and "exorcising demons" to rope in the masses and to capture followers. Some lawless religious believers have also taken advantage of their legal status to engage in numerous evil activities which are harmful to the State and the people, and some of them have already been punished by the people. Religious belief is politically protected by law, but in a world outlook, religious belief and superstition both belong to the category of idealism.

According to the stipulations of the constitution and relevant policies, people have the freedom to believe in religion. At the same time, they also have the freedom not to believe in religion. The Party constitution stipulates that Party members must guide their actions with Marxism-Leninism-Mao Zedong Thought. Adhering to the four basic principles is the common demand on each and every citizen. Feudal superstitions are what each and every Chinese person should oppose. Lawbreakers who take advantage of superstitions to swindle money out of and injure people should be punished according to law. This is both natural and right. As for the Party members and State cadres, since they have taken Marxism-Leninism-Mao Zedong Thought as their guiding ideology, they cannot at the same time lead the masses to look for a "savior" in the "kingdom of heaven." Since they have become public servants of the people, they must wholeheartedly rely on and believe in the masses, and should not at crucial moments, such as when combating drought and providing disaster relief or controlling flooding and dealing with an emergency, pray for blessing and protection from gods and buddhas. This is also both natural and right. Our Party constitution has been adopted and has become effective. Marxism-Leninism-Mao Zedong Thought embodies atheism and opposes theism. The reason feudal superstitions are rampant and the broad masses of young people and working people are hoodwinked by gods and spirits in certain localities is often the ineffective leadership of our Party cadres. In any locality where religious activity is not normal, the reason is also often related to the fact that certain of our Party members and cadres have not adhered to Marxism-Leninism-Mao Zedong Thought and cannot draw a clear line of distinction between a world outlook and religious idealism, and have adopted the attitude of making concessions and exercising forbearance instead of struggling against the phenomenon of taking advantage of religion to carry out illegal activities.

We Marxists must always remember two points: 1. Marxists are atheists, who not only oppose feudal superstitions, but also cannot endorse the world outlook of religious idealism. There has never been the least ambiguity about this point; and 2. Marxists must respect freedom of religious belief, show sympathy for those who believe in religion, form a united front with patriotic personages of the religious circles in the patriotic work of building Socialism, and cooperate with them on a long-term basis. There also has never been the least ambiguity about this point. It will be wrong if we catch sight of only one of these two points, because in this way we will run theoretically counter to the principle of historical materialism, and this will be detrimental to the building of Socialist modernization in actual life.

Document 116

Do Away with Feudal Superstitions

NCNA, 28 December 1982. Translated in FE 6235, 18 January 1983, and reprinted in China Study Project Documentation No. 11, June 1983, pp. 44-47 (excerpts).

In recent years, there has been a tendency for feudal superstitious activities to regain ground in our rural areas and outlying regions. We should pay great attention to the various feudal superstitious activities, which are harmful to our production and construction and to the people's physical and mental health, polluting the general mood of society and affecting our stability and unity. In the course of building Socialist spiritual civilization, cadres at all levels and CCP and CYL members should boldly and assuredly propagate among the people dialectical materialism, historical materialism (including atheism), Communist ideology, and new morality and practices. They should patiently and carefully do ideological work, do away with feudal superstitions, and protect the people's interests.

In their letters to us, many readers ask us to explain what feudal superstitious activities are, our Party and government policies toward them, and the relationship between doing away with feudal superstitions and implementing the policy of freedom of religious belief. After asking the opinion of the departments concerned, we hereby give the following explanation, in the form of questions and answers, for your reference.

What Are Feudal Superstitious Activities?

So-called feudal superstitious activities primarily denote unscientific, absurd activities, such as begging for the advent of gods or immortals, practicing planchette writing or divination, expelling ghosts in order to cure sickness, praying for rain and for an end to natural disasters, practicing physiognomy and other fortune-telling tricks, and practicing geomancy. These activities are carried out by sorcerers, sorceresses, physiognomists, fortune tellers, or geomancers. They take every opportunity to spread fallacies to deceive people and defraud them of money or other property, they are harmful to our production and construction, to social order, and to the people's physical and mental health. These feudal superstitious activities have a very long history in our country. In the feudal, semifeudal, and semicolonial society, the reactionary ruling class did its utmost to support and use these activities to deceive the people, in order to consolidate its reactionary rule and protect class interests. In our Socialist society, these activities usually combine closely with remaining feudal ideas and feudal clannish activities to undermine the social order and poison the people's thinking.

Moreover, many of our people, particularly those in rural and pastoral areas, beg gods or practice divination for offspring or for an end to distress or sickness because they lack scientific knowledge and adhere to longstanding, bad old habits. Such superstitious activities also play a negative role regarding our country's production, construction, and social order. However, their situation is quite complex, and in certain localities they are quite popular. We should deal with them specifically, according to specific situations.

What Is the Policy of the Party and State Regarding Feudal Superstitious Activities?

The Party and State always oppose feudal superstitious activities, firmly ban all feudal and superstitious organizations, and strike at feudal superstitious activities, which harm the national interests and people's lives and property. Article 165 of the "Criminal Law of the PRC" stipulates: "Sorcerers and witches who perform superstitious acts for the purpose of spreading rumors or swindling people out of money and property will be sentenced to imprisonment for not more than two years, detention, or surveillance. In grave cases, the offender will be sentenced to imprisonment for not less than two and not more than seven years." Article 99 stipulates: "Those organizing and using feudal superstitious beliefs, superstitious sects, and secret societies to carry our counterrevolutionary activities will be sentenced to imprisonment of not less than five years. In less serious cases, they will be sentenced to imprisonment, detention, surveillance, or deprivation of political rights for not more than five years." Therefore, all outlawed, reactionary, superstitious sects and secret societies, and sorcerers, witches, and so forth are forbidden to resume activities. Those who spread fallacies to deceive people, swindle people out of their money, or otherwise harm them will be strictly suppressed and punished according to the law.

Those who practice physiognomy, fortune telling, and geomancy as an occupation will first be educated and admonished, and helped to work, earn their own living, and stop cheating people with their superstitious activities. If education and admonition prove ineffective, they will be banned according to the law.

Owing to social, cultural, and other causes, superstitious beliefs remain to varying degrees in the minds of a considerable portion of the masses. This should be solved mainly by popularization of scientific and general knowledge, and patient ideological education systematically to increase their knowledge and consciousness. As to the people who have been fooled and have participated in feudal superstitious activities, we must draw a strict distinction between them and the sorcerers and witches spreading fallacies to deceive people, harm them, and swindle them out of money, and we must not treat them indiscriminately in the same way. . . .

What Are Undesirable Feudal Customs?

Undesirable feudal customs are old customs and habits among the people, grown out of traditional feudal concepts, which to a very large extent have retained elements of feudal superstition. For example, when someone dies, survivors dress themselves in hemp, wave flags to call back the spirit of the dead, and burn paper money, paper figures, and paper horses; in marriage, people ask fortune tellers to weigh the match, based on the "eight characters"; and [people follow] the practices of greeting the gods, offering sacrifices to ghosts, driving out evil spirits, and so forth in observing traditional festivals such as the Spring Festival, Qingming, the Dragon Boat Festival, Zhongyuan (the fifteenth day of the seventh lunar month), and so forth. These undesirable feudal customs waste the people's financial and material resources, poison the social atmosphere, and are detrimental to the building of Socialist spiritual civilization. . . .

How Should We Deal with Those Dealing in Superstitious Items, and State or Collective Enterprises, Units, and Individuals Making Things Convenient for Feudal and Superstitious Activities?

It must be reiterated: No state or collective enterprise, institution, or unit (including rural commune, brigade, and team, as well as residents' organization in an urban neighborhood), or individual without authorization, is allowed to produce, sell, or sell on a commission basis, such superstitious items as paper money, Daoist magic figures, and bamboo slips for divination, or facilitate feudal and superstitious activities, such as by providing places, transport, and materials for such activities or making propaganda for them. Violators must be investigated and severely dealt with according to the seriousness and consequences of their individual cases. Cadres and party and CYL members must not participate in, or support, such activities, and violators must be severely dealt with according to government, Party, or CYL discipline and, in some cases, must also be punished according to the law. . . .

As for religious items specially needed for religious activities, government-appointed units should produce such items, according to their prescribed variety and quantity, and sell them to those prescribed by relevant regulations. With approval by competent authorities, temples, Daoist temples, and churches may also sell a certain quantity of religious items and tracts. Supervision and control over the units dealing in such items must be strengthened, and violators of policies and regulations must be educated and checked.

Will Doing Away with Feudal Superstitions Affect Implementation of the Policy of the Freedom of Religious Belief?

Religious belief is different from feudal superstition, and our Party and State have always adopted different policies toward them. In religion, we respect the right of the people of all nationalities to enjoy freedom of religious belief [and to] protect legitimate religious activities, and have proclaimed this a long-term policy. This is explicitly stipulated in Article 36 of the "Constitution of the PRC" and Article 147 of the "Criminal law of the PRC." Some people regard feudal and superstitious activities and legitimate religious activities as the same thing, thinking that all such activities belong to the realm of "freedom of religious belief." This is entirely mistaken.

The Party and the State have adopted the policy of freedom of religious belief because religion is a longstanding, complicated matter, concerning millions of people of various nationalities. Only by firmly implementing the policy of freedom of religious belief will it be conducive to the stability of the country and the unity of the nation; only thus will it be able to fully arouse the enthusiasm of the religious masses so that they will work hard together with all the other people of the country to build a modern, powerful Socialist state with a high degree of civilization and democracy.

Document 117

Marxism Is the Best Way To Cure Feudal Superstition

By Ren Jiyu, in China Daily *(in English), 6 July 1983.*

We must differentiate between religion and feudal superstition. Religious activities, such as those of Buddhism, Islam, Christianity, and Daoism are legal. Their representatives take part in our government.

Feudal superstition is different, and such activities as dancing in a trance, witchcraft, and fortune telling are illegal. Our policy is to protect freedom of religious belief, but not feudal superstition.

But from the world-outlook point of view, both religion and feudal superstition are inimical to Socialism; they hinder the spread of Marxism-Leninism. For instance, whom should we rely upon to build Socialism? Marxism tells us that we should rely on the laboring people, or on workers, peasants, and intellectuals.

Both religion and superstition say that if you want to get anything done, you should rely not on people, but on God. One of the basic differences between religion-superstition and Marxism is that the former seeks the protection of God or some supernatural power, while the latter relies on our own force to transform the world.

Our Socialist system has just been established; it is far from perfect, and some questions, such as employment, education, love, and marriage among young people, are not so easy to answer in a short time. We are also likely to commit mistakes in our work. Some people thus meeting with setbacks tend to seek solace in religion.

Some people point out that in Western countries some famous and well-educated scientists also believe in God. How can this be explained?

Our opinion is that a scientist is also a man, a member of the society. When he is working in his laboratory, he is a scientist. But when he leaves his laboratory, he is a member of society.

As an ordinary member of society, he will meet with social problems, and some of those problems cannot be solved by scientific knowledge alone. And scientists, like other members of the society, many turn to religion for consolation.

In recent years, there is a phenomenon worthy of our attention. Some Western scholars say that Chinese civilization and morality are better than their own. Last summer such scholars held a symposium on Zhu Xi, a philosopher of the Song dynasty (960-1279 AD). Taking part were scholars from Canada, the United States, Japan, Hongkong, and our province of Taiwan. Some of the conferees raised Zhu Xi to a very high plane.

One of the reasons some Westerners want to learn from us is that they cannot solve some of their own social problems, such as unemployment, juvenile crime, divorce, and old age. They turn to the Orient for some panacea.

Feudal Leftovers

China was ruled for a long time by the feudal system. Many feudal ideas and outdated habits still exist. We did not experience capitalism. We jumped into Socialism from semifeudalism-semicolonialism. We gained time, but on the other hand we entered Socialism with the heavy burden of feudalism.

Because of the prolonged existence of the feudal patriarchal clan system, democracy is not fully developed. Because we never passed through the stage of capitalism, some of us tend to regard feudalist ideas as Socialist ones. For instance, feudal family relationships can easily be transferred intact into a Socialist society like ours.

The basic reason why some of our young or weak-willed people succumb to the bourgeois way of life is that they lack Communist education. Some comrades hope to restore some of our old traditions to combat unhealthy foreign influences. That is pure wishful thinking.

We should analyze our traditions carefully. Some of them are good, others are bad. For instance, the patriarchal system, the small-scale peasant ideology, conservatism, and empiricism are left over from the small-scale peasant economy. Social development will not allow us to go back to a former historical stage.

If feudalism could stop capitalism, then capitalism would not be born. If Socialism is not superior to capitalism, then it will be impossible to build Communism. If you try to fight capitalism with feudalism, you are bound to fail. The only resistance against bourgeois decadence is a firm Communist world outlook.

[Ren Jiyu is the former director of the Institute of World Religions.]

Document 118

Religion Is Not Superstition

Letter to the Editor of China Daily *(in English), by Bishop K.H. Ting, President of the China Christian Council, in* China Daily, *14 July 1983.*

Editor:

May I express my disappointment at the publication by such an esteemed paper as the *China Daily* of the article "Marxism Is the Best Way to Cure Feudal Superstition," 6 July, which actually devotes much of its space to misrepresenting religion? It starts off rightly by saying that we must differentiate between religion and feudal superstition, but does not go on to point out the difference, not in a scientific way, anyway. Instead, in the main body of the article, the two are lumped together as one and the same evil to be cured. Once the two nouns are even hyphenated.

This article asserts sweepingly that people, by virtue of a belief in God, are necessarily opposed to reliance for the building of Socialism on workers, peasants, and intellectuals and are inimical to Socialism. That is making a political case of a religious conviction. Your readers are either likely to be either religious themselves or to have religious friends and hence will feel offended by the caricature. The article gives a wrong impression of how religions are regarded in the People's Republic of China and provides a theoretical support for acts alienating our religious people. Religious believers can be good Chinese citizens, too. The long-standing policy in our country is exactly to ensure religious freedom so as to unite believers as well as nonbelievers in the common task of Socialist upbuilding.

K.H. TING
Nanjing, Jiangsu

Document 119

Carry Out the Policy of Freedom of Belief and Oppose Feudal Superstitious Activities

By Ya Hanzhang in Guangming Ribao, *20 April 1981. Translated in China Study Project* Bulletin *No. 16, July 1981, pp. 21-23 (excerpts).*

When we talk about feudal superstition, we usually mean telling fortunes by using eight diagrams, feeling a person's bones and looking at his appearance to forecast his future, practicing geomancy, reading horoscopes in search of an elixir of life, exorcising spirits to cure illnesses, planchette writing, offering sacrifices to gods, beseeching gods to bestow children on people, offering prayers to gods to ward off calamities and to ask for rain, and so on. These are dregs handed down from the old society in our country. After nationwide Liberation, much work was done to eliminate them, and they basically no longer occupy any important position in the people's spiritual lives. However, during the ten calamitous years, these dregs floated to the surface again. It is noteworthy that today, after the downfall of the "gang of four," and when the focus of the work of the whole Party has been shifted to the modernization program, the various kinds of feudal superstitions are still spreading through the country. They not only corrode the ideology of the people, but also sabotage production, disrupt social order, and even endanger people's lives. Therefore, if we do not struggle against feudal superstitious activities, they will directly affect the four modernizations.

Since the smashing of the "gang of four," various kinds of feudal superstitious activities have been spreading unchecked. There are various reasons for this. An important one is that many cadres still cannot distinguish the difference between religion and feudal superstition. They think that anything involving the worship of spirits and gods is religion. Thus, they think, incorrectly, that the policy of freedom of belief should apply to feudal superstition and therefore allow the practice of feudal superstitious activities. Some cadres turn a blind eye to these activities and do not attempt to stop them. There are a small number of cadres who even speak up for feudal superstition, saying: "We should not get involved with the masses' practice of feudal superstition because the masses have the right to freedom of belief." "Policies for man have been gradually implemented. Why can we not implement policies for idols?" There are many similar sayings.

We must first make it clear that religion and feudal superstition are apparently two different things. What is feudal superstition? It is what was mentioned at the beginning of this article. They exist in China and they exist in foreign countries, too. A recent news report said that in capitalist countries where science is highly developed there are people who tell fortunes by computer. This may be termed superstitious activities carried out with the aid of modern technology. . . . Similarly, religion exists in China as well as in foreign countries.

A religion (the three major world religions in particular) has a complete and systematic religious philosophy and religious doctrine. It has well-organized religious organizations, religious bodies, religious systems, religious rites, and religious activities.

Religion differs from feudal superstition in many aspects, but the most fundamental one is: Religion is a way of viewing the world, while feudal superstition is a means by which some people practice fraud.

When we say that religion is a way of viewing the world, we mean that it has a concept about the creation of the world (including the creation of mankind itself). It says that everything in the world has been created, arranged, decided, and controlled by God (or Allah or the Creator). If people desire happiness, the only way to achieve this is to believe in God and to restrain their words and deeds strictly according to religious doctrines and canons in order to gain eternal happiness in the life to come. This world outlook is, of course, wrong, but pious religious believers consider it correct.

Feudal superstition also talks about believing in spirits, gods, and the mandate of heaven, but its aim in mentioning these is to make people believe in order to cheat others out of their money and possessions. Feudal superstition only answers a few difficult problems (as in planchette writing, fortune telling, and so on) or grants things that are requested (such as holy water, holy medicine, children, and so on) or relieves the temporary sufferings of the sick people (as in exorcising spirits to cure illnesses) or predicts your good or bad future, destiny and luck in a certain year (as in fortune telling). Therefore, we say that feudal superstition is not a world outlook but an extremely foolish and ignorant activity and an indecent means by which professionals in feudal superstition cheat others out of their money and possessions so that they can live parasitic lives. These activities are in essence a disguised form of man exploiting man, and as incompatible with the Socialist system as water is with fire. Therefore, the Party and the State have all along adopted different policies for religion and feudal superstition.

After nationwide Liberation, the Party and State adopted a policy of banning feudal superstition and adopted the policy of educating and reforming professionals in feudal superstition.

Feudal superstition has a history of over several thousand years in our country and a deep social influence in society. So it is not easy to wipe out. We must be ideologically prepared to carry out a protracted struggle against feudal superstition.

In struggling against feudal superstition, besides exposing the absurdity and fraudulent nature of feudal superstitious activities and banning professionals in feudal superstition, we must conduct atheist education among the masses and publicize scientific knowledge.

The struggle against feudal superstition is not isolated, either. It should be coordinated with various kinds of work. For example, places where witches and wizards are most active are usually places where there are few doctors and not enough medicine. If we make an effort to develop public health in these places, the activities of the witches and wizards will certainly find fewer adherents. It should also be pointed out that the spreading of feudal superstitious activities is also related directly with the slackening of ideological and political education among the masses, especially among the young in some places. Therefore, in places where feudal superstitious activities are common, the Party leadership there should pay special attention to strengthening ideological and political work and earnestly grasp the struggle against feudal superstition.

Document 120

Need To Strengthen Rural Political Work Is Urgent

By Zhang Guoqiang, Hebei, Hengshui Ribao; *reprinted in* Xin Shiqi *(New Era) No. 6, June 1981. Translated in FBIS No 211, 1981, pp. 33-34.*

I have learned through a news-coverage trip that at present the political work in the countryside is in a run-down condition, resulting in failure to convey promptly the Party's line, principles, and policies on agriculture to the commune members. During the past year, in some communes no congress of members has been held, nor have the commune members been organized by the Party organizations of some brigades and production teams to study the documents of the Party Central Committee and their superior Party committees. This failure to keep cadres and commune members informed of the Party's current agricultural policy has adversely affected the development of rural work and agricultural production. For example, the wired broadcasting system formerly welcomed by commune members is now in bad shape, with its poles fallen to the ground, the lines disrupted, and the loudspeakers silent. The transmission lines between the county and its communes and between the commune and its brigades have been disconnected. The formerly popular blackboard (wall) bulletins produced by brigades and production teams have disappeared.

The failure to strengthen the political work has given rise to unhealthy trends and evil beliefs. In many places, fortune tellers, astrologers, and other types of feudal superstition have become active. Theft, burglaries, and gambling have become common in some brigades and production teams. There was a male commune member in a brigade in Henghsui County who had searched for doctors to cure the pain in his abdomen for years without success. One day, when he heard a witch spread the word that she could cure his disease, he immediately sent a car to bring her from Henghsui Township to his home, and then he was told to burn incense and offer sacrifices in her presence. Later, she treated a youth plagued by headache in the same village in the same way. The witch nonsensically told the youth that his headache was caused by a fallen tree located near an old temple east of Bao Village that had hurt a certain deity, and that his headache would go away if he replanted a tree there and offered five white sheep as sacrifices at the temple. The youth did just what he was told. In this manner the woman fortune teller deceived the people for several days until she had satisfied her appetite with enough food and drink and cheated enough money out of the villagers' pockets; then she disappeared, leaving her patients just as sick as before her arrival.

The prevalence of such unhealthy trends and evil beliefs reminds us of the urgent need to strengthen our current political work. To this end, cadres and commune members must be organized to study the documents issued by the Party, in order to unify their thinking behind the Party's line, principles, and policies. Meanwhile, all the propaganda media must be fully mobilized and put to good use. This propaganda and education work must be conducted in a lively and realistic manner. Rural grass-roots Party organizations must boldly assume responsibility and take effective measures to deal blows to and prevent the growth of feudal superstitious activities and other unhealthy trends in an effort to insure the thorough implementation of the Party's line, principles, and policies.

Document 121

Local Officials' Superstitious Behavior Criticized

Nanfang Ribao, *Guangzhou, 29 March 1986. Reprinted in FBIS, 28 August 1986, pp. 64-65.*

Wu Quan County standing-committee vice-chairman Liang Rurong and others participated in such a large-scale superstitious feudal activity, the so-called ancestral sacrifice, that it was shocking. Although this was a rare, isolated appearance, its effects are still especially abominable, so it is a rare, negative example.

Such traditions of the masses as the Qingming grave sweeping, the commemoration of ancestors, and the encouragement of descendants are humanly sensible and beyond reproach. But the graveside offering known as "southern snake goes to sea" is completely beyond the limits of normal activity, and thus is typical of feudal superstitious behavior. It mobilized over twelve thousand participants, dispatched over 140 motor vehicles, slaughtered over 160 pigs, and made a big noisy hubbub. It both wasted human, material and financial resources, adversely affecting production, and incited a feudal, clannish mood among the masses, endangering social order. As a Communist Party member and leading cadre, Liang Rurong should have prevailed upon the masses and prevented this. The masses are reasonable, requiring only that local Party members, particularly those who are leading cadres, reason with them and explain the danger. This kind of erroneous, feudal, clannish, and superstitious activity is completely avoidable.

But how did Liang Rurong and the others handle it? They competed to take the lead in abandoning all their Party learning, employed public vehicles to proceed to the cemetery personally, participated in the activity, led the rites, gave speeches, and felt honored rather than ashamed! At present we must take responsibility for the Party's style of work from top to bottom and strengthen the building of the Two Civilizations. What Liang Rurong and the others did runs counter to this. It seriously undermines the Party's style, blackens the Party's image, and pollutes the social atmosphere. With respect to Liang Rurong and the others, rectification is indispensable.

So, why did Liang Rurong and the others do this? Did they think that participation in this large-scale feudal and clannish activity would bring honor to their ancestors? Was the use of official vehicles a display of "government authority"? This reveals precisely their erroneous thinking. It is the appropriate outcome of the evil legacy of going in for ostentation, an erroneous ideological work-style, and feudal ideology. This shows how the slackening of the transformation of one's worldview, the failure to check the climate, circumstances, and erroneous ideology, can lead to serious violations and errors.

In Party rectification, the Central Committee has told us again and again that under the new circumstances and in the new social environment the decadent ideology of capitalism and feudalism will make inroads among us to such an extent that some previously vanished oddities will return. The matter of the participation of Liang Rurong in the ancestral sacrifice should sound the alarm once more. Every one of our comrades must not be light-hearted about the invasion of capitalist and feudal ideology but must strengthen ideological transformation, conscientiously rectify the Party's style, and struggle resolutely against all manner of evil winds and noxious influences.

Document 122

Movie Magic Shakes Superstition

China Daily *(in English), 30 January 1986.*

It happened one night in Shandong Province on China's east coast. A movie theater in rural Sishui County was showing *The Tricks of Witch Doctors*—and one was in the audience.

When the documentary ended and the lights came on, an old man believed by many locals to be a wizard stood up and addressed the audience.

"What the film shows is true," he said. "Give up your superstitions and I won't fool you again."

Two thousand kilometers to the southwest, in Sichuan Province, the film attracted another large audience. The village was Hongguang, in Anxian County, where earlier in the year forty-one people who could not swim drowned after a local wizard had told them to jump into a pond. Said a local film distributor: "If only the film had been shown earlier . . ."

In China, only one in five people has access to a television set, and film remains a central medium of mass communication. Sometimes the information films convey—particularly science and education films—can change lives. Nearly thirteen hundred copies of *The Tricks of Witch Doctors* have been sold.

Nearly half of China's science and educational films are made by the Beijing Science and Educational Film Studio. It produced fifty-three movies last year, the most in its twenty-five-year history.

Zhang Qing, deputy director of the studio, said the increased production "is in response to the rapid increase in demand."

"The need is particularly urgent in rural areas," she said. "More and more peasants have come to realize that they can learn from films how to develop agriculture in a scientific way.

"Since many peasants are still illiterate, showing films can be a shortcut to teaching them science and technology."

For example, she said, peasants in many districts had learned how to make their drinking water sanitary from the film *Simply Built System of Running Water in the Countryside*, and *Pig-Raising Technology* had encouraged peasants throughout China to raise pigs with leaner meat.

Document 123

How To Curb Superstitious Activities

An interview with a "responsible person" of the Ministry of Public Security, in Nongmin Ribao, *Beijing, 17 April 1987. Translated in FE 8554, 29 April 1987, and reprinted in China Study Project* Journal *2:3, p. 46, December 1987 (excerpts).*

Q. How should we deal with superstitious and feudal activities?

A. Curbing feudal and superstitious activities is a protracted and arduous task.

1. We must strengthen the building of Socialist spiritual civilization; vigorously spread scientific and cultural knowledge; extensively conduct propaganda and education on the legal system; actively carry out activities to transform social traditions; advocate civilized, healthy, and scientific lifestyles; and resist the growth and spread of feudal and superstitious activities.

2. We must draw a demarcation line between feudal and superstitious activities and normal religious activities. According to stipulations in China's Constitution, citizens have freedom of religious beliefs. In China, Buddhism, Daoism, Islam, Catholicism, and Christianity are protected by the State's religious policy. Religious believers are allowed to conduct religious activities in religious places. However, all reactionary secret societies and witches and sorcerers are banned and prohibited from resuming their activities.

3. As for those who take fortune telling and the practice of geomancy as their profession, it is necessary to educate, advise, and help them make a living through their own labor and ask them not to engage in such feudal and deceitful activities anymore.

4. It is necessary to select some typical cases of people taking advantage of superstitions in order to carry out illegal and criminal activities, and to expose their fraudulent nature and harmfulness in order to increase the ability of the masses conscientiously to resist feudal and superstitious activities.

5. As for those who commit such crimes as swindling others out of money and property, raping women, and cruelly injuring or killing others by taking advantage of superstitions, it is necessary to punish them severely in accordance with the law of our country.

Section II

Atheism and Religion

Introduction

Atheism is a frequent subject for newspaper stories, editorials, and theoretical and historical studies in Chinese periodicals. The theory and practice of atheism is taught in the schools and in books and journals intended for young people, while the China Atheists' Association promotes research, writing, and discussion meetings. Examples of recent publications are a 365-page book, *Zhongguo wushenlun shigang* (Outline of the History of Atheism in China), published in 1982, which traces the history of atheistic theory and practice back to the Zhou dynasty, and Ya Hanzhang's *Wushenlun he zongjiao wenti* (Questions of Religion and Atheism), first published in 1964 and republished in 1979.

Merely prohibiting feudal superstitious activities is not enough. "We must educate the masses and especially the peasants on historical and dialectical materialism, and . . . the ideas of atheism. Developing propaganda education on atheism and breaking feudalist superstitious ideas are important issues in Socialist spiritual civilization."

Education on atheism "is social education carried out among the masses through various kinds of propaganda and public opinion under the Party's leadership and through the system of Party, political, industrial and public organs, and women's federations, for the purposes of guiding the masses . . . to create material and spiritual civilization of a high caliber without placing hopes on deities and demons."

It is not true, as some people think, that simply breaking with superstition, giving up belief in gods and ghosts, and understanding dialectical and historical materialism are sufficient. Beyond that, "atheist propaganda and opposition to feudal superstition is [an essential] task," not just the task of theoreticians, thinkers, and propaganda departments, but "something that should concern the whole of society."

However, Party members must take the lead in promoting atheism. "Every CCP member must be a confirmed Marxist and a materialist atheist. He must resolutely conduct a lifelong struggle to build Socialism and realize Communism." While they must support the people's right to believe or not to believe in religion, CCP members "are at all times responsible for adopting various methods to propagate materialism and atheism."

411

Document 124

Be Good at Educating the Masses on Atheism

By Shi Yousin, in Hongqi *(Red Flag), 16 January 1987.*
Translated in FE 8491, 13 February 1987 and reprinted in China
Study Project Journal *2:2, August 1987, pp. 32-34.*

On the occasion of the New Year Spring Festival, we should all pay greater attention to the work of removing superstition and changing the customs and habits of the times. Previously it was absolutely necessary for us to follow the law in prohibiting the resurgence of feudalist and super-stitious organizations and the restorationist activities of patriarchal forces, as well as to punish those illegal elements guilty of fanning superstitious sentiments and thereby cheating other people out of their money and harm-ing people. But, in the long-term view, what has been done so far has not been sufficient. We must educate the masses and especially the peasants on historical materialism and dialectical materialism, and be particularly good at teaching propaganda on the ideas of atheism.

Developing propaganda education on atheism and breaking feudalist and superstitious ideas are important issues in Socialist spiritual civilization. Socialist spiritual civilization is scientific and progressive; it cannot rest on a foundation of ignorance and backwardness. The "decision of the CCP Central Committee on the guidelines for the establishment of a Socialist spiritual civilization" has pointed out clearly: "In the vast urban and rural areas, it is necessary actively to change the prevailing habits and customs, advocate a civilized, healthy, and scientific life-style, and overcome the ignorant and backward ways that still exist in their customs and habits. All undesirable practices in marriage ceremonies and burial services must be reformed and feudalism and superstition be demolished.

The ignorant and backward practices in social customs and habits, such as performing Buddhist or Daoist rites to save the souls of the dead, finding out if the "eight characters" of the male and female suit each other in becoming husband and wife, worshiping the sky and earth, listening to the words of fortune telling, seeking advice from the deities, believing in Feng-Shui and Yin-Yang doctrines, and so on, are all related directly or indirectly to the concepts of theocracy that are embedded deeply in the minds of the people by the old society. All superstitious activities may be traced to the spreading of ideas and concepts about the existence of demons and deities. In certain localities, illegal elements can stir up the masses to contribute funds for superstitious activities and thousands upon thousands of people will not begrudge traveling long distances to far-off places in order to pay homage to the deities, while heresies can easily spread rumors of common people becoming gods and deities overnight. Witches and sorcerers, relying on their sermons and talking about gods and demons, can make a comfortable living by deceiving people. All this is because in the minds of the people there exists forever a supernatural being, a deity who is above all.

It can thus be seen that if we do not pay great attention to propagating atheism among the masses and do not help people get rid of the concepts of gods and deities and the bondage of superstitious ideas, then not only will superstitious activities not be suppressed and the development of a spiritual civilization be impeded, but also normal production, life, and social order will be hampered.

Some people may think that since we are committed to the policy of freedom in religious beliefs, and must employ common ideas to mobilize and unite people of various races, including the believers in religion, then we should not spread propaganda for atheism among the masses. Some other people may contend that carrying out this type of propaganda education inevitably will hamper the enforcement of the policy of religious freedom and impede the union with the believers in religion. These views are incorrect. This is because the education on atheism mentioned here is a sort of ideological-political work and is social education carried out among the masses through various kinds of propaganda and public opinion under the Party's leadership and through the system of Party, political, industrial, and public organs and women's federations, for the purposes of guiding the masses to study science and not superstition and to depend on the Party's leadership and the masses' own strength to create material and spiritual civilization of a high caliber without placing hopes on deities and demons.

We have no intention of preaching atheism in religious places or debating with the religious people on whether deities exist, or to interfere with normal religious activities, or to force religious people to give up their beliefs. This kind of education demands that superstitious activities must be differentiated from normal religious activities and certainly cannot mistake religious activities which are permitted by policy and laws for superstitious activities to be criticized and opposed. Naturally, we cannot mistake superstitious activities for normal religious activities and duly protect them. This kind of education does not hamper, but is beneficial to, correct enforcement of the policy of religious freedom and to strengthening political union with those who hold religious beliefs.

In carrying out propaganda and education on atheism we cannot repeat the former erroneous method of "opening wide the road of great criticism." Nor can we hope to achieve great results through calling large report meetings or opening classes to air certain philosophical principles. Rather, we must depend on finding ways and means such as those which the people can readily accept for their guidance. According to the experiences gained in certain localities, the following measures may be advocated.

First, uniting with policy education through changes in propagating and enforcing the Party's guidelines and policies and helping the masses to give up their superstitious ideas. Peasants in some localities, when they are well off, go to temples to worship deities, thanking them for their blessings. When they are not yet well off they go to temples just the same to worship the gods, seeking their blessings in order to bring about a change in their fortunes. This situation illustrates well the need to break superstitious habits through policy propagation and to implement policy through the demolition of superstition. Our Party members and cadres should become the lecturers and propagandists in this respect, just as Comrade Mao Zedong did when he led the peasants' movement, personally convincing the peasants to rely on agricultural unions and not on gods, talking with feeling and reason and making people glad to accept and believe.

Second, uniting with scientific and general education. When illegal elements fan superstition, deceive people, and cheat them out of their money, they invariably take advantage of the weak points of those in the masses who have no culture and do not understand science. A newspaper reported a case in which a witch undertook to "drive out the demons and heal the malady of a sick person." She pretended to have caught the soul of the demon responsible for causing the illness and allegedly placed it inside a paper doll prepared beforehand. She then thrust a knife into the paper doll, which immediately displayed blood stains. In reality, the paper doll had been painted with a certain Chinese herb which, upon contact with the knife — which had been painted with a salty ingredient — caused a chemical reaction producing stains the color of blood. As regards illegal elements of this kind, we should not only deal with them in accordance with the law but also make known to people the trickery involved. By so doing, the circle of people believing in ghosts and demons will shrink, while the number of people who believe in science and like to study science will increase.

Third, uniting with and enriching the cultural and recreational life of the masses. In many localities, there is a sizable shortage of various kinds of cultural facilities such as cultural halls, libraries, places of entertainment, and sports or recreational grounds; and cultural and recreational life of a popular nature is exceedingly rare. This has caused a number of youths, who lack the necessary spiritual interests, to turn to playing fortune-telling games or seeking advice from deities to find satisfaction and fun from feudalist practices of this kind. They have even gone to churches and temples to quench their thirst for knowledge of the unknown. This will require our Party and political organs to pay close attention to the building of a spiritual civilization and to perform earnestly certain deeds which can help to break superstition and to change customs and habits.

Last, uniting with Party style on rectification and concern for the illness of the masses. It has been found that in places where superstition has been running amok for a long time and has successfully resisted suppression, it is solely related to the existence of improper Party styles. Often, because cadres in localities have waywardly used their power to seek private gains and nobody cares for the people's sufferings and illnesses, and because a situation of this kind has persisted for a long time, and [because of] the people's fear that there is no human remedy for their sufferings, no place of refuge against the disasters, and nothing to rely on in the event of natural or man-made disasters, people have been forced to turn to the gods for help. Or, there may be certain grassroots-level Party members and cadres who take the lead in believing in demons and gods, even going to the extent of forming superstitious cliques in order to make private gains. It is true that there have been few instances of this kind, but their adverse effects have already been numerous and great.

Document 125

Persistently Carry Out Propaganda about Atheism

By Gong Xi and Yi Zi in Liaoning Ribao, *17 February 1982. Translated in FE 6973, 3 September 1982, and reprinted in China Study Project* Documentation *No. 8, May 1982, pp. 41-42.*

"We must tirelessly carry out atheist propaganda and struggle." Lenin said this more than sixty years ago during a discussion of what a magazine's task should be. Even today this phrase, particularly the word "tirelessly," merits serious attention.

When people in our country lacked a relatively systematic understanding of dialectical materialism and historical materialism, they had a simple belief that materialism was no more than an absence of belief in either spirits or ghosts. In fact, such an understanding was expressed by many comrades who wanted to join the Party. They insisted that they had made a clean break with feudal superstition and were, therefore, believers in Marxism-Leninism. While such an understanding is not particularly profound it does express a basic knowledge of materialism. And even today it should never be thought that such a basic understanding is no longer essential. It is, of course, very important to the task of carrying out materialist propaganda that we should be able to solve the problem of both idealist work guidance and subjectivist methods of thinking and work. Atheist propaganda and opposition to feudal superstition is, however, a task that should not be overlooked. The fact is that once propaganda in atheism is relaxed, feudal superstitious activities may again rear their head and begin to pollute and damage the overall social atmosphere.

Propaganda in atheism did not originate with the Communist Party. Everyone is familiar with Xi Menbao, Fan Zhen, and other champions of atheism in Chinese history. However, it was our Communist Party that first wrote atheism on its banner and first made unremitting efforts to promote it, converting atheism into the leading ideology in society. Therefore, the propagation of atheism is not merely a matter for thinkers and theoreticians, nor is it merely a matter for propaganda departments or philosophical circles; it is something that should concern the whole of society. It is obviously a mistake to lump all forms of feudal superstition together in the category of class struggle and try to solve the problem in a hurried and violent fashion. This does not mean, however, that we can treat the matter lightly. As far as both the needs of the struggle on the ideological front line and spiritual and material construction are concerned, propaganda in atheism and opposition to feudal superstition are matters of major importance that cannot be ignored.

Some comrades believe that once science and culture have been developed and once the level of production has been raised, superstitious activities will fade away of their own accord. There is certainly no doubt that the elimination of feudal superstitious thinking depends on economic, scientific, and cultural development. However, we should never forget one of the important principles revealed to us by historical materialism—that ideology is relatively independent. Old ideas never disappear of their own accord and even after the political and economic system has collapsed it may take a very considerable time before they actually "enter the grave." In certain economically advanced nations some people use electronic calculators to work out their horoscopes. And in our own country many feudal superstitious activities have been given a "modernized" gloss. For example, some people now burn cars and television sets made of paper instead of paper horses and carts. Advanced science and technology and a developed material civilization merely provide the material precondition for the elimination of decadent thinking; before it can be truly eliminated large-scale and frequent ideological education must be carried out.

Some feudal superstitious activities directly violate our country's penal code. Sections 99 and 165 of the penal code stipulate, respectively, the punishments for the organization of secret societies and the use of feudal superstitions to carry out counterrevolutionary activities and for the use of superstitions by sorcerers and witches to spread rumors and to gain money by deceit. In our practical life, there are also many feudal superstitious activities which do not violate the law; practices such as receiving spirits, burning funeral paper, superstitious quackery, and divination merely reflect the deception caused by superstitious thinking. This should be the focus of our efforts to carry our propaganda in atheism.

During this period of constructing a Socialist spiritual civilization, it is the responsibility of Party members, the nation's cadres, and enlightened citizens to carry out propaganda in atheism so as to help superstitious people escape from the fetters of feudal superstition and to help establish a fine social atmosphere.

Document 126

Atheist Reflections on Religion

Comments from the Fourth Annual Conference of the China Atheists' Association; China Daily *(in English), 28 April 1986.*

The implementation of China's new religious policy, which reaffirms citizens' inviolable freedom of worship, has lent enthusiasm to the country's tens of millions of religious believers to participate in China's modernization drive. This significant change followed the "cultural revolution," when religion was labeled as "reactionary and superstitious poison."

How should the new religious policy be correctly interpreted in today's China? What is the relationship between religion and Socialism today?

Theory Monthly, an academic magazine, recently carried reports of a discussion on these issues at the fourth annual conference of the China Atheists' Association. The following are some views expressed by the participants at the discussion:

The policy that enshrines citizens' freedom of religion should be the only criterion in dealing with religious issues.

Prejudice against religious believers and organizations arising from the influence of "leftist" thinking must be eliminated.

In order to achieve this, a thorough understanding of the current religious situation in China must be encouraged.

Following Liberation in 1949, religion underwent fundamental changes. Comprehensive reforms to old religious systems made it no longer a tool for the ruling class to dope people.

Since religion will inevitably exist in the current Socialist period, it is a task of great importance to mobilize the enthusiasm of religious people to participate in the country's reconstruction.

Under the leadership of the Party, both believers and nonbelievers can unite together to work for the country's modernization. Some positive moral standards advocated by religious groups can guide believers to paths beneficial to the Socialist society. The study and research of religion can help understanding and assimilate the heritage of religious cultures and enrich overall Socialist cultural development.

This fusing requires religious circles to adapt to the Socialist system and the Party, the State, and society as a whole to adopt a correct attitude toward religion.

Religious believers and patriotic religious organizations can support Socialism and make useful contributions to Socialist development. Religion still holds that human society and nature are controlled by illusory "gods" and urges people to fight oppression and place their hopes for happiness on the "other shore" (*Faramita*).

It is not correct to set the implementation of the new religious policy against the popularization of atheism. Our constitution gives the freedom to believe or not to believe in religion. But citizens also have the freedom to conduct atheist popularization activities in a way that does not violate religious freedom.

Document 127

Communist Party Members Must Adhere to Atheism

People's Daily, *19 March 1982, from* Xizang Ribao *(Tibet Daily).*
Translated in FE 6991, 30 March 1982; reprinted in China Study Project Documentation *No. 8, May 1982, pp. 4-5.*

On 21 February this year, *Xizang Ribao* published a commentator's article pointing out that CCP members must adhere to atheism. The article said that, at present, there are a small minority of CCP members in Tibet (especially in agricultural and pastoral areas) who have misinterpreted the Party's policy of freedom of religious belief as meaning that Party members can believe in religion and have therefore taken part in religious activities or indulged in feudal superstitions. Some turn a blind eye to feudal superstitions, have abandoned the Party's principles, and do not have the courage to propagate atheism vigorously. They are afraid of this and that and are full of worries. Feudal superstitions in some localities have directly affected the production of life and the masses, as well as social stability, much to the dissatisfaction and criticism of the masses.

The article explicitly points out that CCP members have never covered up their political views and openly proclaim themselves as materialists, that is, atheists. They do not believe at all in any fairies or saviors. If a CCP member believes in a religion or takes part in feudal superstitions, this is not only a problem of knowledge, but also one of Party spirit. There will have been a violation of the Party constitution. In their treatment of religious problems, Party organizations at all levels must take a clear-cut stand to educate the vast numbers of Party members to establish proletarian views on religion. On this subject, the article discusses four points.

First, every CCP member must be a confirmed Marxist and a materialist atheist. He must resolutely conduct a lifelong struggle to build Socialism and realize Communism. At present, they must first be prepared to sacrifice everything in order to build a united, prosperous, and civilized new Tibet.

Next, CCP members must have an overall, accurate understanding of the Party's policy of freedom of religious belief. Tibet is a minority nationality region on China's border. Many people have the habit of believing in religions. As a form of social ideology, religion is subject to the process of birth, development, and withering away. It has a development independent of human will, and we cannot adopt a method of just issuing administrative orders to solve the problem. Consequently, toward the vast numbers of believers, the Party and government will implement a long-term policy of freedom of religious belief, and this has already been enacted in the PRC constitution. However, on no account does this mean that CCP members can believe in religion or take part in feudal superstitions. Neither does it mean that CCP members can be allowed to give support to feudal superstitions.

Third, in the course of implementing the policy of freedom of religious belief, CCP members should make it clear that citizens have the freedom to believe in religion, as well as the freedom not to believe in religion and to propagate atheism. People are free to believe in any religion and nobody may interfere. However, CCP members are at all times responsible for adopting various methods to propagate materialism and atheism. This is not contradictory to the implementation of the policy of freedom of religious belief. At the same time, CCP members must make it clear that the Party's policy of freedom of religious belief refers to the proper religious activities of those who believe in religion. That is to say, religious activities cannot go against the four basic principles and cannot interfere with politics, culture, education, marriage, civil affairs, production, and domestic life. As for the smaller number of people who have other designs, who take advantage of religion and superstition to sabotage unity among the nationalities, create public disorder, obstruct production, hold themselves out as mediums, obtain money by deception, take liberties with women, harm the masses, and so on, they have long since transgressed the limits of proper religions and have violated the criminal law of the State. They should be punished according to the law.

Fourth, the CCP is resolutely implementing the policy of freedom of religious belief, but it must also actively develop culture, education, science, and hygiene. When the standard of the people's knowledge of culture, science, and hygiene has been raised, they will automatically have a correct understanding of, and attitude toward, religion, and feudal superstitions will gradually lose their *raison d'etre* and market.

Section III

Socialist Spiritual Civilization

Introduction

The idea of "two civilizations" under Socialism in China, material and spiritual, is not new, although it has been raised to the level of a campaign promoting Socialist Spiritual Civilization in recent years. In 1979 Ye Jianying, then chairman of the Standing Committee of the National People's Congress, said, "While building a solid material foundation, we want to raise the educational, scientific, cultural, and health levels of the whole nation, foster lofty revolutionary ideals and morals, develop a rich and many-sided cultural life and thus build an advanced Socialist culture and ideology" (*Beijing Review*, 10 November 1986, p. 17).

Socialist Spiritual Civilization was highlighted in the documents of the Twelfth Party Congress, held in September 1982, and appeared as a theme for frequent articles in the press in subsequent years.

Resolution Four in "The Guiding Principles for Building a Socialist Society with an Advanced Culture and Ideology," adopted at the Sixth Plenary Session of the Twelfth Central Committee of the CCP in 1986, begins: "Socialist ethics mean essentially love of the motherland, the people, labor, science and Socialism," and continues further on, evoking memories of the "cultural revolution" slogan to "Serve the people": "Socialist morality rejects both the idea and the practice of pursuing personal interests at the expense of others. . . . In our public life we should foster Socialist humanism, respect for people [in special need] and concern for their welfare. . . . We should encourage people to observe public order, behave civilly, respect public property, protect the environment and the country's resources and fulfil their duties to the state and community. . . . Bad wedding and funeral customs have to be changed and superstitious, feudal beliefs and practices must be eradicated. . . . As a higher stage in human moral progress, Socialist ethics naturally incorporate all the best elements in the various ethical systems and traditions developed throughout history and reject all decadent ideology and ethics."

China opened its doors in the early 1980s to joint business ventures and tourism, and the flood of visitors brought with them the "spiritual pollution" of capitalist societies which they had fended off for over three decades by a policy of self-imposed isolation. The Socialist Spiritual Civilization and

420

Anti-Spiritual Pollution campaigns, with their moralistic slogans and social-hygiene projects, were attempts to stem the tide.

Spiritual Pollution and the "Three Bad Categories" of People

In October 1983, Deng Xiaoping, China's paramount leader, raised the issue of spiritual pollution at a closed session of the CCP Central Committee. Shortly thereafter, Deng Liqun, head of the Central Committee's Propaganda Department, speaking with foreign journalists, listed four categories of spiritual pollution: spreading things that are obscene, barbarous or reactionary; vulgar taste in artistic performances; seeking personal gain, indulgence in individualism, anarchism, liberalism, etc.; and writing articles or delivering speeches that run counter to the country's social system.

Lin Ruo, the provincial Party secretary, speaking to a CCP forum in Guangdong, said: "Spiritual pollution is . . . spreading all sorts of decadent and moribund ideas of the bourgeoisie and other exploiting classes, and spreading a mood of nonconfidence in the cause of Socialism and Communism . . . . The struggle against spiritual pollution is the current fighting task of the theoretical and literary and art circles, [and] is closely related to Party rectification. . . . Some [writers] have commercialized spiritual products, going after money in everything, not hesitating to produce vulgar things. Some people are propagating humanism and humanitarianism" (*Nanfang Ribao*, 8 November 1982, p. 1).

Party purification, he said, required the weeding out of the "Three Bad Categories" of Party cadres: "leftists" who had risen to prominence in the "cultural revolution"; factionalists who promoted the "leftist" ideology of Lin Biao and the "gang of four"; those who had indulged in beating, smashing, and looting during the "cultural revolution."

Lin Ruo also warned against the "unhealthy tendency of Party cadres to 'look for money in everything. . . .' " Some, affected by "decadent bourgeois ideas," have even gone so far as to "doubt and negate the superiority of the Socialist system and the bright prospects of Communism."

"THREE ARDENT LOVES," "FOUR POINTS OF DECENCY," AND OTHER MORALISMS

Following the penchant for coining numerical slogans, the organizers of the Socialist Spiritual Civilization campaign promoted the "Three Ardent Loves" (love for the CCP, love for the Socialist motherland, and love for the PLA); the "Four Haves" (to have ideals, morality, culture, and discipline); the "Four Emphases" (emphasis on decorum, personal hygiene, discipline, and morals); and the "Four Points of Decency" (decency of mind, decency of language, decency of behavior, and decency of environment [public hygiene]).

"FIVE-GOOD FAMILIES"

"Five-Good Families" are honored with this title because they are judged to be good at adhering to the four basic principles, good at social conduct by following discipline and obeying the law, good at civility and courtesy by observing unity and friendliness, good at changing old customs by preferring late marriage and delayed childbearing, and good on the job by looking after the collective.

THE SIX "DO NOTS"

In 1985, authorities in the Shenzhen Special Economic Zone bordering Hongkong, overwhelmed by the influx of Western commercialism and popular culture, formulated an "Outline for Building Spiritual Civilization" as a bulwark against moral temptations, which included the "Six Do Nots": do not violate the policies of the special economic zone; do not smuggle or buy in order to resell illegally; do not seek ill-gotten wealth; do not depart from the correct stand or from national or personal dignity in dealing with foreigners; do not practice bribery or accept bribes; do not jeopardize family harmony and conjugal love (*Nanfang Ribao*, 21 November 1985, in FBIS, CSO: 4005/415, Nov. 1985, pp. 75-76).

THE "TEN MUSTS AND MUST NOTS"

In a report to the Seventh Provincial People's Congress in May 1988 (Shaanxi provincial broadcast, 21 May 1988, FE 0163, in China Study Project *Journal* 3:2, August 1988, p. 23), Hou Zongbin [unidentified] proposed "Ten Musts and Must Nots" to promote Socialist moral values: one must get rich through hard work and not forget honor at the sight of money; one must work selflessly for the public interests and not make use of one's official power to seek personal gain; one must work conscientiously and show a strong sense of responsibility, never being derelict in one's duties; one must foster lofty moral values and not be bent solely on profit; one must work with and help others, rather than care only about one's own interests; one must be sincere with others, not suspicious and jealous; one must bravely fight against bad practices and not make concessions; one must show an enterprising spirit and not seek ease and comfort; one must be impartial and not enrich oneself at the expense of public interest; and one must be industrious and thrifty, and not live extravagantly.

Where are these various campaigns now? While occasional references to Socialist spiritual civilization and the dangers of spiritual pollution do appear in the press, they are not, at this time, at campaign pitch.

Document 128

Chinese-Type Modernization: Building Socialist Spiritual Civilization

By Pang Yongjie and Li Shanquan, staff members of the Economic Research Center of the State Council, in Beijing Review *(in English), 2 May 1983, pp. 16-19 (excerpts).*

China's modernization program entails the building of a Socialist spiritual civilization simultaneous with the building of a Socialist material civilization, concomitant undertakings which are peculiar to the Chinese way of modernizing the country. The twin tasks will ensure the attainment of the modernization goal.

Since the shift in the emphasis of its work to the modernization drive, China's well-wishers around the world, while acclaiming the momentous decision, have expressed worries nevertheless. Many wonder if the process will rob China of its fine revolutionary spirit, court the "spiritual pollution" intrinsic in capitalist societies, and derail the modernization program in the end. Such worries are not unfounded.

As early as September 1979, the Party Central Committee called for parallel construction of economic and spiritual civilizations, with each promoting the other. For, it is held, the building of a spiritual civilization is crucial to maintaining the Socialist aspect of modernization, facilitating the consolidation and development of the Socialist economy, forestalling any possibility of "Westernization," and preventing China from going capitalist.

Together with the four modernizations, Socialist spiritual civilization has been included in the fundamental law of the land and the constitution of the Chinese Communist Party, the ruling party, as a program of action for the entire Party membership and the people throughout the country.

Implications

The term "Socialist spiritual civilization" refers to the nature of all that is implied in spiritual civilization under the Socialist system. It involves two fields of construction, ideological and cultural. Its quintessence lies in Communist ideas, which places it worlds apart from capitalist spiritual civilization.

Ideological construction concerns ideals and moral values to be advocated and fostered among China's 1 billion people. Through the study of Marxism and education in Communist ideals, an ever-increasing portion of society will acquire a revolutionary outlook on life and the world and will become well-educated, well-disciplined workers imbued with lofty ideals and moral integrity. The aim in society as a whole is to develop new human relationships characterized by unity and mutual assistance and to establish new social morals and customs.

Cultural construction covers such areas as education, science, literature and art, the media, public health, and sports. It is built within the framework of the Socialist system, guided by Marxist theories and Communist ideas, and is different from capitalist culture in that all of its fruits belong to the people and serve the public and the Socialist cause.

New Term, Classic Concept

Some may ask: On what grounds did you invent the term "Socialist spiritual civilization," as it is not mentioned in any Marxist classics?

It is true that this term does not appear in Marxist literature. But didn't Marx and Engels, when speaking of humanity entering upon an age of civilization in new dimensions, predict that history is bound to witness a higher-state civilization characterized mainly by the abolition of class exploitation? By that time, they projected, products will flow in abundance; people inspired by Communist values will develop their talents comprehensively and freely; all traditional ownership of the means of production and related concepts will be abolished and discarded; and education, science, and the arts will enjoy a full scope of development.

Lenin, too, repeatedly expounded on the significance of Communist education, morality, discipline, and attitude toward labor. The basic task of Communism, he pointed out, is to help educate the laboring masses to overcome outmoded habits and customs left over by the old system; and knowledge of all sciences, technology, and arts should be obtained to serve Socialist construction.

Mao Zedong contributed much to this discussion as well. He issued a call to build a civilized and progressive China dominated by a new culture.

Ideological work, as he saw it, is the guarantee for accomplishing economic and technical advances.

The task of building Socialist spiritual civilization was defined on the basis of these principles and the summary of historical experiences gained after the founding of the People's Republic. It was set forth at a time when new policies were formulated for a new period of historical development.

Relationship with Economic Construction

What is the relationship between the modernization drive and the building of a Socialist spiritual civilization?

Just as a Socialist society develops in the direction of Communism, so the success of China's modernization drive hinges not merely on the accumulation of material wealth but also on the heightening of people's Communist consciousness and revolutionary spirit.

Economic construction, or the building of material civilization, lays the groundwork for the construction of a Socialist spiritual civilization. Without the former the latter would be out of the question.

Socialist spiritual civilization in turn provides an impetus for economic construction and guarantees its growth with the current orientation.

In China, the tumultuous ten-year "cultural revolution" confounded right with wrong and good with evil, sapped people's confidence in Marxism and Communism, and opened the floodgates to bourgeois individualism and anarchism. Although things have improved in the last few years since we began to set right the wrongs in all fields of endeavor committed during this period, it will be quite some time before we can remove all the after-effects of this "revolution" from people's minds.

The new policy of opening to the outside world and stimulating the domestic economy, adopted after China switched to the modernization drive, has boosted the economy significantly and raised living standards. But the influence of the old private-owner mentality and decadent capitalist ideas from abroad also left their ugly marks because we overlooked our ideological work.

Facts show that if one buries himself in economic construction to the neglect of building Socialist spiritual civilization, he will run after things material and may even be interested only in material gains. Thus he turns himself into a slave to material things, leading a rich yet spiritually meaningless life, a life which impels him to cheat, rob, and kill.

Failure to check this tendency, rather than mobilizing the nation to work as one in economic construction, would lead China astray, on the road of lopsided development, and weaken, or even scuttle, its Socialist economic foundation, reducing the Socialist modernization drive to nothing but a pipe dream. . . .

Today and Tomorrow

What problem does China face in building the Socialist spiritual civilization?

Over the last few years, China has adopted a series of measures, including publicity and educational efforts, to build Socialist spiritual civilization.

We have advocated the "five stresses" (stress on decorum, manners, hygiene, discipline, and morals) and the "four points of decency" (decency of mind, which means cultivating a fine ideology, moral character, and integrity and upholding the Party's leadership and the Socialist system; decency of language, which means the use and popularization of polite language; decency of behavior, which means doing useful things for the people, working hard, being concerned for others' welfare, observing discipline, and safeguarding collective interests; and decency of the environment, which includes paying attention to personal hygiene and to sanitation at home and in public places). In addition, we have designated March this year, and March every year, as Socialist Ethics and Courtesy Month.

Designed to foster fine life-styles among our people, these activities have achieved initial results in correcting undesirable social practices. Furthermore, we have commended those who have worked selflessly and made outstanding contributions to society, combated bourgeois liberalization, and cracked down on crimes in the economic sphere. All these have enabled the people to learn from the advanced, distinguish the right and good from the wrong and evil, and fortify their confidence in Socialism.

However, it is no small job to build Socialist spiritual civilization in a country where the economy and culture remain relatively undeveloped and where the "cultural revolution" has left such deep scars. At present, our Party's style and civic virtues leave something to be desired, and more so do our science, culture, and education. Moreover, the influence of capitalist ideas is spreading in the wake of expanding exchanges with foreign countries; and the philosophy that "money is everything" still has quite a following among the populace. We need to be on our guard.

Beginning in autumn this year, in order to strengthen the building of the spiritual civilization, the Chinese Communist Party will initiate a self-education process to consolidate itself in an all-round way. It expects to bring about real improvements in the Party's style within three years by which to influence and improve ways of doing things throughout the society.

Further nationwide efforts will be made to publicize the "five stresses" and "four points of decency" and the "three loves" (love for the motherland, Socialism, and the Party), especially during the annual Socialist Ethics and Courtesy Month. People in both urban and rural areas will be urged to consciously promulgate and observe rules and regulations for morally important issues so as to involve an ever-expanding circle of people in building spiritual civilization. In this way social mores are expected to be fundamentally improved.

Investment in various cultural undertakings will be increased and systematic cultural education popularized.

More important, further efforts will be made to educate the whole nation, particularly the cadres and the young, in Marxism-Leninism and Mao Zedong Thought, in the Party's program, and in revolutionary traditions, as well as in Chinese history.

All citizens will be urged to be conscious of their rights, duties, and ethics. Education in professional responsibility, integrity, and discipline will be conducted in all trades and professions.

Sustained education will enable the people to enhance their Communist consciousness and guard against the influence of capitalist ideas.

Through the concerted efforts of the entire nation, China will steadily increase its material wealth and will bring up generation after generation of people with high Communist values. This is not only our wish. It is a goal we aim at in our Socialist modernization drive.

Section IV

Marxism as a Faith

Introduction

Some Party and Youth League members, referring to the constitutional guarantee of freedom of religious belief for all citizens, have been asking why they are not allowed to have a personal religious faith. The answer is unequivocal: "Party members are not ordinary citizens, nor are they ordinary workers among the masses; they are the vanguard of the working class, with Communist consciousness, who maintain ... loyalty to and faith in Marxist scientific truth and in no way believe in religious theology."

What should they believe in? "A Communist party member must guide his own life and work by firm belief in, and by adopting the standpoint, viewpoint, and methods of, Marxism, Leninism and the thought of Mao Zedong in order to correctly understand society and nature." A Party member "should be an atheist fighter, using dialectical materialism to expose the illusions of theism and lead the people to gradually dispel the fog and bondage of religion."

Document 129

Communist Party Members Cannot Be Religious Believers

In Zongjiao Mantan *(Discussions on Religion), Zhejiang People's Publishing House, third edition, 1984, pp. 124ff (excerpts). Translated by Donald MacInnis.*

In recent years situations have arisen in a number of places where Communist Party members, even some basic-level cadres, have become religious believers. They read the Bible, offer prayers, solicit donations, build shrines and temples, and worship Buddha [*qiu shen bai fo*]. Some of them not only take part in religious activities themselves, they also pull other people into their religion, increasing the membership. These actions have a very bad influence on the masses.

We must understand that this is not a normal phenomenon. The appearance of this phenomenon is due to errors of the long-standing "leftist" leadership, in particular the negative consequences of the wrecking of the Party's constructive work caused by the counterrevolutionary gang of Lin Biao and Jiang Qing; it also is a result of relaxing of our work in politics and thought, and neglecting the education of Party members in the basic teachings of Marxism and the Party. This should arouse the full concern of all levels of Party organs and the broad membership of the Party, because it reflects the ideological confusion of certain Party members and some new aspects of religious activities at the present time. . . .

Our Party is the party of the progressive working class; not only is it a Party founded on the working class, but it is also a Party that uses the weapons of Marxist theory. A Communist Party member must guide his own life and work by firm belief in, and by adopting the standpoint, viewpoint, and methods of, Marxism, Leninism, and the thought of Mao Zedong in order to correctly understand society and nature. This is the Party spirit which is required of every Party member. . . .

So a Communist Party member should be an atheist fighter, using dialectical materialism to expose the illusions of theism, and leading the people to gradually dispel the fog and the bondage of religion. To give up this fighting task and believe in religion is to abandon the Party's scientific worldview and to lose the advanced nature of a Party member. . . .

Party members should be the vanguard of the working class, with a Communist consciousness, firmly based in the long-range ideals of Communism and of total struggle. Under the leadership of the Party's correct way, direction, and policy, they should give themselves completely, with whole heart and spirit, to spreading the spirit of serving the people, uniting with the masses, immersing self in hard work, plunging wholeheartedly into the great struggle to build a modernized nation, and in every way giving full play to the role of being a model and vanguard, to research new conditions, to resolve new questions, and to use their own wisdom and two hands to clear away the obstacles to building a modernized nation on the road ahead.

But religion is vigorously preaching that the real world is illusory, insignificant, and that human life is "like the life of a mayfly," brief and ephemeral, without meaning. Religion induces people to give up interest in the present life, and to cease all efforts to find happiness and prosperity in this world. If a Party member believes this kind of propaganda, how can he give himself to the untiring struggle of the Party in the cause of modernizing China? How can he be a vanguard of the working class worthy of the name? . . .

In summary, if a Party member believes in religion, he is going in the opposite direction from the Party and is not worthy to bear the name of Party member. A Party member should arm himself with a scientific worldview, and become a materialistic, atheistic, heroic fighter who never stops in the struggle to bring about the highest ideals of Socialism and Communism. . . .

It should be pointed out that the stipulation in our national constitution on freedom of religious belief refers to citizens of China. Party members are not ordinary citizens, nor are they the ordinary workers among the masses; they are the vanguard of the working class, with Communist consciousnesss, who maintain an important criterion of the Communist vanguard, namely, loyalty to and faith in Marxist scientific truth and in no way believing in religious theology. If one believes that religion is a private matter as it relates to the Marxist party, and that freedom of religious belief is all right for Party members, then one is downgrading the Party to the level of any ordinary mass organization and downgrading Party members to the status of any ordinary citizen; how can one then speak of the vanguard nature of the Party and the leadership example to be set by Party members? If one says that some Party members insist on believing in religious theology because they enjoy the freedom of religious belief of ordinary citizens, then he is arranging his own funeral as a Party member. Since he cannot enjoy his "freedom" and at the same time remain in the Party, he must resign from the Party. . . .

Some comrades ask, "Can members of the Communist Youth League believe in religion?" The answer is also negative. We know that the CYL is a mass organization of vanguard youth which assists the Party under the leadership of Marxism, Leninism, and Mao Zedong thought. CYL members should assiduously study and acquire knowledge of culture, theory, science, and technology, establish a historical and dialectical materialist worldview, faith in science, love of truth, and a wholehearted ideological commitment to serve the people; they should strive to be shock workers in building a Socialist material and spiritual civilization, rather than religious believers who reject the world. By its very nature the CYL determines that its members cannot at the same time be religious believers. . . .

Document 130

An Interview with a Woman on a Bus in Yunnan Province

By Donald MacInnis, May 1988.

We were traveling on a packed minibus between Dali and Xiaguan in May 1988. I spoke with a woman who was traveling with her husband, an electrician, and small son, a fourth-grader. She was about thirty-five years old.

I asked her about the local Buddhist temples. She described two local temples, one the Guanyin Temple (which we later visited), the other, the Gantong Temple, on a nearby mountain, about half an hour's walk from the highway. A third temple in Xiaguan, where she lived, has no resident monks or nuns, she said. The temples were badly damaged by rampaging Red Guards, she said, but are now being restored with government help and generous contributions from Buddhist laity.

"We have three religions in the Dali district: Islam, Buddhism, and Christianity. Now the policy of the government and the Party is freedom of religious belief for everyone."

"Are there no other religions?" I asked. "What about Daoism?" "No," she replied, "there are no others."

She was a bright, articulate person. I asked if she were a senior middle school graduate. No, she had only finished sixth grade, because of the "cultural revolution." I asked if she were a cadre. "No," she said, "I'm just a bookkeeper in a factory."

She asked if I were a Buddhist. I said I was not, and asked if she was a believer. When she replied in the negative, I asked, "Do you believe in any religion?" She replied, "No." So I asked, laughing, "Do you believe in anything?" She replied, "Yes, I believe in Marxism-Leninism." For a person who was neither a religious believer nor a Party cadre she was well-informed about religion and religious policy.

My final question was, "Do you want more children?" She replied, "No, one is enough. Children are trouble for parents, and expensive to raise. Anyway we have too many people already in China. They say one billion, but it is really one and one-half billion."

Youth and Religion in China Today

Introduction

Thousands of letters poured in to the magazine *Zhongguo Qingnian* (Chinese Youth) in response to a letter written in 1980 by Pan Xiao, a despairing young woman who asked, "What is the meaning of life?" She had related how her own high values and hopes for a life of service had been dashed by bad experiences during the "cultural revolution," how friends had betrayed her, and how she had failed in her search for the meaning of life:

Oh, the path of life, why is it ever narrowing as one walks along? As for myself, I am already so tired now. It seems that slackening for a moment would mean total destruction. Indeed, I did stealthily go to watch the service at a Catholic church. I struck upon the idea of shaving my head and becoming a nun. I even went so far as to consider putting an end to my life — I am extremely confused and self-contradictory (Donald MacInnis and Mary Lou Martin, *Values and Religion in China Today* [Maryknoll, N.Y.: Maryknoll Fathers and Brothers, 1988], p. 81).

While it has been said that Pan Xiao was a fictitious person, and her letter created by the editors, the response was real enough, echoed in the pieces selected from *Chinese Youth Daily*, *Shanxi Youth*, and *Chinese Youth*, for inclusion in this section.

Several of these selections are letters to the editor, with the editor's response. How should we deal with Youth League members who start going to church? Why do seemingly sensible Youth League members go to a temple, kowtow before a statue of Guanyin, and burn paper spirit money? Why is religion still allowed to exist in China? Should we expel Youth League members who take part in religious activities? What about young people who decide they want to become monks?

The answer often begins with a standard Marxist explanation of why religious phenomena still exist. Even though the exploiting classes have been eliminated, influences from the old society still remain. Suffering still exists in today's society, and many other reasons, such as family influence, peer pressure, or curiosity lead people to religion. But the main reason, according to two of these respondents, is spiritual distress caused by social problems stemming from the "ten years of chaos" [the "cultural revolution"].

The social disorder of those years upset the old, stable order into which these young people had been born and raised. Angry and resentful after the traumatic experiences of those years, they have become disillusioned with Marxism-Leninism and search for other answers to the meaning of life. Finally, the turmoil of those years shattered social discipline, allowing superstitious practices to creep back in again.

"The 'cultural revolution' is over, but it has caused profound damage. All the same, although those crying to God and the devotees of Buddha are not many, nevertheless religion moves a sizable number of young people. . . ." In any case, it is said that religion is an "artificial flower" that will not bring real happiness. However, even though religion runs in the opposite direction to Marxism, Youth League members should use methods of patient persuasion and guidance, respecting the beliefs of religious comrades, while at the same time establishing a "scientific worldview and outlook on life by strengthening the propagation of Marxist atheism and teaching them about socialism."

Young religious believers should not be patronized or sneered at. Rather than putting pressure on them, Youth League members should get close to them, make friends with them, and share their own feelings about work, study, and life; lead them toward an atheistic viewpoint; and draw them into the League's cultural and athletic programs.

As for those who turn to religion as an escape from personal problems, "we should extend to them the concern and warmth of the Youth League and revive their hope for a good life in the real world."

Superstitious activities are in no way to be condoned, for they are really harmful to young people. Superstition affects their ability to think rationally, it wastes their time and money, and it obstructs social progress by diverting them from learning new ways, such as scientific farming.

The League should treat members who are religious believers with kindness and patience, giving them a period of education to see if they will change. "As for those who persist and do not change, even after our patient help and teaching, there are certain proper organizational ways to handle the problem without hurting their feelings."

Document 131

What Should We Do about Communist Youth League Members Who Go to Church?

Letters to the Editor, Chinese Youth Daily, *6 April 1982, p. 3. Translated by Tam Waiyi and Donald MacInnis.*

Comrade Editor:

A church in a small town not far away from our village was reopened the year before last. At first, only some old believers took part in its activities. But in the past two years some young people have become Christians, attracted by the church's activities, such as telling Bible stories, singing hymns, etc. Our Youth League branch felt this was a difficult problem to handle. We're afraid of violating the policy on religion if we interfere in their activities, but it's not right if we just ignore this. Please tell us what to do.

Liang Jiadian

Comrade Liang Jiadian:

Since the implementing of the policy on religion and the resumption of religious activities, Youth League branches in many places have encountered the problem raised in your letter. Why should freedom of religious belief be protected? We have to trace this back to the origin and development of religion. In primitive society, people had a fear of inexplicable natural phenomena, such as thunder, lightning, tidal waves and earthquakes. They created a belief in the supernatural as an explanation for these natural phenomena.

After the emergence of a class society, people put their hope in "gods" for help from the cruel class oppression. The ruling classes over the past centuries also used religion as the spiritual pillar on which to support and safeguard the system of exploitation, which in turn led to further development of religion.

Although the exploiting classes have been wiped out in our country, the influence of the old society is still there, and our social system still needs improvement. Relationships among people are far from perfect, and mankind's power to control nature is still very limited. People have not yet abandoned the idea that "people do things, but heaven decides things."

Meanwhile, there is still the influence of class struggle in our country. As long as these natural and social origins of religion exist, the dying out of religion is impossible. Only a person's self-consciousness can change the religious belief that is lodged in the mind. Thus we should keep close to these young religious believers, and unite with them, rather than give them a cold shoulder and look down on them. Although they have different beliefs, they have the same goal as we do, which is to build a prosperous motherland.

But in saying this, we don't mean that the Youth League branches should wash their hands of this business. The Youth League takes Marxism as its guide. Marxists view religion as a kind of superstition; they view the world outlook of idealism, and the pessimistic and helpless philosophy of life which is promoted by religion, as harmful for our correct understanding and our struggle to transform nature and society. So the Youth League should take it as an absolute responsibility to promote atheism and to arm youth with dialectical materialism and modern science.

Of course we cannot rely simply on forced instruction or violent methods to fulfill this task, but should use lively teaching methods and rich scientific information. I read such material not long ago.

In the suburbs of Shanghai there is a famous church [Catholic shrine at Sheshan]. In March 1980, a few counterrevolutionaries hidden inside the church made up the rumor of "Apparition of [luminescence] the Virgin Mary," which attracted quite a few Christians to go there on "pilgrimage" to see the "holy light" and ask for "holy water."

But none of the young people working in the microwave station of the long distance telephone system near the church became religious believers. How did the Party and Youth League branches of that unit handle this matter? Besides giving them lessons on materialism, on the origins of mankind, and on the makeup of elements in the world, they carried out an on-the-spot investigation, together with the nearby observatory, to expose the truth of this "holy light." It turned out that sunlight reflected from the great glass expanse of the observatory window would reflect off the green glazed tiles of the church roof, causing a kind of halo visible to those standing in front of the church. But when the observatory window was shaded, the "holy light" would disappear.

As for the "holy water," it was just a stream of ordinary spring water, and was even polluted by nearby residents who washed their feet in it! After learning the truth, these young people no longer went to see the "holy light" or asked for the "holy water."

Besides providing information for young people, we have to try to make Youth League activities as rich as possible. As you said, some young people go to church because they are attracted by Bible-story telling and singing. Why can't we make our activities more attractive? If word gets around that there is a well-run youth club or "Youth Home" [qingnianzhijia], there will be fewer young religious believers.

There may be specific reasons that lead young people to religious faith; for example, the frustrations they meet in the roadway of life, such as the problem of gaining a place for advanced study, employment problems, and disappointments in love and marriage. Some turn to religion because of family disputes, and some because of protracted illness. They fall into depression, and feel helpless when their difficulties remain unsolved. If they don't get immediate care and help from the organization then, they will probably turn to so-called gods for help.

We must patiently and carefully help these young people, warmly assisting them to find solutions to problems which can be solved. As for problems that seem insoluble at the moment, we must show them a reasonable explanation and try to create conditions favorable for a later solution. We must use our efforts to bring them to the warmth of the Party, making them realize that the problem cannot be solved by asking the gods for help, but that only by relying on the organization and taking a positive attitude can one have a bright future.

Of course, while doing ideological education we must be alert. If we discover anyone deluding people with false rumors while wearing the cloak of religion, upsetting stability and damaging unity, and swindling people of their money, we should immediately report it to the relevant department and ask the government to deal with it according to the law.

Document 132

What Do They Really Believe In?

Letters to the Editor, Chinese Youth Daily, *6 April 1982.*
Translated by Tam Waiyi and Donald MacInnis.

Comrade Editor:

On 21 March, I went to Lin Yan [Inspiration Rock] Temple in Taisha for archaeological studies with teachers and students from the history department of our university. At noon, I was visiting cultural relics inside the Rock Temple in the "Lin Yan Guanyin Rites Place" of the Main Peak, when several Communist Youth League members came in, carrying the Youth League banner. They put the bright League banner on the floor in front of the stone statue of Guanyin, then knelt on the banner and kowtowed to the Guanyin statue. They took bits of paper from their pockets to get fire from the incense brazier, while murmuring words like, "just to show a little bit of our heart." Then they walked out of the temple with the burning papers and threw them into the woods outside. I was shocked by their behavior.

These Youth League members did not inspire love for the motherland through their visit to the temple. Neither did they benefit from the culture created by the hard work and wisdom of the working people of ancient times. Instead, they knelt on the League banner to worship Buddha. I don't know what they really believe in. Perhaps they were doing something without thinking, but it was not right, even for fun. The Communist Youth League is the school where we learn Communism, and the League banner is the symbol of the Youth League organization. Every League member should take a serious and respectful attitude toward it.

It's warm springtime now, and the flowers are blossoming. Many young friends like to go on outings at this time. As a veteran member, I appeal here to all Youth League members, don't do anything that would damage the image of the League organization during Youth League Day activities, or while on trips to the countryside. We should treasure the glorious name of Youth League member and be pioneers in the building of spiritual civilization. Youth League organizations should also strengthen the education and guidance of members. Meanwhile, we should also care for cultural relics and protect flowers, trees, and crops when we go on outings.

Zong Xijun
Shandong University

Document 133

Why Does Religion Still Exist in Our Country?

By Xiao Hai in Chinese Youth Daily, *27 March 1982 (excerpts). Translated by Tam Waiyi and Donald MacInnis.*

Some young readers have written to us asking why religion is still allowed in our Socialist country. They want to understand the Party's policy on religion and related matters. We publish here Comrade Xiao Hai's article as a reference for young comrades.

Editor, *Chinese Youth Daily*

. . . The word "suffering" speaks for the great majority of exploited people. That is why early Buddhism attracted many people among the masses caught in the caste system, and later developed into a world religion.

The most influential religion among the world's three major religions is Christianity, which now has more than 350,500,000 believers. Under the rule of the Roman Empire, Christianity began to spread among peoples of various nationalities in the first and second centuries A.D. At first it was a religion of slaves and ordinary citizens. Later it was used by the exploiting classes as a spiritual pillar in their control over people. The Christian Bible talks about "original sin" and the "sufferings of Jesus." This, in fact, expresses the bitterness of people who are suffering under the double exploitation of social forces (the ruling classes) and the forces of nature.

The same is true for Islam, another of the world's three great religions. Even today, the great majority of people in the world are living under systems of exploitation and suffering bitterness in many ways.

So two-thirds of the world's people are religious believers today. In 1978, the world was shocked by the mass suicide of nine hundred religious believers of the "People's Temple" in the United States [sic], the majority of whom came from the working masses and were helpless under the tortures of poverty and loneliness.

Understand Correctly the Religious Phenomena in Our Country

In Socialist China, religious believers are only a small minority of our people, and the number will grow smaller as our country develops. This is mainly due to the establishing of a Socialist system based on public ownership. Under this system, people have become their own masters, and can control their own fate, while following the road which leads to the complete elimination of bitterness and difficulties.

At the same time, Marxism is the prevailing ideology, providing guidelines for our Party and our country. However, the actual number of religious believers in China is not small. Besides cognitive, nationalities, and historical causes, the basic reason for this phenomenon is found in its social origins. The legacy of social evils left by the old society has not yet been wiped out, a brand-new system has not yet been fully set up and perfected, the economic backwardness of the country has not been fundamentally changed, and the standard of our people's education is not high.

Furthermore, there have been various mistakes and frustrations in our work. The unhealthy tendencies of bureaucratism and "connectionism" still exist, causing real difficulties and suffering in the economic life of our people. Under these conditions, some people will readily turn to religion to express their distress and seek for a spiritual way out. They do this without fully understanding the great significance and bright future offered by Socialism and Communism, nor have they firmly made up their minds to overcome difficulties and expose bad practices, together with the Party and people.

In the situation of life today, there are many reasons why some young people join religious activities, such as family influences, peer pressure, or curiosity. But the most obvious reason is their spiritual distress. The various social problems left over by the ten years of chaos [the "cultural revolution"] have frustrated the hopes for higher education, employment, marriage, and other matters for many of them. But our political-thought work among young people has been unable to satisfy their needs, so youth lack effective guidance. In their distress they begin to think that their own roadway of life is becoming increasingly narrow, so in their disillusionment some of them turn to the kingdom of religion in their search for a new future.

A young man from Fujian Province was under the influence of his religious family from childhood, but he had not believed in religion for a long time. During the "ten years of chaos" he was "sent down to the countryside" [as a rural laborer]. One by one, he saw his friends return to the city because they had "connections," until he was the last one of their group to remain. Because he had no "connections," he had to "put roots down" there in the village. He had other problems that could not be solved. As a result he was lonely and spiritually depressed. Concluding with a sigh that man's fate was out of his own hands, he finally became a devout Christian.

We can see from this that the social origins of religion have not been totally eliminated in our country, and that the continuing existence of religious activities is not strange, but inevitable.

The national constitution stipulates that citizens have freedom of religious belief, and the Party and government are implementing policies to protect this freedom.

As for treatment of religious believers, we must realize our responsibility, which is to understand and care for them. If we question the Party's policy, or simply try to impose a ban on religious activities, that would not only fail to abolish religion, it would also contradict the constitutional guarantee of freedom of religious belief. To do so would be unrealistic in our present and historical situation, causing extremely harmful political consequences which would undermine stability and unity, and harm the fundamental interests of the Party and the people.

An Artificial Flower

Although there are reasons for the existence of religion, and we do have freedom of religious belief, religion is, in fact, an artificial flower. The world's religions differ in many ways. Each has a dreamland of its own creation — the kingdom of heaven, the other world, the other shore, paradise, etc. Each has its own idol — God, Allah, Buddha, etc. People have worshiped and prayed for thousands of years, but who has actually seen the power of gods or the realization of a "kingdom of love"?

The artificial flower of religion will not bring real happiness to people after all. Religion paralyzes exploited people's will to fight; that's why the ruling classes throughout history have tried their best to support, foster, and make use of religion as a means to safeguard, in the name of God, their position as exploiters and oppressors. Religion is used by them to make the people obedient and long-suffering, willingly serving the oppressors as their cows and horses.

In our Socialist nation, religion runs in the opposite direction to Marxism, which directs the progress of our Party and our country. The pessimistic and helpless personal outlook and worldview fostered by idealism directly controls the thinking of religious believers, ungirding and undermining the faith and fighting will of the people to overcome difficulties in the building of the four modernizations.

Marxists have always taken a critical attitude toward religion. Some religious beliefs belong to ideological questions, and only by using the method of patient persuasion and guidance can these be resolved. In dealing with religious believers, we should, on the one hand, understand and respect their beliefs, while on the other hand, we should lead them to see their own future and personal interests, and help them to establish a scientific worldview and outlook on life, by strengthening the propagation of Marxist atheism and teaching them about Socialism.

At the same time we should show concern for them by helping them to solve their practical problems, and attract them away from religion toward Socialism. Of course, we can really wipe out religion only by greatly improving the forces of production and by building a Socialist material and spiritual civilization, which will completely cut the social roots on which religion survives. With the evolution of Socialism and the approach of communism, and the continuing development of human understanding of society and nature, religion will weaken day by day, and finally die out.

Document 134

How To Treat Young Religious Believers and Other Young People

Chinese Youth, *September 1983. Translated by Tam Waiyi and Donald MacInnis.*

Comrade Editor:
Not long ago a gust of religious wind was blowing through our place. People from several hundred miles away flocked to religious activities, including some young people.

As a Youth League cadre I do not believe in any religion. We are going to punish those League members who took part in religious activities by expelling them. As for new applicants, we will not accept them if they have ever participated in religious activities. We are not sure whether this is proper and suitable or not. Please give us your advice.

Xiao Chang
Huiyuan County
Anhui Province

Comrade Xiao Chang:
Your letter raises questions that need to be addressed in our society. There really are young people who believe in religion or take part in reli-

gious activities now. Although they are few in number, this problem should be viewed as a new topic for study in the work of the Youth League.

The Party and government in our country allow citizens the right to believe and practice religion, and this right is protected by law. This point must be made clear. But the Youth League should keep in mind the glorious mission of propagating Marxism, promoting atheism, and uniting and educating the majority of young people to be new Communists. Our basic attitude should be to never use administrative orders to ban religious activities, or to ignore the influence of religious ideology on young people.

The reasons why young people believe in religion or take part in religious activities are complex. These include the effects of the "ten years of chaos"; the influence of family members; the ups and downs of life; etc. Religion, as a social ideology, "is the product of society," and people's attitude towards religion is, after all, decided by "people's social conditions, social relationships, and social existence." Thus, our attitude should be one of caution in dealing with the problem of young people's religious beliefs and religious activities; we should do our political-thought work well, help them to establish a worldview based on dialectical materialism, and free themselves from the bondage of religious ideology. We should deal with this problem according to each actual situation, rather than adopt simple measures, especially with young religious believers among the national minorities.

First of all, in dealing with these young people, we should not give in to our feelings and look down upon or sneer at them, nor can we draw a line between them and us, putting pressure on them to leave the League organization. Using forceful measures would only injure their self-respect and raise feelings of resistance, while affecting the implementation of the Party's policy on religion. We should get close to them, using correct methods and our own initiative to make friends with them; to share with them our feelings about our work, study, thinking, and life; to bring them under the influence of an atheistic viewpoint; to encourage them with good reports about the four modernizations; and to draw them in with good cultural and athletic programs so as to enrich their lives.

As for those young people who are looking for a way out of their personal dilemma, and convert to religion because of distress, emptiness, difficulties, and frustrations in their personal lives, we should extend to them the concern and warmth of the Youth League organization and revive their hope for a good life in the real world.

But we should also teach them that, although we permit and protect the right to take part in religious activities, religion must not interfere in educational, judicial, administrative, or marriage matters. Religious activities must not upset the normal order of society, production, and daily life. We should teach young people to be alert for those few people who use religion to harm social stability, unity, and the four modernizations. We should also dissuade young people from joining any large religious meetings that would interfere in the social and productive order noted above.

Here we must show how two situations have to be treated differently. The first is to differentiate between young people who take part in religious activities and those who are real believers. The second is to differentiate between young believers who are Youth League members and those who are not.

Our constitution stipulates that citizens have freedom of religious belief. This policy applies to ordinary citizens. Communist Party members and Youth League members are atheists who must believe in Marxism and Leninism. This is determined by the constitutions of the Party and the Youth League, and by the nature of the two organizations. The Youth League organization must firmly stick to this principle, holding high their bright-colored banner and avoiding ambiguity. In consideration of the actual situation today, we should be strict in taking in new members, and should avoid using pressure on those who are religious believers or have strong religious feelings to join the Youth League.

As for those League members who already believe in religion, we should give them a period for education and wait to see if they change. It is not right to simply expel them, or to order them to resign from the organization. We should expect results from our ideological work with them. As for those who persist and do not change, even after our patient help and teaching, there are certain proper organizational ways to handle the problem without hurting their feelings.

Document 135

Advice to Friends Who Want To Become Monks

Letters to the columnist "Nanbudao" (Dauntless), Shanxi Youth, *September 1987. Translated by Tam Waiyi and Donald MacInnis.*

I have received over a hundred letters from young friends who said that they wanted to become monks, mostly from Sichuan Province, since beginning this "Dauntless" column in *Shanxi Youth*. Although I have already answered this question, the letters keep flowing in. The day before yesterday I got another letter which was forwarded to me from the Xuankong Temple in Hengshan. I always say that I won't laugh without reason, but with these letters I have got to the point where I can't laugh anymore at all.

Most of these friends who have written to me about becoming monks have lost their faith in life after frustrations in love affairs, failure to be accepted for university study, and employment problems. Completely despondent, they want to put their troubles behind them and find shelter in the shade of Buddha. This seems like a very childish idea to me. Don't you know that everyone meets up with misfortune at some time or other? Some people, thinking only of themselves and their own misery, become pessimistic, cry out in despair, and give up; but others, equally miserable, think of others, their work unit, the motherland, mankind, and, instead of giving up hope, retain their optimism and self-confidence.

We all know how Sun Bing [Sunzi] wrote the famous *Arts of War*, completing the book only after great personal suffering (Sun was a well-known general in ancient China who was persecuted by the imperial government when false accusations were lodged against him); and how Beethoven, because of his strong determination, composed many masterpieces after becoming deaf. ... If all people were like you, deciding to become monks when they run into difficulties, think of all that wasted youth, intelligence, and loving parental care. The great inventor Edison said, "Every problem has its solution. If you find yourself in a situation with no solution, then you have only yourself, a fool and a lazybones, to blame."

Now another word. Every temple has strict rules and restrictions for accepting novices. A religious career requires people with a strong sense of commitment. People like you, who easily turn pessimistic and lose hope when faced with difficulties, will not be welcome in the household of Buddha. Moreover, the holy religious places still belong to this society; they are not a paradise or peach orchard in another world. I'm afraid that you won't get away from your troubles there.

Finally, I give you these words of encouragement from the poet Pushkin: "Be patient for now in this unhappy time. Have faith! A happy day is coming soon."

Document 136

There Is Not One Reason Why We Should Hand Our Fate Over to Gods and Ghosts

By a Youth League secretary in a special column in Chinese Youth, *December 1986. Translated by Tam Waiyi and Donald MacInnis.*

We can see, on the one hand, new thinking and new ideas developing in the minds of young people in China today, while on the other hand we can also see the dark shadow of backward and corrupt thinking circling over people's heads. The idea of "supernatural powers" [*shenquan*] is one of them.

So-called supernatural powers refer to feudal superstitious activities that people are always talking about. In the early 1920s, Comrade Mao Zedong called the "supernatural powers" of feudal superstition one of the four ropes that bound up the Chinese people, particularly the peasants. He thought that the "supernatural powers," together with the powers of the clans, of politics, and of men over women, represented the whole patriarchal feudal system and its way of thinking.

In old China, the "supernatural powers" referred to all kinds of gods, from the Jade Emperor up in heaven to the King of Hell. The "supernatural powers" received what seemed to be a fatal blow after the founding of new China, and they disappeared for years, but recently there are signs of their revival. Feudal superstitious activities are happening not only in the backward mountain and rural areas, but they are also gradually spreading into the cities and suburban districts. Shamans and sorcerers have picked up their old trades again, spreading untruths and deceiving people, openly challenging science and civilization with their backward, ignorant, primitive, and even intimidating methods. Cases of insulting women, damaging farmland, and treating people's lives with utter disregard have occurred with increasing frequency.

In April 1979, it was said that a river in a county in Sichuan Province contained "magic water," and that the mud and trees along the riverbanks were "magic medicine" that could cure any disease. Within half a month, countless numbers of people had flocked to the river to get this "magic water" and "magic medicine." Six or seven thousand people came on one day alone at the peak of this frenzy, and thousands of young trees along the riverbanks were pulled out and wheat fields destroyed.

In 1980 a sorcerer in a township in Sichuan Province, "under the guidance of" supernatural powers, led more than a hundred people to "fly up to heaven" by jumping into a river with heavy stones tied to their bodies. More than seventy people drowned, many of them young persons.

In a prefecture in Sichuan, hundreds of thousands of people, most of them youths, travel every year to a certain "Guanyin Stone" in March in order to see the "apparition of gods."

Why Feudal Superstitious Activities Are Becoming More and More Prevalent in Some Places

The reasons for superstitious activities can be found by tracing back through thousands of years of feudal rule—the feudal ideology is very strong and deeply rooted, and it will take a long time to completely wipe it out. Since the implementation of the "responsibility system" in urban areas, some people, under pressure from severe competition, are unable to analyze correctly the frustrations and failures they encounter in their productive work, such as natural disasters, so they simply regard all misfortunes as "fate determined by heaven," or as the "punishment of the gods," so they feel they have to go to the gods for protection.

Backwardness in the development of education, science, and culture is another reason for the spread of feudal superstitious activities. Young people are bound to meet certain frustrations in their education, employment, marriage, and family planning. When they make a choice which proves unsatisfactory, or when they want another chance, they ask the gods to make the decision for them.

Another reason for the spread of feudal superstitions is the existence of various problems in the Party and in social morality. In many places the local authorities do not interfere with superstitious activities at all, and some Party and Youth League members even follow along with everyone else in believing these things. When young people lose their correct spiritual footing, they will "become disillusioned with the real world" and turn to belief in "gods" as they search for psychological equilibrium.

Feudal Superstitious Activities Bring Great Harm to Both the Current Reforms and the Psychological Health of Young People

To a great extent, reform means the reform of people's minds and the renewal of their thinking. But feudal superstitions put serious limitations on people's capacity to think. Science is a force of production. If a laborer does not believe in science, but in gods, he will not break loose from the bondage of "traditional farming methods" and "hand labor." Feudal superstitious activities also waste a lot of people's money and energy. In a certain township each person paid from 900 *yuan* to as high as 2000 *yuan* each year as "tribute to the gods." Many families could not afford these expenses, but, fearing the power of the "gods," they had to do their best to pay them, thus holding back the Party's policy of prosperity for everyone.

Many young people become victims of feudal superstitious activities. In this year alone, eight young women have died as a result of "fortune tellers' " nonsense. Young people are also the first victims in the clan fights that are generated by feudal superstitious activities. When young people begin to worship the gods, their hearts and minds fall under the shadows of ignorance and mysticism. Once they are made captives of the gods and ghosts, they will no longer be new youths with the "four haves" [have ideas, knowledge, intelligence, and consciousness].

Facing the challenge of feudal superstitious activities, Youth League units should take the lead, standing firm in the fight against them. The media should pay special attention to their social effects, but should not overpublicize them, in order to avoid serving unconsciously as their propaganda tools.

The Youth League should be actively concerned about each youth, helping them to solve their personal problems and difficulties. When the Youth League is truly understood and relied on by young people, they will not turn to "gods."

These words from the *Internationale* say it well: "We have never had a savior, nor do we rely on gods." The current reforms point to a bright future for us all, but we, and we alone, must pursue that happy life. There is no reason why we should place our fate into the hands of gods and ghosts!

Document 137

Why Did They Change and Become Theists?

By Du Feng in Zheng Ming *(Hongkong) No. 27, January 1980 (excerpts). (Translator not known.)*

A University Opinion Poll

Some months ago in a university in Shanghai, a group of students underwent a carefully controlled opinion poll. Among the topics investigated was "What do you believe in?" The answers included "Marxism," "atheism," "theism," and "fatalism." The conclusions of the investigation showed that those believing in some kind of fatalism were in the majority, with quite a few theists.

The results caused a sensation. How could a generation of young people, brought up under the red flag, believe in fatalism, and even believe in God? They have never met any priests or pastors [since all churches and temples had been closed for over a decade]; they have not heard sermons or assisted at prayer meetings. They may have, while out sightseeing, chanced upon a temple or pagoda, but what difference would there be in that from roaming around a public park or visiting a museum or zoo? Thirteen years ago these young people rampaged through temples, pagodas, and churches, rebelling, and denouncing the "four olds," destroying in no time statues of Buddha, chasing Buddhist nuns and battling monks, smashing to bits innumerable priceless religious sculptures, carvings, murals, bas-reliefs, etc., all of inestimable artistic value.

Nevertheless, in the course of time, some have become theists and believers in some kind of fate. For someone who has lived outside the turbulence of those thirteen years, this transformation is inexplicable. But the writer of this article fortunately took part in those thirteen years of turmoil, and therefore with his own eyes saw the younger generation's evolution from nonbelief to belief.

THE YOUNGER GENERATION'S PENCHANT FOR FORTUNE TELLERS

I well remember the very first time I encountered the younger generation's belief in fate and theism, which took place at the end of 1968. That was the high tide of the "up to the hills, down to the countryside" campaign, when innumerable young people were forced to go to the countryside. In oil-lamp-lighted semidark little farm huts, I saw young intellectuals grouped together using poker cards to tell their fortunes. I could not but ask them, "Do you really believe in forecasting the future, telling fortunes, calculating life's destiny?" One said, "Walled in, purposeless, dejected, can't we amuse ourselves?" But another said, "I believe in fate, so why not work out our horoscope and see what fate has in store for us?"

After that I noticed that the younger generation's penchant for fortune telling developed more and more, not only among those young intellectuals sent up to the hills and down to the countryside, but also in the cities among young factory workers. Even students entered into the ranks of those searching for good fortune, trying to discover the future.

The methods of divining the future became quite sophisticated, what with Xia dynasty-type tortoise shell engravings, astrology, and mourning-clothes divination; all these methods delighted the youths who delved into those star-gazing explorations. The Shanghai fortune telling customs were comparatively more deeply rooted than elsewhere. Some fortune tellers, old hands and real professionals, went so far as to request payment, such as one dollar for an "eight-character" divination. Still more spicy, some of these fortune tellers were ready to cast lots to figure out Chairman Mao's ultimate demise! These activities soon encountered repression from Public Security, and not a few fortune tellers were arrested. All the same, in spite of repression and control, fortune telling has not been eradicated. . . .

GUANYIN IN CANTON, AND TEMPLE OFFERINGS IN CHENGDU

After the "cultural revolution," when the disorder and turmoil had ended, one might have thought that these things ought to have ended also. But in the spring of 1979, after I had already been in Hongkong for two years, I went back to the mainland for a visit as a tourist. . . . While sight-seeing in Chengdu, the capital of Sichuan Province, I encountered, in the Wen Chu Temple, the same kinds of things as in the Yingtan Guanyin grotto. The Wen Chu Temple is situated to the north of the city of Chengdu. It is a well-known temple, and people say that of the whole area in and around Chengdu, it is probably the most famous. While still outside the temple, I already recognized the heady smell of burning incense, . . . At the temple there were big crowds, pushing and jostling, coming and going. . . . Proceeding upward across two lesser temple structures, going up across two ramps, one comes to the main temple. This has three enormous venerable Buddha statues, and in front of these there is a long, long table. Spread out on the table were many wine bottles, and I could not help feeling somewhat downcast, for on going in a bit further, I could see that all these bottles were filled with oil, being offerings made by the faithful. Food is strictly rationed on the mainland now; edible oil is rationed to five ounces per month per person. But here are the faithful making these offerings, and one wonders how they can offer up one full bottle, about one catty [about a pound] of oil! Does this not testify to their sincerity? In this main section of the temple many were kowtowing. A young lady about twenty years old particularly aroused my attention, smartly dressed, in fact quite elegant, and holding in her hand joss sticks, but seeming rather hesitant to bow down before the crowd. However, encouraged by her friends, finally she too, with a jerk of her head, fell down on her knees on the straw mat and bravely banged her head three times on the floor. . . .

WHY? HOW CAN WE EXPLAIN THIS?

Having gone through some ten years of doing away with all theism, and the erosion of all the old culture, how does it happen that the younger generation turns around and picks up the notion of God again? I think there are several reasons. In the first place, those ten years of turmoil more or less obliged an individual to seize his own destiny, there being a feeling that there is a superior cause, a belief in destiny, the course of one's life, is somehow controlled from above, that beyond the contingencies of this life there is a force which controls one's life.

Before the "cultural revolution," life was peaceful and stable, supported by [social] structures. Young people were only required to study to get results. All that was needed was to know enough of the classics and the orthodox Communist thinking to wheedle a fairly acceptable future place in society for oneself. The "cultural revolution" drastically changed all that. Moreover, with the "up to the mountains and down to the countryside" campaigns, young people sensed all the more that the destiny of their lives was under the influence of an unknown, mysterious, omnipotent force. So quite a few people fell into the murky obscurantism of theism and fatalism.

Another reason was the young people's aversion, detestation, horror and revulsion against Marxist-Leninist ideology provoked by the ten years of wickedness, evil, and turmoil of the "cultural revolution." They were forced to seek a new directive, that de facto put religion and fatalism back on the market. But from what I can see, the mainland youth generation has only the slightest understanding of real revealed religions like Christianity, Buddhism, and Islam. Very few of them have ever studied the scriptures. Devotees of Buddha hardly understand the sutras. As for God, they have only a vague, blurred, confused image of some all-powerful force.

Third, the "cultural revolution" disorders allowed a lot of things that had been wiped out to resurface, such as divination and that sort of thing. Naturally, the fact that these things have persisted is due to the turmoil and laxness of control during the "cultural revolution." But these are only external factors, whereas the real causes were the first two given above.

The "cultural revolution" is over, but it has caused profound damage. All the same, although those crying to God and the devotees of Buddha are few, nevertheless orthodox religion stirs a sizable number of young people. Thirty years ago, Communism's mighty attraction caused many young people to abandon religion and turn to Marxism. At that time, innumerable students of religiously-directed schools joined the revolution.

So today Communism must again think of defeating religion and fatalism, as well as all kinds of religious beliefs, including those which are wayward and rebellious, while at the same time restoring the freedom of religion and the rights of citizens to their beliefs as contained in the constitution, which abhors all coercion. . . .

GLOSSARY

Weights and Measures

1 *mu* — ¹⁄₁₅ hectare or ⅙ acre
1 *catty* (*jin*) — ½ kilogram or 1.1 pounds
1 *li* — ⅓ mile
1 *yuan* — U. S. $.27 (1988)

Administrative Units

cun — hamlet
xiang — village
zhen — market town
xiang — county
qu — district, region

Terms and Abbreviations

ahong, imam — Muslim clergyman
CPPCC — Chinese People's Political Consultative Conference
CCPA — Chinese Catholic Patriotic Association
CBA — Chinese Buddhist Association
CDA — China Daoist Association
CIA — China Islamic Association
CCP — Chinese Communist Party
CYL — Communist Youth League
PRC — People's Republic of China
Panchen Lama — Bainqen Lama (died 1/28/89)
TSPM — Three-Self Protestant Movement

Selected List of Sources

Asia Focus — Hongkong: Union of Catholic Asian News (weekly).

China Study Project — London, Edinburgh House: CSP *Bulletin* and *Documentation* (1979-1985); *Journal* (from 1985, three times a year); press and radio reports and other primary sources on religion and religious policy in China.

China Daily — Beijing: English-language newspaper.

Fa Yin — Beijing: Journal of Chinese Buddhist Association.

FBIS — Washington, D.C.: Foreign Broadcast Information Service.

FE — London: BBC Summary of World Broadcasts: The Far East.

Jinling Xiehe Shenxueyuan Yuanzhi (Nanjing Theological Review) — Nanjing Union Theological Seminary (biennial).

JPRS — Washington, D.C.: Joint Publications Research Service.

Renmin Ribao — Beijing: People's Daily.

Shijie Zongjiao Ziliao (Materials on World Religions) — Beijing: Chinese Academy of Social Sciences (monthly).

Tian Feng (Heavenly Wind) — Shanghai: China Christian Council (monthly; focus on Protestant church and theology).

Tianzhujiao Yanjiu Ziliaohuibian (Compilation of Catholic Research Materials) — Shanghai: Guangqi Society (periodical).

Tripod — Hongkong: Holy Spirit Study Centre, Hongkong Catholic Church; bilingual (bimonthly; primary focus on Catholic church and theology).

Xinhua (NCNA, New China News Agency) — Beijing.

Yunnan Shehui Kexue (Social Sciences in Yunnan) — Kunming: National Minorities Institute (periodical).

Yi (China Message) — Hongkong: an independent Catholic bimonthly.

Zhongguo Tianzhujiao (The Catholic Church in China) — Beijing: the Chinese Catholic Patriotic Association and the Catholic Church Affairs Commission (bimonthly).

Zhongguo Yisilanjiao (Islam in China) — Beijing: China Islamic Association.

Zhongyang Minzu Xueyuan Xuebao (Journal of the Central Nationalities College) — Beijing (periodical).

Zongjiao (Religion) — Nanjing: Center for Religious Research, Nanjing University (biennial; focus on Christianity).

Zongjiaoxue Yanjiu (Studies and Research on Religion) — Chengdu: Religious Research Center, University of Sichuan (periodical; primary focus on Daoism).

Zhongguo Shehui Shiqidi Zongjiao Wenti (Religious Questions under Socialism in China), Luo Zhufeng, editor — Shanghai Academy of Social Sciences, 1987, 268 pp.), from which several documents have been translated for inclusion in this volume, will be published in full by M. E. Sharpe (Armonk, NY) in 1990, translated by Zheng Xi'an and Donald MacInnis.

Index

and growth of religion in a class society is class oppression and exploitation.

Apart from the social sources of religion, there are conceptual sources. The spiritual substances worshiped in religion are the abstraction and idolizing of objective matter in human perception, infinitely expanded and then presented after deification, isolating them from nature and objective reality so that they become something absolute, the ultimate cause of the universe — that is, God.

THE SOCIAL-HISTORICAL FUNCTION OF RELIGION

In a class society, the social historical function of religion is very complex; it must be analyzed in a concrete and matter-of-fact way, examining the effect of each religious event on the historical process. Historically, the reactionary exploiting class used religion as a spiritual cornerstone for its domination; however, some revolutionaries also used the banner of religion in their struggles, therefore religion helped, to a certain degree, in advancing historical progress. . . .

RELIGION AND SCIENCE AND CULTURE

Religion has made an important contribution to the advancement of mankind's knowledge and culture. It is closely related to science and social ideologies such as philosophy, literature, art, ethics, etc. Human perceptions of nature and society in earliest times were represented by witchcraft, mythology or religious concepts. In literature this took the forms of poetry, music, dancing for the gods, painting and sculpture. In ancient Greece and Rome, the outstanding architecture was found mainly in sacred temples, tombs and memorial halls. In such cultures, the religious and secular spirit were merged. . . .

Throughout history, religion has influenced each race in spirituality, culture, science, ethics, morals, and customs. In seeking "natural law" and a means for immortality, Daoists objectively contributed to the development of medicine, chemistry, and astronomy. *Chantongqi* is a widely recognized early work. The "Sketch of Zhenyuan Miaodao" recorded the earliest gunpowder experiments in human history. It is widely acknowledged that Daoist theory contributed to Chinese medical theory, and the laboratory skills of the Daoists contributed to the maintenance of health and the curing of diseases. In the ethnic minorities regions of northwest and southwest China, religion has been central in their history, culture, ethics, morals and customs. There are ten ethnic minorities in China's northwest where virtually all the people are Muslims. Although Islam is a foreign religion, it adapted to Chinese traditional culture while keeping its unique characteristics. It has become an indispensable part of our national culture, contributing a great deal to the history, culture, medicine, astronomy, mathematics, and calendar science of China.

Buddhist culture in Tibet is a fundamental part of Tibetan culture, where it has made great contributions in medicine, calendar science, literature, handcrafts, art, painting, sculpture, and the like. The Potala Palace and the Jokhang Temple are masterpieces of architecture. Tibetans adopted the calendar of the Buddhist Mizong sect, combining it with the duodecimal cycle system of the Hans. It accurately records the agricultural seasons.

While Christianity had the reputation of being the tool of the imperialists after coming into China, it did make real contributions to the spread of Western science and culture, for example, establishing hospitals, schools, publications, libraries, and the concept of equality between men and women.

The Characteristics of Religion in China

China is a nation composed of numerous ethnic nationalities and religions, including both primitive shamanistic religions and world religions. The world religions, Buddhism, Islam, and Christianity, all came from outside China. Once established in China, they interacted with Chinese traditional culture and with each other, forming religions with national characteristics. Daoism, a native Chinese religion, spread beyond China to adjoining regions. There has never been a single dominant national religion in China as in some Western nations. China's rulers throughout history followed a policy of tolerance, supporting and protecting religion.

Religious believers today form only a small proportion of China's population. In the northwest and southwest provinces, where national minorities predominate, religion and government administration overlapped over long periods of our history. Religion is closely related to the culture of the national minorities, where believers form the majority of the population.

Among the Han population, which forms the majority of China's people, the main religious tradition is belief in predestination, or fate, and the worship of ancestors. This is the reason why Buddhism and Daoism have never become dominant religions in China. During the Xia, Shang, and Zhou dynasties, great political and economic changes took place. During the earliest agricultural period in China, the people combined their own hard labor with prayers to heaven for favorable weather. In *Shangshu Hongfan*, it is written, "Their concern is lords, people, and clergy." The will of God and the will of man were placed side by side. After the Zhou dynasty, the Confucianists advocated "governing by virtue, and respect for heaven but not blind belief in heaven." The predominant orthodox ideology throughout Chinese history has been to "respect the gods and immortals, but keep one's distance from them," from the *Analects* of Confucius. Each emperor called himself the Son of Heaven, with all imperial authority granted as a divine right and the imperial power transcending even divine power. The imperial policy toward religion had two purposes, both to use religion and to keep it at a distance at the same time.

Relationships based on blood ties became important after irrigated agriculture was introduced. A patriarchal social system based on kinship and